"Captures the joys and challenges of world cruising, and wraps them in a highly enjoyable read. Zeke provides unique insights into rally cruising, boat partnership, life at sea, and the conundrum of crew. His sense of humour and immense generosity of spirit overcome obstacles to bring an eventful circumnavigation to a well-deserved happy end. Experienced sailors will learn something here; non-sailors will too."

Jimmy Cornell, *Author and world cruiser extraordinaire*

"Glorious! I felt like I was aboard, every nautical mile."

Molly McGrath, *Editor, Pink Eraser*

"Whether it is the granite islands of the Maine Coast or the coral atolls a year's sail away, Zeke ties them together in his 'one ocean' view of our world. This engaging sailing odyssey takes us to fascinating shores, while gently asking what is the meaning of home."

Angus King, *US Senator from Maine*

"Boats are like Shamans...they move between worlds. In all great mythic traditions, a vision quest must be done alone or amongst strangers...for one must be lost in order to navigate the renewal and becoming."

Stephanie Rayner, *Renowned artist, lecturer, boatbuilder*

"Thank you, Zeke, for sailing to Tuvalu and writing about your personal experiences here. Climate change is a matter of survival for our citizens and our culture. I hope readers take to heart your message of One Ocean, One Planet, One Future. Save Tuvalu to save the world!"

Enele Sopoaga, *Prime Minister of Tuvalu*

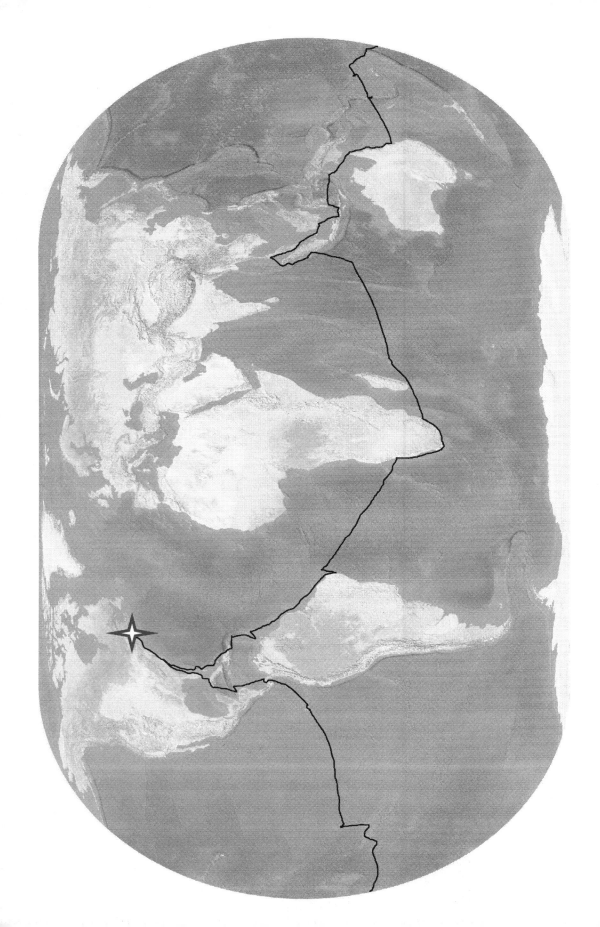

A
SATISFYING SAIL
AROUND THE WORLD

Zeke Holland

ISBN: 978-0692127322

CONTENTS

A Note About Sailing Terms

This is not a technical book; it is a story to be enjoyed by all. But inevitably sailing stories are full of sailing terms that might be unfamiliar. In most cases I believe the reader can gather enough from context, without definitions. If you want to learn more, many sailing glossaries are available online, such as www.schoolofsailing.net/glossary.

A Note About Color

This book is published in black-and-white to keep the cost low. You can enjoy all the photos from the book in color at the companion website: **www.satisfyingsail.com**. There you can also read/leave comments, and you can contact me. And if you wish you can order a full color edition of the book. Cheers!

Zeke

WELCOME ABOARD

Whether sailing off the beach on a summer afternoon or enjoying a week's cruise of the coast and islands, I hated the turn for home. I wanted to keep going. Yet when an opportunity arose to sail without turning back, to continue around the world, I hesitated. The prospect before me looked nothing like what I had imagined. I applied the deathbed test: "At the end of my life, looking back, would I regret it if I let this opportunity pass by?" "Yes?" said my inner voice, "Then go for it. And name the boat *No Regrets*."

I thought I might bake bread during my night watch, between 2300 (11pm) and 0300 (3am). That way I wouldn't interfere with the cook-of-the-day preparing meals, and I'd be heating the galley at the coolest part of the day. Plus it would provide a diversion for me on what seemed, at sunset, like it might be an uneventful four hours.

At 2300 when I took over from Bill, I was in my usual just-woken-from-insufficient-sleep fog. Bill asked if I wanted to shake out the reef in the mainsail, since the wind had gone very light. Also he pointed out an unusual vibration/sound that he couldn't identify. I went into the galley in search of the source of the sound. What I found instead was water on the floor! A quick check below the floorboards showed water there, but not a lot. The water must have come from above, not below; not urgent. Setting the water question aside, I checked the fridge and freezer as potential vibration sources. Nope. Venturing into Tim's sleeping area, I found it. His bulkhead-mounted fan was running on high speed – white noise, to help him sleep. One mystery solved.

I tasted the water on the galley floor – fresh, not salt. My eyes jumped to our drinking water spigot; a small but steady stream was running from it. Yikes! It was far too easy to brush against that lever, accidentally opening that valve and losing precious water. A check of the starboard water tank showed it nearly empty. The port one was full. The stream of water explained the empty tank. But the stream ran into the sink, so why was fresh water on the floor? A mystery to be investigated in the morning.

Bill was still waiting. What about shaking out the reef? I didn't want to go outside; it had started raining. "Sure, let's do it now while two of us are awake." Leaving the comfort of the pilothouse, we stepped into the wet cockpit and raised the full mainsail. Bill disappeared below toward his berth. A moment later Tim appeared from the opposite hull; the noise of the winches had woken him. Assured that nothing was wrong, he retreated to his berth.

The rain stopped; the wind returned. We were moving nicely now. Eight and a half knots through the water, but the GPS indicated only six and a half over the ground. Two knots of current against us? That seemed like too much for here in the open ocean. Was it real, or was it that our through-the-water boat speed was over-reading? Maybe both were factors; not a problem for tonight.

The chart plotter showed three ships nearby. One was already clear of us, but the other two were overtaking us, and this required my attention, to be sure we stayed clear of both. By the time the second one safely passed, there was a new "blip" headed our way.

The wind was now blowing 20 knots. Maybe the reef should go back in the mainsail. Or was this just a passing cloud with a little wind of its own? I'll wait, I thought, and watch both the wind and the approaching ship.

Did I really think I was going to be bored on this watch? Baking bread could wait until tomorrow.

I investigated what was left in the snack locker. No cashews or Snickers bars left, so I munched on Saltines and peanut butter.

It was getting hard to stay awake. The last hour of this middle-of-the-night watch could seem interminable. I checked the time; it was 0147. Crap, the last hour hadn't even begun!

The ship passed; no new ones approaching. The wind was steady at 17 knots. We were doing fine with no reef. A big cloud approached, however – blotting out a patch of stars; registering deeper darkness than the ambient moonless sky. It was 0158.

At this point of my watch, I was just hanging on, waiting until I could sleep. I didn't want anything to happen. I hoped the wind wouldn't change. I hoped no more ships appeared. I just wanted an hour and two minutes to pass uneventfully. I forced myself to stand and go out to the cockpit and scan the empty horizon.

I put away the peanut butter and crackers. I checked the charge level of the batteries. Our hydrogenerator had chafed through the line that holds its propeller in the water; it was out of commission tonight. The batteries were getting somewhat low, but happily I didn't have to listen to the hum of the generator. Our wind-powered generator was doing well, but it couldn't keep up with the current draw of the electronics and autopilot. It was 0217.

My eyes were burning. I closed them for a few seconds. I wished I dared to close them longer. How do single-handed sailors survive, I wondered. Earlier we had sailed past a huge floating thing – some sort of drum, perhaps. It was big enough that it would have done serious damage if we hit it. We didn't see it until it was already alongside. At night, there was zero chance of seeing such a hazard in time to avoid it. All small boats on the ocean take a calculated risk. It was 0228.

Outside again, the constellation Orion was about to set, soon to be followed by the Milky Way. The infinity of stars was amazing. Beyond amazing. I wished my eyes were sharper; I wanted to see more; I wanted to see the multitude of faint celestial dots that could only be seen in the pure blackness that humans used to experience. An airplane blinked an ironic trail northward. The North Star was low in the sky; lower each night, tracking our progress south. I stared upward trying to keep my eyes wide and was rewarded with a shooting star – a good one, leaving a trail glowing in the sky for a second before it was gone. Was I the only human to witness the blazing end of that cosmic pebble? It was 0237 when I went back inside.

I jerked awake! How long was I asleep? Only for a moment. I forced myself to take another look around. No ships. No wind change. No big devoid-of-stars cloud patches. I was on the home stretch now…counting down the last remaining minutes until 0255, when I would wake Tim. Spent, but satisfied, I would wait those last 5 minutes for his appearance in the pilothouse. I would brief him on the conditions, wish him an enjoyable watch, then head for my berth and melt deliciously into sleep.

Looking back, the three of us made a pretty good crew. That is, when we were on passage – sailing through the nights, busy, focused. We were all experienced sailors. If the weather was fair, I lost no sleep worrying about Bill or Tim on watch alone. We had our 4 hours on, 8 hours off watch schedule, and our one day on, two days off cooking schedule. We had our common goal, to safely reach our next destination. And our common enemies – foul weather and gear failures. We made a much better team at sea than we did in port, where our differences collided.

We were not exactly friends, after all. We had met "on the Internet" nearly two years before. People said, "You're going to sail around the world with two guys you barely know!? Are you crazy?" I would reply, "You think it would be better to go to sea with family members? Or to jeopardize a good friendship?" This might elicit a funny reply, but accompanied by a serious look that said, "I'm glad it is you doing this, not me!"

Exercising the Option

Two years before setting sail, I sat in bed with my wife Hallie, she reading a book and I reading an article in Cruising World magazine. Provoked by something in the article, I muttered, "When I sail around the world, I'm going to focus on the sailing, and only stop in a few places, like Cape Town and South Australia." Hallie will deny it, but I remember her reply. "You're not going to sail around the world. You're getting too old for that."

I said nothing. But her comment *really* got my attention! I had always thought I might sail around the world; I held it as an option that I might exercise in the future. The idea that the option would expire soon was a wake-up call. I knew she was close to the truth. I didn't have many years before my physical abilities would decline, and my internal drive wane, and it just wouldn't seem worth it to go for the "big one." Without even looking up from her book, Hallie had just changed our lives.

≈≈≈

"When are you going to retire?" came the challenge from my men's team. Every man should have a men's team, but I know it is rare. We are eight men who have met for an evening every other week for 35 years. We support each member in being the man he aspires to be – the husband, the father, the professional, the human. Together we have faced most of life's big events. We know each other in some ways better than we know ourselves.

I had just reported achieving a financial goal I set 14 years earlier. My intention from 14 years back was to retire when I reached this goal, but now I was comfortably working three days a week, with no plan to stop. The team challenged me on this. "Why are you continuing to work if you've met your financial goal?" "What is your purpose now?"

I didn't see anything wrong with continuing to enjoy my work, continuing to have an income. Besides, the dollar target that I had set 14 years prior didn't look so big and "safe" as it did back then. The threat of permanently shutting off the income spigot changed my perspective on finances. A teammate said, "I know when you're going to retire. It will be when something shows up that pulls you away, rather than you choosing to get out."

The thing that would pull me away was just beginning to take shape. I still thought things would proceed in a logical order; that I would continue working for two or three more years, find the right boat, and take another two or three years planning and preparing.

≈≈≈

Thirty years earlier, Hallie and I had sailed across the Atlantic aboard a 43' monohull (conventional single-hulled boat, as opposed to a catamaran with two hulls, or a trimaran with a main central hull and two smaller outrigger hulls). As we spent day after day sailing downwind in the trade winds, I was wishing we had a multihull (catamaran or trimaran). Monohulls have weight added in their keels to keep them from tipping over. Multihulls rely on the stability of their shape, so they have no ballast, and they are generally lighter and faster. I was sailing in the perfect trade winds, downwind all the way, dragging 9,000 pounds of lead ballast across the ocean. And rolling from side to side in the waves, making it hard to get dressed or cook or handle the sails or even sit and read. A multihull would be faster and more comfortable. A multihull would be my next offshore boat.

Thirty years on, I was getting ready for that next boat. I lusted for a large (perhaps 50') trimaran, for great sailing performance. But it wouldn't have adequate accommodations if I went cruising with Hallie, especially if we invited friends. A catamaran would do better. But it couldn't be a "condomaran" – one where all the design tradeoffs favored accommodations over sailing qualities. These thoughts led me to the Atlantic 42 (42 feet long) and Atlantic 46 catamarans designed by Chris White.

I googled "chris white atlantic catamaran" and happened upon a message board post from a guy in Vermont. He was looking for a partner to share ownership of an Atlantic 42 for cruising on the coast of Maine. The Atlantic catamarans were not production boats; there were maybe twenty of the 42's built. Yet this guy wanted that specific design, and he wanted to sail in my home waters. I had to contact him. That's how I met Bill, via the Internet. We had a nice exchange of emails, and we agreed that our goals overlapped only in that we had similar taste in boats, and we love the Maine coast. We ended with, "Good luck. Stay in touch."

I flew to Florida to look at an Atlantic 46 that was for sale. My reaction? "Holy moly, that is a BIG boat!" The idea of trying to maintain all the systems aboard scared me. Instead of enjoying a year of fast sailing I would be spending a year repairing things and being scared about what would go wrong next. I met with designer Chris White, who offered some perspective. "Yes, it's a big boat when tied to the dock. But it gets small very quickly when you're sailing offshore!" I needed to think it over.

I got another email from Bill. "A guy responded to my post; he just bought an Atlantic 42 on Chesapeake Bay. He wants to sail around the world, and he's looking for a partner. Want me to put you in touch with him?"

I was not looking to co-own a boat. I was thinking if I couldn't line up friends, I might sail solo. How would that work with shared ownership!? On the other hand, talking with Bill had warmed me up to the idea of sharing costs. Yes, I wanted to connect with this guy. That's how I met Tim, via the Internet.

Many, many emails and phone calls later, plus two days of sailing with Tim in Maryland and a lunch with Bill in New Hampshire, the three of us had formed a partnership. Yes, *three* of us. The opportunity was irresistible to Bill, too!

≈≈≈

Tim, Bill and I became equal owners, equal partners. Contrary to all sailing convention, we had no single captain. We agreed to sail westward around the world. We further agreed to participate in a rally called the Blue Planet Odyssey (BPO), organized by world-renowned sailing authority Jimmy Cornell. The concept of a rally includes:

- A predetermined itinerary, and boats rendezvousing at key places along the way
- Rally organizers assisting with route planning, with clearance into foreign ports, and with services/tours ashore
- Mutual support among the sailors
- A fun social community

The BPO had an additional important component: to call attention to global issues of climate change. The voyage would encompass 2 ½ years, with less than two years until the start in Key West, Florida.

This was not what I had envisioned. Not by a long shot!

As for not doing it alone: What a relief! Bill and Tim both seemed to be good at troubleshooting problems and doing repairs. The fear of "too much boat to maintain" eased. And splitting the costs three ways made a great boat affordable. Bill would only sail as far as Australia, as he would have to arrange a limited leave of absence from his job; but he would continue to own his 1/3 share of the boat.

About making many stops along the way and taking longer than I had anticipated: This idea was growing on me. One of the reasons I had been reluctant to "sightsee" was that I didn't want to deal with the logistics of taking a boat into new countries and staying in unfamiliar ports. The BPO rally would handle much of that for us.

About not having the freedom to go wherever I wanted along the way: Although commonly we think of freedom as avoiding commitments, there is also a freedom that comes with being committed. When Hallie and I sailed for a year, we had a strict itinerary because we were meeting friends/family all along the way. We met cruisers who thought we were nuts. But as those sailors perseverated about whether it was time to leave or not, and whether to visit island A or island B, I didn't see them having any more fun than we were having. I was okay with following an itinerary designed by Jimmy Cornell.

About leaving sooner than anticipated: There was my "pull" to retire!

≈≈≈

No Regrets

South Atlantic Ocean

Mid-afternoon I was feeling awfully hot, and I spent some time sitting and doing absolutely nothing. I needed a shower, both because I was getting stinky and because I would feel much better after. But I wanted to wait until the sun was lower. No point in just getting heated right back up again. So, I sat. "Don't just do something," Buddha might have said, "Sit." But this wasn't meditation; it was the opposite – unconsciousness.

When I judged the sun low enough, I came out of my coma, grabbed a towel and soap and a bucket. I sat on the slightly-private transom steps and poured a bucket of seawater over my head. The water temperature was up to a pleasant 81 degrees. Then a little soap, a saltwater rinse, and then a freshwater rinse. And drying in the setting sun and breeze. Life was good again. I asked Nora to put on some music, and was delighted with her choice of The Band, followed by an even better choice of Clapton Unplugged. Now, as we liked to say on *No Regrets*, "It hardly sucked at all!"

MAINE

The three of us sailed *No Regrets* north from Chesapeake Bay to Rockland, Maine, where we would moor her for the summer, do some of the coastal cruising that Bill wished for, and get to know our new vessel. The Blue Planet Odyssey required a prior passage aboard the boat of at least 500 miles. This offshore jump to Maine was just long enough. We had a lot to learn about the catamaran and the plethora of electronic gear, and limited time since we all still held jobs. A few days at sea was a good way to get acquainted with the boat, and with each other. The boat and the crew passed this first test; our future looked promising.

Having *No Regrets* in my home state meant I could do some sailing in glorious Penobscot Bay. At the first opportunity Hallie and I went for a cruise over a long weekend. The very first time we entered an anchorage, I got distracted by problems lowering/furling the big mainsail by myself, while Hallie dutifully steered the course I had given her. Suddenly I realized we had gone beyond where I intended; I ran to check the chart, just as we clipped a submerged rock and broke a daggerboard! Oh well, now I felt properly initiated…to the tune of a $1,000 repair.

Another day we were sailing upwind, getting ready to tack as we approached the rocky shore. I held my course until we were 100 yards off, and then turned the wheel to tack. Nothing happened! The boat was merrily charging toward the rocks, and I couldn't steer. In a second my panicky brain ran through the options. Easing sheets to spill the wind would slow us down, but the wind and current would still put us on the rocks. Starting both engines and putting one or both in reverse to stop/turn could work, but there wasn't time. Maybe the nut securing the wheel was loose, and I just needed to tighten it. I quickly felt for the big nut, and indeed it was loose enough for me to turn by hand, but that made no difference. Maybe I could engage the autopilot to steer. The autopilot had a hydraulic steering connection separate from the wheel, so it should still work. Wait! That's why the wheel was doing nothing – the autopilot was already engaged! I hit the "Standby" button to disengage the autopilot, turned the wheel, and tacked the boat. And slowly returned my heart rate to normal. I don't think Hallie even noticed that an emergency had come and gone in the space of a few seconds. But the skipper clearly needed to get more familiar with his boat!

I had some pleasant sails; Bill made the drive from Vermont for some, too; and Tim joined us from Pennsylvania for one weekend dedicated to work aboard. But before long we were sailing to a boatyard in Belfast that had a big enough Travelift to haul our 23' 6" wide catamaran out of the water for the winter. We had our engines inspected there, and the yard's recommendation was to replace them. True, one was hard to start and had low compression in one cylinder, but we thought replacing them was a crazy idea. In time it would seem less crazy. Much of the following summer focused on those engines.

Departure Minus 4 Months

Our second summer in Maine was winding down, and *No Regrets* was stuck at another boatyard. Aside from sailing from one yard to another at the start of the season, we had done no sailing all season. The major work undertaken was replacing our low compression engine with a lightly used engine that a mechanic had offered at a reasonable price, and servicing the saildrive transmissions that turn the propellers. One thing led to another. The yard recommended that we replace the corroded wiring in the engine rooms. We agreed, without realizing that the yard didn't actually have the resources to finish this work when promised.

We had been waiting a month, unable to use the boat. After many delays and a constant stream of apologies about how busy they were with emergencies, they scheduled a "sea trial" to demonstrate that the new engine and wiring were working. The dreaded but half-expected phone call came that Thursday morning. "The boat isn't ready…," followed by more apologies and excuses and stories. We rescheduled for Friday. Sunday we had to move the boat to another yard, because there was more work waiting to happen there. But we couldn't very well take the boat away with the job unfinished. We were between a rock and a hard place, and the stress was building.

By Sunday the job was "almost" finished. The mechanic from Yard 1 agreed to finish the work at Yard 2, but we would have to pay his travel time. What choice did we have? At Yard 2 we installed a new hydrogenerator (a device for generating electricity by towing a propeller through the water) and repaired a cracked davit (structure for lifting/carrying the dinghy out of the water).

I thought we were going to do some summer sailing on the beautiful coast of Maine, but that just wasn't happening. Now we were trying to get free of the boatyards in time to head south to New Jersey. Tim was going to live aboard there for two months before we all headed on south.

Departure Minus 3 Months

Some of the promised yard work never happened. Nevertheless, we left Maine as planned. Tim and Bill would do the week-long trip to New Jersey; my son Jesse and I were aboard for the first three days.

Winds were extremely light; the engines got a workout. The new/starboard one developed a disconcerting "shudder" periodically when run at full RPM. The mechanic was nice enough to take our phone call on Sunday, and he asserted that it must be a problem with the fuel delivery. We decided to continue with that engine running at reduced RPM. We made it through the day and into a beautiful night as we approached the Cape Cod Canal. Then, just through the Canal, we compounded our engine problems. Believing the fuel gauge that registered three gallons left in the tank, we ran that new engine dry! This is a troublesome thing to do with a diesel engine because you can't simply add fuel and start it again; you have to "bleed" the system to get the air out. We weren't prepared to deal with that on the fly; we called and lined up a mechanic in New Bedford. We anchored for a few hours' sleep and started again in the morning with just the port engine.

This time we checked the fuel level the way we should have before, dipping a dowel into the tank to see how much was left, rather than relying on the gauge. But the port engine started losing power; then running fine for half an hour; then losing power more frequently; until we decided to stop it, too. The morning was calm, and we simply drifted while half the crew took the dinghy ashore to buy fuel in two jerry cans, and the other half replaced the port fuel filter in the hot engine room. The fuel filter that came out was full of crud. We clearly had dirt and/or algae in our tanks. This might explain the "shudder" in the starboard engine as well as the loss of RPM on the port engine. But what to do about it?

With our partially replenished fuel supply and our clean fuel filter, we proceeded under one engine toward New Bedford and our appointment with the mechanic. As we approached the congested harbor entrance, with large fishing vessels approaching from ahead and astern, the one operable engine again started to lose RPM, and then died! We swung the boat out of the narrow channel and hurriedly dropped an anchor, leaving us swinging so close to a navigational buoy that we had to push off from it.

I had anticipated that a predicament like this might happen; I had the dinghy (with its 20-horsepower engine) ready to lower quickly into the water. We did so now and tied it alongside. The hourly opening of the harbor swing bridge was approaching, and we were anxious to connect with the mechanic before the end of the day. While anchored, we did a test run of "pushing" the boat with the dinghy. It seemed to work, so we raised anchor. We radioed the bridge tender to tell him we were coming, with limited maneuverability. He cautioned that he could not hold the bridge open if we were slow arriving. The Coast Guard chimed in, saying that the current had already turned against us, and suggesting we not attempt to come in. A commercial rescue/tow boat was now circling us, vulture-like, and adding to the radio traffic to offer their (expensive) services.

This was tricky going, with the helmsman unable to control the power directly, and the dinghy man unable to hear or see what was going on, and the swing bridge being held open for us (despite what the tender said) while a line of cars waited impatiently for it to close... We made it. And with some additional awkward maneuvering, we made it gently to the dock. What a day!

Trying to get through the drawbridge with time of the essence, with two disabled engines, while the Coast Guard advised against it, and the commercial towboat waited for failure, was our first group action under pressure. It provided a glimpse into our personalities and ability to work (maybe) together. Without hesitation, Tim had taken the helm. Not because he was captain; we didn't have a captain. It was somewhere between leadership and needing to be in control. Perhaps in part it was his training as a physician. Or simply his out-front personality. Both Bill and I tend to hang back to evaluate the situation before stepping into a role.

I went into direct-action mode. I had prepared the dinghy in advance for quick deployment in case of trouble, I had launched it and lashed it alongside when trouble arose. Then I jumped into our makeshift "engine room" – standing in the bucking inflatable boat, adjusting its 20-horsepower push, and trying to assist with the steering. From the dinghy I was unable to see what was ahead or what was happening in the cockpit, nor could I hear the helmsman.

Bill was the utility guy, raising the anchor, going for lines and fenders, seeing what else was needed, ready to take orders. Jesse relayed communications between Tim and me, since we couldn't see or hear each other. It was chaotic, but I thought we showed reasonable teamwork.

But shortly after, when the pressure was off, relaxing with a beer, Bill exploded at Tim! Bill was a mild-mannered gentleman; his outburst was a stunning surprise. Apparently I had missed some of the "fun" by not being able to see or hear the action in the cockpit. There had been a lot of radio chatter, especially between Tim and the commercial towboat. Tim was a talker and a joker, on the radio as well as face to face. It was unnecessary chatter in our emergency, plus uncertainty regarding what was Tim's plan versus what was kidding around, that sent Bill over the top. He had said nothing in the moment, which was just as well. Good for him, I thought, for letting it erupt later, when it was safe.

Tim was thin-skinned; he got defensive when criticism came his way. But he understood what didn't work, and agreed that he would do better next time. Good for both of them, I thought. Maybe this crew would work out...

The mechanic bled the starboard engine for us and got it started again. The boatyard agreed to "polish our fuel" (to clean the crud out) the following day. Jesse and I caught a bus home. We left Tim and Bill with a weather forecast that promised a delightful summer cruise down Long Island Sound, and with our best wishes for two working engines.

Departure Minus 1 Month

With some more cleaning of fuel filters along the way, they made it. Collectively, we were learning how to keep our vessel functioning. For two months Tim lived aboard in New Jersey, and did more preparations, especially focusing on our SSB (long distance) radio and email systems. Meanwhile Bill was preparing for his leave of absence from his software development job, and I was preparing to retire from mine. Then I hit a glitch…

An abdominal pain didn't go away, and I arrived in the emergency department about the same time that my appendix perforated. Two hours later the appendix was gone. I gradually worked my way back up to speed. It was only a minor setback. But everyone had the same thought, "What if it had happened at sea…?" Recovering from surgery was not fun, but this one did have that silver lining. It could have been MUCH worse. Now there was one fewer thing that could go wrong on the voyage. Preparation carried to the extreme…?

My hospital stay was intense. I've long wrestled with how to live a good/purposeful life. That theme was amplified by some heavy drugs. I had vivid dreams of being visited by individuals embodying Good and Evil. In my altered state I witnessed the enormity of the pain in the world, and the heroism of the people who bear witness and offer compassion. In my little way, in my limited capacity, I chose to stand with them – on the side of Good and peace and compassion.

What difference did this vision make? It was a reminder that as long as I still have a working body, I have choices to make, big and small. Those choices are the purest expression of who I am. So choose like it makes a difference! And it might have been the first crack in the armor that had surrounded my heart and cloaked my feelings for most of my life.

Seventh Graders

The Blue Planet Odyssey was more than a collection of boats sailing around the world. It also aimed to raise awareness of the global effects of climate change and the most urgent issues facing our oceans. There was an educational component, and participants were encouraged to reach out to local schools and connect with students and teachers.

I dreaded the idea of talking with students. What did I know about the health of our oceans, about passing this along to others!? With schools having rigid curricula and schedules, why would they take time for me? And what could I say to students that would make any difference?

It helped that my cousin was the superintendent of the nearby Lewiston Public Schools. I could at least talk with him about it. He connected me with a teacher in the middle school, and she and I arranged a face-to-face meeting. My first question: "Is this something you actually are interested in pursuing, or were you ordered to meet with me!?" She gave a wry smile, avoided the direct question, and assured me that her team was interested. I came away thinking, "OMG, what have I gotten myself into?" She planned to work my voyage into the curriculum; I would provide updates along the way; students could post questions on the blog or via email, and I would respond. We scheduled a date for me to introduce myself and tell the 100+ seventh-graders about the trip.

Despite my initial reservations, it was a blast! One doesn't need to be an expert on climate change to share stories about the impact of sea level rise on small islands and island cultures. One doesn't need to be an expert on education to get kids interested in a voyage around the world! The students were engaged and asked a wide range of questions.

Have you ever seen a great white?
Is there such a thing as a two-headed shark?
Will you have a translator aboard?
Do you carry bottled water?
How do you take a shower?
How does the bathroom thing work?
What if you fall overboard?
Do you need a license to sail the boat?
Will you see a Galapagos Tortoise?
Are you concerned about the Ebola virus?
Why is the climate change stuff happening?
You're going to be sailing for HOW LONG!?!?

I think our connection worked. I got their interest in the upcoming voyage. And I think they understood my fundamental message: the oceans are all interconnected, and they have a profound impact on our little planet, the shared home of all humans. I summed it up for them in what became a tagline for our voyage: "One Ocean, One Planet, One Future."

SOUTHBOUND

Departure Minus 3 Days

Hallie and I used to live in a cohousing community, where we built a house and did most of our child-rearing – a beautiful place and delightful people (see www.two-echo.org). I had a small boat-building project in the basement. When we moved out, I decided to keep building the boat (ever so slowly) in the basement, while we rented out the rest of the house. But when the round-the-world plan took hold, the house needed to be sold and I needed to start letting go.

My boatbuilding project went to long-term storage in a barn. The house I had designed, that I loved, was passed to a new owner. My ties with the community receded. Then one day our beloved cat Edward didn't come home, and a search turned up his remains in the woods. Then I sold my old boat, that my father and I had purchased jointly a few years before he died. I sold my car, which had served me unfailingly for four years of zipping between my home in Maine and my office in Massachusetts. And then came one of the biggest "letting go" events – turning in my laptop, surrendering my business email address, cleaning out my office, saying goodbye to my coworkers and walking away from my job (and my income!) that had been a central focus of my life for 28+ years.

So many changes; I wanted to curl up into a ball and just try to breathe for a couple days. But no time for that. I had a day and a half to pack and organize as best I could what I was leaving behind, before Hallie drove me to New Jersey, to the boat. Now it was time to let go of the comforts of home. Sitting on the sofa watching a favorite TV show, eating dinner that was easily prepared in a kitchen that didn't move, with fresh food readily available a few minutes away… Plentiful hot water for a shower anytime. Gathering with friends. Meeting with my men's team. Being with Hallie. Sleeping with no worries about the wind shifting and the anchor dragging. Yikes, I thought, was it too late to turn back??

Onward. No regrets.

Departure Day!

Eighteen months of planning; it was time to execute the plan. The Blue Planet Odyssey was scheduled to depart Key West in two months. In addition to sailing over 1,000 miles to get there, we needed time to prepare/repair and provision.

We left Longport, New Jersey, on November 7, with winds blowing 30 knots and gusting higher. Sailed the night under jib alone – flying minimal sail due to the high winds. We were blessed with a bright moon, and we made good time. We stayed "outside," meaning we did not go the more protected, but longer, route up Delaware Bay and down Chesapeake Bay. We all used scopolamine patches for seasickness, and glad we did. Glad, too, that our boat had a pilot house, providing shelter from the heavy spray and cold.

Delaware…Maryland…into the mouth of Chesapeake Bay. We got a peaceful night's sleep in Norfolk, Virginia, near "Mile 0" of the Intracoastal Waterway (ICW) – the protected chain of rivers, inlets, bays, sounds, and canals that stretches from Mile 0 to Mile 1,236 in Key West.

We entered the ICW and turned into the Dismal Swamp canal. This was a new experience for me – motoring mile after mile through a straight ditch. But it was far from dismal; the trees and the water and the sky were serene. We spent the night tied to shore in a back alley off the canal. What a strange place for a big catamaran to be!

Day 7

One week aboard. Life wasn't easy. Trying to live with two men, each with our distinct lifestyles; in a small space; gear everywhere; endless projects; an occasional shower. Trying to adjust to getting up with the sun and going to sleep many hours earlier than my old routine. Missing the comforts and relationships of home.

We spent a full day at a boatyard in Oriental, NC, because we once again had dirty fuel stalling one engine. The yard polished our fuel through a filtering system all day long. We changed the oil in both engines, which was a messy job. Any job in our cramped "engine rooms" was messy. We started working on problems with the plumbing of our heads/toilets, more work still to be done there. We brought a dead fuel gauge back to life. We failed to fix our wind speed indicator, which worked occasionally, but mostly not. We rigged for a bracket to hold our outboard motor securely, rather than leaving it on the dinghy when we're at sea. A productive day.

Day 20

With a combination of sailing "inside" (on the ICW) and "outside" (on the ocean, overnight jumps of many miles), we arrived in Charleston, SC. For five days we enjoyed the good food, friendly people, interesting history, and architecture. Bill's daughter Nora met us in Charleston, to sail with us for a week.

We left at dawn in the rain, back on the ICW. One engine overheated. Tim determined that the belt for the cooling water system was loose. He tried to tighten it, but it continued to overheat. No big deal, we only needed one engine for tootling along the ICW. Then the second engine overheated, and we had another emergency anchoring drill – in the rain, and strong wind, and strong current.

Inspecting the filters in the cooling system, we found them full of gunk. In retrospect, we should have anticipated that, since the place we stayed in Charleston was so shallow that our props stirred up mud from the bottom. After cleaning the filters, the engines were happy. Another lesson learned.

We navigated some fascinating creeks. Up one, through a cut, down the next; current with us, then against us. Without GPS and a good chart, one could go in circles here!

We anchored late-afternoon in a middle-of-nowhere creek. The wind and rain came up hard just as we were anchoring, and everything on the boat got wet. But in spite of the problems, I was happy to be underway again after our Charleston respite. It even occurred to me while we were setting the anchor in the driving rain that it was rather humorous how much I was enjoying it!

In Beaufort, SC, we stopped at a delightful marina across the bridge from downtown. Showers. Laundry (more importantly a dryer). More good food. Fun walking around town. We stocked up with treats from the bakery and headed out once again in the rain. Though it was calm as we motored down the Beaufort River, strong northerlies were predicted. We wanted to take advantage of that wind and knock off some miles, so we went offshore. It made for a challenging night; rain squalls and gusts to 40 knots; occasional bone-jarring crashes of waves against the side of the boat. The crew did not hold up well, even with Scopolamine.

We put in at St Augustine, FL. By noon we were relaxing, eating the rest of the treats from the bakery, and drying everything out in the sunshine. We were making good time toward Key West, but a different sort of problem arose…

In or Out?

Tim was always up early. When Bill and I awoke, Tim had already been at the computer keyboard for an hour or two. "Guys," he said, "I may have made a mistake!"

This was not a usual greeting from Tim; it was ominous. Tim continued, "We've been thrown out of the BPO!"

The Blue Planet Odyssey had not been looking as rosy as when we registered and sent in our payments. The number of entrants was smaller than expected. The educational aspect of it didn't seem to be kicking into gear. Jimmy Cornell had planned that our first stop would be Cuba, but our application for the American boats to go there was denied (by the USA). And it seemed to some of us that Jimmy wasn't providing information readily.

I suspect most entrants were so focused on preparations that they simply relegated the BPO planning to Jimmy; we would all get up to speed in Key West. But some entrants were expressing discontent in email exchanges. Tim included. While we were sailing south, others suggested Tim contact Jimmy with certain

concerns, and he did. He asked Bill and me to review his email in advance. It
began as follows:

> I am writing on behalf of several registered BPO participants who have
> become more than a bit anxious about several elements of our planned
> voyage. Please know that this email outlining these concerns is sent in all
> ways honoring your incredible work and experience with endeavors of this sort.
> Nonetheless, in the last couple of months, issues have remained unanswered
> and as the days approach for our departure it seems all the more critical that
> they be resolved.

The email listed four open issues that had been raised in conference calls.
My communication style would have been different, but Tim seemed to state the
concerns without getting into blame. Bill and I gave it the nod, and off it went.

Next morning Tim announced our expulsion. I got juice, sat down, rubbed
sleep from my eyes, tried to guess what Tim was talking about, and asked for
the whole story.

Jimmy had responded to the email, but not with answers to the concerns.
Rather, Jimmy wanted to know which BPO participants Tim was speaking for.
This rubbed Tim the wrong way, and without consulting with his sleeping
partners, he sent an email back that described the request to name names as
"McCarthyism." (Bill and I were at this point shaking our heads and hoping
maybe we were still dreaming.) That crossed a hard line with Jimmy. His reply
explained that he was deeply offended, and that he had learned from experience
that you cannot have one "bad apple" in a sailing rally, as it will ruin the
experience for all. He cited the rules we had agreed to, which authorize him to
expel any boat for any reason, provided he returns their entrance fees. Where
should he send the check, he asked.

Our world turned upside down. We had been preparing for the BPO for
18+ months. Tim and I had lined up students to follow our adventures and learn
from us. The BPO is what had kept the three of us together and on track. Without
the Key West departure date looming over us, we never would have made it this
far on schedule. NOW WHAT???

Breathe. Stay calm. Think.

An unexpected idea germinated. Maybe getting thrown out was a good
thing! The BPO fees were not small. We didn't need a rally to sail around the
world. We could still retain our connections with our classrooms. We already
had the benefit of Jimmy's expert input on a good circumnavigation route and
timing of the seasons. The BPO had helped us get ready to go; now our returned
fees could pay for a good portion of the trip.

Alternatively, we could "beg" to be taken back. I could volunteer to be
spokesperson for *No Regrets*. We could acknowledge to Jimmy that Tim's
statement was uncalled for, we would apologize, we would remind Jimmy that

throwing Tim out of the rally meant throwing Bill and me out, too. Plus he would be expelling all our students. We could offer that Tim would no longer send emails to him; that all *No Regrets* communication would be through me.

Should we beg, or take the money? We spent some hours wrestling with this question. The consensus: we were committed to our plan, to the rally. Tim apologized, and I begged for leniency on account of the additional people affected beyond just Tim. We also contacted Doina, Jimmy's daughter, and another person who had worked for Jimmy, asking if they could intercede on our behalf. With some reluctance, Jimmy allowed that we could come back into the fold.

The question of whether to fight to be reinstated, or take the cash, was a useful one. To varying degrees, we had all been complaining about BPO services and communication. Now we had the opportunity to choose, in or out. We chose in. Time to stop griping and make it work!

One Night at Sea

It's never just one thing going wrong that gets you into trouble…

Sailing south along the Florida coast from St Augustine, we had one of the most delightful sailing days ever, and the forecast was for continued clear skies and 15 to 20-knot favorable winds. As the sun set we took down our spinnaker and sailed with the more easily controlled "screecher" (a big forward sail, that can be rolled up with minimal fuss if the wind gets too heavy).

After sunset the wind increased and shifted aft, until it was almost directly behind us. In that situation the mainsail "blankets" the forward sail, causing the latter to lose its wind, collapse, and occasionally fill with a jarring crash. So we rolled up the screecher and sailed with just the mainsail. The wind continued to build on Bill's watch. He put in a reef (decreasing the exposed sail area), and he gybed the boat to head offshore, to clear Cape Canaveral.

At 2300 I started my four-hour watch, after fitful sleep due to the increasingly rough conditions. Bill briefed me that in the course of gybing, our apparent wind indicator was partially damaged. A sensor on the masthead transmits the wind direction to a display on our instrument panel. It still "worked," in the sense that it was consistent, but it showed the wind from astern as though it was from ahead! Consequently he was ignoring the instrument display, and looking at the vane on the masthead to determine the wind direction.

Not long after Bill turned in, I judged that we had made enough distance off from Cape Canaveral, and we should gybe back to run parallel to the coast. It's a bit of a process to gybe, especially when you're not entirely clear-headed. I first checked the instrument that reads the true wind speed. It read 15 knots.

This seemed much lighter than what we had been experiencing, so I decided it was a good time for the maneuver.

Out in the cockpit the wind seemed much stronger than 15, but I still figured that if it went down to 15 even for a moment that was a good sign to proceed. I sheeted the main traveler in to amidships. With the mainsail pulled in that way I could tighten the starboard running backstay, to support the mast when the sail/boom comes crashing over to the new/port side. I left the running backstay tight on the port side also, figuring I would release it after the sail came across. Then I switched the autopilot to "standby" and turned the wheel to starboard. The big mainsail did its expected crash over to port. In the big seas I did 30 seconds of erratic steering to find the right new course, and set the autopilot back to "Auto." Then I eased the starboard side traveler line to let the sail out on the new side. I went back into the pilot house to see if our new course would allow us to sail parallel to the Florida coastline.

There was a JOLT and a BANG in the rigging!

Fearing catastrophe, I rushed back outside. Nothing appeared to be wrong! But a quick survey revealed that the port side running backstay had disappeared. I had neglected to release it before I eased the traveler out on the new side. The entire force of the wind in the big sail had pushed against that runner until something gave way. The good news: on the new gybe we didn't need the port side runner. The bad news: if we needed to gybe back later, and the wind was still blowing hard, the mast wouldn't have the protection provided by the runner, and we could potentially be at risk of losing the entire rig!

Let's review what had gone wrong so far... We expected the more moderate winds called for in the weather forecast, and we weren't prepared for a rough night. Bill's first gybe had somehow damaged the apparent wind indicator, making it difficult to set/hold our course relative to the wind. I had believed the true wind speed indicator when it showed 15 knots, without putting two and two together – that in order for the instrument to compute the true wind speed it factors in the apparent wind angle. The damage to the apparent wind indicator was causing it to "think" the wind was coming from ahead (and thus it subtracted out our boat speed) when in fact it was coming from behind (so it should have added our boat speed). When it read 15 knots, it was really blowing about 30. I let myself be fooled into thinking there was a lull, even though my senses told me the wind was blowing hard. Then I omitted a step in the gybe, resulting in breaking the port side running backstay.

What next...?

On a course to sail parallel to the coast, the wind and seas were now coming from almost dead astern. The seas were building, and we were surfing at speeds that we hadn't experienced before. At one point the knotmeter indicated a boat speed of 17 knots. Fourteen knots or more was becoming common whenever a big wave lifted our sterns and the boat accelerated downhill. Fast can be fun; but this was not fun, it was hairy. The seas push the stern of the boat this way and that, and the autopilot can't respond quickly enough to keep the boat on a steady course. If the boat "yaws" to starboard, it doesn't much matter, except that our course goes closer to shore. If it yaws to port we risk an accidental gybe, where the wind gets on the back side of the big mainsail, and the sail and the heavy boom come flying across the stern of the boat out of control, potentially breaking the remaining runner. Or something more serious.

In most situations we would reduce this risk by setting a course a little closer to the wind. The boat would have to turn further before gybing, thereby giving the autopilot time to respond. But such a course would point us back toward the Florida coast, and before long we would have to gybe out to sea again – a dangerous prospect without the port side runner. On the other hand, if we didn't change course, we faced the even greater risk of an accidental gybe. The heavy weather spinnaker would have allowed us to sail our desired course with no risk, but rigging the spinnaker was complex, and not something we wanted to attempt in the dark. Some line would become tangled and create a new set of problems. The working jib alone would have provided enough power to keep us moving fast, but I had two concerns about that solution. First, it would not be easy to get the mainsail down while sailing downwind. I certainly could not do it alone; I was very reluctant to wake Tim or Bill in the middle of my watch; and I wasn't even sure that two of us could safely do it in these conditions. Probably we could with some assistance from the engines, but the second concern was that we really should have both runners when flying just the jib in this wind.

It was my hope that we could hold the course parallel to the coast at least until the wind eased. Hope is a poor strategy, but I didn't have much else. I rigged a "preventer" line, holding the boom out to port, so if we did gybe accidentally the boom would not fly across the stern with damaging force. We sailed very close to the desired course for the next hour and a half.

During this time I learned to interpret the apparent wind angle shown on our instruments. Although it was wrong, it was possible to compute the correct angle from it. Doing the mental adjustment was easier than constantly looking up at the masthead vane. I got pretty good at it; the mental calculation became automatic. But then an odd thing happened. The instrument showed that I could bear off a little further away from the wind, and thus away from the coast. Good. Then it indicated that I could *still* bear off a little further. I believed that the wind was changing, allowing us to more easily sail the course we wanted. It seemed that my hope was realized, and I felt deep relief.

Then the boat gybed! At the time I couldn't understand why this happened, but there it was. The wind was on the wrong side of the mainsail, the boom/sail held in place by the preventer, which had minimized the impact. The boat was effectively "hove to," with the wind blowing over the side, and the boat drifting sideways. It was relatively peaceful, except for the waves and my mental turmoil still trying to understand what caused the gybe. Maybe we were getting a new wind in my hoped-for direction but with gusts of the old wind.

In any case, what to do now? Normally one would ease the sail out on the starboard side, which would start the boat sailing again, and then make whatever adjustments needed. But I didn't want to do that without the port side runner. And with no forward movement through the water, we couldn't steer to tack or gybe. I decided it was time to wake Tim and have a second brain ponder the situation.

The solution was simple: start an engine and get moving enough to steer downwind and gybe back. I could have done that myself, if I was thinking clearly. Oh well, it was a relief to have Tim say he would start his watch early and I should get some sleep. Tim managed to sail along the coast with just one instance of rounding up into the wind and again having to start an engine to get going again. The "hope strategy" worked out.

In the morning it became clear why we had gybed. The apparent wind indicator still showed the same angle as it had the night before. It had frozen up entirely. I had been making mental wind angle calculations based on a display that no longer had anything to do with the wind! Also in the daylight we retrieved the errant running backstay, and found that it was a shackle that had broken. Easily replaced.

In the end, no problem – just another wild night at sea.

This photo shows the failed shackle from the running backstay, next to a good one. The pin has been screwed back in, after we found it on deck (far from the backstay) the next day. So the pin must have unscrewed, allowing the "U" portion of the shackle to open. When it let go, the pin became a projectile that happened to end up still on the boat.

Once I understood that the pin had unscrewed, it occurred to me to check the backstay on the other side of the boat. That shackle pin was also loose! Note in the photo that the good pin is now properly secured by a wire so that it cannot unscrew. I believe that someone working on the rigging, perhaps a year or more earlier, had left the job incomplete. And we failed to notice.

Key West or Bust!

It was dark when we made the inlet for Ft Lauderdale. We motored up the very narrow New River in the dark, surrounded by a confusion of lights.

Mansions loomed by the water, yachts parked right and left. With relief we found our reserved downtown parking space. There we experienced a steady stream of visits by people walking small dogs.

Aside from the dog walkers, Ft Lauderdale seemed to be about an over-the-top display of wealth. Expensive real estate and expensive megayachts. So, encountering a group of Buddhist monks made for an interesting juxtaposition... We watched them make an elaborate mandala sand painting, and later ceremoniously destroy it. They poured the sand into the river, so the good energy would spread to the ocean and the world. One Ocean, One Planet, One Future!

At Ft Lauderdale we said goodbye to Nora. We had a pleasant sail to Key Biscayne and No Name Harbor, and then decided to do one last overnight sail to reach Key West.

Tim took his usual 0300 to 0700 watch; he was the natural early riser. There was just a hint of dawn when he woke Bill and me to say we were off Key West, and we needed to get the spinnaker down. We pulled on clothes and got to work lowering the sail, and then took a look at our position on the chart plotter. We were several miles beyond the entrance to Key West! We were going to have to motor back against the wind and waves and current for two hours.

"Tim, why didn't you wake us up *before* we were directly off the Key West entrance!?"

"I wanted to let you guys sleep as long as possible," was the reply.

Tim, you have a heart of gold, but you can be a knucklehead!

The mooring area was on the far side of the island. Some of the route was dotted with fishing buoys, similar to Maine lobster pots but with smaller floats. At one point we heard a sharp POP! from the area of our starboard propeller, and looking astern we saw shards of one of the foam buoys. Further along, both engines suddenly stopped. We were entangled with *two* buoys/lines at the same time – one on each propeller shaft. How we could manage to do that remains a mystery. We certainly could not have done it if we tried!

For the third time since leaving Maine, we hastily dropped anchor with both engines out of commission. Bill volunteered to jump in, and he managed to clear one prop. The other one was so tightly jammed that he couldn't get the line off. We cut that line and tied the buoy back on so the fisherman wouldn't lose his gear. We could clear the jam later, continuing with one engine for now.

Arriving at the mooring field (rows of many mooring balls and many boats), we surveyed the area and chose a mooring to pick up. This is a routine maneuver, but it takes some practice to learn how nimbly your boat turns and how quickly it decelerates. Ideally, you come to a complete stop just as the mooring ball comes even with the bow. We didn't quite make it, so Bill turned to make a big circle and a second approach. With only one engine, the big circle didn't go as planned. Our prop clipped another mooring, fouled on it, and the strong wind pushed us into the bow of the attached boat. A big stainless steel anchor roller on his bow punched a hole through our side!

We were in no immediate danger. The hole was well above the waterline. To avoid further damage we tied alongside that boat, while the owner watched, drank his coffee, and wondered what to make of us. There didn't appear to be any damage to his boat. But we were still fouled on his mooring, with his mooring line around our prop. Bill went back in the water and wrestled with it but couldn't free it.

With the other owner kindly providing a dinghy service, we pulled a long line out to the mooring we were originally aiming for, a couple hundred feet to windward. Hauling in on this line took the pressure off of the fouled mooring, and Bill got us free. Then we hauled ourselves up to the new mooring, making profound apologies for our intrusion!

I dove to cut free the remnant of line that was still jammed on one of our props. Tim was already on the phone locating a boatyard that could fix our damage. He made an appointment for that afternoon. We all needed to "chill" for a while to regain our equilibrium, but we couldn't afford to miss the appointment. We set off again for Stock Island, back around Key West.

Key West seemed to be littered with derelict boats. One was sunk, with its mast still showing above the water. One was completely covered with birds. Several looked like they had been there for decades, with no maintenance. As we were taking in these sights, not paying proper attention to our course, we went aground!

We needed only three feet of water to float. It was low tide, which was good – we could simply wait and we would float off. But we had an appointment! We started rigging the outboard on our dinghy, so we could take an anchor out to deeper water and haul, or "kedge," the boat off the shallows. A local workboat happened by. Her skipper sized up our situation and offered to pull us off for $50. We hesitated only briefly; accepted the offer; he made good on it. He also gave us some names of people in the area who do good boat repairs.

Without further incident, we made it to the boatyard. There we discovered that their Travelift (movable crane for lifting the boat out of the water in slings) was only 24' wide. Our boat was 23' 6". I wasn't sure if that included the rubrail or not. Either way, that didn't leave much of a margin! The hands at the yard were confident they could safely lift the boat. Our confidence was lower, especially given how much had already gone wrong in one day. But…they did it.

Now we were sitting "on the hard," getting our bottom repainted, which happily we wanted to do anyway, and negotiating for the repairs to our topsides. Plus various other projects, some of which were more conveniently handled out of the water. We would be stuck there for a week. We rented bicycles and had fun riding around the town and trying out the local restaurants. But I'd rather be afloat. Have you ever watched the TV show Cougar Town? I felt like the guy living on his boat in a parking lot…

Who Pays?

Back in the talking stage, the three of us wrote and signed a Partnership Agreement. This was a modest three-page document, not something done by a lawyer. I did run it by a lawyer friend, and he suggested that it should be rewritten by a lawyer! But we opted for a simple and clear (hopefully) statement of our intent, rather than a bullet-proof volume of legalese. After all, I argued, if we end up in court we will have already "lost." Our focus instead should be making sure we all are on the same page. Here are some important excerpts from the document.

- The purpose of this partnership is to jointly own, maintain and sail the Atlantic 42 Catamaran *No Regrets*, and to complete the Blue Planet Odyssey circumnavigation.
- All decisions about the schedule/use/location/maintenance/ equipment/sailing route/etc, and about the administration of the partnership, will be made by consensus whenever possible, and our intention is to achieve this in almost all cases. If consensus cannot be achieved then decisions can be made by a majority vote, except where noted in this agreement that consensus is required (as for a change of ownership, or a change in this agreement).
- The boat and its equipment will be maintained in good working order, and fully insured.

- Day-to-day expenses (food, fuel, supplies, fees) will be shared equally by the partners aboard the boat. Other expenses will be shared equally by all partners, whether aboard or not.
- Since the primary purpose of this partnership is to jointly participate in and complete the BPO, no partner can withdraw from the partnership and its expenses prior to the completion of the BPO, without the unanimous agreement of the other partners. If the boat is withdrawn from or cannot complete the BPO, this no-withdrawal provision continues until the boat is returned to the USA or Caribbean waters, or the boat is sold or lost. If it no longer works for a partner to participate (e.g., for health or family reasons) he can try to replace himself, and the other partners will make a reasonable effort to accommodate such a replacement. However, since individual personalities are an important aspect of making this partnership work, there is no guarantee that partners will agree to accept a replacement candidate.
- The boat will not be sailed or motored without a partner aboard, except by agreement of all partners. Whenever one partner is aboard, he shall be the captain. Whenever more than one partner is aboard, one shall be designated captain. Captaincy will be recorded in the ship's log.
- All partners share equally in any after-insurance damage or loss.

I think we did a good job coming up with our agreement, and I think it served us well. There is more tale to be told about it, however. The last item was in play now, as a result of our botched entrance to Key West.

That short sentence about sharing a loss equally was the most debated point in the design of our rulebook. We tried repeatedly to draft wording to say who is at fault when something bad happens. Try as we might, we always came up with a "what if" scenario that didn't fit the rule. For example, we tried to say that only those partners who are aboard the boat are responsible for a loss. But what does "aboard" mean? What if one partner has gone ashore and another is on the boat when the anchor drags and the boat goes up on a reef? What if the boat is hit by lightning – are those aboard at fault? In the end, we gave up the idea of "fault," and wrote our "share equally" sentence. In retrospect, this was a mistake.

Bill had been at the helm when we put a hole in the topsides, and although he was hampered by having only one engine, he clearly misjudged our approach. Was he at fault? No matter, our agreement was "no-fault."

But wait! When I hit a rock in Maine and broke a daggerboard, I paid for the repair. There was no question about who was responsible; the other guys had nothing to do with it. I wasn't about to send them a bill for my mistake. Despite our no-fault clause, maybe there was an unspoken range of fault. Maybe it should be up to a possibly-at-fault partner to claim fault?

To complicate matters, when we contacted our insurance company, we learned that we had never notified them that the boat was being sailed in the winter, rather than being laid up in a yard. The insurance would not cover the claim! Our cost was not limited to our expected deductible amount. Who was responsible for our cost above the deductible?

I wondered if Bill would claim fault and offer to pay. He clearly blamed himself. In fact, he was so miserable about his causing it that my focus was on giving him some emotional support. We were exhausted; we had only one engine; we didn't stop to make a clear plan; forgive yourself. He didn't offer to pay, and I thought that was the end of the matter. But it would come up again halfway around the world...

FINAL PREPARATIONS

30 Days to Scheduled BPO Start

The week on the hard was in many ways our most challenging week so far, and relief was not yet in sight. The repairs to our hull were nearly complete – just waiting for the last coat of interior paint. The work looked good. In fact, too good – the repaired surface had a nice gloss that was long gone from the rest of the hull.

What had been difficult about the repair was the epoxy and fiberglass dust within our living quarters. But worse, we were parked next to a large steel workboat where they were grinding the bottom and welding on cooling tubes. For our first days on the hard, with the wind blowing from the east, the noise was annoying, but we could live with it. Then the wind shifted to the north, and their grinding dust covered our boat – ugly and black and into everything. We tried to ignore it, but it became intolerable.

We complained to the yard manager, who reluctantly agreed to move us to a new parking spot, while muttering, "It's a boatyard. That's the gamble you take at a boatyard." We didn't know if we would be charged for the move; we thought it best not to ask…

While stuck in the boatyard, we tackled dozens of projects. Mainsail cover removed and taken to sailmaker for repair. Cracked hatch covers replaced. Mounts reinforced for handrails and cleats on the transoms. Lightning protection system installed at the base of the mast. Electronic chart plotter removed from the cockpit and sent to the manufacturer for a recall/fix. Propellers cleaned/painted. Electric winch switch repaired. Fender boards made to protect the sides of the hull when tied to concrete docks. Dinghy cover made to protect from sunlight. Outboard motor mount completed, to keep the heavy engine secure at sea. Control lines rigged for our new hydrogenerator. Wifi booster antenna mounted. And more.

We thought we were down to the last project that was time-sensitive – getting a mechanic to diagnose why our starboard engine (the "new" one, installed in Maine) was increasingly difficult to start and belched black smoke when it did finally start. The mechanic did a compression test while we watched, and one cylinder was bad. He asserted that the engine had more hours on it than we had been led to believe, and it needed serious work. We agreed to have him remove the engine so he could work on it in his shop. Pulling the engine through the hatch was no small feat!

We watched as the mechanic pulled the engine apart and demonstrated a long list of problems with it. What we thought was a nearly-new engine needed to be rebuilt! And…some of the parts were on back order from Japan. Tim began calling all over the country for parts, but the outlook was not good. We needed to recalibrate our expectations about getting off the hard.

23 Days to Scheduled BPO Start

Bill and I flew home to spend Christmas with our families. Tim had family fly in to visit on the boat. We came close to finishing up our many projects, but unfortunately the boat was still on the hard. It was tentatively scheduled to "splash" the next day. I didn't like leaving Tim and guests with the challenges of getting the boat operational again, and getting settled on a mooring as we had tried to do 16 days before. But, so be it.

The engine had been rebuilt. It was running in the shop, to be installed that day. It would have cost us less to install a brand-new engine when the boatyard suggested it a year before, than to go through all the work in Maine and Florida. Oh well; it's all Journey, and we had learned a lot along the way.

For the hull repair we were still waiting for the interior finish coat of paint; the paint was on order. Buffing our topsides was half done; the guy doing the work was nowhere to be found. The bottom paint for some reason hadn't quite been finished; we could finish it ourselves. The sailmaker was supposed to get our repaired sail cover back to us.

We had purchased a new life raft six weeks before, but we were still waiting for delivery. We were still working on getting insurance to cover our world cruising. There was a lot still to be resolved. Still, at our "Christmas break" it felt like we were very close to where we needed to be.

We had sailed 1500 miles down the East Coast, including some challenging conditions. We had learned a lot about the boat – both its gear and its handling. The three of us seemed to comprise a good crew – effective and generally fun. It had been a good "shakedown," and I believed we would be ready for what lay just over the horizon in the new year.

The 7th graders from Lewiston Middle School sent me some excellent questions. Here they are with the answers that I came up with.

Emma: Are you going to run out of money, since you had all those unexpected repairs?

We each set aside money for the long trip, including money for "contingencies" like major repairs. But we've certainly spent a lot more than we expected so far! We might find we didn't allow enough for contingencies. If we run low, we will still find a way to complete the trip, but it may change our financial plans. For example, I'm not planning to go back to paid work when I return home, but maybe I would have to get another job for a while to bring in more income.

Renee: How is the culture different in South Carolina?

My impression is that people in South Carolina, and in the South generally, are more outwardly friendly than in New England. They are much more likely to say, "Hello, how's it going?" when you simply pass them in the street. And more likely to make eye contact and smile. I think this is an aspect of traditional "southern hospitality." I don't think people in New England are unfriendly, though – just more "reserved."

There are far more African-American people in South Carolina than in Maine. Where we were in Charleston the mix seemed to be about 50-50. Blacks and whites appear to get along with each other very comfortably, at least on the surface. I find this interesting, given Charleston's history as a center of the slave trade. I was told that half of all the slaves brought to North America came through Charleston. The people in this area seem to have accepted this as an unfortunate part of their history, but it is in the past – a lot has changed in 150 years. On the other hand, some people still identify with the Confederate South, and may still resent the "aggression" of the North in the Civil War.

Alia: What will your next stop be?

Originally the plan was for our first stop outside the USA to be Cuba, just 90 miles from Key West. But due to the trade embargo the US has against Cuba, this was not allowed. You may have heard that President Obama is relaxing the restrictions on travel to Cuba, but he does not have the power to lift the trade embargo, so I believe we are still not permitted to go there. Instead, the first stop on the Blue Planet Odyssey is Montego Bay, Jamaica. We do not expect to stay there long. It is mostly a place to rest after our first long-ish passage at sea – about 800 miles, I think – before we continue on to the San Blas islands in Panama.

Ahmed: Have you gone snorkeling?

Well, yes, but not the kind of snorkeling you have in mind. We thought we might do some snorkeling in the Florida Keys between Miami and Key West. But we had very strong easterly winds at that time, which stir up the water and make it difficult to see the reefs and fish. The commercial snorkeling trips were all canceled. We ended up sailing by without stopping. Since arriving at Key West, I went "snorkeling" to clear a lobster trap line from our propeller. That's all so far, but I expect we'll have many chances coming up to do more interesting snorkeling.

Katelyn: Will your trip go overtime since you had this unexpected delay?

Although we've had unexpected problems and spent an unexpected amount of time "on the hard," I wouldn't say we've had a delay. We allowed time for working through problems, and we actually arrived in Key West ahead of our plan, due to the jumps offshore and through the night, rather than staying on the Intracoastal Waterway. The all-important date is January 10th. That is when we, and most of the other Blue Planet Odyssey boats, are scheduled to leave Key West and the USA. As long as we can be ready to go then, which of course we plan to be, then we're still good.

Jordyn: Thanks for telling us about your Thanksgiving. Will you be having a New Year's Eve party?

Bill and I will be traveling back to the boat on New Year's Eve, arriving just after midnight. So we won't be joining a traditional party. But in the sense that New Year's celebrations are about new beginnings, we will be right there – beginning our "odyssey."

6 Days to Scheduled BPO Start

The Big Day was approaching. All but one of the boats leaving from Key West were there, and the last was expected shortly. Jimmy Cornell was there, with his boat *Aventura*, and his wife Gwenda and daughter Doina. We had our first BPO briefing, plus a social gathering. I looked forward to getting to know the other crews better. So far I was just trying to remember names and who was on what boat.

Two boats had just withdrawn. One due to health issues of the owner, one due to lack of funds. Both crews were there, and delightful people. Very disappointing that they wouldn't be voyaging with us. The size of our fleet was much smaller than originally planned. It looked like seven boats would leave from Key West. That was including Jimmy, who would be sailing on a different schedule, but meeting us in Tahiti. There would be six boats leaving from Martinique and joining us in Panama. Three other boats were leaving from other points and would join the fleet in the Pacific.

We still had issues to resolve. Number one on the list was of course engine-related. The rebuild of the starboard engine was completed, and the boat returned to its liquid element. But, believe it or not, on the sea trial to test that engine, the other one started to smoke and make unsettling noises! The port engine went to the shop to also be rebuilt. Could we get it back into the boat and tested in time for the scheduled start? No one could say.

Some said our engine rooms were cursed, and we were going to suffer ongoing problems. I preferred to think that, like getting my appendix out, we were doing some serious preparation, and things were going to be better for our efforts. It would have been naive to think all the problems would suddenly stop, but I did think we were doing everything we could to improve the situation.

We started finding places to stow gear that had never had a proper home. That made me happy – finding places for things. And, in fact, finding out exactly what things we had. We discovered that we had 6 inflatable life vests with safety harnesses, plus 2 more without harnesses, plus 4 additional harnesses (not inflatable). Of the twelve total, we gave 6 away to the boat next door. Better to have less stuff, and be clear about what it was and where it was… We did an initial big shop for non-perishable food; we planned to do another toward the end of the week for perishables (though not much room was left in the galley for stowing more).

Another potential hurdle was our safety inspection, that would be done by Jimmy Cornell. We had prepared for the inspection, but a lot would be open to interpretation, and Jimmy would be doing the interpreting.

Things were going to start happening in rapid succession. I knew that many smaller items would get pushed off the list as the deadline approached. It's all Journey…

Our engine woes did not let up. When the mechanic opened up the port engine in his shop, he said, "You know this engine isn't the same size as your

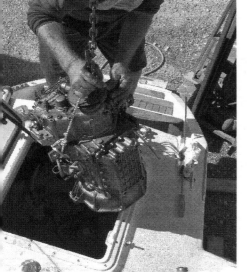

other one?" What?? He asserted that the engine he rebuilt earlier was 20 horsepower, and the one he was working on now was 27. Our engines were supposed to be 27. So…the "lightly used" (not) engine we had installed in Maine wasn't even the right size…? We didn't believe it. It looked the same, and the Maine mechanic had told us it was a direct replacement for what we had. We climbed into the engine room with a flashlight, and there it was stamped right on the engine block: 20 HP.

"If you want," said the mechanic, "I can put a 27-HP engine on your starboard side. My girlfriend has one in her boat. I rebuilt it last year. She wants me to give her a bigger one anyway." Crazy. But maybe.

4 Days to Scheduled BPO Start

More bad news. The cylinder head for our port engine rebuild was not available, back-ordered from Japan. The old head had to be sent to Miami to be reconditioned. This was going to add days that we didn't have. We tried to rent a car to drive it to Miami, but we found there weren't any rental cars available in Key West. We shipped it overnight. Our mechanic got the shop in Miami to promise to move it to the front of their queue. But it was becoming apparent that we were not going to be ready for the BPO start on Saturday.

We were on the hard once again, for work on the saildrives. Frustrating, but lucky that we could schedule it on short notice.

2 Days to Scheduled BPO Start

No chance that we could make the Saturday start. The cylinder head that was sent to Miami was found to have a crack. Luckily our mechanic had the foresight to also send our old engine head (from the starboard engine, where we bought a new head for its rebuild). It was inspected and passed muster; was on its way back to the mechanic. With only a little luck we would get back in the water Monday. Then we needed to give the engines a thorough workout before leaving the area. If everything worked (did it ever...?) we might start chasing the fleet Wednesday or Thursday.

1 Day to Scheduled BPO Start

Although we were not ready to start, we were doing better than some of the other entrants. Originally Jimmy Cornell was concerned that we might have too many boats to be manageable for going to small islands. Of that initial burst of interest, only about 15 boats actually registered for the rally, with about half planning to start from Key West. At least two had dropped out. The one that was short of funds was hoping to start later and catch the fleet in Tahiti. Wishful thinking? We now heard there was some uncertainty about yet another boat. In the end we would be one of only four or five BPO boats to start from Key West, plus there was one Pacific Odyssey boat (sailing only as far as the Marquesan Islands in French Polynesia). The fact that we would be several days late in departing seemed like a minor point in this context.

We got our repaired saildrives back in place. Our rebuilt port engine got tested in the shop, was working in record time, and got put into the boat. Both engines needed to be wired to the electrical controls again, so we couldn't use them yet. Nevertheless, we went back into the water and got a tow from the boatyard to the marina where the other BPO participants were docked. We hoped we would be able to use both motors by Monday, so we could test them and leave maybe mid-week.

Jimmy completed our safety inspection. He summarized his review with, "It's better than I expected." We balked at that "compliment," but he explained that given our problems, he hadn't expected us to be done with our safety preparations. So it was indeed a compliment that we were ready. He had one suggestion for an improvement to better secure our propane tanks, which was a good suggestion, and would not be difficult to do.

In the evening we had the "captain's briefing" before the BPO start the following noon. Suddenly it felt very real that we were about to head off around the world, despite our delay. Routes and winds and currents and forecasts and starting time and daily radio check-in procedures and satellite tracking devices and information about arriving in Jamaica and in the San Blas islands off of Panama. Wow! Was it safe to start dreaming about tropical islands…? First we needed to think about food shopping!

Jimmy and Doina Cornell completing our safety inspection

ISN'T IT DANGEROUS?

Most people believe it is dangerous to sail a small boat across an ocean. There certainly are hazards. But offshore sailing today is very different from just a few decades ago, before GPS and other satellite communications. Technological advances have reduced many of the dangers. "What's the worst that can happen?" was a quip I would cheerfully toss at the crew when we faced an unknown. But it is a serious question at preparation time. Let's look at what could go wrong, and how we addressed each contingency aboard *No Regrets*.

Hitting a Reef

There is simply no excuse for this anymore. We have GPS in our cars, and of course we have GPS in our boats. We have chart plotters that display an image of a chart, and the boat's position is clearly displayed thereon, with pinpoint accuracy. Almost every spot in the world has been charted in amazing detail. Especially offshore, there is no reason one should ever hit a rock or reef.

What if the electronics fail? What if the batteries die? These are contingencies that must be planned for. On *No Regrets* we had multiple backups. We carried two iPads with built-in GPS and loaded with charts. These provided nearly 100% of the functionality of the primary chart plotter system. If we somehow lost these first three systems, we had a battery powered satellite tracker that would give us the coordinates of our position, and we could plot that on one of our basic small-scale paper charts. We also had a battery powered VHF radio that included GPS position reporting.

Boats with functioning chart plotters have still been known to sail onto a reef. How? One scenario is that the person on watch falls asleep, and the autopilot sails the boat into harm's way. Hmm, falling asleep at the wheel is not a hazard unique to boats, and in fact 99%

of the time it carries no harsh consequence on a boat. Another scenario is the navigator failing to "zoom in" to see small details on the electronic chart. A chart display cannot show every detail for a large area on its display. If the navigator chooses to display an entire ocean, a small offshore reef could go unseen. Like falling asleep at the wheel, the crew simply should not allow this to happen.

There needs to be a second/backup source of power. Most yachts have at least an alternator on an engine, plus solar cells and maybe a small wind generator. *No Regrets* had all of these, plus the second alternator/engine, and a hydrogenerator that produced electricity by dragging a propeller through the water. We also had three separate banks of batteries: the house batteries that were for general use, a starter battery reserved just for starting engines, and an electronics battery to optionally power the electronics separate from the house battery.

Hitting a Ship

Not many years ago, the risk of being hit by a ship at sea was a major concern. No longer, due to another modern technological advance called AIS (Automatic Identification System). AIS is a radio-based system that enables nearby vessels to know your presence, your boat name, the size/type of your vessel, your position, your heading and speed, and other details. All large commercial ships have AIS. Smaller yachts should at least have a receiver (so they can know about ships and stay clear). Many, including *No Regrets*, also transmit their information.

Large commercial vessels can usually be "seen" via AIS long before they are spotted on the horizon. With that much lead time, plus their heading/speed information, there is rarely an excuse for a "close call." Occasionally there are complicating factors, due to course changes and navigational obstructions, but AIS also makes it easy to get on the VHF radio, hail the ship by name, and work out the plan for staying clear.

More worrisome nowadays are fishing vessels. Many range far offshore, and most do not carry AIS. They may be pulling nets behind, making unexpected course changes, and their attention is likely on things other than approaching boats. Ergo, it's still necessary to keep a careful lookout!

Hitting Something Else

There are things in the ocean to hit that might not be seen by a lookout, especially at night. We've all heard of floating shipping containers, and there is other "junk." It is rare, but hitting something like that at high speed could put a sizable hole in the boat. Boats have sunk after collisions with whales, as well. I don't think there's much to be done about these hazards, other than to prepare. One nice aspect of a catamaran like *No Regrets* is that the boat won't sink. So a collision could be disastrous, but we would probably be able to continue limping along. A traditional monohull, on the other hand, might sink. The only answer to that is to have a life raft at the ready.

Wild Weather

Wind, waves, and lightning are all threats. The first step in mitigating these risks comes in the planning stage. You don't embark on a passage in a hurricane-prone region during hurricane season! Warming oceans have increased the length of the storm seasons worldwide; this change needs to be factored into the plan. Modern technology comes into play, in that we can almost always know what is coming. Whether via satellite or SSB radio, we can download wind, wave, and weather reports and predictions. In most cases, predictions are good enough to allow sailors to anticipate and avoid storms.

Bad weather can be extremely uncomfortable, and seasickness can be a major factor compounding other problems. (It's never simply one thing gone wrong that gets you into trouble…) But the major risk for a catamaran is capsize. Unlike most monohulls, if a catamaran flips over, it is not coming back upright. But it's not going to sink either. There is a safety trade-off between the unsinkability of a good catamaran and the uncapsizeability of a good monohull.

Capsize can be caused by wind or waves. Except for rare occurrences such as microbursts, one can adjust/reduce the sails to deal with heavy wind. It is more difficult to mitigate the risk of huge waves. Many catamarans carry "drogues," which can be towed behind the boat to slow it down and keep it from surfing into the wave ahead, or turning side-to and being rolled over. We chose not to carry a drogue; we judged for the route we were traveling there was a vanishingly small chance of encountering capsize-inducing waves.

Lightning can kill a crew member, zap all the electronics aboard, start a fire and/or blow a hole in the boat. One can have endless arguments among sailors/experts as to how to protect a boat from lightning. We did some research and chose an approach that bonds the aluminum mast to a metal spike pointed toward the water between the two hulls. The theory is that a strike would follow this route and arc to the water. We never put it to a good test…

Some sailors disconnect as many devices as possible in an electrical storm, and small devices can be put in the oven. The oven should act like a Faraday cage, protecting the electronics inside. Most importantly, crew should stay away from the metal rigging of the boat.

Medical Emergency

As I was made acutely aware just before leaving, a crewmember could rapidly develop appendicitis, and it could become life-threatening in short order. In bad conditions, falls are not uncommon, perhaps resulting in broken ribs or a head injury. For conditions that are not life-threatening, sailors should have some first aid training, and carry a well-stocked medical kit. In our case we also carried a doctor (Tim)! If my appendix had perforated at sea, we would have been calling for help.

Falling Overboard

Of all the risks, I believe this is the greatest. At night we commonly have only one person awake, and the boat is on autopilot. Someone could go overboard and wouldn't even be missed for up to four hours! We might be 40 miles away at that point. I try to make my crew conscious of the danger by telling them unequivocally, "If you go overboard, you are dead." I lighten things up a little by adding that consequently we have a rule at sea: "No swimmers."

We all have harnesses that we can wear, and we rig "jack lines" that allow movement on deck while being securely attached to the boat. But few cruising sailors wear (and attach) harnesses religiously, ourselves included. Especially on a catamaran where the water seems to be so far from the cockpit, due to its wide beam and its stability. Yes, sailors use harnesses when conditions are violent, but as my father only-half-jokingly used to say to me, "Of all sailors recovered after falling overboard, half of them had their zippers down…"

My lifejacket/harness rig included a small AIS device. When turned on (after falling overboard) it would broadcast a distress signal on the same AIS system that locates ships. It would trigger an alarm on any AIS system nearby, though it is limited to 2-3 miles. There are also personal devices that transmit a distress signal by satellite. For mid-ocean, I think there is only one boat that has a chance of recovering you, and that's the one you fell from. The AIS signal is the best chance to alert your crew of your situation and your location. It would still be a long shot, though. The alarm wouldn't waken an exhausted crew.

Pirate Attack

This is another risk that you live with in several areas of the world. There are a few things you can do – primarily avoiding the highest risk areas, and traveling in company with other boats. Some boats carry firearms, but I seriously doubt they help in most cases, and they could make a dicey situation worse. We had none. Some boats, including *No Regrets*, carry pepper spray. That's not going to help if you have a boatload of armed pirates intent upon coming aboard. But it may help if a local fisherman gets it in his head to rob you.

When Things Go Really Wrong…

Most yachts carry an EPIRB (Emergency Position Indicating Radio Beacon). Although the name says "radio," new units communicate via satellite. When things have gone totally wrong, and you need help, you can flip on the EPIRB. Some units will come on automatically if they are immersed in water; ours required a person to flip the switch. Once activated, authorities are alerted. Of course, if you are in mid-ocean they may not be able to help you in time. And if help does arrive, you need to be prepared to leave your floating home behind, if you haven't already.

While the EPIRB is the ultimate form of calling for help, there are many other ways to communicate from a boat. Short distances between boats calls for a VHF radio, which is standard equipment, and which includes an emergency hailing channel that boats are required to monitor. Most offshore boats have a high-frequency radio. This can be SSB (single sideband) or "HAM" (amateur radio) or both. On *No Regrets* we also had a satellite tracker device (provided by the BPO so they could track our position on their website). Like the EPIRB, the tracker works anywhere, and can send the boat's GPS coordinates. It can send short messages to your contacts, or send an emergency notification. If our boat were to break its mast, the VHF and the high-frequency antennas would end up in the ocean. We carried a second VHF radio with a deck-mounted antenna (plus two handheld units), and we carried an emergency antenna that could be stretched out on deck for our SSB radio. Many boats would also carry a satellite telephone or other means of satellite communication. We did not, but we felt we had adequate systems and backups for communication.

An inflatable liferaft is a must-have for passage-making boats that can sink. For an unsinkable boat like ours, the value is not so clear. If your catamaran were engulfed in flames, you would be happy to have a liferaft (though if the weather isn't too nasty, your dinghy would also be an option). After a capsize, maybe a liferaft would provide better shelter than your swamped upside-down boat. I would have considered going without a liferaft for our voyage, except that the Blue Planet Odyssey required one. Some boats have a built-in space to store the raft. Ours did not, and its home was a large locker near the mast. This could present a challenge if the boat were upside down, to get it out of the locker to deploy it. To help with that, we carried a dive mask in our ditch bag.

Ditch Bag

Most boats carry a waterproof bag or other container that is stocked with essential items and is ready to grab on short notice in an emergency. The liferaft probably has a few items packed inside it – some seasickness pills, some sunscreen, some water, a small knife. Our ditch bag held dozens of additional items: a small medical kit, a jar of peanut butter, more water, a hand operated water purifier/desalinator, a Leatherman multi-tool, a coil of small rope, fish hooks and line, a handheld VHF radio with GPS, reading glasses, a cutting board (for using the knife in an inflatable boat!), dive mask and snorkel, flashlight, batteries, laser flares, plus we kept our EPIRB there.

So, Is It Dangerous?

There are more hazards to think about than when you drive your car across town at rush hour. Hard to say if it is more dangerous, though. You choose a seaworthy boat, you equip it properly, you plan a good route, you get good crew, you learn and prepare. Then you minimize the risks that you can, and you follow your dreams with a light heart.

≈≈≈

THE RALLY BEGINS

The day had finally arrived, for those who were ready. Jimmy Cornell aboard *Aventura* left the dock first, to preside over the starting line. The BPO Rally wasn't a race. But when sailboats are within sight of each other and/or have a common destination, let's just say they are comparing their sailing performance. Some in a laid-back way, some in a hell-bent way.

Jimmy had hoped to sail the Northwest Passage from east to west, and then meet the fleet in the Pacific. Sailing the Passage was aligned with the goal of raising awareness about climate change. But after sailing to Greenland and into the eastern end of the Passage, it was unclear whether the ice would clear a path through or not, and to be safe Jimmy had turned back. Now he had joined us in Key West. But he would not be leaving with us, as he was to show his new boat at the Miami Boat Show. Then he would try to catch the fleet later in Tahiti.

Second off the dock was *Tahawus*, a 54' Amel ketch, sailed by Norm and Klaudia, with her two boys. They were in the Pacific Odyssey, sailing in company with us for just the first 5,000 miles or so.

Next out was *Chapter Two*, a big and luxurious 45′ Lagoon, and the only other catamaran starting from Key West. Sailed by Pat and Janet, with Sue and John as crew.

Then came *Ransom*, a classic old Hinckley 49. Sailed by Tim, Ceci, Pip, and Daphne.

Gypsie was next; Benjamin and Joseph aboard. But their departure was only for show. They were the crew in need of funds, hoping to go later along with Jimmy.

Last to go was *Gusto*, a beautiful custom boat that we had first seen back in Belfast, Maine.

Well-dressed but forlorn at the dock was *Joyful*. Jeff and Anne's crew backed out the day before. They hoped to find new crew and depart later with *Aventura* and *Gypsie*.

Remaining at the dock also was the 48' *Imagine*, withdrawn due to health issues.

And *No Regrets*, with both mechanic and electrician spending their Saturday doing a lot of swearing and trying to get us going. Supposedly both engines were now working. Still some wiring issues to be sorted out.

The three left-behind crews went out to dinner together. It was a nice way to simply acknowledge that, well, "Here we are," each for different reasons and each with different plans, but all part of a community of voyagers.

Scheduled Start Day +1

It was hard for us now, watching the positions of the boats on the BPO tracking website, while we remained behind. We had some positive news (the rebuilt engines ran okay for a couple of hours of sea trial) and some setbacks (electrical issues related to wiring the engines into the existing systems). One day at a time…

Scheduled Start Day +2

Just for a moment, I thought about abandoning our boat/crew and offering to crew aboard *Joyful*… But no, that was not the journey I was on.

We made an updated plan to address our remaining issues:

1. "Trade in" our too-small engine that we got in Maine (and just had rebuilt!), for the mechanic's girlfriend's engine of the right size. He says he can do this in 5 hours on Wednesday! I know this sounds crazy, as it introduces new risks of things going wrong, but we are leaning toward doing it anyway.

2. "Trade in" our two new alternators for a different type that can be wired into the boat's existing systems, rather than require a different/separate solution. Hopefully this can also be done Wednesday.

3. Speak with a service expert about our watermaker, which made bad-sounding noises when we tested it yesterday, even though it successfully produced fresh water. The goal is to either be reassured that the noises are normal, or take it apart again and figure out what we did wrong when we serviced it.

4. See if we can understand why the hydrogenerator, which we tested yesterday, does not show up on our electrical systems monitor as charging the batteries, despite the fact that it appears to be generating current. We may decide that since it is working (apparently), we won't worry about the lack of confirmation on the monitor, but it would be nice to eliminate this mystery.

5. Stock up with fresh food and go.

We hoped to be off within one week of the original start date. This would still put us in a better position than many of the entrants. The tracking chart on the BPO website showed that one of the 4 boats that left Saturday for Jamaica had turned back! An email said they have technical issues, but we didn't know any details. That put us in "4th place" in our little fleet. Of course, it was not a race.

Scheduled Start Day +4

Installed the rebuilt starboard engine, but the guys didn't finish before quitting time, so no confirmation as yet that it worked. Electrician was working on remaining electrical issues. Bill and I took a lot of the day off to bicycle into old Key West and look around at the architecture and eat yummy food.

Other BPO boats and "Rally Control" contacted us to ask if we had left yet. That they were even thinking of us brought some cheer. They would arrive in Jamaica soon. We would probably skip Jamaica, to make up some of our lost time. We would catch the fleet in San Blas, islands off the coast of Panama.

Scheduled Start Day +7

We had more ups and downs. Both engines were running okay. But now they were not charging the batteries. An urgent call to the electrician resulted in their working fine when he arrived... Just like taking your car to the mechanic!

Then there was a blockage in a fuel line, but that was something we knew how to track down ourselves. Bottom line…we planned/hoped to leave tomorrow.

We borrowed a car for a major food shopping trip. In the afternoon we "stopped work early" to go into town with our fellow BPOers-still-in-Key-West. We checked out the Seafood Festival (artists, rock band, and…seafood), and walked to the sunset pier where the tourists and the street performers mix. It was a fun time, and it felt like the right way to spend the night before departure. A touch of sadness saying goodbye to our new friends, hoping we will see them again.

The plan was to leave for a "sea trial" in the morning. If all went well, we wouldn't return. Instead of not going until we were ready, we were turning things around, and "going unless we had to return." And did we ever feel ready to go – to complete our escape from the clutches of Key West!

We were considering a stop in Cuba. President Obama had just announced that relations were thawing, which was exciting. But it was still against the US government's rules to take a yacht there. We had spoken with several people who had sailed there anyway. Tim was strongly in favor; he had visited Cuba multiple times in the past. If we did go, we didn't want our satellite tracker documenting the fact, so it would be turned off at certain points.

Goodbye Key West, Goodbye USA!

We were ready. Ready enough, anyway. Key West felt like quicksand; like the edge of a black hole; like Hotel California. Relax, it beckoned; it's warm here; it's charming; time is flexible; why get all twisted in a knot? Stay. I was haunted by images of the derelict boats we saw when we arrived. The mast of one reaching upward from its sunken hull; another smothered with birds and guano; the many boats on foul moorings, and on makeshift cradles ashore. Boats that were clearly never going anywhere else.

We must resist! We were on a mission; we had to break free. We left Key West mid-morning to a fanfare of conch shells and blaring boat horns. There were waves from friends and from people I had not met – inhabitants, perhaps, of the boats caught in the grip of the Key West black hole. If our "sea trial" had gone badly after such a resounding farewell, I would have been reluctant to return to the same marina!

But things went well. I was SOOOO happy to be moving again!

It was a beautiful sailing day. As dusk settled, we were gliding across a peaceful Gulf Stream, flying our big spinnaker. We did some fiddling with the hydrogenerator, trying to get it working consistently. We had a fully stocked freezer for the first time, so we were drawing more current than in the past. We needed the hydropower or we would have to run engines to charge the batteries.

During Bill's night watch he was hailed on the VHF radio by an invisible Coast Guard vessel. They must have been close by, since they referred to us as a catamaran. But no lights or AIS signal on their part. They asked a lot of questions about the boat, the crew, and our destination (Panama, of course). Then off they went, apparently, still unseen.

Day 2

In the morning we put in at Club Hemingway, near Havana. We all wanted at least a taste of Cuba. We also had a problem with the control system for our port engine. That conveniently gave us a justification to stop for repair.

Quite a parade of officials came aboard. All very nice, but all asking for "tips." In addition to cash tips, one gentleman searching the boat took a liking to Bill's deodorant, which fit neatly into his pocket. He asked directly if he could have it; it was a small thing, but I didn't feel like I really had a choice. We also had to pay for visas and a sailing permit, and of course a docking fee in the marina. This is all the stuff I didn't like about cruising, that I thought would be good to have Jimmy take care of for us. But this time we were on our own.

Clearing in with the Medical, Customs and Immigration officials, I was scared. I've always been uncomfortable not speaking the local language. Add to that the general fear of officials who have power over you – maybe confiscating your boat and/or detaining you for reasons you don't fully understand. Or merely charging you some inexplicable and unreasonable fee. Add to that the uncertainty that it was still against US rules to sail to Cuba. On top of all that, I had a cold and a slight fever. The first hurdle was a medical clearance, and the form expressly asked if anyone aboard had a fever. I said no, of course. But the doctor came equipped with an infrared forehead thermometer and took our temperatures. He took mine last and chuckled, "A little high. The capitán must be feeling some stress."

Whew!

The first time I arrived at a foreign port, decades ago, and faced the unfamiliar check-in process in a foreign language, I asked the English-speaking skipper of the nearest boat if he had any advice before I met with the authorities. "Yes," he said, "Smile. Don't laugh." These three words have been my check-in mantra. Be demurely friendly; take it seriously. I would say little, be deferential, use "Sir" frequently.

It became apparent at this first set of *No Regrets* formalities that Tim had a different approach. He wanted to have fun with the officials, learn something new. How often do they find drugs on yachts? What drugs are most problematic locally? What do they think about the political party currently in power? Do they feel that their government addresses their needs? In addition, he liked to joke with the officials. Suggesting that we had a large stash of drugs aboard, for example. The person in uniform would have the same did-he-actually-just-say-that look that I did. Tim would keep right on smiling and kidding, and before you knew it, he was best buddies with the guy. It seemed to work, but I was pretty sure the "captain's stress fever" worsened.

We paid our "tips," and we were in. We had an interesting meeting with the Comodoro of Club Hemingway, who told us a long history of yachting in Cuba. We took a taxi to downtown Havana and had a walk around. The city felt like it had a story to tell; one should live there a year to absorb the rhythm, the soul. Ah well, we were only there for a day, peeking in.

We spent hours tracking down the engine control problem. In the end it was just a loose wire connection to a terminal strip deep in our electrical locker. We managed to get underway around noon. Our destination was uncertain. We had heard there was great cruising on the south coast of Cuba. On the other hand, we had also heard that we would only be allowed ashore at a handful of designated areas, and they weren't the areas attracting us.

Also in question was whether we would try to go to Jamaica, as the other Key West boats had done, or skip it to make up lost time. The three boats ahead were about 400 miles from San Blas. We had 800 miles to go, if we went direct. Six additional boats were on their way from Martinique, and their distance-to-go was similar to ours. But they would likely have more wind than we, and from a more favorable direction.

When we got to the western tip of Cuba, we had to choose. A nice breeze came up just there. It would have been in our face for cruising Cuba, but just right for a course to Panama. None of us cared much about Jamaica. So, with a touch of disappointment about not seeing more of Cuba, we set the course for Panama.

Over the next several days of sailing, one of my most enjoyable activities was answering more questions from the 7th graders.

So many problems with the boat; why not sell it and get a new one?

Several reasons…The first is cost. We bought a 15 year old boat because that's what we could afford. A new boat of a similar type would cost 2 to 3 times as much and be beyond our means. Also, remember that we thought we had taken care of our major problems last summer. By the time we discovered that was not the case, it was too late to switch boats even if we could afford to do so. It takes time to equip a boat with all the right gear and "get to know her."

Have the other boats had a lot of problems?

As far as I know, the other boats have not had the kinds of problems that we have. (But we haven't spoken with the boats coming from Martinique yet. They will rendezvous with us in the San Blas Islands off of Panama.) The boat *Gusto*, also from Maine, had problems with their electronics, possibly due to a lightning strike. They turned back to Key West for repairs. We're hoping to see them restarted soon, but according to the daily position report we get over the radio, they are still in port. One boat had to withdraw due to health concerns. One boat is indefinitely delayed due to crew problems. Another is indefinitely delayed due to a shortage of money. So there are many kinds of problems that can arise. Ours appear to be manageable (though we were in doubt about that for a while!).

What kind of weather are you expecting on the 800 mile tour?

This is a major topic of conversation on board right now. When we cleared the western tip of Cuba, we thought that we would be able to sail a direct course to San Blas. The winds along the way commonly blow from the northeast, but we've had southeast winds. As you probably know, a sailboat cannot sail much closer to the wind than 45 degrees. Catamarans, ours included, cannot even sail that close unless the water is smooth. We've been doing a lot of bouncing around, sometimes with spray blowing over the bows, and we're feeling pretty uncomfortable. Not much desire to cook or eat. We're hoping for a wind shift soon. Wind aside, it is mostly sunny and warm.

How far away from you will other boats be at any given time?

The three boats ahead of us that left from Key West have been staying close together – probably within sight of each other. But we are 400 miles behind them. We saw one sailboat as we rounded Cuba; it was headed west to Mexico. We've seen perhaps a dozen ships since we left Cuba. We have to pay attention to them – where they are and where they are headed, so we can be sure to avoid them. Once we catch up with the other boats, I expect we will commonly be within a few miles of one or more, except for the long ocean passages, where the boats will likely spread apart.

Did you go through the Bermuda Triangle?

Nope. Maybe on the way home…

What kinds of personal conflicts have you experienced onboard?

The three of us have gotten along remarkably well. As Bill suggests, we have a "common enemy" (engine problems, etc.) that brings us together. But I don't think we need a common enemy to get along well. It can be challenging to live in a small space, with little sleep (when at sea), and still be considerate of others, but so far, so good.

Have you seen any sea animals yet?

Very few. Many people saw manatees when we were in Key West, but I always seemed to come along just after they swam away. One dolphin paid a visit this morning. We have flying fish now, which are fun to watch. Sometimes they seem to glide endlessly, just above water. We caught two fish that were mackerel-like, but bigger than what I've seen in Maine.

How old were you when you first went sailing, bought *No Regrets*, and decided to sail around the world?

I learned to sail when I was 13, when I joined the Sea Explorer Scouts. My father had been a sailor, and he was very supportive of my sailing (he bought boats that I could use!). When I was in college I crewed on a boat crossing the Atlantic. Later Hallie and I bought our own cruising boat, left our jobs, sold our cars, sold our condo, and for a year we sailed across the Atlantic and back. I thought maybe that would be enough to satisfy my urge to cross oceans, but the idea of sailing around the world has always hung around. I was 59 when Hallie made a comment about my getting too old to do a circumnavigation. That spurred me into action, and my partners and I bought *No Regrets* a few months later (nearly two years ago now), and signed up for the Blue Planet Odyssey.

What places do you look forward to visiting most?

I tend to get more excited about the passages (between places) than about the places themselves. I think that is rather unusual; for many sailors the boat is the means of visiting cool places more than a means of crossing an ocean. But I find the Panama Canal intriguing, and the idea that we will cross from one ocean to another via a man-made "ditch" definitely has my interest. The Galápagos Islands are high on my list, due to their abundant and varied wildlife. French Polynesia is up there due to its classically beautiful, romantic allure. Australia has always seemed like a cool place. I've been there, but only on a business trip, so I saw the sights of Sydney only.

Is the saying, "Red sky at night, sailor's delight; red sky in morning, sailors take warning" true?

Hmm. It is true enough that the saying sticks around and sailors notice the red skies. But like most weather predictions, it is often wrong. At sea we get weather forecasts via the SSB (single sideband) radio, along with our email. The forecasts include both a textual description of the general weather patterns, and charts that show the predicted wind direction and strength. These, too, are often wrong, but they are probably more useful than relying on sayings.

Landfall

We had beautiful sailing into Porvenir, San Blas Islands, east of Panama. For $100 apiece we got through Immigration and acquired a local cruising permit.

Before the anchor was even set we were visited by local Guna people in boats ranging from outboard skiffs to dugout canoes, offering lobsters and molas (embroidered fabric designs). I sent them all away; told the mola ladies to come back tomorrow. They were still nearby later when we were settled, so I waved to them and they paddled over. They asked (in Spanish) if they could come aboard. Of course. I didn't realize that the invitation was assumed to extend to another boat full of mostly teenage girls as well. No problem. They brought dozens, maybe hundreds, of molas aboard with them. It felt like a line had already been crossed; I was going to have to buy one.

An older woman pulled out one mola after another from a tub, and showed me not just the design but the detailed stitching on the back. I nodded appreciatively, though I didn't know enough to judge the quality of her work. I chose one quickly, so she would stop pulling them from the tub. Twenty US dollars, she said. I wondered if I was expected to haggle over the price. I didn't want to offend; I also didn't want to be seen as a fool. With my limited Spanish I offered to give her $20, if I could take their picture. Yes, they said. But the older women hid their faces. Then, to my surprise, the teenagers asked me if they could take selfies on the boat! Out came the cell phones, and photos and giggles. Dugout canoes and cell phones; what a world we had entered!

I got my twenty dollars' worth, just from the experience. No matter that we saw similar molas later for $10. Maybe their quality was inferior. But regardless, it was worth paying double to buy direct from the artist in her dugout canoe. That hastily chosen mola is framed on my wall, and I smile every time I see it.

I was happy. Happy to be anchored and anticipating a good night's sleep. Happy that we had places to explore, anchorages to find, reefs to snorkel. Panama! We had come a long way from Maine! I heard there was a blizzard back home; here it was hot, hot, hot.

Hemingway ate here. So did we.

The older-generation Guna ladies: Yes, if you buy a mola you may take our picture; we'll just hide our faces.

SAN BLAS ISLANDS

We were thinking of moving to one of the nice reef areas to the east. But first, Tim suggested that we visit the island/town where the Guna ladies had paddled from. I hesitated, wondering if "outsiders" would be welcome there. But one of the great things about traveling with Tim was his uninhibited interaction with anyone and everyone. I got to tag along and see where it led.

The town consisted mostly of houses with thatched roofs, plus some with metal roofs and water catchment systems. There was no fresh water on the island – only rainwater or water brought from the mainland. I was surprised to see a sign near where we landed, indicating crafts for sale. As we ventured further, along paths winding between closely-spaced houses, there were more signs…for stores, for the church, for the school, for a meeting house, for the medical clinic.

Enter Nestor, who spoke reasonably good English (slightly better than our Spanish), who introduced himself and adopted us. We bought him a cold beer; he answered dozens of questions. He guided us to the bakery, where the bread would be ready in 15 minutes. Ten minutes later, when they still said 15 more minutes, Nestor suggested we go to <u>his</u> island, Nalunega, just across a short stretch of water. We went, we visited the store there, we bought hot empanadas, we said no to many, many molas, we saw the school (closed for vacation), and then Nestor asked if we would like him to prepare a dinner for us in his house that evening. Yes!

We went back to the first island, Wichubwala, to pick up our bread. Nestor took his dugout canoe, and Tim rode with him. Bread in hand, we crossed a few yards to another island (or is it just some structures built over the water?) to buy lobsters for the meal Nestor will make. Finally we got back to *No Regrets*. It had been a much bigger outing than anticipated, and I was hot and tired and thirsty. But what a great opportunity to learn how the Guna people live!

When we returned in the evening to Nalunega, there was much more activity than earlier in the heat of the day. Lots of kids running around, lots more people on the paths among the houses. And a basketball game, complete with referee! I was going to ask if people played soccer, but I realized there was no space on the island for it. Nestor reported 700 people live on the island, which was at most a 3-minute walk from end to end.

Solar panels sprouted between the thatched roofs. They attached to car batteries, wired to LED light bulbs. And an occasional TV! There were even some satellite dishes, but Nestor said they don't always work; his set was primarily for DVDs for the kids.

Dinner was lobster (the tropical kind with meat in the tails only, not to be confused with Maine lobster!) and coconut rice and breadfruit and beans. All delicious! Nestor did the cooking. His wife helped with serving. His daughter minded the younger kids in a hammock. It was apparent that all sleep in hammocks that were swung up into the rafters to make room during the day. Clothing was stored hanging from rafters. Most of the cooking was done in an adjacent structure, and the results were carried in to us.

Nestor showed us his passport, which had several stamps in it. He was proud of it, and he spoke of going to Columbia next, to work for a while and then return. He said he goes to Panama City to work, but Panama City is "not good." Tim asked about the city of Colón – was it a dangerous place for "gringos?" Nester considered this for a moment and said, "For Gringos, sí."

We tried to ask if the community has been affected by sea level rise, but he didn't exactly understand the question. Yes, he says, last November when the winds blew hard from the east, parts of the island were flooded. We asked about what the young adults aspired to – did they want to stay on the island. I couldn't fully understand his answer. Many go to Panama City. At first I thought he said that the Guna customs are retained by them, but then I think he said the opposite.

My impression of life on Nalunega changed dramatically during the course of the day. My predisposition was to think of the people as poor, and unhappy. But the people seemed to be quite happy. The children were beautiful and playful and appeared to be very healthy. My idea of "poor" morphed as I saw more of their lives. Were they lacking anything they needed? Would they wish to trade places with any of us??

About sea level rise… Nestor's community, and the rest of the San Blas island group, will be among the first to be washed away. The islands are sandy cays only a few feet above water. And that's the high ground! Several of the cays are completely covered with rickety homes, and more are built over the water on stilts. In the distance is the mountainous backdrop of mainland Panama, clearly an entirely separate world. I suppose it is good that these people have cell phones, and the young people can probably integrate into the mainland society. But that's also the shame of it, that *a whole culture is going to disappear.*

Thursday

We headed east to the more classic sandy cay anchorages behind the reefs. But first came engine issues. The starboard alternator was putting out low amps, like 10 instead of 80. We spent some time investigating this, to no avail. Then the starboard engine failed to generate much thrust, just when we needed it in the process of raising the anchor. For some long seconds we were seriously thinking we might have another collision, or end up on the reef to leeward. Then the engine started running properly. Bad injector…? It remained a mystery, as did the alternator output.

These travails were quickly forgotten, as we anchored in a fabulously beautiful spot, the sound of distant surf on the reefs as a backdrop. A sandy palm-covered cay a short distance away; an unimpeded wind keeping things cool. Bread was baking; chicken was thawing; sprouts were ready to eat. We all had the feeling that we had 'arrived.'

Friday

Some work on the wind generator (successful), some snorkeling, some troubleshooting of the alternator (unsuccessful), and a lively social gathering aboard *Chapter Two* of the four crews that left from Key West. The big catamaran easily accommodated all of us.

Arrived!

Saturday

Another lively social gathering on BBQ Cay, with nearly all the BPO and Pacific Odyssey crews. So many names to learn, and who is on which boat!

As our small flotilla of dinghies pulled up on the beach of the tiny island we were greeted by a welcoming committee of two locals who demanded $3 per person to visit the island. This was unexpected; no one had money with them. Some thought it was fair, like a park fee (the island was nicely groomed). Others thought it was crazy and we should go elsewhere. Others thought it was reasonable but questioned who the two were, and what right they had to ask for money. It got a little testy. I hurried back to the boat (ours was one of the closest) and got money to pay for everyone. Suddenly everyone was "amigos" and we had a good time.

Sunday

Wondering how the Patriots did in the Superbowl…

Monday

Sailed 10 miles southeast to another section of the San Blas islands. Took the dinghy up the Rio Diablo, which provided jungle-like scenery. Birds calling from the tall trees. Several dugout canoes on the river, paddling upstream to get water to bring back to the Guna island just offshore. We towed a very friendly young guy a mile or so up the river, and on our way back we towed two canoes a mile or so downstream. Another paddler laughed at our new friends, asking if they were too tired to paddle.

Tuesday

Switched alternators between the two engines, as a final confirmation that our problem was in the alternator. It was. We ordered a new one that hopefully would get through to us in Colón next week. Moved to a beautiful anchorage in the Coco Banderos group of cays. Drinks with fellow BPOers aboard *Om*, a catamaran joining us for the Pacific Odyssey.

Wednesday

Lots of snorkeling. Saw a ray with an extremely long tail. Looked menacing but it paid no attention to me.

The previous night we had anchored directly in the lee of a small island, which was nice for protection from waves, but we didn't like the greatly diminished wind. It felt much hotter, plus we lost the power from our wind generator. So today we moved a couple miles west, and anchored "out." That is, instead of anchoring in the usual protected spot, we anchored behind the barrier reef, with nothing but the reef and its surf between us and the open ocean. It was somewhat bouncy, but that was okay with me, so long as I had a steady wind blowing through my hatch.

Thursday

Our last day in San Blas. A beautiful day of not doing much but snorkeling. I discovered a wreck (steel boat, maybe 50 feet long) on the reef nearby. That was unexpected and cool. Tim saw a shark (about 5') in the same area. Luckily he (Tim) had already had a long swim, so it was an easy decision to return to the boat. Tim also saw sea turtles, but by the time he pointed them out to Bill and me they were gone.

We bought a fish from a local boat. We tried to do that once before, but after "placing our order," they never returned with a fish. The guys today returned with quite a selection. We had a big dinner plus applesauce cake and fresh pineapple for dessert. A little celebration of our time in San Blas, which had been very pleasant. It was a delightful cruising ground, and I liked the local Guna people.

As usual I was happy with the thought of moving on. I wanted to get to Colón, get the boat well provisioned, do laundry (everything I wore or slept on was salty), take a real shower, collect the equipment that had been sent to us at huge expense, and then I wanted to "do" the Panama Canal!!

Friday

Beautiful/fast sail about 50 miles to Portobelo, just 20 miles from Colón. As we rolled along with the 10' waves I was thinking about how a good sailor is always thinking about what could go wrong, yet one wants to be present and enjoy the "now." An interesting balance…

Saturday

This day was about exploring Portobelo and learning a little history. We were told that when the Spanish took (traded, stole, plundered) gold from Peru and Ecuador 400+ years ago, that it was sailed north to Panama City, and then brought over the mountains by mule train to Portobelo, where it could be loaded onto ships for Spain. That explained the big forts and cannons on both sides of

the harbor. We also visited the church that is the home of the "Black Christ." I had always thought there was only one Christ, but Portobelo claimed another, and he was black. The statue was reportedly thrown overboard by superstitious sailors aboard a ship beset by bad luck, and it was pulled from the sea at Portobelo. Miracles had since been attributed to it, and busloads of tourists/pilgrims came from throughout Panama to see the statue and pray.

Over dinner at Captain Jack's restaurant, the *Ransom* crew told us a story about their time in San Blas. They went to anchor at an island, and two Guna men came out and demanded a $10 fee to anchor off their island. We had all paid big bucks for official cruising permits, allowing us to anchor anywhere in San Blas. But the local guys didn't care about that. The *Ransom* crew spoke good Spanish; they tried to reason with the men. The boat was simply anchored for the night with nobody coming ashore, and thus they were not using their island. The locals would have none of that, and so the fee had to be paid, given the unspoken threat that a dinghy might be slashed in the morning, or some such retribution. This experience, plus the ubiquitous sloppy handling of trash by the locals, colored *Ransom*'s San Blas experience. They concluded that the Guna culture was threatened by more than just sea level rise.

More questions from my seventh-graders…

Do you guys have to do daylight savings time on the sea?
Time at sea is an interesting thing. The three of us could declare it to be any time we want, and it wouldn't much matter, *except* that sometimes we have scheduled radio calls with other boats. Our time has

to be in sync with their time or we miss the call. If their boat is far east or west of ours, then it might be in a different "time zone," and saying we're going to have a call at 3pm could lead to confusion – 3pm their time might not be the same as 3pm our time. (In California, for example, it is three hours earlier than in Maine, so 3pm on the West Coast is 6pm in Maine.)

In order to avoid this confusion at sea, sailors refer to UTC time. UTC stands for the French phrase for Universal Coordinated Time. This used to be called Greenwich Mean Time, referring to the time in Greenwich, England, and it may also be called Zulu time. All of these refer to the time at longitude 0 degrees. If another boat agrees to a radio call at 1600 UTC (4pm at 0 degrees longitude), each boat can figure out what time that is locally. In our current time zone (same as Maine), we are 5 hours earlier than UTC, so it would be at 1100 (11am) local time. UTC time does not get adjusted for daylight savings. So once Maine goes on daylight savings time, the difference between Maine and UTC will become 4 hours instead of 5 hours.

To keep things simple, many boats at sea just set the clock to UTC time and stop thinking about what time it is locally, so you don't have to keep converting back and forth. In that case the crew doesn't have to "do" daylight savings time, until they interact with people ashore. Then they have to get in sync with everyone else.

What do you mean by "gringos?"

In most of Latin America, including in Panama, "gringo" generally refers to any citizen of the United States. In some cases it is applied primarily to white people, but not exclusively so. It sometimes is used in a disparaging way (an American who does not respect the local culture, maybe doesn't speak Spanish or doesn't try to, who expects things to be like what they are accustomed to in the USA instead of adapting to the local ways), but often it is simply referring to one's origin. The three of us aboard *No Regrets* are gringos.

How long do you think it might be before global warming goes into full effect?

This is a hard one! First of all, the term "global warming" is not used much anymore, because when Maine has a winter with record snowfall and cold temperatures, it doesn't appear that "warming" is occurring at all. Usually the term "climate change" is used instead. This is all-encompassing of temperature variations, shifts in rain and snowfall, length of seasons, and other factors that scientists tell us are changing primarily due to increased carbon levels in our atmosphere. Climate change is not intrinsically a bad thing, and in fact we know that there are huge changes to the climate over thousands of years due to factors that are mostly beyond human control (e.g., volcanic eruptions; ice ages). But climate change is very disruptive. It will change the coastline; it will force people near the coast out of their homes; it may cause droughts that will destroy traditional farmlands; it may cause floods; etc. So climate change is generally considered "bad" in the context of things under human control (like how much coal and oil we burn), and "just the way it is" in the context of "geologic time" (many thousands of years).

I am no expert on climate change. But my belief is that the effects caused by humans burning fossil fuels are already happening and cannot readily be turned back. We know that the average ocean water temperature has been rising. This causes the water to expand a little, and the only way it can expand is "up," so sea level rises slightly. We also know that Greenland and Antarctic ice has been melting, which also contributes to sea level rise. I think these trends cannot quickly be reversed. So even though they have not yet caused widespread disruptions, I think we will see incremental changes/disruptions over many years to come, even if humans were to reduce the burning of fossil fuels now.

One aspect of the Blue Planet Odyssey is to raise these questions and call attention to them. We need to think about the possible long-term effects of our collective behavior, and push our leaders to make well-informed policy choices.

Is it easy to sleep on the boat?

Sometimes yes, sometimes no. When we are in a marina like we are now, where the water is calm and the boat is well protected, it's pretty much like sleeping at home. When we're sailing in substantial waves, it is much harder. It becomes noisy, the boat can toss you around on your berth, and occasionally a wave will slap the side or bottom of the boat with a jarring thud that is almost impossible to sleep through.

But on passage we get into a rhythm of sleeping when we can. Even when it is rough we eventually become so exhausted that we sleep, or do something close to it.

When sailing in smooth waters it can be delightful to lie in your berth and feel the energy of the boat moving, and the gentle surge of the ocean, and this can put one right to sleep. But smooth waters generally means "along shore," which usually means short day sails, and thus we are not often trying to sleep in these conditions.

If you had all the money in the world, what would you buy for the people on the island, and why?

I'm going to assume by "people on the island" you refer to the local Guna people on the San Blas islands. When Jimmy Cornell planned the Blue Planet Odyssey, he wrote to an administrator of the Guna and asked if there was some way that we could contribute. Jimmy was thinking of helping to build something – a school or a water catchment system. The response he got was that they didn't want our help with such things, and if we wanted to help we should contribute money to a scholarship fund to help send some young people to college.

I'm very skeptical about efforts to help other people, other than to help them do what they are committed to doing anyway. I think a scholarship fund to help students who want to attend college is a good idea, and that is one thing I would do. Other things tend to have unexpected/unintended consequences. It's tempting to give outboard motors to people paddling canoes, but this might cause big (and potentially troublesome) changes in the culture that I couldn't foresee.

What kind of transportation did they use on San Blas island?

Almost all transportation is by boat, and in most cases the boats are dugout canoes (some with little sailing rigs) or larger skiffs with outboards. There are no cars, because the individual islands are too tiny. I don't recall even seeing any carts or wheelbarrows. There are small airports on a couple of the islands, usually with one small plane per day coming/going to the mainland.

Portobelo

PANAMA CANAL

The excitement about the Panama Canal grew as we approached Colón and saw dozens of ships in the distance. Their AIS signals generated a thick swath of triangular icons on chart plotter screen. Most of the ships were anchored, waiting to transit the canal, or in some cases to be loaded/unloaded in the port. It was an odd video game, trying to identify the one or two ships that were moving, that needed to be avoided!

Crossing the swath of ships, we arrived at Shelter Bay Marina. Ahhh, showers and laundry services and a restaurant!

Our new alternator was successfully (and expensively!) delivered. We installed it, and it worked. A new propeller for our hydrogenerator also arrived and was installed. We discovered two broken bits of rigging hardware, and fellow sailors promised to help us with replacements. We also noticed that the bolts holding the stays for the sprit (where the jib connects) were starting to bend. The connection for these stays was not very well designed; we hoped to come up with a better solution before heading into the Pacific. In other words, we had boat projects still.

There were also BPO things to do. For starters, this was the first place where the Key West boats and the Martinique boats were together at a marina. Lots of socializing, both on boats and at the restaurant, as we all got to know each other. For some reason our crew seemed to have an affinity for the Martinique crowd more than the Key West contingent. Not that there was anyone we didn't like; and we knew that the distinction about where boats started would soon fade away. Jimmy Cornell was also in town, and planning some of our activities.

We had an excellent briefing by Jimmy about the wonders to come in the Galápagos, the Marquesas, the Tuamotus, the Society Islands (which include Tahiti), and even a little hint about what he was cooking up for Indonesia. We also had a less pleasant briefing about the administrative requirements for entering the Galápagos, which were onerous and at times nonsensical, and which seem to be changing almost daily. Boats had been turned away for not complying with unreasonable requirements that they didn't know about in advance!

But first, the Canal. Transit through the Canal had many prerequisites. Each boat required, in addition to the "master" of the ship, four line handlers. We would have to hire two. Four 125' long 7/8" lines were required. We had no lines that big, but the BPO would provide them, plus tires to be available as fenders. A measurer had to come in advance, and ask lots of questions about the boat, measure its length and width, and provide an official number to identify it for Canal purposes. We had made it through this step. All the BPO boats had to be measured before the Canal Authority would schedule our transit.

Jimmy had been pushing the authorities to grant transit quickly; there could be many days between completing the measurement and a scheduled transit date. Then on Tuesday the Authority gave us permission to transit on Wednesday. Wait!! No one was ready; provisioning was not done; projects were in mid-stream. Jimmy had to reply that we couldn't go that soon!

The revised plan was for 6 boats to start Saturday and complete Sunday; the remaining 5 to start Monday and complete Tuesday. Ideally, our fleet of 11 boats would all go together and fill an entire lock, but with the revised schedule they could not take us all at once. Every boat required a Canal pilot, who gives directions where to go, how fast, how to tie up in the locks, etc. But the coming weekend was Carnival! They had to cancel some scheduled vacations to accommodate us at all. *No Regrets* was in the second group, which reduced the time pressure on us and our incomplete projects. Our two extra days wouldn't help much, though, since they were Saturday and Sunday, when we wouldn't be able to get any materials or outside assistance.

Field Trip!

We were busy, but we would carve out a full day for a once in a lifetime field trip. Jimmy arranged for a bus to take the Odyssey participants to see the

Panama Canal expansion project. New/larger locks were being built to accommodate larger ships. We would also visit Panama City, see Balboa (where the Canal begins/ends at the Pacific side), and meet the president of the Panama Canal Authority.

The Panama Canal was completed 100 years ago, after decades of work, and horrendous loss of life to disease. The Canal is 48 miles long. It runs approximately north/south; the north end is the Atlantic/Caribbean side, south is the Pacific. The path makes use of a large lake that was created via dams as part of the canal project. There are locks at each end of the Canal, to raise vessels up about eighty-five feet to the level of the Gatun Lake. The lake also supplies the water to operate the locks.

The dimensions of the locks (and to a lesser extent the clearance of the bridge at the Pacific end) determine the maximum size of a ship that can transit. The design of some ships is based on these dimensions; such ships are called "Panamax." Panamax ships are big (close to 1000 feet long, 106 feet wide, with a draft of 41 feet), but there are larger ships that are unable to transit the Canal.

A project was underway to build new, larger locks alongside the existing ones, to accommodate the larger ships. The addition would also facilitate maintenance of the 100-year-old locks, since it would become possible to close them down when needed, without closing the Canal entirely. The project had experienced some delays but was expected to complete in another year.

Jimmy had arranged for us to visit the site of the new Atlantic-side locks. Shortly before the trip, he was informed that we would not be allowed to enter the construction site. But Jimmy had connections. He made a call, and within minutes our trip was back on track.

Our bus route required that we drive across the (existing) canal. At the Atlantic end there was no permanent bridge, so driving across was accomplished via a single-lane movable bridge that was swung into place when no ship was approaching.

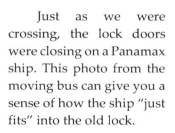

Just as we were crossing, the lock doors were closing on a Panamax ship. This photo from the moving bus can give you a sense of how the ship "just fits" into the old lock.

On to the construction site of the new north-side locks. Jimmy introduced his friend Dave Wilson, an American ex-pat, a sailor who fell in love with Panama while living on his boat, and a project manager for the construction effort. We kept Dave busy for the next hour or two with endless questions.

From our initial vantage point we could see three huge retaining pools for holding the water released from a lock as a ship descends. The retained water would be re-used to fill another lock. This design (which has been used for hundreds of years, but not at this scale!) would allow the new/large locks to operate with about the same amount of water loss as the old locks. But the new locks would accommodate three times more tonnage of cargo in the transiting ship(s).

Thought Experiment

Which uses more lake water for the locks: the transit of a few small yachts or the transit of a Panamax ship? Be sure to consider that both an UP and a DOWN is required to complete a transit. As Tom and Ray of *Car Talk* used to say, write your answer on a twenty dollar bill and mail it to me...

The water retention was more about preserving the depth of the lake, to accommodate large ships, than it was about the environment. Yet the project design also included a serious focus on the environment. For every tree cut to make way for the new channel, two were planted. And a contractor was hired for the sole purpose of moving individual animals, from spiders to crocodiles, away from the construction area.

Dave described the process for relocating a 20' crocodile. First a lasso was secured around the head or tail. Then a second lasso around the other end. Then several more lines around legs and body, and a loop was tied around the jaws. Then 4 or 5 men jumped on the animal's back – it couldn't run with this added weight. The legs were "hog-tied," and the animal could be moved to the new location. At that point the process was reversed. Except that the men remained on the croc's back to prevent its running, until all lines were removed. Then on the count of three, the men *ran*!

We bussed to the interior-end of the new locks, to a narrow strip of land with Gatun Lake on one side. On the other side we looked down into the length of the new locks. Dave explained that we were standing on the "plug," which had been a source of sleepless nights of the project. It was this strip of land that would be excavated last, and until then it prevented Gatun Lake from spilling into the new locks (potentially killing workers, destroying the work, and draining the lake such that it might require several years of rainfall for it to fill back in after constructing a new plug). The plug had been reinforced with concrete shafts and was constantly monitored for any sign of leaks. As anyone knows who has built dams at the beach, if a leak gets started the dam will wash away, with little hope of stopping it.

One of the notable features of the locks were the "gates." Instead of having opposing pairs of swinging gates, like the old locks, the new locks would have recessed gates that slide out across the channel (and which can be moved into different recesses for maintenance purposes). The gates were built in Italy. They weighed up to 4000 tons each! One hundred feet tall, 180 feet wide, 10+ feet thick. Four gates were secured upright on the deck of a ship to transport them from Italy, and a special dock was constructed in Colón to unload them.

Here is a gate on its way to being inserted into position in the side of the lock. The scale is hard to fathom. Remember the gate is 100 feet tall. Notice the car 2/3rds of the way to the gate – it looked like a toy!

On the bus, Dave said "if they don't stop us" we were going to drive down into the locks! We would be among the first to "transit" the new canal. We got some surprised looks, but nobody stopped us. We had some time for the experience to sink in as we drove across the isthmus to Panama City.

After changing from shorts to dress pants (or at least the best we had on board), we went to meet with El Presidente of the Canal Authority. We met around a very official-looking conference table, with one person from each crew at the table, and others in chairs around the room. Enter señor Jorge Luis Quijano, who was a delightful guy and spoke fluent English (studied in Texas). After some pleasantries about sailing he asked if we had any questions. Tim (of course) had a question. "I have a controversial one… Nicaragua…?"

In Nicaragua they were (maybe) building a canal to compete with the Panama Canal. Our host had obviously addressed this issue many times, and it was interesting to hear what he had to say about it. The Panama Canal was a huge part of the Panamanian economy – extremely profitable, so of course they were paying attention to any competing alternatives. There was the possibility of ships using the Northwest Passage. Climate change had made this route more feasible. But it remained a risky proposition; a ship might approach the area only to find the route closed by ice. Or worse, find themselves caught in the ice. Another alternative was Cape Horn, but that was far out of the way, as well as being plagued by severe storms. And there was "the other way around." I.e., travel from China to the US East Coast by sailing west, via the Suez Canal, instead of east via Panama. This last option, especially, was primarily a time/cost/fuel financial calculation. Big ships, by the way, paid more than a quarter-million dollars to transit the Panama Canal.

Señor Quijano was very diplomatic about the Nicaragua project. He said it would require excavating 10 times the amount of earth excavated in Panama. The Panama Authority had a pretty good idea, based on very recent experience, what it took to dig a big ditch. The Nicaragua schedule was to build it in five years. Señor Quijano said to accomplish that they would have to import half a million laborers, and build all parts of it at once, which would add many challenges. And he asserted that there was insufficient demand to support two canals, so if another one was built they would have a price competition, and thus the financial return expected in Nicaragua would probably not be realized. The strong suggestion was that their plans were unrealistic, and the project would not be completed anytime soon.

≈≈≈

The first batch of six Odyssey boats completed their canal transit. We were scheduled to transit with four other boats the next afternoon, probably reaching Gatun Lake after dark, and spending the night there. Then an early start, and into the Pacific by late afternoon. It was all rather uncertain because of Carnival, a major holiday. We couldn't count on people showing up and keeping promises after they'd been out partying all night…

The boat was probably more ready than it had been for any departure to date. New alternator was working. Oil had been changed (earlier than recommended, but if we didn't do it here, we might have trouble finding a place to dispose of the old oil). Replacement for a broken fitting on the boom was procured and installed. Newly fabricated fittings to improve the strength of the screecher side stays arrived and were in place. Missing bolts in the jib roller furler had been replaced. New propeller was installed on hydrogenerator. We had topped up our diesel fuel and filled our water tanks.

We did our big provisioning run to the supermarket in Colón, an hour's bus ride away. Because we were spending $500, the supermarket offered a van to bring us back to the boat. I was uncertain just how long we were provisioning for. Could we get food (that we wanted to eat) in the Galápagos? In the Marquesas? But really it didn't matter. We couldn't pack any more food on the boat anyway. Our lockers were *full*.

Emotionally we were all ready to go. A week at the comfy marina had been enough.

To the Pacific

Happy crew about to leave Shelter Bay: Tim, David (friend assisting with line handling), Zeke, "Gato" (hired line handler), Bill.

Going up - Gatun Locks. Next day passing through Gatun Lake to the Miraflores Locks
at the Pacific end.

Lines heaved from far above

As we were lowered, the ship in the adjacent lock was raised.

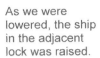

At the last lock; water up.

Water down, gates opening.

We were through and into the Pacific Ocean!

We anchored near Panama City, while Tim went to clear out with Immigration. We still had one other pending quest. We had dropped off our old alternator with someone who claimed to be able to fix it. We hoped we could retrieve it before we set sail for the Galápagos!

Tim returned with unhappy news. Our Panama cruising permit was issued with a wrong date, indicating that we would depart two days earlier. The authorities wouldn't let us check out! We would have to make another visit to the authorities in the morning to get a new cruising permit (!); then we could check out. And no word yet on our old alternator.

Had Enough of Panama Yet?

Such was the greeting the next day among the BPOers, as we tried to sort out the administrative SNAFU that prevented many of us from getting permission to leave. All our "zarpe" permits were written with our original planned departure date. We were two days beyond that date, due to the change of plans for transiting the canal. Thus we no longer held valid permits, and without a valid permit Immigration would not issue permission to leave.

We got our alternator delivered to us by the repairman in the morning. No charge (pun intended) for either the re-work or the shop-to-dockside delivery! And then we got a call from Tim on the radio; he had managed to get our passports stamped, even though some of the other boats were still stuck in the administrative mess. We were good to go.

Panama City

GALÁPAGOS

Tim had some vague intel that there was a Whole-Foods-like store across Panama City. We teamed up with the *Maggie* crew and took a taxi in search of it. No luck. But we saw a "gourmet delicatessen" along the way, with a nice-looking restaurant next to it. We had a farewell dinner and then browsed the bounty of the deli. We bought upscale cold cuts, cheese, and chocolate. Good stuff, but our provisions didn't include much in the fruits and veggies department. The Galapagos were roughly six days (900 miles) away; bound to have fruit; not so sure about veggies.

Day 1

Got underway in the morning. Sunny, hot and no wind. Motored a few hours until a little breeze came up directly behind us. Up went the big spinnaker and we had a pleasant day of sailing. Mid-afternoon the wind picked up and we started zipping along at nine knots. Almost immediately we got a bite on the fishing lure we were trailing. It ran all the line off our reel before we got to it; we were lucky the fish pulled free of the hook rather than taking our gear.

Not to worry… within minutes we had another strike, and this time we successfully landed a small tuna. Maybe twenty inches long and five pounds. We made nori rolls with sticky rice, plus empanadas and salsa on the side. Lots of tuna left over for another meal.

Evening was beautiful, blowing a comfortable (for going downwind) twenty knots, and we continued to fly the spinnaker into the night. Bad idea… Though the night was clear, the wind gradually increased, and with it the waves began to build. By the middle of my watch (Bill and I switched watches, so I now had 1900 to 2300) things were getting hairy. Wind 28 knots. Boat speed hit 17 knots, surfing on the waves. We were overpowered, but I didn't want to wake the others (if they were able to sleep in the mayhem), so I tried to wait it out. But the waves were pushing the boat off course faster than the autopilot could adjust, and the spinnaker would occasionally collapse as we headed up too far, and then collapse the other way as we would bear off too far. We were risking breaking something (probably the spinnaker), so finally I called, "All hands," and we got it down. Ambling along under jib alone, at about 6 knots, was *much* more peaceful!

I know I'm repeating myself, but I was SO happy to be moving again!

Day 2

A day of just the sun and the ocean and a few pelagic birds and us. Vast emptiness; profound aloneness.

Day 3

Light winds, no clouds, intense sun. We were at 3 degrees north latitude, less than 200 miles from the equator. A major daytime activity aboard was finding comfortable places to sit in the shade. The sun was uncomfortably hot by 8am. It was a welcome relief when it set, and I could enjoy the sliver of setting moon, brilliant Jupiter, uncountable stars, and the occasional satellite or shooting star.

We sailed very close to the Columbian island of Malpelo – a huge steep rock in the middle of nowhere. Some authority hailed us on the radio, asking who we were and where we were headed; I'm sure we violated some Columbian territorial restriction. "Mal pelo" translates to "bad hair." I wondered about the name. In the morning we saw many seabirds that must nest on the island (there being no other place for many, many miles). I imagined that the island was covered with birds/nests, and that got me wondering if the name came from someone having a bad experience with birds flying overhead…

We saw a pod of whales. They were small (pilot whales?), but one put on quite a show by repeatedly jumping nearly clear of the water! Naturally by the time I got my camera the jumper had ended his show.

Once we were clear of the coast we had a 1-knot current in our favor, which was a great boost. We had analyzed the expected currents online before departure and planned our course accordingly. If you are interested in the winds and currents, check out www.earth.nullschool.net. This site provides a wonderful visual representation of both wind and current anywhere on the planet. I wished we could access it when we were at sea!

Day 5

Beautiful day. Winds forward of abeam blowing on us and keeping us cool. Many dolphins in the distance, including one jumping clear of the water, but they showed no interest in us. One ship on the horizon.

Light winds during the day had me convinced we could not make our destination by tomorrow night. But after dark the wind picked up, and we were doing 9 knots to windward in reasonable comfort. If this wind held (which seemed unlikely based on conditions so far) we could still make it. Not that we were in a hurry to arrive, but we wanted to enter the harbor in daylight. We didn't want to approach after dark and have to heave to (or drift), killing time until daylight.

A red-footed booby (a bird) roosted on our sprit stay all night, and he returned the next night. Tim kept inviting him toward the pilot house and offering him things to eat, but he seemed content just to perch and get a free ride. In addition, I could see in the moonlight three more birds "leading the way" – flying just ahead of our jib. Sometimes they broke away and flew off, but before long they were back. It was eerie seeing them silently fly by in the moonlight.

We would cross the equator during the night, after my watch. I was disappointed because I wanted to be awake at the time. Silly perhaps, but I thought it would be cool to watch the navigation system show 0.00 latitude and switch from North to South...

Day 6

We arrived just before dark. Anchored in Baquerizo Moreno on San Cristóbal, we made a grand dinner. We would visit the Customs/Immigration authorities in the morning.

Five and a half days was excellent time. We were lucky with the wind – we motored just one night, and we had no squalls. Relative to other boats we made better time than most, but two had arrived six hours before us. We guessed they motored a lot, but we didn't really know. I liked that they, more than we, were now perceived by fellow ralliers as the fast boats. Better, I thought, to start with the bar set low, and beat expectations later.

We had our first Galápagos wildlife experience almost immediately, while we were relaxing in the cockpit as dinner cooked. Tim heard a sound behind him and turned around to find himself face to face with a sea lion! The sea lion had climbed up our transom steps and boarded without asking permission.

It was hard to believe we were in the Galápagos. Unfortunately, we were

in a relatively busy harbor with too many lights and too much noisy nighttime activity. But to think we were in the Pacific Ocean, that we had crossed the equator, that we were now in the fabled islands of incredible animals and Darwin's inspiration – wow!

Red-footed booby that spent the night perched unsteadily in the wind, and returned to do it again the following night

Land ho! San Cristóbal

Kicker Rock

It grabbed our attention when we passed it on our approach to San Cristóbal. The Spanish name was Sleeping Lion; I had no idea why the English and Spanish names were unrelated. Its cliffs not only plummeted down to the water but continued straight down into the depths. Exciting just to see the formation and the seabirds on and over it, but the real treat was the snorkeling. Three ocean currents meet at the Galápagos – a warm one from Panama, that helped us arrive quickly; the cold Humboldt Current that flows up the coast of South America; and the deep ocean counter-current that drifts eastward, opposite the surface current that would push us toward the Marquesas soon. That confluence leads to a great abundance of sea life, as nutrient-rich cold waters mix with the warm.

Snorkeling next to a sheer wall, with the sunlight illuminating the many living colors, plus zillions of fish...quite an experience! Tranquil sea turtles ambled below, while sea lions darted by inches away, sometimes scaring the dickens out of me, when one suddenly appeared next to my face. In the depths were a few sharks, non-threatening yet evil-looking. There were fish of many colors, and if you dove down 10 feet there was a school of little fish so dense it almost seemed solid. All the while frigate birds were soaring overhead. We swam around the rock's perimeter for an hour until we were exhausted as well as awed.

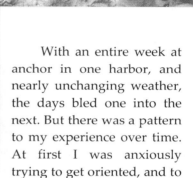

With an entire week at anchor in one harbor, and nearly unchanging weather, the days bled one into the next. But there was a pattern to my experience over time. At first I was anxiously trying to get oriented, and to quickly choose a first tour. I didn't like to wait and hear everyone else's stories that begin, "You *have* to do/go/see…" Next came figuring out what else I really did "have to" do (Kicker Rock), and doing it. By then I felt that I'd had enough of the place, and I wished we were moving on. But it wasn't yet time to go. Then I found myself settling in. I now knew my way around; there was nothing more that I felt the need to do; the people were friendly; the pace was slow and I was finally starting to match it.

The Galápagos are famous for their finches, which were one of the species (actually they evolved into 13 species on the islands) that got Darwin thinking about why/how they had developed different beaks, adapting to the foods they were eating. I found it rather amazing that a mating pair of finches somehow made it to these islands in the first place. Recent "invasive species" aside, the

only animals in the Galápagos were ones blown 700 miles off course, or that could live for a long time drifting (perhaps on a downed tree) in the current. Tortoises yes (they can go a long time without fresh water), frogs no (amphibians cannot last long without fresh water), for example.

We motored the 40 miles to Puerto Ayora on Santa Cruz Island. Dolphins paid us an always-welcome visit.

Instead of staying on Santa Cruz island, I arranged an overnight side trip to Isabela, mostly in hopes of seeing Galápagos penguins. Yes, penguins at the equator! Thanks to the Humboldt current. In addition, I liked the idea of getting some time away from my partners, doing something on my own, and staying in a room with a real shower. I left early, the morning after arriving in Santa Cruz, before other BPOers got their own Isabela trips in place.

The "ferry" was a challenge. No tickets. My name went on a list, and an agent helped to find the right boat. My boat had been changed, reason unknown, so it was useful to have the help of the agent. I found it stressful, though, to have to meet someone I didn't know (and would he really show up on time?) on a dock at 6:30am in order to get aboard. Then two hours mostly in the sun, packed in with 25 others on a boat with three massive outboards, occasionally pounding over the waves. Thankfully it was a relatively calm day. [The return trip turned out to be full of bone-jarring pounding, and sick passengers…]

Another agent met me at the other end and got into a taxi with me to see me to my "hotel," provide me with a map, and make sure I knew how to meet my afternoon tour. The hotel was tiny and simple and nice – included hot water in the shower, should someone want it (actually I did, after snorkeling).

I saw the penguins, got some unique photos of them juxtaposed with cactus plants in the background. Later, however, I found that my camera settings had been scrambled. My prize-winning penguin shot was not to be.

I went to dinner at the Booby Trap, rated #1 on Trip Advisor, where I was the only customer. I rented a bike for $2/hour and rode out of town, up to the "wall of tears" – a pointless wall of chunks of volcanic rock built by prisoners in a penal colony in the 1940's/1950's. Felt good to ride a bike, and then to spend some time alone with the iguanas on a beautifully desolate beach.

≈≈≈

Being in the Galápagos, and seeing the fascinating wildlife was cool, of course. But I don't want you to be left with romantic notions that might not be met should you ever go there, so here is a less-than-romantic view. First, there is the matter of getting in. Half a dozen officials came aboard and required lots of redundant forms to be filled out, and payment of many hundreds of dollars in entry fees. You are not allowed to actually sail/anchor in the wonderful places. In our case we were limited to the two largest ports – Baquerizo Moreno being the smaller and nicer of the two. I heard it was possible to get permission to visit three other islands, for additional dollars.

The harbors were not pleasant. Larger tour boats came in, bringing an oil slick and a stink and their excessive lights and generators. Sometimes you could both hear and smell a generator running on shore at night. There was rarely any wind. With our wind generator useless, and our solar panels relatively small, we had to run our own engine periodically to keep our batteries charged.

Dinghies were not used here – you called on the radio for a water taxi to take you ashore or aboard. While it was nice that we didn't have to rig/use our dinghy, and the dollar per person fee seemed reasonable, it meant there was no "casual" getting around and visiting the other boats. One had to plan their comings and goings. In Puerto Ayoro radio calls for the taxi didn't seem to have much effect – you had to wait until one was in the area and hail it directly.

Then there were the sea lions in Baquerizo Moreno; they quickly lost their charm for us. On shore, where they hauled out in large numbers, they stank. In the harbor, they were difficult to keep off of the boat if your boat had steps up the transoms. When they got aboard, they shed and they sh*t. They also competed with each other for nice haul-out spots, with occasional middle-of-the-night raucous commotions on deck when one tried to displace another.

But here is the major point. Getting to the "good stuff" mostly required hiring a tour, at substantial expense. Thankfully there were a few places nearby that were accessible on foot or by bike or taxi, but they were limited. The concept of "exploring" the Galápagos mostly consisted of selecting which tours you wanted to sign up for. The wonders were undeniable. But they were fed to you by a guide who could tell you most of what you would see before you saw it. There was a touch of Disney in it, even though it was all real.

There are ever-increasing numbers of visitors (and residents) in the Galápagos. How can they experience the wonders, without destroying those wonders? The Galápagos administration was clearly making an effort to preserve the ecosystem. The animals and the environment appeared to be largely unaffected by the visitors. But one could no longer explore and discover on one's own. More restrictions will likely be needed as more airplanes, more cruise ships, and, yes, more yachts, bring added pressure to bear.

As some have quipped, the most destructive invasive species is human!

Time for us to leave. I wished we could have cruised to more remote areas, and yet it was a pleasure to be there. The wildlife was awesome. The people were very friendly. I sat in the cockpit after a delicious meal aboard, watching the moon rise, enjoying the coolness after sundown, watching the monohulls rocking in the swells (being glad I was on a catamaran), listening to the distant music getting started ashore…and thinking how satisfied I was…just being there. At the same time looking forward to what would be next.

We did our provisioning, topped up the fuel tanks, picked up a last batch of laundry, got our "zarpe" paper that said we could leave. We received our BPO sailing instructions. We had a drink and dinner with our fellow rally crews. Then at 8am we all got our passports stamped, and off to sea…

≈≈≈

"Hey Tim, how did the big green fender work for keeping the sea lions off the boat…?"

LONGEST PASSAGE

Between the Galápagos and the Marquesas lies 3,000 miles of uninterrupted ocean. It would be the longest passage of the circumnavigation. One thousand miles per week was our prediction; three weeks at sea.

The BPO had scheduled a noon "start" – mostly a chance for the shore crew to come out and take photos of the boats. We were anxious to go – arrived at the start area an hour early. Should we keep going or wait for the others? We decided it would be good form to wait. That gave us a chance to clean most of the crud off our waterline that had accumulated in the dirty Gálapagos harbors. But when noon arrived and most of the other boats were still motoring toward the start, up went our sails and off we went. There was a surprisingly pleasant wind, and we made the most of it.

It was not a race, we were frequently reminded, and we reminded ourselves. But in fact, for us, it was two races. The most important one was to make the best possible crossing given whatever conditions we encountered. In this race I judged we were doing very well. The winds were unusual, challenging. We kept the boat moving nicely (though our course may have appeared erratic), taking advantage of whatever was available.

Our second race was against the other boats. For starters we wanted to prove (to ourselves) we were faster under sail than the other catamarans. We had invested in a boat reputed to have good performance, trading off the luxurious accommodations of the other catamarans. Now we hoped to "cash in" on the performance aspect. Happily, those catamarans were increasingly falling behind us. But two monohulls pulled ahead. *Blue Wind* was reputed to be a racing boat, or at least equipped with racing-quality sails. I had never been aboard and had barely spoken with the crew, so I didn't know what to think of them. *Tahawus* was a fast cruiser and was 54 feet long to our 42. We wanted to prove (to ourselves) that we could go faster than they, in certain conditions. We had not yet found those conditions. We were going fast but they were going equally fast, or slightly faster.

Our second day/night out the winds went very light, as expected near the equator. Boats started motoring. That struck me as "cheating." I had to rethink my notions about that. This was not a race. The goal was to have a safe and fun passage. Boats carried a limited amount of fuel. Part of the calculation for success was how much fuel to burn now versus having it available later. We could expect more wind later, when we worked our way south into the trade winds. Now was an effective time to use some fuel and get closer to those winds. We started an engine.

Most of the boats went about the same speed under power, but *Tahawus* was faster and pulled further ahead. We held our position ahead of the "pack," so when the wind came up, we got it before most of the others. The wind gradually increased each day, allowing us to stretch ahead of them, while *Tahawus* stretched their lead over us.

Settling In

During the day I did a lot of staring at the horizon. I half expected to see something, but there was just ocean and more ocean, an occasional bird, and lots of flying fish. I saw a whale spout once, but it remained in the distance, taking no interest in us. We didn't see another boat after Day 2, nor did we expect to after that. We had a lot of pleasant idle time. I had a book to read, but it didn't feel right to read it. I didn't want to be distracted; I wanted to be fully present, sitting and watching the ocean go by.

Life was smooth aboard. The first days I felt lethargic – just a touch of seasickness. When that passed, I felt a surge of energy. I baked bread. Our bread from the Galápagos had already turned moldy. But my bread was a hundred times better than the crap we bought there anyway. I didn't understand how such interesting people could put up with such lousy bread!

On my night watch, the night was black – no moon, no stars. We were scooting along at 9+ knots with no fuss at all. Very cool that our boat could move like that, though eerie to be speeding into blackness.

I was very, very happy to be exactly where I was!

Seeking Trade Winds

The passage wasn't going the way I pictured it. No surprise, right? None of the places we visited had matched my preconceived notions of what they'd be like. But having crossed oceans before, I thought I knew what to expect at sea. After a few hundred miles sailing or motoring SW from the Galápagos, we would hit constant trade winds of about 15 knots, and zip along on a broad reach under spinnaker for the last two-thirds of the trip. Going into our sixth day, we were still looking for that constant trade wind, and we had yet to set a spinnaker. The wind was often only 7 or 8 knots – very light. Plus at times it changed direction 45 degrees and/or nearly stopped blowing altogether. Where were the trade winds!?

What strategy would make the most of the situation? The wind would normally be stronger further south. And when the wind was light, we would sail fastest on a close reach – going across the wind rather than with it. So we continued to sail SW, further south than we had planned, further south than the two boats ahead. Soon we would have to turn west for the Marquesas. Would our additional "southing" give us a payoff, or were we sailing a longer route for no benefit?

We made our guesses about the course/speed/distance trade-offs based on "grib files" – wind predictions that we received via the SSB radio, in a .GRB file format. (GRB stands for Gridded Binary, but nobody remembers that, or cares.) With a really good radio connection we might receive a grib file in a minute or two. But often at sea the file would require more than half an hour to download. Sometimes we would lose the radio connection midstream and have to start over. The file would show us the wind predictions in six-hour intervals, for several days.

What was the basis for the wind predictions? Meteorologists have developed amazingly good weather models, but they require an accurate reading of the current situation to predict the future. How much actual data was available in mid-ocean, away from major shipping lanes? How much was interpolation? We carried a drifter buoy aboard, to be deployed when we reached 108 degrees west longitude. Once deployed, it would be transmitting weather data from one more mid-ocean location. Other BPO boats were going to deploy buoys at other longitudes. But my guess was that there weren't very many inputs coming from our part of the ocean.

Based on the grib files from the previous two mornings, we expected to see a trough of confused and light winds to our north, and gradually stronger winds as one moved further south and west. Jimmy Cornell likes to say that the .GRB file extension stands for "garbage," and we should ignore the predictions. Or at least not "outsmart" ourselves by taking the predictions too seriously, and making course changes on account of them. Yet that was exactly what we were doing. So far the gribs seemed to be helpful, but the jury was still out as to whether our "southing" would pay off.

On a long passage I could stay in communication with Hallie via email-over-the-radio. This method of communication was slow, both in the data transmission speed and in the fiddling to get a decent radio connection. I expect cheaper satellite services will make radio email obsolete very quickly, but we used it heavily and happily. Hallie forwarded a fresh batch of questions from my 7th graders back in Maine.

In Science class we are learning about adaptations and evolution, especially with Darwin's finches on the Galápagos! It's funny how you mentioned them in your blog, what a coincidence! Have you seen any finches with noticeably different beaks? What do you think about their evolution?

I'm afraid all the finches look pretty much the same to me, other than the coloring of males/females. Many of the finches I've seen have been in the towns, often hanging around restaurants. Do you think their beaks will eventually adapt to foraging human-food…?

Have there been any recent droughts that affected the finches?

I don't know. I will relate one thing I learned, though, that impressed me about the impact of climate change. About 30 years ago there was a very strong "El Niño" year – where the usual ocean currents are disrupted, and with them the weather. Our guide on one of our tours said that in this one year 90% of the coral around the Galápagos died off. He attributes this to the ocean currents. One day the waters would be cold, brought north by the Humboldt Current. The next day the water would be warm, from the Panama Current. Coral can live in both temperatures, but he believes the constant switching back and forth killed the coral.

This year is a strange one; we are now in the rainy season, but there has been almost no rain. There was a lot of talk about this among locals, though no one seems to know why or what the impact might be.

Were the iguanas mean?

For the most part the iguanas ignored people. Though the tourists didn't ignore them, we never touched them or tried to scare them. I did have one "spit" at me once.

Were you able to touch any of the animals on the islands?

There was a strong local ethic of not touching animals, and we almost always adhered to that. I did touch the back of a sea turtle that was swimming with me. He (she?) didn't care; maybe even liked it.

What was your favorite part of being in the Galápagos?

Three things come to mind. First, the sea lions were a hoot – very entertaining. But that got old quickly as they "invaded" our boat. Second, visiting the island of Isabela (going by ferry and spending the night there in a little hotel) was fun. The town was smaller and life seemed more relaxed, and it was fun to explore a little on my own. But the winner has to be snorkeling around Kicker Rock, where both the cliffs above and the cliffs underwater were incredible.

> **What is your favorite place you have been so far?**
>
> Hard to choose one. Some of the places in the San Blas islands were interesting and fun. The Panama Canal was a cool experience. Parts of the Galápagos were unique and wondrous. Another favorite is right where I am now – in the middle of the ocean, where there is nothing around but more ocean, and the night sky is amazing in its brilliance and its vastness!

Broken Shroud

I awoke to the best wind so far on the passage. So, why were we motoring…? Perhaps it was related to the downpour we were in? It was the first heavy rain since leaving the States. But no, the rain was just a passing squall. We were motoring, I was informed, because during the night we broke our starboard lower shroud (that keeps the mast from flexing in the middle). It parted just above the "Norseman fitting" that connected the wire cable to the turnbuckle (which tensions it), which in turn attached to the chainplate that attached to the hull. Without the mast supported half way up by this shroud, it was unsafe to use the sails.

Yikes! We had no spare mast! And we were 2,000 miles from anywhere. Going all the way under power, besides sounding like a miserable idea, was not possible – we only carried enough fuel to motor about 500 miles, and we had probably used a quarter of it already in the light stuff at the start. What to do?

The remaining cable was in good shape, except for the last inch or two. My first thought was we could bend it around a thimble and use cable clamps to secure the loop, and then lash it to a shackle attached to the chainplate. I found that we had no suitable cable clamps. (Note for shopping list…)

Second option: we could rig a line in place of the wire cable. Where the cable attached to a tang on the mast we could put a shackle on the tang and attach the line. But the line we had would stretch under load – probably enough that it wouldn't support the mast adequately.

Third option: Bill thought we could take the Norseman fitting apart, clean it, cut off the last two inches of wire cable, reattach the Norseman fitting to the good wire, and still have enough thread on the turnbuckle to connect it all back together. Tim was hesitant to trust the wire or the Norseman fitting, so we decided to try this approach while also rigging a backup line. Belt and suspenders.

We looked through our reference books and found that Nigel Calder's "Boatowner's Mechanical and Electrical Manual" (our bible for engine issues) described how to properly connect Norseman fittings to wire cable. Having never done this before, our thanks went out to Nigel. Tim and I took turns going aloft to rig the "suspenders" line, but after reading Calder and replacing the Norseman fitting, we decided the "belt" alone was a satisfactory solution. Within a few hours we were sailing again.

In the meantime, we tried to send an email to Rally Control to alert them to our circumstance, and to ask if a rigger could be found in the Marquesas to help us out. The email failed to send. Our Sailmail radio-based email system informed us that our service had been cut off. We had used too much connection time (presumably downloading too many weather files). What timing! It's never just one thing going wrong that gets you into trouble...

Our satellite tracker (that reported our position on the Cornell Sailing website) was capable of sending short messages. We got a message out, also explaining that we couldn't use Sailmail. Before the day was out we got a message from Sailmail that we had been temporarily granted unlimited service. Was this the "Cornell influence" at work? However it came about, we were very grateful (and we would cut back on file downloads).

Naturally we inspected the rest of our shrouds, and found that the port side lower had a broken strand in the cable. We decided not to wait for it to also fail. We cut off the last inch or two and reinstalled the fitting just as we did on the starboard side. This process went surprisingly smoothly and was completed just as it was getting dark.

Our two "new" shrouds were now getting a test, as we sailed through the night with our first taste of the trade winds.

Cookies

Fresh food and a hot shower. From past experience, these were the things that made it worthwhile arriving. If not for these benefits, I'd prefer that the sailing continue indefinitely.

After nine days at sea, I was hearing the call of those benefits. But their song was not so compelling as in voyages past. *No Regrets* had amenities that I'd never had before: a refrigerator, a freezer, a watermaker. Okay, I had a fridge on past boats, but never one that I relied on for an ocean crossing.

True, we were running out of fresh fruits and vegetables. But the freezer was well stocked with meats and cheese. We had freshly baked bread. We had cold beer and soft drinks. Sure, a dinner at a restaurant sounded good, but I would happily forego it for another night's beautiful sail under the stars in the warm breeze. I did miss having a regular supply of cookies though...

With a watermaker aboard, we used water much more freely than I had in the past. We didn't have to ration our supply over three weeks, plus potential delays. We took showers! Not like showers ashore, but at least a freshwater rinse every couple of days, to remove the salt. Wonderful!

Upon completion of our 3,000 miles, would I be happy to arrive, or disappointed that we had to stop? I wasn't sure yet. Probably it would be both. Sorry to see it end, and happy to have cookies!

Halfway Day

Day 10, around dinner time, we crossed the halfway point. To celebrate, we made a coconut carrot cake (with no recipe – why didn't we have a cookbook on board…?). It was delicious.

It had been a beautiful day, the breeze a little cool, the blues of the ocean and sky seeming to have extra richness. The wind had been light. These light winds could be frustrating, but today I didn't much care, as it was a joy just to be gliding smoothly along at a tranquil six knots.

Tim took the relative calm as an opportunity to work on our port engine, which acted up the day we left the Galápagos. (We had a two-minute conversation about turning back, but we figured we didn't really need the engine for the ensuing three weeks, and repairs in French Polynesia seemed equally plausible as repairs in the Galápagos.) We had diesel fuel getting into the engine oil. Our hypothesis was that the fuel lift pump diaphragm had failed (a common problem, according to our Calder reference book). We carried a spare, and switching to the spare was Tim's project of the day. He was successful, apparently, but it would be another day before the gasket goo hardened, before we could try it. We couldn't detect any problem with the old pump after removing it though, so another hypothesis might be needed.

Bill took the relative calm as an opportunity to put an adhesive patch on our torn screecher. We had been using the big sail in stronger winds than it was designed for, and the consequence was a two-foot long tear in it. Now it was patched, but we weren't sure how strong the patch adhesive was, so we would only be using the sail in light winds. Our winds were mostly light, but they would come and go. When they came, they were sometimes too much for the screecher.

I baked bread and the Halfway Cake.

Being halfway, it was Bill's opportunity to say if he wanted to switch night watches with me. He had taken the "dark watch" covering the middle of the night, and let me have the after-dinner watch. I suggested we go half the way with that schedule and then decide about the second half. Bill was happy to continue doing the dark watch; I was happy to continue with the early watch.

It was a beautiful night. Just enough chill in the wind for a fleece over the T-shirt and shorts. Intense stars. No moon. Venus low in the western sky, casting a reflected glow on the ocean. The bowl of the big dipper pointed toward the North Star, now well below our horizon. Opposite it the Southern Cross pointed at the empty space where the "South Star" would be if there was one. The Milky Way was rather dim in the north, growing brighter in the south, and brightest just before the Southern Cross; then petering out at our southern horizon. There was a faint glow about 20 degrees west of the Milky Way, and 20 degrees away from the south celestial pole – no individual stars discernable, but a patch of lightness. I'd never seen that before, and I wondered about it. It must be a cluster of an unimaginable number of stars, an unimaginable distance away… Our Spaceship Earth is so tiny…

I saw an occasional shooting star. And *there*, a star was moving! A satellite heading south right past Orion's belt. Funny how it is hard to spot satellites, but then suddenly one jumps out at you. At least, that's my experience. This one passed behind the jib. I didn't want to move from my reclined position on the cockpit seat, so I waited what I estimated was the right interval and then tried to find it again on the other side. But even when I knew it must be there, I couldn't spot it.

Contemplating things celestial…the vernal equinox had occurred…the sun was increasingly north of our position. Facing north to greet the sun – disorienting for a Northerner like me!

Trade Winds at Last!

Finally, we had the expected trade winds. For 24 hours they blew 13 knots. We wanted another five knots, but we were happy to be moving well again. We had just the spinnaker up, which made for very easy going. Just set it and forget it, so to speak.

In fact, this was the first day that I'd felt rather bored. During the night a control line for the hydrogenerator broke, and I thought I had a repair project for the morning. But come morning I found that Bill had already fixed it during his watch. (Pretty impressive, hanging over the back of the boat alone at night…) Morning brought a problem with our electronics, where some of the wind and speed information wasn't getting displayed. But a "reboot" of the system set that right. There wasn't much route planning/strategizing to be done, now that the wind was steady. I wasn't planning to cook or bake. Not much on the agenda.

We entertained ourselves for a while with ideas about getting more sail flying. Our spinnaker wasn't especially big, and we could use more power. We dropped the mainsail when we flew the spinnaker because the main blocked the spinnaker's wind, and we sailed just as fast with it down. But there was a big gap between the bottom of the spinnaker and the deck – could we come up with a way to capture the wind that escaped there…? We tried setting our storm jib. We knew it wasn't very big, but we'd never flown it before. This was a chance to learn something. It was good to go through the exercise of rigging it, in case we ever actually needed it, but it was so tiny it didn't make any discernible difference in our speed.

We brought the storm jib down and tried flying our small spinnaker "under" the bigger one. This didn't seem to catch much wind, and it interfered with the big spinnaker; we judged the net difference to be zero. Then we tried pulling the small spinnaker aft, close to the mast, inside the furled jibs, and off to one side. This actually seemed to work. That is, it increased our speed by half a knot. Not pretty, since it was rubbing up against the headstay and the big spinnaker sheet and sometimes other things, and it had the potential to get fouled and make a mess. We brought it down for the night. I doubted it would ever go back up unless we got back into the racing mindset, which we lost when everyone started motoring back on Day 2.

I had a dozen or so books on my iPad that I wanted to read, but my iPad got a saltwater bath the day before we left Galápagos, and it died. I had been reading the few old-fashioned printed books that were on board. I was on the last of the novels. After that...reference manuals...?

One thousand miles to Hiva Oa.

Next Boat...

I spent an hour or two sitting atop the pilot house (where it was shady), watching our wake streaming out behind – a continuous river disappearing into the sea. A continuous river stretching some 5,000 miles astern, back home...

Thoughts of "back home" were often about food, and usually a comfy sofa, either in front of a favorite TV show or overlooking the ocean from our Maine cottage. But this time my thoughts meandered to another favorite topic: boats. What kind of boat would scratch my sailing itch after this adventure...?

Thoughts began with my little trimaran, 2/3rds built, sitting in storage in a barn. If I completed that project, and then took it a step further to outfit it thoroughly for backpacker-type cruising, it could satisfy my desire to sail over the horizon – to Downeast Maine or perhaps Canada. A huge plus for that boat would be its low cost. Even with complete cruising gear it would be the least expensive option by far. But it had its drawbacks. I'd want a little autopilot, so I didn't have to steer 100% of the time. So I needed a battery, and a way to charge the battery. And a little boat like that had no good way to carry a dinghy for getting ashore. I could lash a small kayak on the cross-beams. Ugly, but workable. And potentially the biggest drawback: it would accommodate me only – not a boat for cruising with Hallie.

To get a boat for cruising together, we would need a reasonable galley and an enclosed head. There was a big trade-off between interior space and my desire for a trimaran. Trimarans had exciting sailing qualities but very little space. There were some nice ones in the 30 – 35-foot range that probably had enough inside for the two of us to be reasonably comfortable.

But…only the two of us. What about sailing with friends? If we went a little bigger we could have a "guest room" and be able to accommodate another couple. Probably not a trimaran at that point, as its size would get unwieldy and its expense would be exorbitant. Maybe a catamaran? Hey, maybe like the one I was on?

But if we went that big/expensive, maybe we should be thinking about living aboard. We could migrate along the Intracoastal Waterway, which I found quite enticing on the way south. Living aboard would change the equation in big ways. Sailing qualities would take a back seat to space and comfort. Maybe it wouldn't even be a sailboat at all. We saw some nice "trawlers" on the ICW that seemed like ideal vessels for that environment, where one has to motor most of the time anyway.

Boats are always a compromise. Whatever we did, I would lust after other boats that could do other things better. I would just have to keep contemplating this question that had no right answer, and kick it around with Hallie a few times…over the next 15,000 miles…

Counting Down the Days

We had told people the passage should be expected to take 21 days. That was calculated by assuming an average of 6 knots…approximately 150 miles per day…approximately 1,000 miles per week; 3,000 miles = 3 weeks. We tended to be conservative in such estimates; I was hoping to make it in less than 21 days. I thought we could average better than 6 knots. I had visions of logging a few 200-mile days in the trade winds.

The 200-mile day still eluded us. We had done 190 twice, but we had some very light winds on other days. It was Day 17, and we had about 450 miles to go. Three more days.

After 2,500+ miles and 17 days, we converged with *Tahawus*. They were a speck on the horizon, occasionally rising above the ocean swells. The two of us were sailing "neck and neck." We pulled ahead, they pulled even, we pulled ahead, they were gaining. We did better in some wind strengths; they did better in others.

Our solitude was gone. I couldn't help looking at them, or at the general area where they would appear if I stared long enough. At this point we were preparing (mentally) for reentry anyway. Finishing up the favorite foods, since we didn't have to stretch them out beyond three days; learning about the anchorage, and what would be required for formalities in entering French

Polynesia; realizing that we didn't know anything about cruising in the Marquesas. Happily, as part of the BPO rally, we had someone meeting us at Hiva Oa who could help us get oriented.

Arrival in Hiva Oa

We saw the first isles of the Marquesas in the afternoon, still 50 miles distant, and watched the sun set behind them. As we got close the wind went very light, and we motored the last 30 miles. *Tahawus* was behind us, but we knew they could go fast under power. For a while we ran both engines to stay in front. Then we spoke on the radio and agreed we would finish together. Very satisfying.

When it was getting dark we cut the engine so we could enjoy a quiet dinner, some nice music, and the islands in the twilight ahead. Then motoring on in the moonlight. The islands seemed so much bigger than the little dots on the chart! Very dramatic in the night. As we closed with the south coast of Hiva Oa there was suddenly an almost overpowering fragrance of shore – of flowers – of exotic South Pacific lands. A dramatic change from the constant scent of the sea!

We anchored outside the little harbor. It was rolly out there, but we didn't care. At dawn we would move into the harbor and anchor bow-and-stern so as not to swing, because the harbor was tiny. Then we all would go ashore at 8am to take a shuttle into the town and clear in at the gendarmerie.

At anchor it was sweet to have a drink together in the cockpit, the steep hills of Hiva Oa outlined against the moonlit sky. We were feeling good about what we had accomplished, enjoying our arrival in this already-special place.

Blue Wind and *Tahawus* in Hiva Oa

≈≈≈

MARQUESAS

As I learned in the Galápagos, I don't do very well initially in new places. It started well, going ashore to meet Luc and Jackie, the BPO representatives there. They were wonderful; they greeted us at the dinghy dock with baguettes and fruit. Luc drove us three miles into town and helped us get through the formalities, which we had been led to believe would be very simple. No; it took most of the day, lots of waiting around, lots of money put into a bond that somehow we would get back upon leaving, all handled in a language that I didn't understand (French).

I greatly disliked not speaking the language. Oh well, I just followed Tim and Bill around – they seemed to be happy as could be in this place even though they didn't speak French either. Tim, as always, engaged with everyone. When he couldn't communicate well with two ladies gaving us a ride back to the harbor, he sang a song that he knew in French. They loved it!

I felt better by the end of the day, back on the boat. We jumped into the water and scrubbed the hull for an hour. A "beard" had grown in three weeks at sea. It surprised me that barnacles and green algae would take hold and grow while we were moving. I could blame some of it on the Galápagos but much of the growth was up the side of the hull, where it was wet only when sailing. Cleaning it was difficult but it was fun work. Then came a bottle of French wine, a baguette, two kinds of French cheese, and star fruit. *Now* I had arrived in French Polynesia!

I liked things even better a day later, despite spending a large part of the day trying to upload video clips with no success. The island's only gas station was a short walk from the dinghy landing, and it had a "mini-mart" with baguettes and cheese and fruit juice and a reasonable selection of canned/dry foods. And ice cream! The place where I got Internet access was the "signal station," out on a point, high in the air, with an extraordinary view of the ocean and the islands and the approach to the harbor. It had a picnic bench in the shade – wonderful place to struggle with slow Internet access. More cleaning of the hulls followed; greeting the next boat to arrive (*Chapter Two*); dropping off our laundry with a woman who promised to return it clean in two days.

We hired a local man named Pifa to give us an all-day tour of Hiva Oa. Pifa looked Marquesan but he had no tattoos. His last name was, surprisingly, O'Conner. His great-grandfather created a homestead on Hiva Oa. Pifa claimed to be related to half the island's population of 2500. He had studied in Hawaii for two years, so he spoke English well. That helped with the tour. He could also speak Russian, Chinese, Portuguese, Spanish and perhaps other languages, in addition to the mandatory French and Marquesan (plus the various dialects of French Polynesia – Tahitian is somewhat different from Marquesan).

The drive to the north side of the island entailed going up over the steep hills, down into a central valley, up over even steeper hills, and down to the ocean. Many of the roads barely deserved the name. Four-wheel drive was definitely a requirement even with the weather dry. Along the way we sampled fruits directly from the trees (Pifa's own, or belonging to some extended family member). The views were spectacular. The houses were simple, their gardens beautiful/bountiful.

Pifa had arranged a lunch stop. There was wild boar (the hunting of which was a major pastime and topic of discussion), goat in coconut sauce, fish ceviche, breadfruit, plantain, bananas, rice, and starfruit juice. What a meal! Despite Pifa's help (like most Marquesans, he was a very big man), we could not finish it all.

Then to a sacred ritual area of the Marquesans. We passed a large flat stone at the top of a high cliff, jutting over the water. This was where a beautiful young girl would be sacrificed to the gods every new moon! We learned that there used to be a community of 18,000 Marquesans in this area, in addition to another rival community on the other side of the island. We saw where the temple was located, where only the priest and the tribal leader were allowed inside. There were large stone tikis depicting the leader, a warrior in front of him, his younger brother behind him, and nearby the one who did sacrifices. Here men were sometimes sacrificed, supposedly voluntarily, so they could join the gods as servants. There was also a large stone tiki of a woman giving birth. There was a tattoo hut, where the first-born male of a family would be tattooed from head to toe over a period of 3 months upon reaching puberty. The tattoos on the chest depicted his family history. Others told stories of strength and courage. These tattoos were the only "written language" of the Marquesans, other than some petroglyphs. Being tattooed by primitive methods was a major trial; not all survived the ordeal.

Pifa was a font of information about the old culture and the history. The name 'Marquesas' came from a Spanish explorer in the 1500's. The pre-European name for the islands meant "land of men," and in this case the "men" apparently did not refer to "our tribe" versus outsiders, but instead to fierce male warriors. Cannibalism was practiced – eating captured enemies and even their own babies if born with deformities. In the mid-1800's missionaries came and told the people they had to stop eating other people. Given the power of the European gods (that gave a soldier the power to kill a man as if by magic without even touching him), this had some sway. The natives dying off in vast numbers (from the European diseases) also showed the power of the European gods, and Christianity took hold. But it was apparent that Marquesans remained very proud of their earlier heritage. French was a second language to them, and they preferred speaking their own language. The tradition of tattoos remained, even if some of the symbols had lost their meanings. They loved their homeland. Who wouldn't? The islands were spectacularly beautiful, food and water were abundant, and the weather was always great!

Jimmy Turns Back

Jimmy had left Florida later than the fleet, with the intention of catching up in Tahiti. He had transited the Panama Canal and started for the Marquesas when we received an email from him stating that he had a personal emergency and had to turn back. He assured us that the BPO would continue, and he would fly into Tahiti to meet us. Later he would ship his boat to Vancouver and then achieve what he wanted most – to sail through the Northwest Passage. Good! We didn't need Jimmy to accompany us around the world, and we were happy to learn of his success.

Manta Rays

Two rally boats had just arrived. Several other boats stopped first at Fatu Hiva but were coming soon. One boat was still at sea. We wanted to be in Hiva Oa with all the crews; celebrate everyone's successful passage. But we had places to go and things to see! Despite misgivings about missing our rallymates, we resupplied our food (beer from Tahiti, meats from New Zealand, cheeses from France), and set off to explore the Marquesas.

We had heard that the neighboring island of Tahuata was a favorite for manta rays; that you could swim with them; watch their magnificent flight through the water. Tim said if he could witness this, it would make his trip! Destination: Tahuata. Objective: swim with mantas.

We had a recommendation for a particular bay on the west side of the island. But there was a town there, and I thought it would be fun to stop in one of the more remote bays a few miles north. We spoke on the radio with another crew that had hired a guide; they had seen mantas near the north end of the island. That settled the matter. The first likely cove had two boats anchored in it. There was room for a dozen more but we wanted paradise to ourselves. We pulled into the next cove. All ours.

We had been warned, and we quickly saw for ourselves, that the wind gusts coming down from the hills ashore blow very hard over the anchorage.

"Williwaws," or their tropical equivalent. No problem, though. The worst that could happen was dragging our anchor, and that would take us out to the open sea and we could just come in and try again. Sometimes with the wind came a quick rain. The fast-moving clouds, the splashes of sunlight (and later a full moon), the force of the gusting wind – this place had a warrior spirit.

We saw no mantas on the way in. I swam ashore to see if I could speak to someone – there were two huts visible, and clothes hung to dry – but I found no one. At nightfall we saw powerful flashlights at the edge of the cove – divers collecting something, but what we could not tell. By midnight the cove was deserted again.

In the morning I took the dinghy around the point to the cove with the two boats anchored, and asked them about mantas. Yes, there had been mantas in the cove two days before, but not yesterday, and they had not seen any that morning. They explained to me that you spot mantas by their "wing tips," which poke up out of the water a few inches when they are near the surface.

Heading back to the boat, I saw a rock ahead as I rounded the point. No, I thought, if it were a rock, there would be waves breaking over it; it must be a shark fin. It took me a few more seconds to recognize that my "rock" was what we were searching for – wingtips of a manta. I spotted two rays, close to the surface, just a few feet away. Quickly – to the boat to rally the snorkelers!

It seemed to take forever for Tim and Bill to get into bathing suits, apply sun lotion, dig out masks and fins. By the time we returned to the "rock" I held little hope of finding our quarry. But there they were – wingtips ahead. Not knowing what to expect, we let the dinghy drift and we slipped into the water.

WOW – the creatures were sooo cool! Massive, yet graceful. Not in any hurry, not deterred by our presence, they slowly flapped their wings and flew. They had huge mouths, wide open, taking in water and filtering out the plankton food. The water flowed out through slots on their undersides. Their backs were black; their bellies whitish with black spots; their mouths white. One glided toward me...directly at me...mouth wide...I was scared but enthralled. Reminding myself that they eat only plankton, I stayed still. As she got close, she banked into a wide turn and slowly disappeared. When the next one came, I dove down as far as I could and turned to look up as it flew overhead. Awesome... Magnificent...

Chilled and tired, we returned to our mothership. Tim's goal had been achieved before noon. We stretched out in the sun, no other humans in sight, and tried to absorb this amazing place.

Vaitahu

Late in the afternoon after seeing the mantas, a small powerboat approached us. Aboard was a couple with a son, perhaps eight, and daughter, perhaps nine. We had our usual language barrier, but they indicated that they wanted a small amount of gas for their outboard, and they would trade a short stock of bananas for it. We siphoned a gallon out of our tank and into theirs. They indicated that tomorrow we should sail to their town of Vaitahu just two miles away, and they would have more fruit for us. Tim communicated that he would buy ice cream for the kids.

The bay off of Vaitahu was dramatic, beautiful. There were three sailboats anchored, and room for fifty more. Fantastic rugged slopes crashed down from the clouds to the sea – covered with lush green, coconut palms in the valleys, a tiny village at the bottom.

Tim and I took the dinghy to the landing. The rocks were sharp and there were swells; we hoped our little stern anchor would hold the dinghy safely off. Stepping ashore, there was the boy from yesterday, and a man who explained that the boy's family had gone to pick pamplemousse (grapefruit) for us. Tim gave the boy an entire box of snack/energy bars. The boy didn't know what to make of that, but as we all walked toward town we passed his house. He scampered up a little hill to it and ducked inside, reemerging with just one bar in his hand.

We had little success communicating with the boy. But he understood ice cream, and he led us to the store. I thought it odd at first that the store had no sign; of course no sign was needed in a tiny village. As we were buying his treat, his family appeared, carrying fruits and vegetables. Communication was very difficult until we were joined by Cameron.

We had been told to look up Cameron. I assumed he was a local, but in fact he was a surfer dude from Hawaii who has spent much of the past 20 years in Polynesia. He seemed to be friends with everyone. We chatted at length about the goals of the Blue Planet Odyssey, and whether or not there was any direct evidence of sea level rise in the area. He said no, even though he has no doubt it was happening.

I asked about Internet access in the town and he said, "Here." We got the wifi password and tried it out, but it was even slower than what we had found in Hiva Oa. Certainly not capable of uploading photos; it barely supported email.

Cameron let us know that the store owner was inviting us to lunch across the street. We hesitated; Bill was still aboard the boat. But this was an opportunity not to be missed. It turned out that LOTS of people were invited to lunch, including the crews of the other 3 boats at anchor. What an amazing spread! Ceviche, whole raw fish sliced so you could eat it off the bones (with coconut milk, they suggested), breadfruit in a goo like poi (in coconut milk), cooked bananas, rice, grilled chicken, sausage, olives, nuts, mangos… We had brought along one of the soccer balls that we carried to give as gifts, and with Cameron's help we asked our host if we could give it to his son. "Give it to all the kids," Cameron translated.

We were in the right place at the right time to get an authentic Polynesian experience – and it was a treat! We even packed lunch "to go" for Bill, plus two mangos to augment our bag of fresh fruits. Back at the boat we ate one of the grapefruits, which was without question the best I'd ever had. I couldn't help but wonder, could it get any better than this? Would this be the best day of the entire circumnavigation!?

Dolphins

Our friends in Vaitahu told us there were dolphins at the next village/bay south, Hapatoni. They said it was a breeding ground, and dolphins appeared there nearly every day. In the morning we motored the 2 miles to check it out. The hills were very steep, and the water depth dropped off quickly. We anchored in about 40 feet, but it felt like we were almost on the rocky shore. The wind coming down the hills kept changing direction; sometimes it was blowing us toward the rocks. I would not want to spend a night there, sleepless. But Bill planned to remain aboard, so Tim and I felt safe going exploring in the dinghy. Later we would move back to our first Tahuata anchorage.

We went out to the mouth of the bay, where we had seen some black shapes from a distance. But when we got there – nothing. We headed further south along the coast. What a coast! Hills more steep and rugged than we had seen, lava cliffs and gullies and chutes and seams down to the waves, caves and odd shapes carved into the lava walls by the sea. Atop the cliffs were shapes that looked like tikis, but I think they were natural lava protrusions. Either way, a spiritual force seemed strong and present.

We motored around a point to the southernmost bay on Tahuata, unnamed on our chart, and it seemed we had arrived in the Bay of Eden. Hills and valleys and coco palms and clouds spilling over the mountain tops and cliffs and caves and green and blue…and not one sign of humanity. Well, no, there were some hard-to-make-out letters painted on the rocks, perhaps the name of the place. But no huts, no boats, no buoys, no gardens, no clearings, no trash, no engines… I said to Tim, "If I were a dolphin, this is where I would come to mate."

We went into the bay, and we saw their fins. I slipped into the water, and there they were – looking up at me from 30 feet below, swimming up to the surface, and swimming away. There were maybe twenty. They mostly kept their distance, and calmly swam in several groups, though twice we saw individuals leap out of the water. We would come close to a group, and they would disappear. A minute later they would reappear 50 yards away. At one point they seemed to be swimming in a circle about 50 feet in diameter. Was that herding fish to the middle? Was it a defensive stance against us? Was it a way of relating to each other? Or was it just by chance? I don't know what they were doing or thinking, but it was special to be in their midst, an honor to be allowed to view them for a little while in their Eden.

Ua Pou

We sailed 60+ miles from Tahuata to the island of Ua Pou, and thus from the southern group of three Marquesan islands to the northern group of three. Here, the BPO reps had arranged for two very full days of activities for the rally participants.

First, a "welcome" – each person presented with a bead necklace – and an amazing spread of fruit. Mangos, pamplemousse, bananas, dried bananas, breadfruit chips, star fruit, pomegranate, guava, watermelon, and probably more that I have forgotten. We used noni leaves as plates, and "toothpicks" made of banana leaf spines to serve ourselves. There was a time, maybe 40 years ago, when fruit was not considered "cool" here. The companies that imported processed and canned foods promoted their wares as better than the local foods, which they suggested were for the animals. More recent economic hard times had led to a revival. Present day Marquesans were proud of their organically grown fruits, harvested ripe, no preservatives – much tastier than what we get at home!

On a guided walk around town, the island seemed wealthy to me. The streets were good (in town, not up in the mountains); there were street lights; a hospital; a school with a soccer field; horses; many 4WD cars. The houses looked to be well built; everyone looked healthy and happy. Much of this wealth was from French subsidy, as the infrastructure was done by the French administration, paid for with the taxes collected in France. Was there a poor part of town? Or people struggling to survive in the hills? If so, we saw no indication of either.

We stopped at an ancestral meeting place – a sort of village green with stone walls. Our guide described a dance that used to take place here. Young men and women would meet and perhaps choose mates. The women would spend several days preparing in the hills, searching out fragrant flowers to use as perfume, especially, she said, "for their most intimate place." At the dance the women would form a circle, the men inside. With great animation, our female guide proceeded to demonstrate the dance of the men. Squatting low and grunting and jumping from side to side, bobbing and swaying, and then bending low and sweeping upward she planted her face in one of our lady's "most intimate places." If the man liked what he smelled, he might choose his mate. Kissing, by the way, was not part of the process. People kiss now because they have seen it in movies and on TV.

Our tour included the Catholic church. It was big and beautiful, but there were no stained glass windows. Instead, there were large openings aloft looking out on the amazing volcanic peaks of Ua Pou. What could be more spiritual!? We discussed how/why the Marquesan paganism gave way to Catholicism, in the 1800's. According to our guide, the original Catholic missionaries were eaten. But the white man brought diseases, as they did in other parts of the world, and a large portion of the Marquesan population died from them. That apparently was an indication that the white man's God was more powerful than the many Marquesan gods, and the tribal chief converted. One person told us that even now many Marquesans do not like to visit the traditional spiritual places; they are afraid of the angry spirits still lurking there.

A presentation followed about the history of breadfruit, including a breadfruit "creation myth." In a time of drought a father magically turned his body into a tree trunk, his limbs into tree limbs, and his head into the breadfruit, and so provided for his hungry family. From that first tree all breadfruit trees have descended. We saw how to carry the fruit out of the hills, how to skin it, how to roast it, how to pound it into a poi. For lunch, there was plenty of breadfruit! Also some dishes we hadn't sampled before: dried octopus and curried goat.

I learned the gist of the Marquesan creation myth. A male god and a female god traveled together, forever over the sea, until one day the female god said she wanted a home. So the male god started creating a house, which is the six Marquesan islands. Ua Pou is the upright pillars, another island is crossbeams, one is the roof, etc. Somehow in the process of doing this the gods lost their godly powers, and they became the world's first people, in their Marquesan island home.

When I asked our guide why he had no tattoos, he lifted his shirt – he had plenty. We were told that tattooing originated in the Marquesas, and that "tattoo" is in fact a Marquesan word. A Marquesan tattoo can tell your life story, using ancient symbols. It starts when a boy turns 15, and every 4 years the tattoo is expanded to tell the "next chapter" of the story. Our guide's tattoo was a work in progress. He said that warriors of old would have tats telling of their conquests. If you were threatened by a warrior whose body tells the story of heroic deeds you might want to simply "submit" rather than confront the man!

Women also get tattoos, but theirs are mostly done around their ears, their mouth, their nose, and in fact around every bodily orifice, to protect themselves from evil spirits. Recently some men have been getting tattoos around their ears, which our guide derided, saying those men are getting "girl tattoos." He explained that Tahitian tats are very different, less macho. Recently Tahitians have been copying the Marquesan tattoos, often without giving credit for their origin. Everyone is welcome to use the Marquesan symbols for tattoos, he said, but their origin should be recognized. He was fiercely proud of the heritage and wanted it to remain distinctly Marquesan.

The second day's activities were to take place in the next village, four miles west. We motored the boat to their bay, anchored, and headed ashore in the dinghy. The locals waved to us, indicating that we should land at the "beach," which was nothing but watermelon-size rocks with crashing waves. No way! We managed to tie the dinghy off a pier, despite surging waves coming in. The rest of our rally crowd had the good sense to come by car from the first village.

The locals wished to formally welcome our group. We were directed to walk 100 yards up the road, out of sight, so we could then approach as a group from away. They blared horns and shouted and chanted. As we got close they formed two lines, which we were to walk between in single file. The mayor welcomed us. The tribal chief welcomed us. Nearly-naked men danced to welcome us. The males in our group were encouraged to join the men and dance. Ignoring the embarrassment of being scrawny white guys with no rhythm, we danced. I thought of my men's team back home; wished they were in this dance. I dug deep to locate my warrior spirit and danced it out. The eruption of laughter among the children only added to the flow of energy, out of the earth, summoned by the drums, through my body, through this tribe, resonating with the gods. The description sounds corny. The experience was not.

That was just the welcome. There were demonstrations of how to open coconuts without metal tools. How to extract the coconut meat. There was wood carving and basket weaving. There was a huge spread of fruit for our welcome breakfast, followed immediately by another huge spread for lunch. There were many jokes about fattening us up, as we were too skinny to be eaten.

We piled into the 4WD cars and headed for a waterfall for a swim. Parking was a challenge, the road being carved into hillside. We found a narrow strip between road and ravine, and walked into the "jungle." It wasn't overgrown like a jungle, but it was so lush that I don't know what else to call it. Past a huge banyan tree. Past a cliff where the banyan roots appear to be holding the earth together. Across the stream – it struck me as disappointingly small; I hoped for a good swim in fresh water. Up the gully, and *there* was the waterfall, a delicious pool at the base. Into the water – cold at first, and then perfect. And yes, deep enough that I couldn't touch bottom as I swam across to the falls. Then the torrent of the falling water pelting down. You could stand under it; almost too much to withstand on your skin. You could also stand behind the falling sheets. Someone insisted that the couples in the group stand behind the liquid curtain and kiss. Sadly, no Hallie there. But what a wonderful fresh invigorating enlivening shower!

Back at the beach, I joined a volleyball game with teenage kids, most of whom were better at it than I. There was a tournament of petanque (bocce), and the team of Tim and Bill won a gift certificate to a restaurant in Papeete. The local ladies clearly outclassed all of us at the game, but we were guests and I think they made sure they didn't win the little tourney.

Dinner had been cooking in a pit since dawn. It was now after dark. But before dinner it was time for the fire dance. The nearly-naked men again, in the dark with torches burning, drums echoing, I imagined being an enemy of theirs, and being terrified. They were big and powerful and tattooed and ferocious. The chief screamed unknown words at us. The drumbeats carried messages directly to the soul. The warrior cries echoed off the fire-lit backdrop of rock cliffs. Torches in hand, they danced, they bellowed, they did choreographed hand-to-hand combat. They were serious about this dancing; they were clearly "into it."

I noticed that one of them got a glowing cinder on his back, and it stayed there unnoticed or unheeded by him. I soaked up the vibe; the drumming and the all-out raw male energy of it all.

The dancers led the way to the fire pit. They pulled off the many layers of banana leaves, and with bare hands pulled out the steaming baskets of fish, octopus, goat, breadfruit, and bananas – for us to devour.

After the feast a Marquesan summoned all the men in our group to the center of the pavilion; we were to do the pig dance. He was a hoot, teaching us how to do the simple moves, but more importantly urging us to go full out with the grunting and shouting and wild boar spirit of it. I think we all did pretty darn well, despite the roars of laughter from the Marquesans, young and old. Then the ladies joined in, men outside in a circle, facing the backs of the ladies on an inside circle. The pig dance continued with the men doing the moves we had just learned. The ladies were to do some of the same moves and grunts, but when the men got to their most macho part, the ladies were to put hands on hips and wiggle, with a touch of…perhaps flirtation, perhaps mockery, probably both…toward the men. A good time was had by all.

Our two jam-packed days in Ua Pou came to a close. I didn't know what to make of it all; it was a lot to digest – figuratively and literally. We were told that the town had never put on such an event before. I was grateful and honored (and exhausted) to have been a part of it.

Nuku Hiva & Marquesa Farewell

The day after the festivities on Ua Pou we sailed the 20 miles to Nuku Hiva, administrative capital of the Marquesas. There were more BPO activities planned there, including a "farewell dinner" for all the Pacific Odyssey crews. They would be continuing on at their own pace, no longer with the BPO.

The BPO events were wonderful, but we were weary of Marquesan welcomes and farewells. We soaked up the information presented about our next destination – the Tuamotus, an island archipelago 500 miles to the southwest. We got fuel and food. We said goodbye to friends that we may or may not see again.

One more thing I had to do before departing. Tattoos are so much a part of the Marquesan culture, and the Marquesas were now so much in my heart, and this day was the last opportunity. Although Doctor Tim advised against getting a local tattoo, especially just before departing (we would be offshore when any infection showed up), I had to do it…

The squiggly cross is a symbol of the Marquesas. The "sharks teeth" represent strength and courage in the physical world, and beyond. On the back are three rows of symbols. One is waves, indicating that I am a voyager. The next is a row of sea turtles; they are protectors. The third row is symbols of men. This could have various interpretations, but to me they represent my men's team back home.

The forecast was for very light winds. We decided rather than be bounced around by waves without enough wind to keep moving, we would just go down the coast to Hakatea Bay for the night. This was a great choice, as spectacular volcanic landscapes are not something we had grown weary of. The bay was sheltered all around, mostly by mountain cliffs that bring Tolkien scenes to mind, with a small beach and one hut. One other boat anchored. The bay had room for many more, but more would have ruined the perfection of the place. Birds could be heard singing from shore, and varying scents wafted by as the breeze shifted this way and that.

The evening perfection gave way to a morning that was intensely hot and infested with little flies. The winds remained light, but we had to get moving. A quiet sail on a relatively smooth sea – we were in no hurry.

I had arrived in the Marquesas with no idea what to expect. Our stay was just three weeks, but they will hold my heart forever. Rugged hills, craggy coasts, ancient spirits, nestled villages, bountiful coconuts, heavenly scents, magnificent mantas, beautiful people.

Ahead lay the Tuamotus – also part of French Polynesia, but we knew they would be dramatically different. The islands are coral atolls, barely rising above the sea. They used to be called the Dangerous Isles, because they could not be seen until one's ship was so close it was at risk of hitting the coral. I was looking forward to new experiences just three days' sail ahead.

Ua Pou

Welcome from the tribal chief and the village mayor. Despite the macho culture, women appeared to be on equal footing with the men.

Giving it our (laughable) best!

Hakatea Bay, Nuku Hiva

≈≈≈

TUAMOTUS

Things had been going so well… Our engines were working. The boat was holding up. The crew did the work, stood watch, cooked the meals, without complaint. However, there was friction between Tim and Bill. They had a knack for "pushing each other's buttons."

For example, the three of us could be working to diagnose a problem or resolve some unknown, and we would get to the point of having to wait to get more information. Maybe we needed a wifi hotspot to google the issue, or we sent an email to a customer service address and we had to wait for a reply. This wouldn't stop Tim from pondering all imaginable answers and contingencies, where some of the options were rather "far out." Bill would say, "We'll just have to wait until tomorrow to get our answer, and then look at the options." Tim would continue his conjectures. Bill, exasperated, would simply walk away, leaving Tim mid-sentence. Buttons pressed and counter-pressed.

Once when we were anchoring in a crowded harbor, Bill and I suggested what we thought was a better spot than the one Tim was headed for. Tim ignored us. Bill complained that Tim was not a master at anchoring, and he should be more consultative and listen to his partners. Defensively, Tim agreed to "do it our way." He headed toward the spot we had indicated, but he didn't fully understand what we had in mind. When we ended up too close to another boat, it was evidence for Tim that we were wrong, and it was evidence for us that he didn't listen. After moving the boat, we all agreed to do better next time, but the level of irritation grew.

To cap it off there was what would later be referred to as "the winch handle incident." But I was asleep for that one, and I didn't learn about it until much later, when it would come up again…

Tim was dealing with a business problem back home and decided he needed to be there to address it. He booked a flight from Rangiroa, one of the Tuamotus ahead. Bill and I would sail without him to Tahiti, and we would cruise the Society Islands for a month. A month is what Tim thought he needed; he would rejoin in Bora Bora.

The three of us had been sharing a small space for months; a little time apart might be a good thing…

We were four days sailing the 500 miles from the Marquesas to the Tuamotus. The wind was very light for two days – a little frustrating, but it made for enjoyable night watches. My early watch was moonless; the stars brilliant on the black fabric of space. Nothing needed tending; just sit and enjoy the peace and solitude and quiet and slow movement, and maybe doze off now and then. The third night brought squalls, and we needed to reef the mainsail. Believe it or not, this was the first time we had reefed since leaving Key West! After several squalls went through, we had good wind the rest of the way.

The Tuamotus are the world's largest chain of coral atolls. Each atoll was once a volcanic peak, the ancient mountain now eroded/submerged, a ring of coral and sand now enclosing a central lagoon. Many of the atolls are uninhabited. We chose one of them: Tahanea. As we approached along the shore, there was one hut visible, but no sign of anyone there.

We were "early" at the pass – the current still ebbing fast. Navigating in the Tuamotus is largely about timing the entrance/exit through a pass to the lagoon inside the fringe reef. Most atolls have one or two passes. Many square miles of tidewater flow through the passes, so the currents can be extremely strong, and when they oppose the wind it can make for steep breaking waves. The Tahanea pass was wide, so we could hug one edge, away from the maximum current and waves. The current was three knots against us, even there.

I didn't fully anticipate what the atolls would be like. I imagined that once you made it through the pass, you were in a placid lagoon, protected in all directions. Yes, the pass was all-important. But once we were inside, we could barely see the palm trees on the far side, miles away. The lagoon was huge! We were protected from ocean swells, but the wind could blow across five or ten miles of lagoon, kicking up waves on the inside.

To get good protection from waves, we would have to motor five miles to windward and anchor behind a different part of the reef. We chose instead to try a semi-protected area near the pass. But there were coral heads *everywhere*. There was no possibility of anchoring in a clear patch of sand, where the chain wouldn't swing against coral.

We checked a little further along the rim, but it was the same. Sandy bottom, with coral heads scattered wherever you look. The coral did not rise high enough to threaten the boat. The concern was that the anchor chain could wrap around a head, potentially eliminating the "cushion" of the chain's catenary and damaging the chain or bow cleat or other gear, as well as damaging the coral. There was no avoiding it; we settled on a pretty spot and anchored as best we could.

The place was beautiful. The place was profoundly remote. The water was clear, the coral in varied colors, including bits of striking purple, and intricate shapes. The sky and lagoon and palm and beach colors were vibrant and classic. It seemed like an ad photo enhanced to be more than real.

It was hard to relax and enjoy it, though. It was not a well-protected anchorage; the lagoon was too big. If the wind shifted and blew hard, we would be in an untenable place, on a lee shore, with the prospect of moving miles in the dark through the coral to get to the sheltered side!

We stayed two nights in Tahanea, with some swimming and beachcombing between. The second morning the wind was howling, but we forged ahead with our plan to leave early, at high water. The destination was Fakarava, another atoll 50 miles away. We had a challenge getting the anchor up. No surprise that it was fouled on a coral head. We struggled until a chunk of coral broke off and freed us. We didn't want to damage coral, but where there were innumerable coral heads about, breaking off a little seemed insignificant.

As we motored toward the pass, we had gusts over 30 knots. And in the pass, the current was already flowing out hard, creating some crazy waves with the opposing wind. Being carried by the current into breaking waves got the morning adrenaline pumping, but there wasn't any real danger for a boat of our size. It was like river rapids; just hold on and keep going.

It turned into a beautiful breezy day. By mid-afternoon the pass at the south end of Fakarava came into view. The tide would be in full flood now, but it would flow with the wind, and carry us in. It was scary to be swept fast by the current into an unfamiliar channel with reefs on both sides. No time to think – just go! The sun was still high enough to illuminate the underwater dangers, and before I realized I was holding my breath, we were in. We chose a place to anchor that looked idyllic; three other boats at anchor nearby.

The spot lived up to expectations. Our anchorage was well protected, in a clear patch of sand (with coral heads all around, of course). The water was clear and slightly cool – wonderful to swim in. The surrounding reef and palms were beautiful. The wind kept us comfortable and helped charge our batteries. There was a tiny village nearby that we would explore in the morning. I was starting to like the Tuamotus!

Ashore you could hear the wavelets lapping on the lagoon side, and simultaneously the crashing surf on the ocean side. The land was narrow, and it never rose more than a few feet above high water. This is an archipelago that will be horrendously affected by sea level rise. Some say that the atolls have a chance because their coral reefs are alive and will continue to grow as sea level changes. But it isn't that simple. The CO2 that we release into the air not only affects the atmosphere, it also gets absorbed into the ocean, increasing the acidity of the seawater. Even a slight increase in ocean acidity has been shown to kill coral reefs. The future of the atolls and the Tuamotuans is bleak, unless we transform our fossil-fuel-based economy *now*.

≈≈≈

Before I grasped the extent of an atoll's lagoon, it didn't occur to me that one can sail for half a day on the inside. The shallow depths can impose limits; beating to windward could be difficult. But sailing downwind along the edge of the Fakarava lagoon was delightful. All the ocean breeze; no waves.

Off the town at Fakarava's north end, we spied most of the BPO fleet. So nice to see our friends again! We dined ashore; we ordered baguettes to pick up in the morning; we bought a few supplies. We snorkeled at a very nice little reef, a short swim from the boat.

Our last stop in the Tuamotus was Rangiroa, 150 miles away. The sailing was ideal. We left in company with two other BPO boats, and quickly left them behind. In fact, we arrived off the Rangiroa pass before dawn, and had to drift for a few hours to wait for good light and reasonable current for entering.

Rangiroa is known for world-class diving. Luckily for us, the excellence extends to snorkeling, too. We snorkeled at "The Aquarium" – a reef that was accessible for beginners yet had an incredible number and variety of fish. I saw shapes and colors of fish that I'd never seen before. Purple fish with long streamers off the tips of the tail; multicolored fish like parrot fish, but far larger than any parrot fish I'd seen; tiny blue fish with brilliant color like neon; a fish that looked like it grew a finger out of its forehead, extending over and in front of its face... The coral, too, had dazzling color and shape.

We did a "drift dive" in one of the passes. Rangiroa is said to have one of the best drift dives in the world. The idea was to take your dinghy out the pass to the ocean when the current was flowing in, then get in the water and drift back (hanging on to the dinghy) through the pass. Allegedly one could see large animals below in the pass – manta rays, large sharks, dolphins, etc. We were disappointed, seeing nothing remarkable.

We went to the Air Tahiti office to make sure Tim was all set with his flight out in three days. Then to the gendarmerie to process his exit and planned return. Surprisingly, based on our Marquesan experience, the gendarme spoke good English. We thought we were just processing Tim's paperwork, but the official said we needed all our passports. Oops, we hadn't brought them ashore. With a shrug he said, "This is paradise." The implication was that it was a French requirement, but here in this tropical outpost...he didn't care.

We visited the Gauguin Black Pearl Farm and learned how black pearls are cultured and harvested. It's a surprisingly complex and interesting process. The oysters grow for 3 years before they "put them to work." Then they pry open the oyster about 1 centimeter, and with surgical tools they make a small incision and insert a small "marble" and a graft of a small piece of tissue from another oyster. The marbles are made from oyster shells from the Mississippi River! The Mississippi shells are shipped to Japan to be cut into the marbles, and then shipped here to the pearl farm. The oysters are put into mesh bags for a month.

If the marble is then seen in the bag, the operation didn't "take." If no marble present, the oyster is added to a string of others, the string is surrounded by a cage to keep predators out, and the whole rig is hung out in the lagoon…for two years. Then the oysters are brought ashore and opened slightly again, and the pearl is taken. This is done by an expert who immediately judges the quality of the pearl. If it is inferior grade it goes into one box, and the oyster goes into a bin to be eaten. It the pearl is higher quality it goes into another bin, and the oyster gets a slightly-larger seed marble and goes back out to the lagoon for another two years.

After learning all about growing black pearls, there was a sales showroom to be visited. There they had zillions of pearls, all sizes and shapes and qualities, and craftspeople to turn them into jewelry. Although Hallie had rarely worn the jewelry I had given to her in the past, I had to buy her a black pearl. I chose an oddly shaped one; I preferred it over the perfect ones. It had some personality, some individuality, some spirit. The perfect ones hardly seemed real.

Where is Paradise?

There were some things 'wrong' with the place. It was way too hot in the sun. The primary activity for several hours during mid-day was to find shade, preferably with a breeze. There was no soft sand – it was all tiny bits of coral, not something you would want to dig your toes into. Pretty much everything except fish was brought in by boat. Supplies were very limited, and expensive. It struck me as funny when we stopped into a store, after a walk in the heat, to splurge on an expensive ice cream bar. "Sorry, no ice cream until the boat comes tomorrow."

And yet, many consider this paradise. I was thinking about what makes it so. Sitting in the cockpit in the cool breeze at the end of the day, watching a beautiful sunset, I came up with one answer. Here, you live outdoors. You feel that you are a part of the natural world, not apart from the natural world. You can swim in cool refreshing water that is clear enough to see the fish all around. You can sit outside with little or no clothing and enjoy the warmth and the breeze. There are no insects interfering with this enjoyment. It might rain, but it will stop in ten minutes, and you'll be dry again in another ten.

I could not live here long. The sun erodes one's will, one's initiative. It becomes too easy to sit and do nothing. I would likely lose the satisfaction that I find in doing my projects (such as

circumnavigating). Not much happens here; not much changes. I would never tire of the weather, but I would not like to be so far from friends and family. And a supermarket with a steady supply of cookies and ice cream and, yes, fresh vegetables, too.

Is there some other paradise for me? Or some aspects of this paradise that I could find or make at home? It is challenging to spend time outdoors in Maine. The mosquitoes and other insects immediately come to mind, and the cold for much of the year. Would it be significantly different further south in the USA? Should I be focusing on building a screened deck with a heated floor and a hot tub and a view…? Would that be my paradise…?

We got Tim off to the airport, no problem. I was surprised when he took his guitar, but he said it wasn't getting used much on the boat, might as well take it home.

Bill and I had a pleasant overnight sail to Tahiti. Jimmy Cornell would be flying in, and we would be choosing the route/schedule for the rest of the BPO rally. And Hallie would be flying in to meet me, our first time together since Key West.

TAHITI

No Regrets spent nine days in the brand-new marina in downtown Papeete, the capital city on the island of Tahiti. Papeete was very convenient. Shops and restaurants and banks (everything is expensive, except baguettes), and the BPO reps Luc and Jackie helping with rides and phone calls and translation.

We got our foresail patched and a zipper replaced on an awning. We ordered a new screecher from a sailmaker in Australia, to be picked up somewhere ahead. We changed the oil in both engines and were able to properly dispose of the dirty stuff, plus additional old oil we had been holding for this opportunity. We had an electrician check our batteries and tell us they were okay. We rented a car so we could drive around the island, plus carry many hundreds of dollars of supplies to the boat. Last good place to shop until Australia, we were told.

The most important activity in Papeete was the much-anticipated meeting with Jimmy Cornell, to update the plan going forward for the Blue Planet Odyssey. The rally had just lost another boat. After sailing to Tahiti from the US West Coast, they decided that offshore husband/wife sailing was not for them. They would spend some time in French Polynesia and then sail home via Hawaii. In addition, the boat that turned back to Key West early on, and the boat that was delayed due to lack of funds – both were out of the picture.

What boats remained? Five were present and planning to continue: *No Regrets* (of course), *Chapter Two*, *Maggie*, *Ransom*, *Libby*. Although not present, *Blue Wind* also planned to continue. Three others were possibly in the mix. *Joyful* had a delayed start, and they were now sailing non-stop from Panama to the Marquesas, hoping to catch the fleet by Bora Bora. We didn't know if they would make it in time and be ready to set right off again on short rest. *Tahawus* had signed on only as far as the Marquesas, along with the other boats in the Pacific Odyssey. They were present in Tahiti, unsure of their future plans. *Coconut Woman* remained in the Marquesas. The lady aboard had suffered mightily from seasickness, sun exposure and insomnia at sea. They had not withdrawn from the BPO, but the writing was on the wall: if they continued across the ocean at all, it would not be at the BPO rally pace.

My expectation coming into the planning meeting was that the remaining BPO boats would each have different and strongly-held ideas about the route and schedule. Some were talking of sailing to New Zealand, which would be far off the current working plan. Some wanted to slow down and spend more time in the Pacific and/or Southeast Asia, perhaps adding a year to the plan. That would not work for me, as I had a home and wife to return to. I expected Jimmy to announce a grand plan, and everyone would grumble that it wasn't what they wanted, and the BPO would unravel completely.

There were surprises in store for me. The first was that Jimmy did not declare an updated BPO route. He asked the participants what we wanted to do, and made suggestions. My second surprise was that the participants went out of their way to come up with a consensus plan. Everyone was flexible. With Jimmy's coaching about what routes/schedules would work and what wouldn't, a consensus plan emerged. The BPO still had life after all!

The biggest aspect of the new plan was that we would sail south around Africa, around the Cape of Good Hope, rather than traverse the Red Sea. Between stories of piracy and the ongoing threat of political/religious strife, the Middle East was simply not a desirable place to go cruising. That removed the Mediterranean from the plan, which was upsetting to some. Shipping their boat from SE Asia to Turkey was an option they could consider.

Another aspect of the plan was an agreement not to sail to New Zealand. We would plan for some extended time in Australia, and those who wanted to visit New Zealand could fly there during that break. Jimmy also hinted about cool things to come in Indonesia, but that plan was not yet fully developed.

The cyclone season in the Indian Ocean was a major scheduling factor. One option would be to move on quickly to Australia and continue aggressively to South Africa. We could be home in one year. I may have been the only one to seriously consider that option. The alternative was a more leisurely voyage to Australia, spending some extended time in Vanuatu. Then more cruising time in Indonesia and Southeast Asia before crossing the Indian Ocean. Home in two years. Because we had to avoid cyclone season, there was no middle ground.

Expecting the BPO to die, I had been thinking of going fast on our own and getting home in a year. But with the BPO still alive, and the continued camaraderie of the participants, I supported the new plan. I didn't look forward to some of the "dallying" ahead, but the schedule would still get me home pretty much as originally intended – two and a half years from departure.

As the planning meeting was wrapping up, Bill and I were approached by a crewmember from the boat *Maggie*. Owners Rob and Carol wanted to try sailing *Maggie* by themselves, so their crewmember Bob was hoping to sign aboard another boat. "I hear you might be looking for crew," Bob said to us.

This was perplexing. Yes, we would need crew when Bill's leave of absence was done and he returned to work. That would be nearly four months away, in

Australia. We didn't yet have a plan for crew at that point. But Bob already knew this. I gave Bob a questioning look as I said, "Well, yes, when we get to Australia…"

Bob looked perplexed now, too. With an awkward, "Oh, okay," he turned and left. Several hours later Bill and I would learn what Bob already knew. An email from Tim informed us that his return (planned for Bora Bora in three weeks) was delayed. He would instead rejoin later, perhaps in Australia, *IF he returned at all*!!!

This news required some adjustments on the part of Bill and me. Having adequate crew aboard was critical. But beyond that, what was the nature of our partnership…the bond of trust…the future of the entire voyage…?

Tim had obviously confided things to Bob that he hadn't yet shared with his partners. What kind of partnership was that? Did he have any intention of returning, even when he left? When he took his guitar home, was that because he knew, or suspected, that he wasn't coming back? I looked through the emails he had sent through our boat account. Normally we respected individual privacy and did not look at each other's emails on this shared account, but feeling betrayed trumps privacy concerns. I found an email to Jimmy Cornell where Tim hinted that he might not return. Perhaps he hadn't known, but he had at least been thinking about it before he left and said not a word to Bill or me. Tim apparently cared enough to speak with Bob about filling his position; did that count for something? Not much. I felt betrayed.

Next day we signed Bob on through Australia.

This was the first time we had to work out finances outside of the three owners. Bob agreed to pay for a third of the food, fuel and mooring costs. Since Hallie was aboard for the next three weeks of cruising in the Society Islands, Bob would come aboard in Bora Bora.

After the shock, it was a relief to have crew lined up for the rest of the voyage across the Pacific. After that…? Would Tim rejoin? Did I want him to rejoin? Could I still sail with him if he wanted to rejoin? What if I was left with no crew at all? Not something to dwell on while cruising in paradise. It's all Journey; something would work out…

Papeete

SOCIETY ISLANDS

Hallie, Bill and I left Tahiti and motorsailed the short hop to Mo'orea. It was a relief to get away from the city and anchor out behind a reef. In the morning we moved on to Opunopu Bay on the north side of Mo'orea. Here was South Pacific classic beauty, plus a great anchorage with clear shallow water, sandy bottom, no coral heads, and a handful of other boats nearby.

BPOers *Ransom* and *Libby* came to the same anchorage. The social planners among the crews noted that there were several birthdays to be celebrated. We had a good time all squeezed into *Libby*'s cockpit for beer and cake. Sue had been bitten by a dog earlier in the day and had gone to a doctor. (Excellent socialized healthcare, of course!) The doc noticed from Sue's ID that it was her birthday, and he wrote a prescription for painkillers and champagne! Sue was in jolly good spirits for her party.

We had entered the realm of tourists. We went ashore to the Intercontinental Resort and had an expensive (but quite good) lunch. The resort had three dolphins in captivity. They did a dolphin show and you could swim with the dolphins. They claimed the dolphins were there for "research and education." We had mixed feelings about this, but we stayed to watch an amazing show.

We snorkeled at the "underwater tikis." An artist carved several stone tikis and placed them in the lagoon, in about 8 feet of water. Interesting way to view an artist's work!

Back at the boat we were below putting groceries away when we heard Terry from *Libby* calling to us, saying that our anchor was dragging! This was an understatement – we were moving rapidly backward toward a deep narrow channel, and in another 50 yards we would be across it and on the reef! We started an engine and reset the anchor uneventfully. But we were incredibly lucky that we were back on the boat, and that Terry was paying attention! Our anchor had never dragged before, once it was properly set – it left us a little shaken, uncertain about what we could/couldn't count on.

We got underway for Huahine, 80 miles away, just as it was getting dark, plus it started to rain, plus it was more bumpy than we had expected. Hallie had a tough night... But things looked better in the morning. We anchored in a very protected channel between Huahine Iti and a barrier island, and stayed three nights. The area had no store, no restaurant, no wifi. Eighty miles had gotten us clear of the tourist areas and into an idyllic clear-water anchorage.

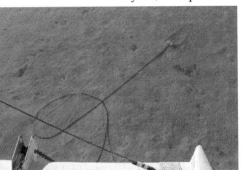

Idyllic, except that the breeze blew one way and the current ran the other. The confused boat couldn't decide which to lie to, so we turned this way and that. At one point we noticed that our anchor chain was wrapped around our anchor. I realized then that this was how/why we dragged in the previous anchorage. Our primary anchor had a 'float' that helped it orient properly on the bottom. But the float stuck up above the sand and could foul the chain if the boat drifted in circles. At least we now knew what to watch out for.

We were visited by Paul, a local who apparently paddles his dugout canoe to greet all yachts that come to his lagoon. Paul was deaf, and communication was very challenging, but he had a "guest book" with entries by hundreds of sailors, to which we added ours. He left us with coconuts and a breadfruit, and the next day dropped off fish as well. We made a local cuisine dinner of fish and coconut rice and breadfruit.

Home is Where the Anchor Is?

I had been thinking more about the alternatives after Australia. There were still two major unknowns: was Tim rejoining, and how would Bob work out as crew. But the aspect under my control was how I felt about traveling at BPO speed versus hurrying back...home. I realized that the feeling of "home" was a big factor. Looking at other boats/crews, in most cases there was a married couple, and in many cases they had sold or at least rented their house ashore. Their boat was their home.

For me the boat was primarily a vehicle for making a voyage. At times I could see it differently, though. Especially with Tim away and Hallie aboard, I could perceive the boat as my home. When I did, I found I was in no rush to be moving on. If I was already home, why rush to go elsewhere? In this state of mind I could imagine being content with the pokey BPO schedule. So I "practiced" being home aboard, and it worked pretty well. Hallie being there was a huge temporary assist, but nevertheless it seemed like something I could learn and develop. I vowed to keep with it and see how I fared after Bora Bora.

≈≈≈

For another week we cruised among the Society Islands. To the town of Fare on the west side of Huahine (food shopping, expensive laundry, and a nice dinner ashore with the crew of *Coconut Woman*). South to Avea Bay (beautiful bay, but it got rolly at midnight when high tide seemed to let waves in over the reef). Out through the pass with impressive surf breaking close by on both sides. At Raiatea we anchored in five feet of water with a flat sandy bottom glowing turquoise for miles. Bill put a stern anchor out by carrying it – on foot!

After a stop at the island of Tahaa, we had a windy sail to Bora Bora, where we picked up a mooring at the yacht club. We had been warned that Bora Bora was sometimes called "Boring Bora," but we enjoyed our stay. The club was nice, with a swimming pool and wifi and good (expensive) food, and less than a mile into town. Better yet was the dancing and drumming. There was dancing right at the club, which we participated in. But even better was the local community practicing every night for an annual competition in Papeete. We could hear the drums from the boat, and if we walked into town for dinner we got to watch the practice. The whole community seemed to be there, dancing or drumming or singing or just enjoying being where the spirit was flowing.

With two other crews we arranged an island tour. Someone joked with our guide about how well marijuana must grow there, and after our next stop he produced a small amount for sale. Normally as visitors we would steer well clear of any and all drugs in a foreign country. Just too risky. But here it seemed natural. The buyer said it was for medicinal purposes…

From the hills of Bora Bora, looking down at the surrounding lagoon, I saw some alluring anchorages. But they would have to wait until "next time around," as we were shifting out of cruising mode and back into voyage preparation.

I said goodbye to Hallie at the ferry to the airport. We picked up Bob at the ferry the next morning. There were a few boat chores to be done; another run to the supermarket. Then to the gendarmerie to check out, and to the bank to get the bond money back that we had to put into escrow on arrival back in Hiva Oa.

We had visited three distinct parts of French Polynesia. The Marquesas were rugged and awesome. The atolls of the Tuamotus were flat; alluring in a very different way from the macho Marquesas. The Society Islands, from Tahiti to Bora Bora, had taken a while to grow on me. But they did, particularly with the drumming, the dancing, and the wonderful friendliness of the Polynesian people. And geographically, with a fringe reef around rugged islands, they had the best of both worlds – impressive landscapes plus calm anchorages.

There was good BPO news and bad BPO news. The bad news: *Ransom* had dropped out, to follow their own timetable to Australia; *Libby* was also out, planning to circle back to the US West Coast; and, as anticipated, *Coconut Woman* was out. The good news: *Tahawus* was in! We also got an update from *Joyful*. They had sailed 40 days straight from Panama to the Marquesas, then direct to Bora Bora where they caught up with the fleet. But their skipper was not well;

perhaps had an unidentified infection; they were not ready to go. Departing as planned from Bora Bora it would be just ourselves, *Chapter Two*, *Maggie*, and *Tahawus*; maybe *Blue Wind* – we were unsure of their plans. I wondered once again if there was critical mass to hold the rally together.

There are many islands in the South Pacific, and many paths a boat can sail going west. The BPOers would rendezvous in Vanuatu, but that was two months and 2300 miles away. Probably we would cross paths in Tonga, two weeks away. As stops on the way there, we chose Maupiti and then Niue. After Tonga, I wanted to head for Tuvalu, but that would require convincing my crew to add an extra thousand miles to the trip; we weren't ready to have that conversation yet.

Maupiti – The Way Life Should Be!

Maupiti lay 25 miles west. The island is part of French Polynesia, but there would be no gendarmerie (or bank) there. Hence the check out from Bora Bora. We departed early to time our arrival for slack current at the pass in the reef.

Maupiti has a challenging entrance. The surrounding reef is relatively low on the south side, so waves from the south can break over the reef into the lagoon. Most of that water flows back out through the pass. Reportedly there could be a current up to 9 knots flowing out. Nine knots was faster than we could go with both motors running. In addition, the south-flowing current might oppose the waves rolling in, potentially creating dangerously steep breakers. When those conditions occurred, even the ferry did not run to Maupiti. If you were at the island when the conditions developed, you would have to wait it out, perhaps three days, before you could safely leave.

Because of the risk, most yachts leaving Bora Bora sail past Maupiti without stopping. That was one reason the place attracted us. The wind had been light and the waves moderate; we were going to give it a try. The pass was narrow, and at the scheduled "slack water" we encountered a 2.5-knot current. Waves crashed on the reef, close aboard on both sides. My hands were white-knuckled on the wheel; I focused on steering right down the middle of the pass. If a wave caught us, the trick would be to surf straight through, and not get pushed to the coral edge. As when approaching rapids down a river, there comes a point where you are committed to proceeding, even though you don't know exactly what lies ahead. An adrenaline rush. And then we were through; the surf behind us; the water colors revealing the channel ahead.

What a place! We anchored in a secure spot with a pleasant breeze, and an unbelievable view of peaks and cliffs. Ashore we found nothing "touristic" – just wonderfully friendly people. There were a couple tiny stores (where you stand at the window and tell the proprietor what you want; you don't go in and pick things from shelves). One small shop offered local crafts – mostly shells. There was one restaurant, not open when we walked by. There was a closed bakery that suggested croissants in the morning. There was fruit for sale. And we happened upon a woman selling cooked fish at the side of the road, and that became our dinner.

Looming overhead was a central mountain and immense vertical cliffs. We were constantly looking up as we walked the street. The narrow ribbon between the cliffs and the water was the town.

The kicker was that we were the only yacht! I knew sailors were put off by the difficult entrance, but I didn't expect to have this spectacular island and lagoon all to ourselves. Relaxing with a sundowner in the cockpit, the idyllic scene was completed: the brilliant full moon rose from the reef, and the cliffs glowed in its majesty.

Maybe humans exist to bear witness at such moments. I couldn't help but think along the less profound line of the Maine state slogan, "Maupiti – the way life should be!"

Raiatea

Bora Bora

Just-dyed pareos drying

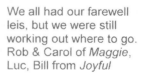

We all had our farewell
leis, but we were still
working out where to go.
Rob & Carol of *Maggie*,
Luc, Bill from *Joyful*

Black-tip sharks won't
hurt you, they say.

Self-portrait

Maupiti

Bob made the climb and took the photo. We are anchored off the ribbon of town.
Between the two islands is the channel to the narrow pass through the surrounding reef.

NIUE

Sailboats fly the flag of their home country on the stern. When they first arrive in a new country, they fly the "quarantine" flag (all yellow) from the starboard spreader (part way up the mast) to indicate that the boat needs to be cleared in by Customs and Immigration authorities. Then the quarantine flag is replaced with the flag of the current country. This is called a courtesy flag.

When we were preparing for the BPO we made a list of the countries we expected to visit, and we looked on the Web for courtesy flags. Most flag companies sold overly expensive flags, made to last longer than we would need. We found one company that sold flags at such a low cost that I doubted they would last through the first squall. We decided to order the inexpensive ones, but only through French Polynesia, so we could test their quality before we ordered more. The flags were fine. But we forgot to place our order for more!

For several days we tried to procure the flags we needed, at least to get to Australia. Well...one benefit of boats dropping out of the BPO was...they had flags they were willing to part with. Indeed, we pulled together a very inexpensive set of flags that would serve us as far as Indonesia. Except...nobody had Niue, which was our next planned stop. Niue is one of the smallest countries in the world (population 1,600), and its flag was not readily available on short notice.

So...time to make our own! The background of the Niue flag is yellow, the same as the international code flag for the letter Q (which is also the quarantine flag). So I started with the Q from our code flag set. The upper left quadrant of the flag was complex, in white, red, blue and yellow. I cut pieces of sail repair material, bought permanent markers, drew the design, and stapled the material on to the Q flag. I wasn't sure it would last long, but it didn't have to – maybe 3 days.

Beautiful Emptiness

It is 1,000 miles from Maupiti to Niue – about a week, and we were four days into it. The weather had been beautiful, the winds light, no rain squalls, so there was lots of time to contemplate…emptiness. No boats. No land. A thousand miles of ocean. Bill had been reading; Bob had been learning everything about the boat. I did a lot of staring at the ocean during the day and staring at the sky at night.

The emptiness was punctuated by little events. We caught a fish the first day. That generated lots of activity: trying to slow the boat down while we reeled it in; all taking our positions on the stern to gaff it and to blow a mouthful of rum into its gills to kill it; filleting it still on the back of the boat, to contain the mess; cleaning up the mess; and of course cooking and eating it!

We hadn't caught a fish since, but we had small tuna swimming with us. I had never seen this before – fish acting like dolphins. They would swim alongside and sometimes in front of the boat. Then disappear for a few minutes, and then they'd be back. We were trailing a lure at the time; I was relieved that we didn't get a strike. Didn't seem right to catch a fish that was being a sociable escort.

The stars of the early night were magnificent. Then the moon would rise and paint its own beauty across the sky. One night I saw six satellites. One was so bright I was convinced it was the space station. But ten minutes later I saw another that was equally bright.

We celebrated Bill's birthday. Bob had brought a two-kilo bag of granola from home, as a gift from Bill's daughter. Bob made a card and wrote a poem to go with it. I baked banana bread.

Receiving emails via the radio was a treat. Missives from family and from the other rally boats. Lots of time to think about family and friends, and future boats and adventures. Lots of time to enjoy emptiness.

My emptiness meditation was interrupted by a yellowfin tuna on our line. An hour later he was filleted. Then I had to finish the loaf of bread I had started preparing earlier. Then I offered to make dinner even though it wasn't my turn in the rotation, because I found an interesting recipe for fish curry. After dinner we needed to get the spinnaker down because the wind was veering too far forward. By then it was time to look for satellites (just for fun). No satellites tonight (we probably missed prime spotting time when we were busy with the spinnaker), but two airplanes. I guessed we were approaching the flight path between New Zealand and Hawaii.

After several hours of busy, I could get back to the emptiness. Stars galore. I learned that the dark area next to the Southern Cross is actually a dust cloud that obscures the stars behind it. Happily, I still had two hours on my watch to contemplate that…

I received another round of questions from the Lewiston 7th graders and took a stab at answering.

- Regarding the color(s) of the water. Yes, very different from Maine! My understanding is that the cold water carries more oxygen, which in turn supports more plankton and/or other microscopic life in the water, with the result that the water is not clear like it is in the tropics. With the clear tropical water, the color is an indication of the depth. Dark blue is deep and safe to sail in. Light turquoise/green is shallow with a sandy bottom – good for anchoring…until it becomes too shallow. Brown or dark patches in the water indicates coral reef or coral heads – dangerous! I love the dark blue and the turquoise side by side.

- Regarding the black pearls – no, we didn't get to keep the one in the photo, but I did buy one for my wife. **Zamzam**, what they do is choose an oyster that has a pretty color around the edge/lip of its shell. They "sacrifice" this oyster, cutting that edge/lip tissue into many little pieces (I think they do 120 pieces from the one oyster). This is the tissue that they implant with the "marble" to start the pearl. For some reason that I don't think anyone fully understands, that little piece of tissue determines the color of the pearl.

- **Chantel**, thinking about the cost of fuel is always wise! The fuel for our engines is diesel, and the fuel for our dinghy outboard is gasoline. Here (and in most of the world) they are sold/priced by the liter, not by the gallon. For diesel we paid 84 French Polynesian francs per liter. To compare that to the cost at home, we have to convert both the currency and the units. For a simple approximation, one franc is very close to 1 American penny, and a liter is just a little more than a quart.

So 84 francs per liter is close to 84 * 4 = \$3.36 per gallon. The local people actually have to pay more. We do not have to pay some of the tax (which can be substantial on fuel), because we are a foreign yacht in transit through the country.

- Hmm, how to answer **Ryan**'s question as to whether my wife was a big help? Yes, in the sense that it was great to be together again, and spend some time talking about people/relationships instead of about sailing. But no, in the sense that she's not much of a sailor, and she's uncomfortable when the boat is moving, even when I think the motion is so gentle that I barely notice it. Let's just say I'm looking forward to having her back (in Australia). There we will be exploring ashore, rather than sailing.

- **Reginald**, the doctor was being funny when he prescribed champagne. But he really did write it on a prescription form. And the woman bitten by the dog really was drinking it when we met with her that evening.

- **Brooke**, yes, with what I know now I would indeed do this again. Probably if I ever *do* sail here again I will do it differently. I will pick certain places, like the Marquesas, where I will stay for a month or more, and I will skip other places. Sailing in a rally has its advantages (partnering with other boats, assistance with clearing into foreign countries, guidance about scheduling to avoid stormy seasons), but a disadvantage is that if you fall in love with a place you can't stay put for a long time – the rally moves on.

- **Ben**, I'd guess that the black tip sharks we've seen range from pretty small up to maybe 80 pounds. We saw one very large nurse shark (I think it was). It was probably 10 feet long and must have weighed at least 200 pounds. The locals do not consider these sharks dangerous, but if I saw a shark that big when I was snorkeling, I would be out of the water quickly!

- **Veda**, I'm never in fear of sinking, because our catamaran would not sink, even if it developed a huge leak. There are other bad things that could happen, like colliding with a ship, crashing on to a reef or capsizing the boat. It's up to us to pay attention and stay safe. There are times when I feel scared, but I know what needs to be done to pull through, so I just need to stay on task and do it.

Niue is a country I'd never heard of before the trip. The entire country is a single island about 13 miles long and 8 miles wide. It is a "raised coral atoll." That is, it once was an atoll like the Tuamotus, but the seabed pushed upward, turning the atoll into a plateau about 150 feet high. The rock of the entire island is limestone – old coral.

Although Niue was independent, in many respects it was a remote outpost of New Zealand. Aside from visiting yachts (there were 4 others during our stay), the only access was by air from New Zealand – two flights per week in the tourist season, one per week the rest of the year. A cargo boat stopped by once a month. The population of the country was 1,600. It had been over 5,000 fifty years earlier, but many people moved to New Zealand in search of jobs.

The last day of our passage from Maupiti was rough – gusts to 30 knots and uncomfortable waves from two directions. Niue didn't have a "harbor" – just an indentation/bay on the west side, providing shelter from the prevailing easterlies, but wide open if the wind didn't follow the script. The bay was deep almost to shore, so it was nearly impossible to anchor. But there were moorings, courtesy of the Niue Yacht Club. The yacht club was not a group of resident sailors. It was a few volunteers helping visiting "yachties" like us. Many yachties in turn supported the club by becoming members. The club had more members than there were residents of the country!

It was a relief on arrival to find clearly marked moorings, and discover that the bay provided surprisingly good shelter from the big seas. Customs, Immigration, Quarantine and Health officials met me on the pier, and I filled out the forms in the back of their van. The pier was the only place to get ashore, and it was not well protected. You took your dinghy (or fishing boat, or canoe) alongside and lifted it out of the water with an electric hoist; parked it on the concrete.

There was a bank, but they didn't exchange currencies; they would provide NZ currency by charging your credit card and adding a fee. There was a pretty good grocery store, and fresh bread, including a sweet coconut bread. There were several restaurants, most open only a few days a week. There was a very helpful tourist information center that provided an island map, and a booklet about the businesses. The yacht club maintained showers next to the pier.

And...everyone spoke English! That was a welcome change for me, whether dealing with the officials or chatting with someone in a restaurant. I would have enjoyed French Polynesia (even) more if I spoke French. Interesting, though, that in French Polynesia I learned basic words (hello, thank you, cheers!) in the local Polynesian language, and used them regularly as a courtesy to the Polynesian people. In Niue everyone just spoke English to white people – I didn't learn a single word in the local Polynesian language.

It was a quiet place, but a fun place to explore. There were dozens of "sea tracks" from the road (on the raised plateau) down to the ocean. These were paths, often with steps to help in the steep parts, to get to the views, the caves, the chasms, the coral formations that shaped the island. We rented bicycles and rode to some of the choice places, per the tourist info.

We pedaled to the Limu Pools and snorkeled there. These pools of water connected to the ocean but were inside a very protective reef. Fresh water also flowed in through the island's coral base. The fresh water was much colder than the seawater. Swimming in the pools you went from warm to cold to warm to cold…every few feet. Or, when it was cold you could dive down just a foot or so to the warm salt water below the cold fresh water. Looking through the water you saw "shimmering" similar to air above hot pavement.

Riding back to town late in the afternoon, I said, "Let's stop at the first burger joint we pass." We saw a bar, and we stopped, but they served no food. What they did have was, according to a little sign, "the world's most challenging golf course; one hole, par one." To understand this we had to walk a short distance out to the cliff by the ocean, where there was a "tee." From there you could see the flag/pin, across a chasm and in a little clearing on an opposing cliff. There was no practical way to get to the "green" – hence the challenge and the par one.

The guys at the bar told us we could get burgers at the town market. That seemed odd, but we pedaled there. The market at that hour was empty, except for one couple…selling burgers. They made an awesome burger! They didn't ask what you wanted on it; it came with fresh tomato and lettuce and pickled beets and a homemade chutney, and was topped with a fried egg. It hit the spot after a long day of cycling and hiking and swimming. And it came with interesting tales of bringing all sorts of fruit trees and nuts and veggies to the island and trying to grow them on their land.

Another night Bill and I ate at a sushi restaurant that served some of the best sushi I've had. I little pricey, but not unreasonable, and a nice treat. The passion fruit ice cream served on a bed of fresh papaya with chocolate sauce wasn't so bad either!

There was a fishing competition going on while we were there. When we went to return to the boat, we found that the electric hoist was being used to lift and weigh the day's catch – we had to wait an hour to relaunch our dinghy. The catch was all yellowfin tuna. Someone said that no mahi-mahi had been caught. I thought it was just us failing to bring in my favorite fish, but I guess they had become scarce. The largest yellowfin weighed in at 76 kilos – about the same weight as me! That one was caught from a powerboat. But most of the fishermen were paddling small outrigger canoes, and I found it amazing to see them bring in 30+ pound fish. It would be exciting to see them get the fish from the ocean into their tiny canoe.

It rained all day one day. I think it was the first "rainy day" (as opposed to passing squalls) we had since leaving Key West! It was pleasant to spend the day doing little. And then it was Sunday, when no work is done on Niue, and no fishing or diving. We bent the norms a little and did laundry on the pier, and snorkeled right off the boat (surprisingly interesting coral and fish between us and the shore), but it was a quiet day. We talked at length with our Canadian crew (Bob) about the differences in government and healthcare between Canada and the USA.

I enjoyed the slow pace on Niue, and I would have been happy to stay longer. I wasn't in such a rush to move on anymore. And whales would be coming to Niue to calve, starting in a couple weeks. They say you can watch them from your boat, right on the mooring. That would be worth staying for. But there was a BPO schedule to meet. Besides, heavy wind was predicted to blow from the south, which could make for a very uncomfortable ride on the mooring. So…we were off to Vava'u, Tonga.

My Niue courtesy flag? Still looked great after flying for six days!

≈≈≈

A "Sea Track" to a sea cave, and somebody's parking space

All the canoes were of
the same design and
construction.

Talava Arches

Yes, we were having fun here with the perspective, while we waited to use the hoist to launch our dinghy; but this fish did weigh as much as I did.

TONGA

Two days downwind sailing from Niue to Vava'u – a group of 60+ islands that comprise the northern part of The Kingdom of Tonga. Winds came up strong and the second half of the ride was uncomfortable, with occasional seas slamming under the bridge deck (beneath our feet, between the hulls) and against the side of the boat. On arrival the wind was blowing right up the two-mile long harbor, with waves slapping against the concrete Customs dock. We knew we were expected to come alongside so the authorities could board the boat – we did so with trepidation. But the authorities understood that it was a dicey position for a boat our size, and they told us to go to a mooring and then dinghy in for the formalities. Very nice.

Kjell was our BPO rep/helper here, and he offered us a mooring at the far (protected) end of the harbor. This turned out to be right in front of his house, and he allowed us to connect to his Internet via the boat's wifi antenna. Our antenna could *just* do it – the connection dropped every few minutes, but for the most part it was better than our usual Internet connection, and certainly was more convenient!

As had happened before in some other new places, I experienced the Yet Another Paradise Blues. Another place where we had to figure out how to navigate through the formalities. Another place where we had to get local currency, find out where to buy food, where to do laundry, how to get around, what local customs we needed to be aware of, etc. This could/should all be part of the fun and adventure, but I had grown weary of it.

We stayed on Kjell's mooring for a week – longer than we had planned. The weather was unparadise-like. Two days were rainy, and the wind blew hard; the locals were complaining about the cold. While stuck in town, we made arrangements to have our newly made screecher sail shipped to us, and a new hydraulic pump for the autopilot.

About the autopilot… It keeps the boat on a set course. We rarely steered by hand. But in waves the autopilot would "wander," sometimes far enough one way to collapse our spinnaker, and then far enough the other way to collapse it again. This had always been a problem, but it seemed to have gotten worse. We gave it a test on a daysail. I watched the autopilot's hydraulic pump and its linkage to the rudders. I could see that when there was a lot of force on the rudder (going fast in waves), the linkage "slipped" from time to time. The seals in the pump were worn. We had a mechanic come aboard and check out the steering, and he confirmed that the pump was at fault, and he said it would get worse until eventually it would be useless. We ordered a new pump from New Zealand and hoped Fed Ex could get it to Vava'u before we departed!

During the week I cheered up, as always. We had some delicious meals at inexpensive restaurants. We got our laundry done. We bought a cruising guide for the area. We shopped for fruit and vegetables at the open market. We shopped for other food, but what was available was extremely limited. Two of our fellow BPOers arrived, so we saw some friends. We invited Kjell aboard to see our boat, and he came with his adorable and rambunctious two-year-old son. Bob played Grandpa for 45 minutes so the rest of us could have a conversation. The two of them hit it off, ran all over the boat and the dinghy, and tired each other out!

We celebrated my birthday. I was surprised and delighted to find a wrapped present from Bill's two daughters. Bob had snuck it aboard when he joined us in Bora Bora! It came with a card that included a poem from Bob. I received another card with a wonderful poem written by my son. Plus several birthday emails. I had never cared much about my birthday, but this felt special.

We planned to leave the harbor on my birthday, to start some local cruising. But I slept late; then had to enjoy my presents; then we went to do a little food shopping. Walking into town from the dinghy dock I noticed an array of shirts for sale, hanging from a tree. Many bore US labels. It took me a while to find the lady who was selling them, but when I did I bought one that I liked for the equivalent of $5. I think that set a tone for the day. A few minutes later at the market, I bought a woven basket and a necklace for Hallie. After buying lots of fruits and veggies, Bob went off to find a bakery with the idea of getting me a cake. I told him I'd rather have cinnamon buns, and to my surprise he returned with exactly that. Plus some coconut buns. Then we decided to go out to lunch…

Is was getting late for going sailing, so we went for a walk instead. Passing Kjell's house, his wife came out with slices of freshly baked banana bread for us, and a birthday gift of homemade granola! Good granola was a rare and prized item on *No Regrets*. How did she know!?

On our walk we met Ian and Keith, an Aussie and a Kiwi. Ian said it is rare to have an Aussie and a Kiwi in the same room without an argument, but the two of them were longtime friends and longtime residents in Tonga. Ian ran a guest house, but also produced vanilla and coconut oil. He was a believer in "zero waste," and he used the leftover coconut pressings to feed pigs and chickens, he cured pork/bacon with coconut husk smoke, he recovered methane from the pig poop, and I can't remember the other half dozen processes that completed a full no-waste cycle. He was quite talkative about the pros and cons of moving to Tonga. In his view you measure happiness/satisfaction on two scales. One was things you could buy, like good wine. In Tonga you didn't fare well on this scale. But the other was quality of life – nice weather, low cost of living, no crime, no city congestion or foul air, no worries. Tonga scored high on the second scale. He liked the balance.

Keith and his wife had moved to Tonga 25 years before, and brought up two children. Friends in New Zealand had questioned the wisdom of raising children there, but he thought the Tongan schools were very good, and the kids thrived. In addition to taking people out to catch big fish, he was licensed to take people out to swim with whales. He said a few whales were present, and many more would arrive within two weeks. Should swimming with whales be on my bucket list? I wasn't sure…

Long, fun, delicious, happy day. We could go cruising tomorrow.

#13

Our first stop was anchorage #13. Probably because there was a bareboat charter operation in Vava'u, all the anchorages were identified by numbers. The numbers were shown on a chart (not to be used for navigation), and we had two

cruising guides that referred to the same set of numbers. Numbers were easier than Tongan names for us pelangi (white folk).

Number 13 was interesting primarily because it was very much like a lake, with a narrow entrance from the sea. The guide said never enter when there are waves, or at anything other than high tide, or when you don't have good sunlight to see the coral. I suspected that they overstated the danger, but with the narrow entrance plus the warnings it made for an exciting pass.

More challenging was anchoring inside. The water was too deep. There was a small beach across from the entrance, and I thought we might find shallow sand there. But by the time our port side depth sounder (yes, we had one on each side) read 30 feet, we were awfully close to the beach. And the starboard side depth still read 50 feet! We explored further and found a mooring. It was in questionable condition, but we decided it was the best option.

The most memorable thing about our stay at #13 had nothing to do with the location. The overriding thing was that it was…wait for it…COLD. Wearing long pants and a fleece. Sleeping under a blanket. Choosing between putting on socks or getting into bed right after dinner. Winter had come to latitude 19 degrees south.

#16

We sailed to #16. Bill declared it one of the most enjoyable sails ever on the boat. The wind was strong but because of the islands everywhere there were minimal waves. I enjoyed a good sleep through much of it, as I was recovering from a flu-like illness that had Bob down for a day or two, and then me. Bill managed to avoid it.

We anchored out where the wind blew hard. Free energy for our batteries, but the howling all night made for troubled sleep. It felt a little weird to be tied to the bottom of the ocean by one rope, and if it chafed through we would be on the coral within a minute! You couldn't worry about this constantly, but when the anchor rode creaked and groaned during the night, I got up periodically to reposition the protective chafing gear and let out six inches of line so it would rub in a new spot…

#11

Sailed in 20+ knots, with double-reefed mainsail, but again in smooth water. Going to windward in these conditions was fun, to Anchorage #11. Loved it! We took a mooring for 10 pa'anga a night (US $5). Nice to be in a secure place where I could get a good night's sleep.

We rented the mooring from the Ark Gallery. The owner/artist was from the US but had lived in Tonga 31 years. She lived on a little houseboat on another mooring and showed/sold her paintings there. She and her husband also did yacht deliveries (mostly back to the US). They had been interviewed by Jimmy Cornell years ago for his book about the experiences of veteran cruisers.

We had read about a Spanish restaurant nearby called La Paella that only did paella, but served it in a multi-course meal, plus music. We had been depleting our own stores for nearly a week, so we asked the artist about the restaurant. She told us that the owner/cook was in town shopping at that moment – if we wanted to go we had to book immediately so she would buy enough for us. She made the call for us, and we were still in time. The artist said one more rather cryptic thing as we were getting into the dinghy to go – that La Paella reminded her of the bar scene in the Star Wars movie!

La Paella provided one of the most enjoyable meals ever, and yes – it did have a Star Wars bar scene quality to it! We dinghied in to a little beach, and walked up the steep path, past the goats. In the restaurant three tables were set. There was a Spanish woman prepping food behind a bar made of huge twisted vines. She nodded toward the table set for three, so we sat. In the corner was an area closed off by what looked a lot like a couple of shower curtains. Odd, but all very pleasant. She came to the table and made sure we understood there was no menu. She would bring gazpacho and a series of tapas, which she would describe as they were served.

Maybe I had been living on a boat with food-by-us for too long, but the flavors were scintillating. Gazpacho had never before stood out as a taste treat. And then the succession of maybe eight (I lost count) tapas, each arranged creatively and beautifully, each a distinct fresh taste. The paella that followed was good, but I wished I could have run through those tapas again! How did she even get all the fresh ingredients, here where there didn't seem to be anything but fruit and some vegetables?

Then the shower curtains were pulled aside, and there was a three-person band. Flamenco? Latin Jazz? No, hard-hitting Delta blues. In Spanish. Or was it? The vocalist (the cook's husband, I think) belted out mostly incomprehensible lyrics. Occasionally I recognized English, and maybe some Spanish, and some I believe he made up on the fly in non-language. It didn't matter, because we were in the Star Wars bar scene.

Did I mention that this restaurant was on a small island, accessible only by boat? The folks at the next table were from New Bedford. Oh, did I mention the dog sticking his nose past the shower curtain during the musician's tune-up, and wagging his tail in time to the music? Or the beautiful black billy goat walking in during the music and rearing up on his hind legs threatening to butt a guest that tried to pet him? All part of the movie. For me it will be strange to watch Star Wars again someday, and think of La Paella, Anchorage #11, Vava'u, Tonga!

FedEx Delivery

We received Fed Ex tracking emails saying that both our new sail and the hydraulic pump for the autopilot had arrived. Faster than we expected…yeah! Bob and I took the dinghy back to town – about 5 miles. Nice to have a big powerful dinghy! We had to wait for Linda the Fed Ex lady to return to her office, and we had to wait for the truck that had the big heavy package, and we had to wait for the paperwork to be completed and the forms printed at the store next door, and then Linda drove us the two blocks to the Customs office where we had to wait for them to verify that we really were a yacht-in-transit so we didn't have to pay import duty, and we paid Linda for the delivery from Tonga's capital island and we paid her to be our Customs agent and we paid the Customs processing fee, and they gave us the boxes. In other words, it all went smoothly, on island time.

Mantas

Back to the boat, but no time to check out the new sail yet, as we wanted to try another anchorage further east. Along the way we saw shapes in the water. Very large manta rays; right next to us! We slowly motored in a circle watching their show all around us, until we had our fill and continued on to Anchorage #27.

The anchorage looked idyllic, but the bottom was too hard for the anchor to dig into. We struggled with the anchor for an hour. It held fine until we backed down hard on it, and then it would skip loose and then grab again, but still not properly set. Finally we decided to leave it and set an anchor alarm that would alert us if we dragged very far. We hoped we wouldn't be woken in the middle of the night, needing to start the anchoring routine all over again. But no big deal. If we dragged it would be into open water, and it was a beautiful night with a full moon.

Our next destination was Lape Island. Along with the three other BPO boats now in Vava'u, we were invited for a Tongan feast. Just 26 people lived on Lape. Most spoke little, if any, English. They had a school with two teachers, and a church. They received aid from many foreign governments. For example, they had photovoltaic panels with batteries to provide lights, donated by the Japanese.

When the residents sought to build a pier a few years ago, they asked for donations, but came up with only 150 pa'anga. Then they had the idea of reaching out to the yachties by putting on a Tongan feast each week, and selling their crafts at the events. The first year they raised 40,000 pa'anga!

We received a brief lesson about the local culture. For example, every Tongan house, whether a poor person's or the king's, *must* have a tapa and a mat, ready for weddings and funerals and other important occasions. Then the feast. Roast pig, of course. Several fish dishes, of course. And an assortment of other tasty things, not all of which I could identify. We happily contributed to the village kitty.

Whale Song

I lay in bed half awake at dawn, thinking that Bob was making very strange snoring noises. I rolled over and tried to ignore it, but the sounds persisted and

I awoke another 10%. I had the thought that his snoring sounded inhuman, and ever so slowly the idea took hold that maybe it was something else. I got out of bed and saw that Bob wasn't even in his cabin. On deck, I saw him securing the dinghy painter, which made no sense to me. Seeing me, he said, "Oh, you heard the squeaks that the dinghy was making?"

We both went back into the pilot house, but I couldn't imagine how the dinghy could make such sounds. "Was the dinghy caught under the bridge deck? Or tied up so tight it was rubbing against the boat?" No, Bob said the dinghy had not been touching the boat. At that point I was pretty sure that the thought taking shape in my sleepy brain was correct. We had been hearing humpback whales!

I darted below to listen again, and sure enough, it was faint now, but I could still hear the sounds coming through the hull via the water. I grabbed my camera, told Bob what was happening, and we went out to scan the surrounding waters. There she was, swimming out of our anchorage. I managed to snap one photo of her before she was gone behind an island. There must have been more, as they were having quite a conversation. And I dare say the pod included a baby, given the high pitch of some of the calls. We just saw the one large humpback. But it made our day!

Another Tongan Perspective

The Kingdom of Tonga is a fabulous place for cruising. Islands everywhere, with protected waters between, and beautiful anchorages. The town had fuel and laundry services and restaurants and a great produce market. It seemed a little strange, though – almost every business was run by an ex-pat. Quite a few Americans, plus Kiwis and Aussies, and the grocery stores all seemed to be run by Chinese. There seemed to be two worlds, one Tongan, one ex-pat. The worlds overlapped, and everyone appeared to get along very well together, but it made me wonder if there was more below the surface. The ex-pats all seemed to love it there. Many had a story about arriving under sail many years ago and never leaving.

Our BPO support person (Norwegian ex-pat) taxied me to Immigration, Port Authority, and Customs, so we could clear out. I asked him about the mix of two worlds. He said, "The cultures are so utterly different that if you aren't religious you would have nothing to talk about with the Tongans." That was an overstatement, of course, as there was always family and the weather, but it provided some insight. He said white people have traditionally been looked up to (after all, they brought the Christian faith), though not so much now by the younger people. He expressed admiration for the family values of the Tongans, mentioning specifically respect for elders.

But his feeling was that he lived in a community of 200 ex-pats interspersed in a larger, culturally separate Tongan community. All friendships and most other relationships were within the group of 200 ex-pats only. He didn't much like the small town feel of a community of only 200, and he said it would be the ex-pats that eventually drive him to leave, not the Tongans.

Clean Sheets

While I dealt with the authorities, the rest of the crew bought frozen foods and bread and eggs, and picked up our laundry. I wanted to put clean sheets on my bed before we left, but discovered that one of the sheets was missing. We didn't have spares, or so I thought. I went back to the laundry shop, where the lady said, "Oh no! I know which boat has it. They had a lot of bedding, and I mixed yours in with theirs." We tried to hail them on the radio, to no avail. She thought they were moored near the charter company, so I got in the dinghy and checked out all boats there. Didn't find them. Went to the charter company office and asked about them. "Yes, they were on one of our moorings, but they left earlier today."

It was time for us to go, so I returned to the laundry shop and gave her the names of all the BPO boats. If the sheet got returned she could pass it to one of them. Off we went, checking the names of all the boats we passed. When we anchored I got in the dinghy and zoomed around toward other likely boats under sail, and to another popular anchorage. No joy. One good thing, though – I saw other BPO boats there, and they told me about a family on the nearby island that had invited us all to another Tongan feast the next day.

Returning to the boat, I felt good that I had given the search a good try, but I wasn't happy sleeping without it. In the morning I tried calling for the boat on the radio, via the morning "net" that most yachties listen to. No luck. I searched deeper into the bowels of the boat and found another set of sheets. Smelly. But the laundry would still be open. So back into the dinghy for another long and wet ride, back to town. The laundry lady told me she hadn't slept, fretting about her mistake. I offered her a chance to make it up to me, by washing my smelly sheets ASAP. Ninety minutes later I told her we were even and she should sleep soundly. Bought gas before embarking on the four-mile ride back in the dinghy.

Bill claimed that because I had taken care of the lack of sheets, we would run into the boat that had mine. He was right. As we were sailing out of the anchorage, they were sailing in. We tried to hail them on the radio, with no luck. So I again jumped into the dinghy for a short wet ride over to them. They were obviously perplexed to see a dinghy pounding over the waves coming at them as they sailed along at 7 knots. When I shouted that they had a sheet of mine, the helmsman's look was even more perplexed. But one face lit up. "Oh, yes! We ended up with an extra one. But, how did you track us down…?"

Updating the Plan

Although we had already cleared out with the authorities, we weren't passing up an invitation to one last Tongan feast. There was only one family living on the island, yet they managed to prepare at least a dozen different dishes for twenty hungry people. Dad played guitar and sang, with Mom accompanying on vocals, and the girls did traditional dancing. A satisfying way to wrap up three weeks in Tonga. In the morning we would provide some epoxy resin to help our host patch a hole in his boat. Then off to…somewhere…

Tim wrote that he would rejoin the crew in Australia, after Bill headed home. Bob was working out very well, but with Tim returning and my son Jesse also joining in Australia, we didn't have a berth for Bob between Australia and Singapore. He would head home for that interval, and then rejoin. I planned to fly home from Singapore with Jesse. I would spend two and a half months at home, while Tim and crew cruised in SE Asia. Then back to Singapore, and Tim and I and presumably Bob would continue westward across the Indian Ocean. It was a lot of juggling, but it seemed workable…

Backing up to Australia, there were logistics to be worked out there, too. When would we arrive? What flights should Bill and Bob book from there? What flights should Hallie and Jesse and Tim book to get there? Hallie, Jesse and I wanted to explore some of Australia by land. What part(s)? How long could I afford to be away from the boat? What work would we want done on the boat during that interval?

But first we needed to make some choices for the near term. Where to go from Tonga? Tokelau was my goal. But it was north and east of our position, and thus probably to windward (and thus uncomfortable sailing in the ocean waves). The reasons to go there were threefold. First, it was one of the places most threatened by sea level rise; as a BPO participant I wanted to help bring attention to that, and I also wanted to see it for myself. Second, almost nobody went there; it would likely be the most remote stop on our trip. Some may have seen that as a reason *not* to go there, but I saw it as an exciting departure from the "milk run" – the standard route that most yachts follow. The third reason to go was that *Drina* would be going there. *Drina* was a boat that successfully navigated the Northwest Passage, and this would be the first chance to rendezvous with her. Jimmy Cornell's daughter Doina and her son would be sailing aboard *Drina*, adding to the fun.

The downside of heading north to Tokelau, and then to Tuvalu, was primarily the added distance – nearly 1,000 miles. It also meant we would be bypassing Fiji. Another issue for us was that our food supplies were dwindling, and there would be little or nothing available in Tokelau or Tuvalu. We would have to stock up in Tonga, which seemed to have less than anywhere we had been so far. Or an alternative would be to stop in American Samoa, on the way to Tokelau. Excellent provisioning there, but a pain to clear in and out of another country.

Bill and Bob were reluctant to go north on the Tokelau/Tuvalu route. Usually I went along with the leanings of the crew as a whole, but this time I asked them to do it my way. They agreed to give it a try. It would all depend on the weather. I agreed we were not going to "knock ourselves out" trying to get there if the winds made it miserable. Everyone was talking about it now being officially an El Niño year, and this would manifest in unstable and unpredictable weather. TBD…

Banyan tree

Treehouse, Mandala Resort

Tapas and dessert at La Paella

Sometimes called "walking trees," this one
looked to me like it was "trucking."

TUVALU

We got underway from Tonga about mid-day, and saw whales blowing in the distance as we worked our way out the maze of islands. We had twenty knots of wind on the beam; fast sailing. Too fast. Once clear of land it became uncomfortable. More importantly, we had allowed three days to get to the vicinity of Samoa, where *Drina* was now anchored, and at this rate it was only going to take two. We had the idea that we would spend a night at anchor in Apia, Samoa, without going ashore. We would avoid going through the formalities, and then we would leave the next morning in company with *Drina*.

An email from Michael on *Drina* said not to try it – that the Samoan officials would require that we clear in and out, including paying a minimum of $100. Michael also mentioned that there was no safe anchorage on Tokelau. When he got there he planned to have a boat pick up Doina and her son Dan, and he would simply drift off the coast for the day.

These prospects did not sound pleasant. We were crashing through big waves with deeply reefed sails; we needed to kill an entire day so as not to arrive in Tokelau before *Drina*; and then to spend another day drifting… We decided to cancel the Tokelau plan. After an hour's deliberation we decided to head for Wallis Island. Wallis is the largest island in the French Territory of the Wallis and Futuna Islands, located west of Samoa and on the way to Tuvalu, where I still hoped to rendezvous with *Drina*.

I had misgivings about withdrawing from Doina's effort to visit Tokelau – a place she had visited as a child, and a place that was severely threatened by climate change. But the next day we got another email telling us that Doina's request to visit Tokelau had been denied! I couldn't imagine why the authorities there wouldn't want the Blue Planet Odyssey support, or simply allow Doina to visit. (Later they would apologize for their mistake.) In any case, suddenly I felt better about our change of plan…

Our cruising guide said when the wind blows hard at Wallis, a very strong current flows out of the pass (similar to Maupiti), so we had some concern about what lay ahead. But the pass presented no special problem. Two other boats were in the anchorage. We dinghied over to the Australian (English-speaking) one to ask for information about where to land the dinghy and how to clear in. We hit the jackpot. They told us all that and much more, and provided us with a hand-drawn map of the places most important to yachties (gendarmerie, Customs, supermarket, restaurants).

We hitchhiked into town (first car picked us up), and cleared in with the gendarme, but the Customs office was already closed for the day. We went to the post office, where they offered 10 minutes of free wifi per day, and checked email – via Internet so slow that it took the full 10 minutes. We investigated the grocery stores, which were far better stocked than in Tonga. Then we hitchhiked back to the boat (first car picked us up) with fresh baguettes and a few other goodies, and invited the Australian couple to join us for hors d'oeuvres. They started sailing their 52-foot boat from Spain seven years ago…and when they arrived 'home' in Australia they planned to keep right on going. I picked up a few tips about cruising and sightseeing in Oz.

Next day we hitchhiked back to town (easy, again), and cleared through Customs. In fact, the Customs official cleared us *out*, too, so that we could leave whenever we wished. Very laid back. He told us we were the 19th pleasure boat to come to Wallis that year. The place was off the beaten track! We also visited the Cultural Bureau, which provided information about the islands, and offered a free tour (for tomorrow). There was no tourism office.

We stopped for a chocolate croissant, bought more baguettes and Camembert cheese; we stopped at the post office for our 10 minutes of Internet; and hitchhiked (easy) back to the boat. The other two boats had left, so we had the anchorage to ourselves. All very relaxed. None of my usual "yet another paradise blues" – especially since I had zero expectations, and no particular schedule…no hurry, no worry.

Wallis found its way into our hearts. The Cultural Bureau tour guide was born on the island but had lived in other parts of the world, so she had an interesting perspective. The fact that she also spoke good English was a big plus. We bombarded her with an endless stream of questions, while we took in the sights.

Ancient peoples lived on the island as far back as 2,000 BC, maybe earlier. Circa 1700 the island was 'colonized' by Tongans, who brought nobles and set up a hierarchical society. They built forts, one of which we visited. Around 1830 Christian missionaries arrived. The first batch tried to impose their own ways of doing things; they were killed. But the next batch was more open to the existing culture, and they were accepted. After several years the local king converted, and then of course everyone did. The Catholic Church provided schools, which added to their acceptance. The number of churches we saw was incredible. Every community had one, and there were lots of communities (not clear to an outsider where one stopped and the next began). There was also a large cathedral. The structures were elaborate and beautiful.

The United States stationed forces on Wallis during World War II. They built a fuel depot that was still used. After the war, Jeeps and other equipment were pushed over a cliff into the deep volcanic lake, which we visited. The crater was remarkable because of its shape – nearly a perfect circle, with sheer cliffs all the way around.

Wallis and Futuna became a protectorate of France in 1961, with a referendum vote 94% in favor. Our guide remembered life before then, with essentially no infrastructure. There was a boarding school at the south end of the island; people got there mostly on horseback. She was sent there at age five, because her mother was sick and needed care in New Caledonia. Our guide said she felt like she had been sent to the end of the earth.

The current population was about 9,000. France had provided roads and electricity and schools and a hospital. Students could complete high school on-island. If they went on to university, they usually went to New Caledonia or to France. Parents were scared to have their children leave the island, as they had heard about the many bad things that happen "out there." Sometimes parents went with the child. Others got Internet (at relatively hefty expense) so they could stay in touch via Skype. The Internet was very slow; it was hard to imagine using Skype! The 10 minutes of free wifi at the post office was just enough to check email; forget doing anything else. Residents were hoping to get an undersea cable laid to the island to greatly boost bandwidth, but it didn't sound like this was coming anytime soon.

The French connection seemed to be welcomed. My sense back in the Marquesas was that there was disdain for the French "colonists," and we felt that it was important to fly the Polynesian courtesy flag and say hello in Marquesan. At Wallis the French courtesy flag seemed appropriate. Good thing, because there were three island districts, each with its own distinct flag, and flying the wrong one would probably be an insult. Of course, we had none of the flags anyway. People seemed happy to have the French support, and French citizenship, and they appreciated our feeble attempts to speak a little French.

Everywhere there were small "plantations." Land was owned by families – plots were all small; no agribusiness. Taro and cassava were the major crops. Unfortunately we didn't make it to the produce market, which was open every day in town…from 5am to 6am! That time worked for everyone going to/from the morning church service. We were told that the singing in the church was something wonderful to behold. Sunday morning the service didn't begin until 7am, but that was still too much of a stretch for me. Going to church would be further complicated by the need to wear long pants, while there was no dinghy dock to allow getting ashore dry.

The caretaker at the Tongan fort brought us green coconuts. The tops were sliced off so we could drink the juice – the sweetest ever. And hold on to that sliced-off top piece, because when he cuts the coconut open for you it is used like a spoon to scoop out the soft meat. I had never been a coconut lover, but these were really good! Our guide mentioned about the troubles of the world,

"When Wallisians hear about people going hungry in other parts of the world, we think, 'If only we had a way to share our coconuts with them…'"

I asked if the Cultural Bureau had specific projects in the works, and she explained that the big projects were trying to train her staff, and to get the politicians to understand that the 15-year Development Plan needed to include a cultural component. Development needed to be sustainable, not only in terms of natural resources but also of the culture and the quality of life that they enjoyed there. She said sometimes new staff would come from France thinking they knew what was needed, instead of listening and learning about the culture. Those people were focused on climbing their own career ladder. I said she must have "seen it all" and know how to deal with such people. She laughed and said, "You never know – your own neighbor may surprise you!"

Talking with Bill and Bob later that evening, we realized we had a nagging question that we neglected to ask: Do Wallisians want more yachts to come? Or was the average of about one per week all they cared to see!? I think more would come if they knew about the island. But we weren't sure if we should tell them!

One last reason that Wallis had become special to us was that our visit was completely outside the purview of the BPO. Not a big deal, but it was the first time since Havana that we were entirely on our own to choose the anchorage, negotiate the formalities, and learn about the place, without information provided to us by Jimmy or a local BPO support rep. A taste of world cruising outside the rally structure.

We cleared out with the gendarme, in preparation for leaving in the morning. He asked our next destination, and we told him Tuvalu. He chuckled and said, "Tuvalu – soon to be underwater!" That was the first time I could recall anyone referring to sea level rise without our bringing up the subject.

Longitude 180

We were two days out from Wallis to Tuvalu. We were sailing northwest, about to cross from 180 degrees west longitude to 180 degrees east longitude. Kind of like crossing the equator – fun to watch the chart plotter climb to 179 59.999W and start counting down with 179 59.999E. You would expect this crossing to also advance the date to the next day, but no. Both Tonga and Wallis were already on the advanced day. Everyone wants to think "the day begins here" rather than being at the tail end of the day. In any case it would be a relief to be clearly over the dateline, and not be trying to figure out what day it was for us versus what day it was for other boats at other islands.

That night we had an impressive show of lightning to the north, in the distance. The wind was blowing 20 and we were going directly downwind, surfing down waves – at one point we hit 15 knots. We were on track to achieve the elusive 200-mile day, and we decided to leave the big spinnaker up as it got dark. Always risky…

We had tuned the settings on the autopilot earlier in the day. It was doing a much better job of keeping us on course, and thus keeping the spinnaker from collapsing. But it was still on the edge when waves pushed us around. I found I was staring intently at the wind instruments, watching the boat yaw in the waves. As we swung close to where the spinnaker would collapse I found myself trying to WILL the boat to turn back. Then as it yawed in the other direction I was again trying to mentally/psychically bring it back on course. I was busy trying to keep the lightning away, too!

The effort to will the universe to do my bidding was exhausting, and obviously useless. So I tried to practice relaxing. "Wiggle my toes and breathe." Trust the universe. Respond when needed to actually steer back on course, but relax and enjoy the ride when the autopilot was doing the work. I did a pretty good job of this – relaxing and taking in the wonder of it all.

Two hours later it was suddenly blowing 30, and I was yelling, "All hands! Wake up!! We need to get the spinnaker down NOW!!!" The autopilot couldn't keep the spinnaker from collapsing, so I began hand steering. Bill turned on our deck light so he and Bob could see the spinnaker lines, but that blinded me. All I could do was stare at the electronic wind direction indicator and try to keep the display pointed dead downwind. My fear was that the spinnaker would collapse and flog itself to shreds or 'explode' when it filled with wind again. Also on our minds was whether Bill and Bob would be able to pull the "sock" down (a sleeve that furls/contains the spinnaker) in a 30-knot wind – a question we had wondered about from time to time. Answer: one person was not enough (he would get lifted off the deck rather than the sock coming down), but two could do it. Good reason not to be single-handing…

Ten minutes later the squall had passed. But we were happy to let the 200-mile day go, and continue at a relaxing 6 or 7 knots under jib alone. The sky cleared; the stars were magnificent; the lightning in the distance continued unabated. What a place to be! We hadn't seen a ship or another sailboat at sea for weeks. Endless waves. Can you imagine the early explorers who had no chart, and never knew what lay just ahead, if anything? We knew exactly where we were, thanks to the miracle of GPS, and I'm pretty sure our charts were complete and reasonably accurate. Even so there was an overwhelming feeling of awe.

Were we really rolling along from an island I had never heard of before this trip, to another island I'd never heard of before this trip? Three odd ducks on a catamaran? Wave after wave welling up out of the blackness behind, raising our sterns, pushing us forward, and melting into the blackness ahead… Sailing through the eerie night toward foreboding flashes of distant lightning? Or was this all a vivid dream and I would be back in the office in the morning?

Once again we were sailing too fast, with wind gusts into the mid 30's. We hove to (set the sails/rudders so that the boat pretty much stayed put, drifting slowly sideways) for eight hours, so we wouldn't arrive in the dark. In the morning it was easy getting through the pass into the lagoon of the atoll, and we anchored next to *Drina* and one other sailboat off the capital town of Funafuti. We cleared in with Customs; they told us we were the 8th yacht to come to Tuvalu that year.

The Customs office was a long way from where we anchored, and after our experience at Wallis we assumed we would hitchhike to it. But it turned out to be not so easy in Tuvalu because nearly everyone traveled by motor scooter. There were a handful of cars, I think mostly for government officials. Nobody walked.

There were only eight kilometers of road, all flat. The highest point in the country is just fifteen feet above sea level, and we never saw an area that high. That was no different from the atolls in the Tuamotus. What was different was that these islands (nine of them; eight inhabited) comprised an entire country. There is no France (Tuamotus) or New Zealand (Tokelau) to provide infrastructure support and/or citizenship. With only ten square miles of land, Tuvalu is one of the smallest countries in the world.

The anchorage was protected, as long as the trade winds blew as expected from the east or southeast. They continued to blow hard, with heavy rain squalls. Everything got damp on the boat, but then at least once a day we got a long period of sunshine, and things dried out.

Maybe it was the wind and rain, but people didn't seem to exude happiness like they did at many of the other South Pacific islands. Many didn't smile at us, or even look at us. Maybe they simply weren't used to foreigners. When we waved and said hello we usually got a big smile back. Especially from the youngsters!

There were no yacht services. A handful of restaurants were hidden around the town. Almost no crafts were for sale. No tourists. No ex-pats running businesses, except for little stores run by Chinese. This was not a playground for people from somewhere else. It was the home of 11,000 people. The homeland and culture of these people were directly threatened by climate change, weather patterns and sea level rise. That was why the Blue Planet Odyssey was here, albeit with the limited presence of just *Drina* and *No Regrets*.

Yes, We Have No Bananas

Tuvalu was full of little stores. They all carried a few imported canned goods, and onions. The biggest one, the "supermarket" also had imported refrigerated apples and oranges and a handful of other items. When we asked about a produce market, we were told, "Friday morning at 5am, near the end of the airstrip." We were also told by a policeman at the airstrip, "Down the main road 150 meters. Open until 8am." Having no fruit left on board, Bob and I got up at dawn and went for it.

Seeing no market in the 150-meter vicinity, we asked, and were told, "Across the runway, on the ocean side of the island." On the other side of the runway we got further pointers to a place where a couple dozen women were waiting with plastic baskets and tubs. Tables were spread out, mostly covered with seedlings, but also cucumbers and lettuce. Someone told us to put our name on the list (we were number 36) and they would call us by number. But not seeing any fruit, we asked, and were told the fruit was already gone. When we asked specifically about bananas, the answer was, "I don't think they have any bananas; they don't have any banana trees..." Further questions led to a description of a market across the runway and down the road on the lagoon side, where we would see bananas hanging; they also sold bread. Our spirits lifted, we crossed the runway again. (When an airplane was approaching, the fire engine would blare its siren, and people stopped crossing the runway.)

We asked several women sweeping in front of their houses. They all gave us puzzled looks, and the consensus was, "Maybe at the supermarket." At this point we had walked in a big circle. But we knew where the 'supermarket' was, and maybe early Friday morning they had fresh produce. Not so. Asking there, we again got puzzled looks, and the most direct answer yet – "I don't know."

Thwarted, with no new ideas about where to try, we headed back to the dinghy. But we ducked into another store along the way. No bananas. Did you try at the supermarket...? The gentleman tending the store was huge, and had a stammer making it difficult for him to get out a sentence, but he had a captivating smile. As I headed back out the door, Bob told him how much I was wanting bananas, but nobody had them for sale. He said something unintelligible but commanding – perhaps "Wait!" in Tuvaluan. He raised up his massive self and plodded out the back door. Probably gone to ask the woman of the house where to find bananas, I thought. But he was gone for a long time. We thought about leaving, but we didn't want to be impolite, so we waited. And when he finally returned it was with a plate of bananas!

Of course we offered to pay him. Of course he said no. I have a feeling the way my eyes lit up and the smile erupted on my face, he received his "payment." In fact, he seemed to take enormous delight in having presented us with this gift. With effusive thanks, we said goodbye and headed to the dinghy with a lighter step. Apparently, you cannot buy bananas in Tuvalu...

Climate Change

As a child in 1978, Doina Cornell had been in Tuvalu when the country became independent. The Cornells made a lasting connection with a local family. Michael on *Drina* had connections as well, from sailing there decades ago. The connections led to a referral to the Finance Minister. Bob and I followed Doina and her son Dan to the Minister's office, and watched and smiled and nodded and shook hands. Doina explained about Jimmy's vision for the Blue

Planet Odyssey, that we were sailing around the world, that we wanted to call attention in our little ways to the plight of Tuvalu... "The Prime Minister is very focused on climate change," he said. "Have you met with him?"

"No," said Doina, "Could you arrange for us to do that?" Wow, she was good at this! We came away with a tentative meeting, to be confirmed the next day.

When Bob and I took Doina ashore the next morning, we were met at the dinghy dock by a messenger. "The Prime Minister would like you to attend the workshop today." No, the messenger didn't know anything about the workshop, only that he was to invite the people from the yachts.

With no idea what to expect, we went to the central pavilion. Yesterday it had been filled with families watching loved ones board an airplane. Today it was filled with chairs. The chairs (with lettering on the back saying they were supplied by the Mormon Church) seemed to be absurdly far apart...until you factored in the size of many Tuvaluans... We were told that the Prime Minister was going to sign the accord for the United Nations Conference Against Corruption.

We got to listen to speeches in Tuvaluan, peppered with English terms like "public sector" and "bribe" and "leadership and management" and "contextualize." The PM's speech was largely understandable from the English phrases, and I found it very interesting. The gist of it was this:

> The spirit of the United Nations Conference Against Corruption is "Do the right thing. And do things the right way." Tuvalu is doing the right thing, in the right way, and we are happy to sign the accord. However, we must also call attention to the problems facing Tuvalu. Tropical cyclones are our biggest threat. We have "development partners" who offer to help us. But these agencies are not democratized. They are controlled by powerful governments and commercial interests. The World Bank must be reformed. The Agency for International Development must be reformed. The development partners think of their efforts as charity. It is not charity for Tuvalu; it is a survival fund.

Here was a man willing to stand up for what he believed was right, and ask the world to stand with him. I liked him.

There was a break for "tea," which turned out to be a feast of interesting food, and weak hot chocolate. The Finance Minister joined us and said he would ask the PM over. So we got to chat with Enele Sopoaga, Prime Minister of Tuvalu. He asked about Jimmy, and he appreciated our concern for Tuvalu. He hoped we would help raise awareness of his country's situation. He said his motto these days was, "Save Tuvalu, save the world." He lamented that although there were funds pledged to help places affected by climate change, the "bureaucracy and paperwork was higher than sea level rise!"

I offered that raising awareness was the main thing we could do, and maybe we should make T-shirts with his "Save Tuvalu, save the world" motto.

He liked that idea, but he quipped that the industrialized countries had scheduled the upcoming Paris climate conference when it would be too cold for T-shirts, and global warming would not be present in people's experience.

The event left me face to face with a familiar personal dilemma. On the one hand, I liked this place, and I liked the people I met, and I liked what I had seen of their culture. When sea levels rise, and warmer-ocean-powered cyclones hit, this country is going to be hammered. People will become climate change refugees, and their culture will be shattered along with their homes. I would be proud to take a stand with Enele Sopoaga, demanding that all the countries of the world "do the right thing" in limiting climate change, and minimizing the impact.

On the other hand, change happens. Forces are already in play that will impact Tuvalu and the world climate (even if the world pulls together and limits the human-driven factors). Is the "right thing" to try to preserve Tuvalu? Or is it to help the Tuvaluans adapt to the coming changes?

Don't expect an answer from me – I don't know. What I can do is write a book and raise awareness of the question. Now *you* know a bit about nine South Pacific atolls and reefs called Tuvalu. I would like to read your comments – what you think is "the right thing" about Tuvalu, about climate change, about related policies of industrialized and developing countries, about renewable energy sources, and about what actions an individual can and should take. If you are uncertain about what to think and what to do, share that, too. You can enter your comments on this book's companion website at **www.satisfyingsail.com**.

Taking Climate Change to Heart

We were invited to the opening reception of the "High-Level Dialogue on the Tropical Cyclone Pam Recovery & Vulnerability Reduction Plan." Representatives of the "donor partner countries" were being hosted by Tuvalu, to discuss the devastation from Cyclone Pam, the recovery effort, and how the effects of future cyclones could be mitigated. It was also a forum to ask for additional assistance. Representatives were present from Australia, New Zealand, Japan, Taiwan, India, the E.U., the United States, plus various United Nations agencies, the World Bank, and others.

We arrived soaking wet from a downpour that began just as we got into the dinghy. I felt out of place. But we got to speak with the Prime Minister again, and we had a very informative chat with his wife. She explained that there was an extremely high "king tide" a decade or so ago, that flooded many areas, and raised the saltwater level under the ground. Coconut and banana trees, which have shallow roots, survived; but the breadfruit trees died. Now breadfruit trees were growing again; they replanted them in raised beds.

She also spoke about traditional handicrafts. Unlike most Pacific islands, there were none for sale here. She explained that traditionally the handicraft skills were kept within a family and passed from mother to daughter. But now most girls were busy with school, and many went off to study abroad. The elder women would not teach the skills to girls other than their daughters, and their daughters were busy, absent, or not interested. The skills/crafts were dying out. She was leading an effort to invite the elders with the skills to come together and teach girls, beyond the family boundary. Hopefully having the First Lady supporting this effort would lead to acceptance of a new way.

I had the thought at the time that the Tuvalu culture was already fading, unrelated to climate change – that maybe there wasn't much here worth preserving. But that thought would change 24 hours later.

The next day was the actual "high-level dialogue." Doina was going to present the PM with a BPO plaque and say a few words. Bob, Dan and I went in tow with her to the morning session, and morning tea.

I could never be a diplomat! I wouldn't have the patience. So many agencies and countries and policies and bureaucracy and grant hurdles and people to thank without slighting anyone. There was $15 billion pledged to a Green Climate Fund, and Tuvalu would be applying for a grant for a few million. But first they were applying for a smaller grant to fund the staff and resources needed to apply for the bigger grant…

Immediate disaster recovery aid, medium-term goals, long-term goals. Seawalls were wanted. Stormproof buildings. Safer access to outlying islands in storm conditions. Training for local tribal leaders, who will have to take the lead in emergencies when communications with the main island/government fail. Questions about how to handle the loss of a family's land – not property "damage," but their land simply washing away. Should they be compensated? There was no legislation covering that situation presently. I found all this overwhelming…the complexity of it all…

In the evening there was a presentation of traditional singing and dancing. There were groups from two islands performing; a friendly competition – one group at one end of the hall, the second group at the other end, they took turns performing. The styles were similar. A relatively simple song/dance would start, as if it were spontaneous. At the end of a short song, they would act as though they were done, briefly, and then take it up again one key higher and with more intensity. This would repeat until you thought they must be done, but it would start once again, rising higher and higher in pitch and fervor. The voices were beautiful, the drumming powerful, the dancing elegant.

They had a unique custom – if you appreciated the singing and dancing you could walk up to the performers and spray them with perfume! The PM's wife was the first to walk among the performers and spray. Spectators were welcome to join the line and become dancers. Some of the cabinet ministers seemed to have allegiances to one island or the other, and they danced with them. The PM also. Some of the foreign delegates joined the dance, notwithstanding that they didn't know the elaborate movements. They were willing to look silly; how cool is that!?

The energy grew and grew; then abruptly they were done. After a silence, the deputy PM got up and said, "Some ask why we want to remain in our Tuvalu homeland. THIS is why! We want to be able to dance for you." I choked up.

I get it that if/when these people become climate change refugees, their culture will rapidly erode. If the world chips in with funding for sea walls that make these islands habitable for another couple of generations, is that worth the cost? Facing this conundrum directly, with the Tuvaluan voices still echoing inside, could break your heart.

Traditional Tuvaluan dancing, drumming, singing that could make a soul care deeply about climate change...

Doina chats with Prime
Minister Sopoaga during
tea

Between conference
presentations was a dance-
in-place break. I think the
US Congress would benefit
from this!

Wallis

The Tuvalu runway was built by US troops during World War II. It is vital to the country (three flights/week), but unfortunately it occupies a large portion of the best land.

In the background are *Drina* and the Tuvalu government offices building – the roof covered with solar panels, of course.

NASTY WEATHER
(FINAL EXAM?)

Modern technology plus an internet connection enabled us to look at the wind conditions near Vanuatu, our next destination, 800+ miles away. There was a low-pressure disturbance there. The wind chart showed windspeeds to 33 knots. That would be an average; there would be much higher gusts. Plus we had found that the predicted wind speeds were often understated.

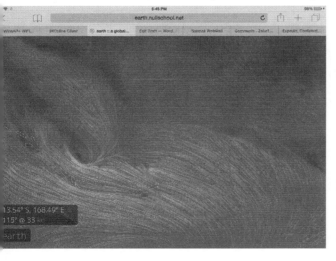

On this wind map, Tuvalu would be at the upper right; our destination was toward the lower left, not far from the brightest color, indicating the strongest wind.

We didn't want to set sail toward bad weather. But modern technology also let us see what winds were predicted for our arrival, roughly five days out. The prediction was for the storm to gradually dissipate, still ugly but with average winds only about 24 knots by the time we would arrive. Of course, modern weather models, as amazing as they are, have not yet produced accurate forecasts for five days out. We decided to delay our departure from Tuvalu by one day, to allow more time for the storm to wither. We could also get one last updated look at the predictions before we left wifi behind, and had to rely solely on forecasts received by radio.

Our destination was Luganville on the island of Espiritu Santo, commonly known as Santo. We assumed we could log 160 miles per day; five days. *Drina* left two hours before us, and the only other yacht at Tuvalu had departed earlier, so we left the lagoon yachtless.

The day was sunny (at last!); the wind perfect in the teens. We tried to catch *Drina* for a photo op before dark. But by late afternoon when we passed them it had started raining. The wind gradually increased, and at times the rain came down hard. At the end of my early night watch, Bill and I put in a double reef; the ride was uncomfortable.

Things started going wrong. First it was the radar, which we used to identify squalls in the night. The radar signal disappeared from our electronics network. I hoped this was somehow caused by the heavy rain getting into wiring connections, so it would eventually come back... Then we got vibration and nasty noises from our hydrogenerator. Upon first inspection I couldn't see anything wrong. I decided to just pull it out of the water for the night, which revealed that our new $200 propeller had only one blade left on it! So we no longer had our primary source of power-when-underway, and we had to start an engine to charge the batteries. When Bill went to stop the engine later, it wouldn't stop. We guessed it needed a simple adjustment to the stop solenoid connection, but not so simple underway in rough weather. Bill had to climb into the hot engine room (itself a challenge in these conditions) to manually pull the stop control.

Still on Bill's watch, he heard another unfamiliar sound, and discovered that the boom was rubbing against a shroud. There was no longer a mainsheet attached to the boom – no line controlling the mainsail! The fitting that connected the mainsheet block to the traveler (slides across the boat on a track to control the position of the sail) had broken. Bill dropped the sail and lashed the boom fast, and we continued sailing with just the jib. We didn't have the right hardware to fix the problem, but with a little time we would come up with something temporary.

Our electronics beeped a warning that the connection to our AIS system was lost. The AIS system (that identifies the locations and courses of ships, and broadcasts our position) appeared to be working fine. But the alarm repeatedly and annoyingly went off every few minutes, and we couldn't find any way to shut it off!

We also lost our boat speed sensor. The pins in a network connector had corroded, and one was broken. We had no way to repair that. Not a big deal, but it meant that our instruments could only show the apparent wind speed, not the true wind speed (because the system needed the boat speed to covert the apparent wind to true wind). We still got our speed determined by our GPS. That night it hit 17 knots several times. Those were momentary readings when we were pushed by a wave, but nevertheless it was *fast*. That was when we were still flying the full mainsail; with just the jib we rarely exceeded 8, which was plenty under the circumstances.

Meanwhile, I was feeling seasick; the worst I had felt since leaving Key West. I just didn't want to move. Or open my eyes. Or be awake. This was the first time that I had thoughts about not wanting to be there. A bed ashore sounded like the most heavenly thing imaginable. But I knew I would get better, and that helped me cope. I always felt sick for the first two days when we were in rough conditions.

Day 3

The day was mostly sunny, and the wind and waves moderate – not a bad sailing day. I felt somewhat better; still not good. Bill seemed to be suffering more than I, but I noticed he has applied a Scopolamine patch, and he said it was starting to kick in. Bob did not seem to be affected by motion at all, and he had been doing extra chores, like dishwashing, on our behalf. Thank you, Bob!

Despite the relatively pleasant day, the weather outlook was bleak. The forecast when we left was for the low-pressure system ahead to dissipate. The forecast had since changed. The system was not diminishing, and it had moved more directly into our path. Winds to 40 knots and seas to 6 meters…this was not something we wanted to sail through. After lengthy discussion about the options, we spent most of the day sailing very slowly south, rather than on the westerly course to our destination, hoping to miss the worst of it. This strategy would position us to have the wind behind us when it really started to blow.

In the evening with an updated forecast, plus an update from *Drina* that they had hove to the previous night to slow down and stay away from the storm, we also hove to. We drifted very slowly NW, comfortable enough that we could sleep. In the morning we would get another forecast and decide whether to continue to "park" there, or head south or possibly west.

We fixed our mainsheet/traveler connection. The radar appeared to have fixed itself. We mounted our old/larger propeller on the hydrogenerator, allowing us to generate power when we were sailing slowly. We adjusted the engine stop switch. On the other side of the ledger, we had a new problem with the throttle on the port engine; it wouldn't slow to an idle. That didn't much matter while we were at sea.

Day 4

The morning forecast was worse – the gale heading directly toward us. It was forcing us to choose between two undesirable options. Heading south would take us into the teeth of it, but we would be able to sail fast through it toward Santo. Heading north should avoid the worst of the weather, but we might then be faced with headwinds en route to Santo.

An email from *Drina* showed their position north of us, and they were heading further north. Our crew held another conference. The wind rose even as we deliberated; we decided it was prudent to head north. It was frustrating that the weather forecast showed we should have winds under 20 knots in our location, and that certainly was not the case. Plus the center of the storm was reported to have a barometric pressure of 1003 millibars, and we were already slightly *lower* than that! Could we trust the weather prediction even a few hours out? It seemed not, and that was a factor in choosing to "run." If we had 30+ knots where 20 was reported, what was the wind like where 35 was reported? We chose not to find out.

We set a goal to reach 10 degrees south latitude. We were at latitude 11, sixty miles south of the goal. The was nothing magical about reaching 10, except that the forecast showed lighter winds there. No, we didn't trust that forecast, but it helped our disposition to have a goal. We sailed with jib and triple-reefed mainsail. We had never used the third reef before.

Day 5

Not so simple to sail north to latitude 10… A tropical depression in the Southern Hemisphere has winds rotating clockwise. We could initially head north with a northeast wind, but the further north we got, the more the wind backed (changed direction counter-clockwise) and headed us (blew more in our face). By daybreak we were sailing west, or even slightly south of west, and we were still 30 miles south of our goal; the wind still blowing hard.

Lots of banging and crashing…difficult moving around the boat, and potentially dangerous as one could be thrown against a bulkhead or a table or down the stairs, and break ribs. Everything was wet, and every hatch but one was closed to keep spray out. The boat started to smell bad. Bedding became damp and sticky. We were covered with salt, as we got doused every time we went outside to make a change to the sails. Bob couldn't sleep in the forward berth (amazing that this was the first time for him, given how violent the motion could be in the bows), so we had to "hot bunk" as we changed watches through the night.

During the night a line that held the hydrogenerator down broke. The nosecone disappeared off of our wind generator. Four times our instruments stopped reporting the wind direction and strength, which was the data we paid attention to most. Each time, after a few minutes, the readings came back again.

Early in the morning we tacked. Now we could head north, though also a little east – away from Santo. Close to noon we were surprised by *Drina*'s signal showing up on the AIS, heading in the opposite direction! We hailed them on the radio; they were concerned about how to get to Santo after the storm moved on, and they decided it was time to make a B-line for the destination. That would take them right through the eye of the gale, but the winds would be light in the eye. What lurked on the other side was the concern. We discussed making a U-turn and going with *Drina*, but we were still in search of lighter winds, and respite. An hour later our wind eased. We decided to heave to once again in the relative calm, and wait 18 hours until dawn – then, after another weather update, go for Santo.

We received the weekly weather synopsis of the South Pacific from Bob McDavitt, a well-respected reporter of weather patterns as they affect yachts. Deep in his report he mentioned "our" gale, gave its location and said it was likely to move slowly south. He described the conditions as "worthwhile avoiding!"

Day 6

A fuse blew in our electronics network, resulting in our being unable to see the wind data. The loss of information was similar to before, but for a different reason; and the blown fuse wasn't about to come back on its own! We tracked it down…eventually…to the bad connector to the boat speed sensor. We disconnected that whole arm of the network, replaced the fuse, and we were back in business. There had been fishing boats some miles off, and they no longer showed up on the AIS system, so we thought the AIS was out. In fact it was working (the fishing boats must have moved out of range while we were focused on the network/fuse), but we didn't know that until a ship showed up on AIS the next morning.

We had a daily check-in on the long-range SSB radio, on a "net" that included the other BPO boats and some others that were sailing a similar route. The radio check-ins were noisy and frustrating and intrusive and inconvenient. It took half an hour just to establish who could hear the net controller and who couldn't. Most of the conversation was about poor reception rather than about boat positions/crew/progress. So we tried an email approach that worked better for most boats. Each crew would send their report in an email to me. At the end of the day I sent out a compilation of all reports, again by email, to everyone on the net. We still did the radio call, but now most boats already had the information they wanted, and we checked mostly to see if anyone was in distress. Here is our own report from the previous night:

> *NO REGRETS* – Position at 0700 UTC is 11 23 South, 173 41 East. Got sailing again this morning after a peaceful night hove to, and headed south to 11 04 S, 174 00 E at 1600 local (UTC+12). At that point we "committed" and turned toward Santo. No longer much in the way of options to do anything but go for the ride. Has been fine so far, though the rain has been Very Heavy. I think our AIS is out (no way to confirm this) and our radar is out, which leaves us blind in the rain. Oh well, no one else would be foolish enough to be here now, right…? Wind has eased to ~25; waves are not bad when you are going with them. We hit 18 knots on one of them. At the time we still had our triple reefed main up; now we have jib alone. Santo, here we come! ETA Friday.

It was an exciting ride. Waves a little less than we had braced ourselves for, but still big. Winds still blowing 30+ at times. We were well on our way to a 24-hour run of 200 miles. But in the morning the wind eased. We weren't ready to risk flying the big spinnaker. We flew the little one, and our 24-hour run ended up being 191 miles. Good, but we had hoped for more.

Things calmed down. Bob caught a fish. I baked banana cake. Under 300 miles to go.

Day 7

If you talk to enough people, or I should say the right person, you *can* buy bananas in Tuvalu after all. We worked it out just before leaving. They were rather expensive ($30 Australian), but that was for a stalk as long as your arm, which was harvested in the bush and brought to us at the dock. They were now the only fresh food on board. We had bananas on cereal for breakfast, banana pancakes for lunch, and I baked a second banana bread/cake in the afternoon. Of course they all went ripe at once. Time to start mashing them and freezing for future banana bread.

Yesterday Bill pointed out that the repair we did on the starboard lower shroud was starting to pull apart. It didn't seem close to failing though, so we decided just to watch it. Today it looked worse. I went halfway up the mast (a challenge in the waves) to secure a line at the spreaders to provide a backup for the shroud. Any chance of replacing a shroud in Vanuatu? Probably not. Would it be safe to sail on like this to Australia? Probably our backup line would hold things together for the 1,000 miles…

The day's activities included cobbling together an arrangement of lines to hold the hydrogenerator down. Our wind had gone light, as we passed through the "eye" of what was left of the tropical depression. So we might be motoring the last 150 miles anyway, and thus charging batteries via the alternator instead.

We switched from the little spinnaker to the big one, in an attempt to arrive before the authorities headed home Friday afternoon. But the wind kept getting lighter, and even motoring all the way would get us there too late. Technically one cannot go ashore before clearing in, and clearing in between Friday afternoon and Monday morning could incur hefty overtime charges. The idea that we might be stuck on the boat for two days after arriving felt like insult being added to injury, after what we had gone through en route.

As we discussed our strategy regarding arrival time, Bill said that this leg of our trip felt like our "final exam," for which we had to use all the knowledge we had gained along the way. It did feel like that! But then we got an email from Luc. (Remember Luc? The BPO rep through French Polynesia, now coming to take care of us once again in Vanuatu.) His email said:

> I arrived in Santo this morning and went already to talk with officials. It is arranged that if you arrive during the weekend, you can go ashore, and we will go see them together on Monday morning – no overtime. Hope you have nice sailing…do not force or stress…and be prepared to enjoy Vanuatu very soon.

Wow – it felt like we were getting 10 points extra credit on our exam! You had to love Luc.

Day 8

We were expecting a close reach in moderate wind; good sailing. What we got was heavier than that, and right on the nose; hellish sailing. The shroud broke. Thank God we rigged the backup line! We sailed most of the night with just a reefed jib, trying to minimize the strain on the rigging. Still we were crashing/bashing into waves, and the biggest crashes were followed by a tense pause…was the boat still sailing or was the mast crumpling onto the deck!? Not much sleep.

The wind generator supports couldn't withstand the crashing, and they slipped, allowing the generator to pitch wildly. Bob woke me to take a look. As the boat pitched, one of the support rods bent ninety degrees. The generator blades careened nearly into the water, and I guessed that a few more waves would put it into the drink. For a minute or two we watched out the pilothouse window; to my amazement it did not break. "Bob, let's get harnesses on and see if we can save it." For 20 minutes we perched on the stern of the bucking boat, yelling at each other over the din, and breasting occasional saltwater cascades. We got lines around the whole rig and secured it aboard. In fact, it was still working!

Fixing the generator mount was going to be a future project. For the shroud we would probably have to do a jury rig until Australia. The last problem on this final exam had been a doozie!

We were not going to make our destination before nightfall. But we were close, and in high spirits – no one was hurt, the mast was still in place, it had stopped raining, the wind was easing, and Bob had again made banana pancakes!

Day 9

Arrived. Anchor down at 10pm, eight and a half days into the five-day passage! Other skippers were right that heading north to Tokelau/Tuvalu would be challenging, in addition to adding 1,000 miles over the "milk run" route. But I was SO glad we did it! Going to Wallis…rendezvousing with *Drina*…helping to bring the BPO to Tuvalu…experiencing Tuvalu first-hand…attending the Tuvalu discussions and dancing…and even having this crazy tropical depression experience – all wonderful.

The weather experience gave me new appreciation for storms – keeping a safe distance, and not trusting the details of forecasts. The heavy weather sailing also gave me a deeper appreciation for the design and construction of *No Regrets*. The boat handled well throughout. If you're going to sail a light-weight catamaran through rough weather, it is going to interact violently with the waves. That strains the gear and the crew. Our crew held up well. A lot of the gear did not. Here's a summary of the failures.

- network short due to bad cable, blowing fuses and taking out our wind displays
- AIS alarms about low voltage and "connection lost"
- broken bolt that connects mainsheet block to traveler
- hydrogenerator propeller broken
- hydrogenerator hold down system broken
- bilge pump for port engine room running frequently
- broken lower shroud
- half a broken bolt found on the cockpit floor – source as yet unknown!
- wind generator nosecone blown away
- wind generator mounts no longer support unit properly
- engine stop switch failed
- throttle not working properly on port engine
- float for anchor line disappeared off of bow nets despite being tied on
- zincs (to prevent electrolysis) broken off their cables
- hatches leaking
- radar lost connection to network in heavy rain
- cockpit chart plotter – freezes just when you need it most
- freezer – died toward the end; had to pitch chicken and steaks overboard

Top priorities for us were showers and laundry. By evening *Drina* would arrive; dinner ashore with our compatriots sounded good. After a day of recovery we would start on our list of repairs. After all, it may have felt like a final exam, but really it was only the midterm.

Winds as forecast (for 5
days out) when we left
Tuvalu; the tropical
depression dissipating

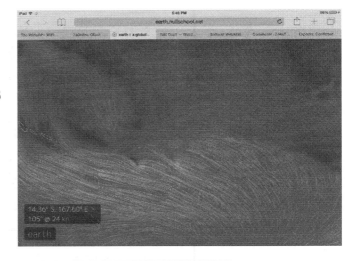

The way it
actually turned
out, with the storm
intensified

Our chart plotter showed
the crazy route we sailed to
avoid the storm, up to
where we turned SW and
"committed" for Santo

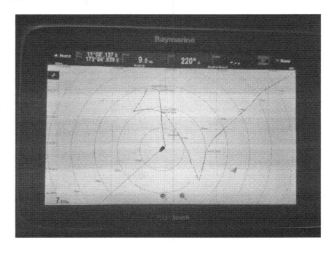

Bob filleting while holding on with his knees
(but with safety harness properly clipped in, of
course)

Taking a 'freshwater
shower' as we surf
through a squall

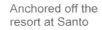

When it rains bananas, it pours

Anchored off the
resort at Santo

VANUATU

Vanuatu? I knew nothing about it. I was relying on the benefits of the rally. Luc had, as always, made major plans for us.

We found a length of galvanized pipe to use as a "splint" for the wind generator support, and Luc helped with arrangements to get hardware to reinforce our broken shroud. Then we were off to explore the Republic of Vanuatu.

It was late afternoon when we anchored in Malua Bay, but Bob swam ashore. He met Ruben, a student at a Seventh Day Adventist school. Ruben gave Bob a lift back to the boat in his dugout canoe. We invited Ruben aboard; he was very interested in the boat. Bob named each sail and many other components, and Ruben repeated each word. But when we invited him to come inside he declined. Maybe it was a cultural thing about entering someone else's dwelling.

In the morning another canoe came for a visit, paddled by a woman named Stephanie. She brought fruit and asked if we could give her rope. This was a common request throughout the South Pacific, usually posed as "for my cow." I think rope was a very tradable commodity. I told Stephanie that we needed all our ropes. She then said she lives in the bush with her children ages 6 and 7, and it was cold (which indeed it had been the previous night), and did we have a blanket we could give her. No…but…I would find something warm for her.

Rummaging below, what I found was my bulky Norwegian wool fisherman sweater, that I had owned for decades, but almost never worn. It may have been TOO warm for this latitude, but probably good on a cold night. It felt right to pass it on to Stephanie, and I did. We came away with pamplemousse, coconut, and a pleasant feeling of passing something along. I loved that sweater, but I sure didn't need it or use it. Giving it to Stephanie released a little positive energy into the universe.

Tisvel

We sailed to a bay that is not mentioned in the cruising guides, by the village of Tisvel. Bob and I went ashore and were warmly welcomed. A woman named Kathy offered to show us the village, and Joseph (who turned out to be the village chief) came with us. Tisvel had 132 inhabitants, including the children…one church (Presbyterian)…pretty little houses…one little store with mostly bare shelves…lots of papaya and mangos and bananas and pamplemousse and of course coconuts, and other fruits that I didn't recognize…cacao (we got to taste the bright white not-yet-ready beans)…running water at 4 community spigots piped from a big tank in the bush…fat chickens…scrawny dogs…a few pigs…bamboo harvested from the bush for building thatched roofs and woven siding. The place was very clean and nicely laid out, and our hosts were proud of it.

Unsure about photo etiquette, I asked if I could take pictures of the village – yes, of course. Then I asked if I could take pictures of the people. That got some giggles and posing. Luckily Bob was using his iPad for photos, because they wanted to see themselves in the images. His iPad trumped my camera hands-down for that.

We asked about the effects of Cyclone Pam and learned that it was their crops that were affected. Nevertheless, Kathy insisted on giving us a large papaya, and she laughed, "No!!" when I offered to pay her for it. We asked Chief Joseph if we could give a gift of a soccer ball for the kids to use. He and two other men wanted to see the boat, so the five of us paddled out in our dinghy to get the ball and to show them our home. No reluctance on their part to come inside – they wanted to see everything!

Our guests assumed initially that we were from Australia. They had no idea where the United States and Canada are. They recognized the names of Tuvalu and Wallis, but they didn't seem to recognize Tonga. They had traveled to other islands in Vanuatu (principally to the cities of Luganville and Vila), but not beyond.

They asked repeatedly if we had wives, and where were they. And how long we had been on the boat. I told one of the men that my wife would be coming to Australia – that I was looking forward to seeing her in three weeks. He gave me a knowing look that said, "I bet you are; long time to be without your woman!"

Later in the afternoon Bob swam ashore again. He met another chief, who said they rarely see white people. Indeed, our presence was special, because a couple of young men invited Bob to drink kava. Kava was usually a social/ceremonial drink, but they said they couldn't drink any because they were about to play soccer. They accompanied Bob, while Bob drank! They assured him he would still be able to swim back to the boat, which he did with no problem. Bob was unusually gregarious at dinner, though, and then proceeded to fall asleep in the middle of sending email over the radio.

It was a quiet night in the bay. There were a few lights on shore – some huts had solar cells for a light and a DVD player, and there were a few people on the beach with flashlights. I could smell the smoke from fires ashore. I wished I could live in Tisvel for a month, to learn what it was really like. Everything seemed very communal…shared…easygoing. Everyone seemed happy. Did these people have no sense of scarcity, like we-who-have-everything do? Or was there another layer beneath the surface, that we couldn't see as we sailed on by?

Kathy and Chief
Joseph in Tisvel

Southwest Bay, Malakula Island

Leaving Tisvel we beat into the wind (with triple reefed mainsail, since we didn't have the materials yet to fix the broken shroud), to Southwest Bay. *Tahawus* and *Drina* were there ahead of us. Just the three of us in a huge protected anchorage. Doina had already met with the Chiefs ashore and arranged for a guided tour of the tidal lagoon by the village.

Taking two dinghies to the beach, we met Principal Chief James. Each tribe, which I believe equated to one extended family, had a chief. A Principal Chief was elected for a four-year term to oversee the entire village. Or in this case PC James oversaw a collection of neighboring villages. To visit the lagoon or snorkel at the reef required permission from the chief. But you wouldn't want to do it without a guide anyway, because what was fascinating was not the lagoon itself; it was the culture of the people around it.

Up the little tidal river we went, James sitting in the bow and pointing which way to go to avoid the shallows, and telling us about the villages and the customs. Past a field with a small heard of goats. Past a large canoe heavily loaded with firewood, paddled by two women. Past men building a guest house atop the steep bank, who hooted and shouted at us in fun, but I never saw them in the dense growth. Past endless mangroves at the water's edge, with paths cut through every so often just wide enough for a canoe to get to the muddy shore, so a family could access their garden.

We stopped for a short walk through the bush to a watering hole, where James demonstrated that you could drip the sap of a certain vine into the water, and it would "clean the water." That is, whatever stuff was floating on the surface would move away from the sap, leaving a clear surface for drinking. James told us about an odd custom: if you killed someone in the bush (not clear to me if this referred to slaying an enemy or to other forms of manslaughter), you placed a certain leaf on your head before returning to the village. This announced the event, and you were expected to go directly to the chief to tell the story. Dan volunteered to wear such a leaf into the village; James assured us he would explain that this was merely a demonstration.

The village was up a well-made set of steps to a plain above the water. We met the local chief (later we learned that he was James' father), and after explaining the leaf on Dan's head we were properly welcomed. That is, the children gave us each a flower, and we each received a young coconut with a reed straw to drink the juice.

We were invited to take a walk into the bush, to see a canoe being built. Before the first missionaries in 1895, canoes (and drums) were hollowed out by

burning the inside wood. Missionaries brought metal tools, and for a hundred years canoes were made with the adze. In recent years, more often than not, the tool of choice was the chainsaw – even for the inside. Our canoe builder was using an axe to strip the bark of a "blue water tree" log. The name did not refer to the distance the canoe would travel. Rather, it was what happens when you put the bark of the tree into water. If you waited a few minutes, the water began to turn blue. They demonstrated this for us. The blue water tree was the best wood for canoes – they would last 15 to 20 years. Canoes were also built from the "white wood tree," but those might last only 3 years. It took a month for a man to build a canoe. Many men were capable of making a canoe, the builder said. But he confided, mariner to mariner, that only a few could make a *special* canoe.

Chief James was the Principal Chief for several tribes. People would come to him for conflict resolution. Many disputes had to do with land rights. When that happened, he would review the history of the families involved, sometimes back many generations, to make his ruling. Asked if people always listened to him, he said, "Yes, they have to listen to me. If they didn't I would refer them to the police!" There were higher level Chiefs, though – overseeing the whole island of Malakula, for example – so it wasn't clear how the appeals process really worked.

The land was owned by the villagers, which was not always the case in South Pacific countries. Women could own land, but only if a family had no boys. Women were expected to move to the villages of their husbands. I imagined this would be a difficult transition because the neighboring village was likely to speak a different language. There were over 200 local languages within Vanuatu! The village on the east side of our anchorage spoke a different language than the village on the west side.

Labo Festival, Malakula Island

Next morning brought the arrival of *Chapter Two*, *Blue Wind*, and *Maggie*. Six BPO boats together! Luc had arranged for a "festival" at the nearby village of Labo. The activities began with dancing, traditional to this area. It had none of the masculine warrior spirit of the Marquesas or the sensuality of Tahiti or the grace of Tuvalu. In fact, its most distinguishing characteristic seemed to be that it was…different! Five ornately dressed/decorated men with…well, see the photos…snaking their way up from the beach, around the drummers in a field, and back from whence they came. They then did two more dances, where the only difference appeared to be the things that they carried. It did not make me want to get up and move my body, but it certainly was unique.

There was a feast, of course. It was almost all starch – taro, yams, sweet potato, manioc, cassava – I didn't know all the variations, but there were all these and more. Some octopus. No meat, and to my surprise no finfish, even though we saw lots of fishing going on around us. We saw how some of the food was prepared – rolled in leaves and stuffed into a length of green bamboo. The bamboo was then placed in the fire. When the bamboo was charred; the food inside was ready.

We toured the village. About 150 people lived there. Once again I was impressed with the beauty and the cleanliness. There were falas/huts built at the places with the best views; these were communal resting places. There were several water faucets, piped from a big tank up the hill. Some houses had water carried by bamboo sluices, direct from a stream. There were a handful of solar panels. I was told that everyone eats together in the dining hall, at least one meal per day, and sometimes three. The kids all looked healthy and happy.

There was a swim at the waterfall, a demonstration of pottery making, a performance of water music (an amazing form of percussion, making a variety of sounds with hands on and under water), and a demonstration of fire making. The village had clearly spent days, maybe more, preparing for our visit. We paid $30 each, feast included. I had mixed feelings about the prepared presentation of the culture. Not that it wasn't real – it was. But it seemed like it was taking the culture out of its natural context. I suppose it was like a "living museum." Of course we would never have seen and learned so much in one day if it were

not prepared/presented for us. And it was great that our money went directly to the village, with no "agent" taking a cut. But I was also glad that I got to see the village of Tisvel earlier, just as a friendly visitor and not as a customer!

Back to My Roots Festival, Ambrym Island

Luc, our grand master of ceremonies and event planner, billed the Labo event as the "small festival," and now it was time to sail to Ambrym Island for the big festival. The big festival was called "Back to My Roots," and it was held annually near the village of Olal on Ambrym Island. Visitors were welcome (we paid), but it would happen with or without visitors – to keep the traditions alive, and as a forum for chiefs to earn their way into higher degrees of chiefdom.

Luc had sent the shroud repair hardware to us via one of the other BPO boats. It got a good test in a stiff wind on the way to Ambrym. We all anchored at the Maskalyne Islands along the way. A canoe paddled by shortly after we anchored, and we had a chat. It was a bigger canoe than I had seen before, and the first I had seen that carried a sail. The gentleman had his garden nearby, but he lived on an island two miles upwind. Easy getting to the garden; hard work getting home. He mentioned that he had also caught some small fish for his dinner. Given how empty our cupboards were, I asked if he had caught enough to sell some to us. He stared at me and said, "You are serious!?"

Yes, my friend, we lived on a boat and had sailed nearly halfway around the world, but we didn't know how to feed ourselves! We caught pelagic fish occasionally at sea, but no little reef fish. Nor did we want to try, because only the locals knew which reef fish were safe to eat. It varied from one reef to the next and eating the wrong one could make you very sick. He sold us the only two fish he had, and turned around to paddle back to the reef, to catch more for himself.

On the morning of the festival we all met ashore and set out with a guide; two miles to the festival grounds. Lots of people and some little shops along the way. Everyone smiling and saying hello. If you looked directly at the children and said hello, you got rewarded with a beautiful smile and a wave. We left the road and followed our guide half a mile through the bush. We were told to wait in a clearing near two carved drums; we were close to the ceremonial grounds.

It was a long wait and we didn't know what we were waiting for, but we had nothing else on our agenda. Presently we were told we would have a traditional welcome, and six volunteers were needed. Having no idea what I was volunteering for, I joined five others. A group of nearly-naked men and women appeared out of the bush. The six women carried flower leis, and the six representatives of our group were welcomed with them. Not a bad volunteer job. Later I would be surprised and a touch disappointed when I realized the flowers were synthetic!

We were led into a clearing that was obviously the ceremonial grounds. Many large carved drums on the periphery; some improvised benches for us; some locals on their own mats. The drums came to life; the dancing began. We were in a very foreign world...

That night from the boat we could see the orange glow of the volcano in the black sky.

The festival had a new quality the next day. Chief Sekor was going for higher rank. He currently wore two boar tusks; the highest chiefs wore three. I expect this was all worked out prior to the festival, but this was the public ceremony. During a portion of the dancing he, and also two lesser chiefs going for advancement, climbed a bamboo tower in the middle of the area. Atop the wobbly platform, they wildly danced and shouted, and the other dancers had the opportunity to hurl coconuts at them! Not many were thrown, and I got the impression the throwers were being careful to miss, but nevertheless I found this an interesting ritual that might have some useful applicability with our Western leaders.

Having survived trial-by-coconuts, Chief Sekor next gave gifts to the village and various families. There was a huge pig, which he was expected to publicly kill by the traditional method of striking it on the head with a special club. There was a pile of yams. And there was cash. A man loudly announced each cash gift – how much was presented to whom. Wow, what if our leaders earned the right to lead through gifting, and all transactions were made public...?

That evening there was yet another feast, and we drank kava. It took me a long time to realize that the local guy next to me, in a T-shirt and baseball cap, was Chief Sekor! Quietly drinking kava in the bar, he looked much less ferocious than when he was dancing, shouting, and having coconuts hurled at him.

The grand finale was the next morning, with the Rom Dance. I couldn't get a satisfactory explanation of what the Rom were, other than scary-but-good spirits, and "We do this because our ancestors did this." We were warned not to get too close – anyone touching the Rom costume would be heavily fined. I guessed that the traditional penalty was even harsher!

The anticipation of the local people, especially the kids, got it cooking. The drummers and dancers were clearly transported to an ancestral world. And the ceremonial aspects of granting power to a chief were fascinating to witness.

Gifting

Rom dancers. Chief Sekor leads the action. Look carefully and you can see his cell phone in his waistband!

The events had been incredible. But I was festival-weary, and happy to get sailing again – an overnight back to Santo. Time to depart for Australia, 1,000 miles away. Luc gave us sailing instructions...farewell dinner...provisions run...clearing out...

I felt anticipation about Australia...a major milestone...hauling the boat...paint and repairs...Hallie coming...Jesse coming...exploring ashore in the Northern Territories...Bill leaving...Bob leaving...Tim returning...sailing with Jesse...Great Barrier Reef...Torres Strait...and then...but no, I couldn't think ahead to Indonesia just yet...

≈≈≈

A great message if you can sound out the Pidgin English. (Please respect the environment; it belongs to me; keep a clean ocean.)

AUSTRALIA

Just before dawn was a wild time, the wind blowing 30, the water roaring along the hulls, and the anticipation of wave after wave approaching in the utter darkness. A wave would lift the sterns and propel us forward. My mind would gauge what our speed would rise to in the seconds that followed. Fourteen knots had become no big deal; when the wave caught us just right we would hit 18. Mostly the sailing was "smooth," in the sense that we were going downwind, riding the waves rather than bashing into them. But occasionally one smacked under the bridge deck and gave the boat a jolt that would have been terrifying months ago. We had grown accustomed to the violence of the seas; what had been terrifying was now merely nerve-wracking.

The forces on the boat had to be immense. Not just the static forces of 30 knots of wind against a reefed mainsail and jib, but the impossible-to-calculate dynamic forces of being lifted and dropped and twisted in every direction. How long could *No Regrets* withstand such torture?

"What's the worst that can happen?" I would ask myself, as though speaking with a new crew. The rig could come down, or the structure of the boat might crack. It would be disastrous, but it would not be life-threatening. Stay calm. The boat was designed and built to take these conditions. Trust it.

We did our best-ever noon-to-noon run of 225 nautical miles.

We'd been within AIS range (~20 miles) of *Blue Wind* for two days. We would watch their little blue triangle on the chart plotter screen start to fall behind; then the wind would change a little and they would catch up. At one point we had almost no wind, and we could see from the AIS that they were making 8 knots. Of course we concluded that they were motoring. Later on, when our breeze freshened, our speed jumped from 5 knots to 10. *Blue Wind* called on the VHF radio asking if we had just started our engines. We had a good chuckle about that; our engines were not capable of pushing us that fast. And they had revealed that they were watching us as closely as we were watching them. We each assured the other that we were not, nor had we been, motoring.

Then the radio conversation turned more serious. James (skipper) said that Ruy (his only crew) was very sick. He asked about our medical knowledge and medications on board. Our "ship's doctor" (Tim) was no longer aboard, of course. We tried to call Tim on Bob's satellite telephone, without success. We sent an email via the SSB radio and were pleasantly surprised to see a reply by the time we had rummaged through the contents of our medical kit.

Tim and James connected directly via satphone. Although Ruy had already taken an antibiotic, Tim recommended a different one. *Blue Wind* did not have the medication; we did. We made a plan with James to get it to him.

When the medical issue first arose, we had altered course to gradually converge with *Blue Wind*. We knew we might be transferring medicine. We also discussed the possibility of transferring a crew member to assist. A crew change might spark a nightmare with the Australian immigration authorities, but that was not our concern at the moment. Transferring a person would be much trickier than transferring a package. In ocean waves it would be too dangerous to bring the boats alongside each other. Probably we would have to get a line across, and then the person would have to go into the water. James declined the offer of crew.

As we were closing the last mile to *Blue Wind* we prepared a package for delivery. We cleaned out an empty peanut butter plastic jar…put the medicine in a sealed plastic bag in the jar…added a portion of just-baked bread in another sealed bag as a nice gesture…tied a small line around the lip of the closed jar…tied the small line to one end of a larger/heavier/throwable line…found a small water bottle that we half filled with water to act as a throwing weight…tied a small line around the neck of the water bottle…and attached that to the other end of the heavier line.

We agreed that *Blue Wind* would hold their course at a slow speed, while Bill conned *No Regrets* under power and approached from astern, passing alongside about a boat-length away. I would then heave the weighted end of the line. If unsuccessful we would be able to retrieve the line and try again. But the first toss was on target – right into their mainsail, so the bottle slid down to James on deck. James then pulled the entire line to his boat, with the payload on the end. We would ask for the line back in Australia.

The transfer went without a hitch, and *Blue Wind* motored at top speed toward Mackay,

Australia, 300 miles ahead. Any offshore sailor would assist another boat if they could. But this experience underscored a benefit of sailing in a rally – having another boat close enough by to help!

Sunday night

Last gorgeous night at sea, and a fitting way to complete our crossing of the Pacific. Flat water, gentle sailing breeze, just-past-full moon, quiet, peaceful. We would arrive at Mackay at dawn.

We were buzzed by the Border Force airplane, and hailed on VHF; they were very friendly and welcomed us to Oz. We cleaned the boat thoroughly and disposed of all fresh foods, in anticipation of a stringent inspection. Fingers were crossed about that. We had already scheduled our haul out for new bottom paint. We were as ready as we could be for our arrival and the changes that would occur.

Monday

Clearing in was an interesting, lengthy and somewhat stressful experience. Five uniformed Border Force officials plus the sniffer dog greeted us. We were to stay up on the bow nets until the dog was done sniffing. That took a while; she got excited about something in our spares locker. So they brought in the drug-and-explosive analyzer device, and determine that an aluminum (aluminium) bracket had traces of pseudoephedrine. Skipper, can you explain that…? No, makes no sense.

Then lots of questions, some seemingly friendly/chatty, but clearly they were trained to keep you talking about your background, etc., and they split the crew from the skipper, so your stories had better check out! The big question up front: "Are we going to find anything aboard that might be an issue? Weapons, plants, drugs…?"

"Well, yes, sir." Internally I repeated my smile-don't-laugh mantra. "We have a 12-gauge flare gun, which we've been told is considered a weapon in Australia."

"No worries, flare guns are fine."

This sounded much more reasonable than I had been led to expect. So I felt hopeful about the next one. "We also have a big store of prescription medicines, since our third owner, not present, is a physician." This turned out to be only a minor issue. They pulled out our two boxes of narcotics and sealed them in an unused locker in the head. When we checked out of the country we would simply have to show that the locker was still sealed.

"There is one other thing. We have a can of bear spray." We had heard that mace and pepper spray were considered weapons, and Bob had alerted me just before the inspection that he had bear spray. Bob is from Canada, remember, so of course he carried bear spray across the Pacific…

The officers spent some time on the phone with headquarters, including reading the ingredients on the can. With apologies they informed us they had to confiscate the bear spray. Later that afternoon we walked past an outdoor bar, and one of the agents was there with a pint. Seeing us, he asked if we'd seen any bears yet. No worries, the Border Force was friendly, courteous, professional, and they didn't give us any further grief about strange substances on our spare aluminum bracket.

Still pending was the dreaded quarantine inspection. The agriculture official was delayed; we had to continue to stay aboard until he showed up. We had been told they would confiscate most food, sometimes even your spices. Also told they would inspect the bottom of the boat with an underwater camera, and if they spotted any barnacles we would have to haul the boat immediately and have it cleaned at our expense. We were also told that if they found any insects, alive or dead, the boat would have to be fumigated, including sealing it all up and us moving elsewhere for two days – again at our expense, of course.

Well, the bloke was nice enough, but he certainly was painfully thorough – went through every locker, inspected all food packages, and tapped all woodwork looking for signs of termites. He found some weevils in a bag of pasta. Uh oh… No worries, he says, these are garden-variety weevils that are already in Australia. He disposed of the bag. Then he took the woven basket that I bought in Tonga and banged it hard on the counter. He proceeded to point out tiny crawly things that had fallen out. This I had feared, as I had seen tiny ants around the basket, and I had sprayed it with an ant poison, but there they were still. Not ants, he says. Booklice; the bane of libraries. Not a problem – he just wanted to show us that they were there…

He ended up taking very little. Our seven remaining eggs, the pasta, and the only fresh produce we still had aboard: a garlic. As he was leaving I asked about the underwater inspection. Yes, he had the camera in his car, but he only used it on the boats with major growth. The "gypsies," he said, who stay in one place a long time and don't clean/repaint the boat.

Whew! Everyone was friendly and heartily welcomed us to Australia, but it was a major relief when it was over. We could take down our quarantine flag and move the boat from the quarantine dock to a slip in the marina.

Tuesday

One day after arriving in Mackay the boat was out of the water and dozens of projects were started. Everyone in the yard seemed to know their stuff. In fact, our experience was much better than at American yards.

I felt an emotional whiplash. Being at sea one day; talking with various contractors the next. From solitude to city. We took the bus to the shopping mall

– just to experience it; there wasn't anything there that we needed. Bob rented a car. I visited a dentist to reattach a crown that had popped off. (I considered myself very lucky that this happened just one day before arriving in civilization!) We had a list of maybe thirty boat tasks/issues/questions. Hard to prioritize, beyond the obvious top items. And what was it all going to cost??

Bill's voyage was done. He had completed what he set out to do; he had a job to get back to. And he was ready; I could tell he had begun to "check out" back in Vanuatu. He never failed to pull his weight, but his enthusiasm had waned. I appreciated that he was still helping with boat chores right through his last day in Mackay.

Bob had already headed home. He had been a great crew. He and his wife planned to cruise with Tim in SE Asia while I would be home. Maybe he would be back for more after that.

I was on my own dealing with the boat and the boatyard, and I found it stressful. But for a little while, my attention would be elsewhere. Hallie and Jesse arrived, and we were about to go traveling ashore, to Darwin and Kakadu National Park in the Northern Territory. After that, Tim would return, Hallie would go, Jesse would stay, and we would sail north, through the Torres Strait, and on to Indonesia.

≈≈≈

I picked Tim up at the airport. It was nice to see him again. But I couldn't pretend that nothing had happened in our relationship; we needed to talk. That turned out to be easier than I expected. I told Tim I felt betrayed by him, and that I expected him to communicate with me about anything that affects our partnership. Tim apologized, and I got it – he meant it. We were in partnership again.

A lot had been done by the yard, in addition to what we managed to do ourselves. The lower shrouds were replaced with larger size wire. The other standing rigging we replaced simply because it was sixteen years old. Hardware that held the screecher at both the top and the bottom was replaced. Its furler line also replaced. We fixed a slow leak in the hydraulic steering. Repaired a torn spinnaker.

We made a new anchor bridle. Our anchor line was turned end-for-end so it would wear in new areas. Both engines and the outboard were serviced. Our folding propellers were serviced. A faulty sensor causing an alarm to sound was replaced. Our corroded speed/depth sensor was replaced. We upgraded a relay that was getting so hot it started to melt. We replaced all sorts of filters. We filled a propane tank. We replaced the wooden mount that held the outboard at sea with a stronger aluminum one.

The freezer was fixed. The vinyl covering on our bows was removed, and the dings underneath patched. The broken propeller for the hydrogenerator was replaced, and the mount was modified so the propeller would sit a little deeper in the water. The cockpit seat cushion that had disappeared on a windy day was replaced. Our broken fishing rod holder was replaced. We rigged another rope clutch on the mast for our spinnaker halyard. We stocked new spares for the fluxgate compass, the valves in the head, and the fuel lift pump for our engines. We procured courtesy flags for all remaining countries on the anticipated BPO route.

We had a freshly painted bottom with high-quality bottom paint. We coated the dinghy with UV protectant. We replaced the bearings in the wind generator. We even updated the labels on some of our electrical switches to make them look better and be clearer.

No Regrets was probably in better shape than when we bought her.

Thursday Island would be our point of departure from Australia. It was about ten days and 800 miles away. Which was unfortunate, because there was great cruising along the way, inside the Great Barrier Reef. We should have allowed more time. Long hops with short stops were also hard on Jesse, who learned the benefits of the Scopolamine patch.

We arrived at Thursday Island on a Thursday, as had William Bligh, who named the island on his epic journey after the infamous mutiny aboard his ship.

TI, as it is more commonly known, is at the northern tip of Australia. Across the Torres Strait is Papua New Guinea. To the east is the Pacific; westward is the route to the Indian Ocean. The geography made it an exciting place for me. I remembered standing atop Gibraltar 30 years before, looking across at Africa and at the ships passing into and out of the Mediterranean. I had felt the pulse of that pressure point of our planet – control Gibraltar and you control the Mediterranean Sea and the civilizations around it. In the age of sailing ships, anyway. Here at the Torres Strait it was not so dramatic, but for me it brought up the same feeling of being at a powerful global nexus.

Our anchorage was in the lee of Horn Island; we took a ferry across to TI. We went to the Border Force office with the intention of scoping out what we needed to do to clear out from Australia. Several forms later we were already cleared. They said they might stop by the boat for an inspection (they were supposed to verify that our narcotics were still in the sealed locker, after all), but we already had our clearance paper and passports stamped.

The people were friendly, and an interesting mix of white and aboriginal, but I did not find the town appealing. Probably it would grow on me if we spent a few days there. But my focus was solely on preparing to leave Oz and begin our Indonesian adventure. The Great Barrier Reef coast of Australia had been big and beautiful and windy and wild (except for the resort areas). Next time around I will spend more time there.

INDONESIA

From Thursday Island it is 650 miles to Tual, Indonesia, where Luc would once again be waiting for us with activities planned. We would be spending seven weeks jumping from island to island in "Exotic Indonesia," as Luc liked to call it. The country extends over 3,000 miles east to west; it has 6,000 inhabited islands; it is the 4th largest country in the world by population.

The 25-knot wind was average for the Strait; we flew our small spinnaker and tried to take it easy. It was Jesse's first time in the open sea, and I was concerned about how he would fare, even with Scopolamine. He was game, but sometimes his face seemed less game than his words, and it was clear that he wouldn't last long if he ventured into the galley!

We were six degrees from the equator. As Jesse and I worked out with a little mental gymnastics, the declination of the sun was $6°$ S – directly overhead. It was very hot during the day; very pleasant at night. One night I was treated to brilliant phosphorescence in the water – our wake glowing in two large streaks, plus a small one from the hydrogenerator. Mesmerizing. And then add dolphins! First heard, as they blew and sucked in air; then seen, as glowing splashes on the dark ocean canvas.

The next night the ocean was glowing from a different source. Dozens of fishing boats alit to attract fish. All congregated in one area. It looked like the lights on a runway as we went by! Their lights loomed over the horizon long after we passed.

I knew Jesse would be very happy when we were once again at anchor. He mentioned the 20-day passage that we did to the Marquesas. "Not for me!" he said. But I very much enjoyed sailing with him. We had never undertaken such a great project together; never "played on the same team" like we did as crewmates. I liked it!

Temporary Patches

The last day of the passage I felt good about two things I did. The first stemmed from a problem with our starboard engine, which we started when the wind died. We heard the bilge pump run repeatedly on the starboard side. Tim and I shared a "That's not good" look. In the engine room, water was spraying all over, apparently from the vicinity of the cooling water pump. We shut the engine down and switched to the other one.

After the engine had cooled, I went in for a closer look. Tim suggested that we couldn't do anything until we anchored, but I thought we should at least look for the cause of the problem. To see much in that area required a mirror, and it would have helped to be a contortionist. But I was able to determine that the culprit was a hose that had slipped up against a belt pulley. The pulley had ground a hole through the hose. With a little duct tape the problem was minimized, and we had some right-size hose to do a proper replacement later. Hooray!

The second problem of the day related to our three-way ownership. Although Bill was done sailing, he was still a partner with obligations toward the boat. A disagreement arose about who should pay how much of the Australia boatyard expenses. We tried to anticipate this day in our partnership agreement:

> Day-to-day expenses (food, fuel, supplies, fees) will be shared equally by the partners aboard the boat. Other expenses will be shared equally by all partners, whether aboard or not.

It seemed pretty clear to me, but Bill had a different understanding, that he would not be sharing the cost of annual maintenance after he left the crew. That was a surprise to me, but it shouldn't have been. Looking back over old email, I later saw that he had expressed this view from the beginning, but we never resolved the difference.

I didn't see this as a major issue. Although it meant that my expenses would be a little higher than anticipated, the fact remained that Bill was helping finance my round-the-world dream. Tim, however, became unexpectedly angry, and refused to "give Bill a break." Why? Two reasons…

Back in Cairns, Australia, Tim had valiantly tried to back into a marina slip when a crosswind was blowing 30 knots. We scraped against the boat in the next slip, doing several hundred dollars of damage. Tim volunteered to pay the bulk of the cost, and I covered the balance. There was no suggestion of asking Bill to contribute. But now Tim brought up our botched entry into Key West. Tim paid for his docking error in Cairns, I had paid for the broken daggerboard when I hit a rock in Maine, but Bill had not offered to pay when he hit a moored boat in Key West.

Key West paled, however, in comparison to the second reason. Remember the "winch handle incident" back in the South Pacific…?

On the crossing to the Marquesas, something occurred during the night while I was off watch, asleep. Tim and Bill were reefing sails in a squall, I think. While Tim steered and adjusted sheets, Bill was winching in the jib furling line. Bill's task was more challenging than you might imagine. When the breeze was up, and the air was spilled from the jib, and it started flapping in the wind, our jib sheets could whip violently, and potentially dangerously, right in the vicinity of the winch. As Bill manned the winch, something happened in the chaos, and the winch handle went flying at Tim's foot. Tim was not seriously hurt, at least physically. Tim interpreted this not as an accident, but as an aggressive act on Bill's part.

The incident didn't get resolved at that time, and with the three of us no longer together it was unlikely to get resolved now. Tim took the opportunity to raise the issue, "piling it on" to the financial questions. He wrote in an email to Bill:

> I am still emotionally festering from your throwing a winch handle at me, a felonious act which I let go at the time but, frankly, Bill, was my major reason for not returning to the boat until you left – granted something I had trouble addressing at the time.

When I read this, I nearly went through the pilothouse roof! Was Tim seriously going to jeopardize the workability of our partnership because he had an upset lingering from thousands of miles astern?? Apparently so, and I let him know I was not happy about it. We were all still partners, I fumed, and we had to work together – not just to do annual maintenance, but for the rest of the circumnavigation and the eventual sale of the boat. Exasperated, I took refuge alone in the cockpit.

I had thoughts about not being able to sail further with Tim. Maybe I could crew on another boat. Or maybe he'd be happy to sell me his share and walk away. Dangerous thoughts swirled in my mind as I sat in the cockpit and tried to calm down. Maybe after some deep breaths I would see some humor in the situation, and appreciate new possibilities…

Tim got the message. Before I embarked on any radical new course, he agreed to yield regarding the current cost allocation issue, and he agreed to set aside his other issues for now. I guess that left problem #2 in about the same state as the water hose – with a temporary patch. I had no permanent repair for lingering resentment over stale issues involving players not-all-present. I expected it would come up again. Still, I was happy with my communication and the resulting truce. If it were only sailing issues I had to deal with, this adventure wouldn't have been nearly so interesting!

We entered the harbor in the dark and anchored next to the other boats. Luc had arranged for officials to come aboard in the morning to clear us in, in spite of it being the Muslim New Year holiday! I was already surprised by the place, even without seeing it in daylight. It appeared to be a small city – a busy working port with generators running through the night. Funny how I didn't realize that I had certain expectations, until we would show up and the expectations weren't met. I thought this would be an out-of-the-way place with little on shore. Oh well, I was up for whatever Luc had arranged. All Journey...

Tual

After two days it felt like I'd been in another world for weeks!

Our first morning we had Quarantine and Customs officials aboard. Very friendly and courteous, but lots of forms (done in duplicate with carbon paper!). Then all the BPOers went ashore and piled into a little bus to go to an ATM, since no one had Indonesian money and credit cards were not accepted. Then we stopped at the biggest store in town, which sold SIM cards. We each in turn wrestled with our electronic devices and SIM cards and data plans to get ourselves connected. Then a brief rest back at the boats before walking to the Raja's house. We were being welcomed by the (now largely ceremonial) King of Tual, with traditional dancing and dinner.

Walking through the street, with Tourist Board escorts in colorful garb, we attracted lots of attention. In fact, everywhere we went we attracted so much attention that it was exhausting just to be around all the excited and friendly people. The dancing was beautiful, and then the real fun began, with everyone wanting photos posed with everyone, smiles everywhere.

On Day Two we visited a school with over 1,000 students, ages 15 to 17. We were cause for complete disruption of a school day! Students were hanging out of windows to see us as we arrived. We were led first to the teacher's lounge, where we found ourselves in a chaotic photo fest with teachers, administrators and some elite students. Some adults stayed on the sideline and looked dignified; others simply joined the fracas.

We divided into small groups to visit individual classes. I walked into one, all eyes on me, and I said a robust "Hello!" An almost deafening "Hello!!" came right back at me. The students were very interested in us, but reticent to ask questions. It was a science class, so we tried to understand what they were studying, and if they ever discussed climate change. It was difficult to determine any of this. Yes, we were told they cover climate change...but I wasn't sure the question was understood.

Before we got any further, my name was called by someone at the door. There was a problem with our boat, I was told. Luc assigned a car and driver for us, and Tim, Jesse and I left the tour to return to the harbor and find out what was up.

The boat was not where we had left it. The anchor had dragged, and *No Regrets* was in the clutches of a nearby matrix of ropes – a seaweed farm. Apparently we didn't hit any of the other boats, and we appeared to be only moderately entangled in the many lines and floats of the farm. Our guide and another local came out with us on our dinghy, and there were three locals waiting for us in their boats tied behind ours.

Everyone had ideas about how to get clear. One of the local guys jumped in the water and cleared some of the lines from our saildrive. But one he indicated needed to be cut. He asked us for a knife, and he cut it. We were clear aft. Next we used the dinghy to put out our second anchor, in the clear water. We pulled ourselves in that direction, but it was apparent that our first anchor line was badly fouled with the seaweed lines. Our diver made another cut, and we were able to pull the first anchor up, but it came up fouled in more lines. I thought we could sort that out, since it was all at the surface, but our guy was at it again with the knife, and then we were clear. We motored up to an open area and re-anchored.

I stayed with the boat, along with two of the locals, while the others went to find the owner of the seaweed farm, so we could make amends. I had a good time trying to communicate with the guys aboard. At their request I gave them some shampoo and body wash.

Tim and Jesse reported back that the owner was very nice, happy to accept an apology, but now they had to go to the pier to meet with someone to settle compensation. Shortly thereafter I got the update that we were being asked to pay damages amounting to 15,000,000 Rupiah (over $1,000 US). Yikes! Tim brought Jesse back and picked me up so we could get to the bank to exchange money before it closed in an hour.

At the bank we had to wait half an hour, so I got to hear from Tim about the dollar figure. Supposedly 18 lines were cut, and a value was assigned per line and to the seaweed growing on it. The seaweed was ready to harvest, so there was a crop loss involved. But there weren't 18 lines cut (there were three that I was aware of), and the value seemed arbitrary. Not clear where the numbers came from.

When we got to the head of the bank line, they wouldn't accept half of my US bills. Any bill with a crease, or an ink stain, or any sort of mark was rejected. We changed as much money as we could, but we didn't have 15 million Rupiah.

Back at the dock, Luc was now there. He suggested that the settlement was negotiable, unless we had already agreed. That was unclear, since the "negotiation" had all flowed in one direction, and I wasn't even there. We got into a discussion with the brother of the owner, who was acting as his agent, about the cuts and the value. It was a long discussion with several people trying to translate. No, 18 lines were not cut, but that's how many lines were lost from production, he explained. But who cut so many lines and why, when it might not have been necessary? Etc. Many people were talking, plus the usual kids watching. But all were sincere and friendly. The brother finally asked, "How much are you offering?" We said ten million Rupiah, which is what we had in cash. He said okay.

Hands were shaken. Bills were counted. A receipt was written. Photos were taken to document the agreement. We apologized for the trouble. I think everyone was satisfied, and we were about $700 lighter. No one got visibly upset, except the tourism ladies who wanted to be sure that despite this very unfortunate accident we would be joining tomorrow's tour.

The next morning began with a trip to the market. Produce, fish, hardware, cell phones, everything...packed tight with people.

"Hey, Mister! Photo, photo!" Over and over again. Everyone wanted their picture taken. It didn't seem to matter that they would never see the photo. The photo culture could not have been more different from what we encountered in the San Blas Islands, where the women covered their faces.

A boat took us through a maze of passages among tiny islands, to a little hidden beach for a swim. The crew and our guides all went in, too. The women went fully clothed, jeans and headscarves included. They all clung to life jackets. One of the young ladies said she didn't know how to swim, and Jesse did the parent/child thing, holding his hands just out of reach and telling her to paddle to him. She did, and with tons of encouragement from Jesse, she was swimming. She was *so* excited and happy, her face radiated a giant smile. Jesse was The Man!

Tuti was a young and beautiful guide who connected with Jesse. When three of the guys said they were going to climb up the cliff (about 25 feet above the water) and jump off, Tuti went, too. Initially the leader of this pack was a local boy full of bravado about it. But when he got to the edge, he wasn't so sure about jumping. So Jesse went first. Then the others went, including Tuti in her jeans and hijab. I found this incongruous, which just showed that I had some false preconceptions about Muslim women. My lesson for the day: being a Muslim woman and covering your body does not preclude your being a thrillseeker!

Baubau

The 650-mile passage from Tual went according to plan, except for another rip in our spinnaker. We were in close proximity with the other boats, which I found made the passage more stressful because, in effect, we were racing. I tried to make decisions (like whether to fly the spinnaker at night) the same as I would if the other boats weren't nearby, but at times that was hard to do.

Baubau (or Bau Bau or Bau-Bau or Bau-bau) was a city of about 250,000. We anchored near a small hotel that had a dinghy dock. Despite this being a Muslim area, the hotel served beer. At Luc's insistence, they kept the beer cold for us. Luc arranged for each crew to have an interpreter/guide, plus there seemed to be extras. They were all delightful, and they constantly wanted to practice their English and ask us questions. I found it tiring, even though they were lovely people who could answer my own questions. If only I could muster the energy to formulate the queries, ask them, and try to decipher the responses.

Jesse was so much better at this than I. He was constantly chatting with the guides, and they adored him. He learned about them and about the city, the language, the customs, their families, their aspirations. He passed some of this along to me, which was nice. But what I enjoyed more was simply watching him interact.

While Jesse and Tim visited a school (where they were asked, "We have no money, so what can we do about climate change?" and "What are *you* doing about climate change?"), I spent the oppressively hot day working on the boat. I took a stab at repairing the spinnaker, but I wasn't confident the fix would last.

In the evening we had a buffet dinner at the hotel (about $5 each, including paying for our guides). Luc told us not to eat too much because after dinner we would take a bus to a ceremony where we would have more food. Little did we know… Luc didn't tell us much, I think because he didn't actually know what we were in for. Nevertheless he exuded enthusiasm and made it seem like it was an opportunity not to be missed.

The bus ride was half an hour winding up into the hills. We knew we had arrived when suddenly there was a big crowd and hundreds of motorbikes. We were celebrities. A few guards kept the walkway passable for us, while hundreds of children and no small number of adults lined both sides and stared at us, took pictures of us, gave us high-fives, and/or smiled bashfully.

A large pavilion was packed with people seated on mats in long rows. Between the rows of people were rows of things resembling large woks on wicker stands, with tops covered in colorful fabric, each one uniquely and ornately decorated. There were hints of foods/drinks poking out from under the covers. Although the pavilion was crowded, there was a people-less area in the middle; we were led there. We each sat in front of one of the decorated woks, and everybody waited.

We were firmly planted in the middle of something, and we had no idea what. One of the guides explained that this was the annual celebration of the harvest. Thanksgiving! We could relate to that, and to the waiting (for what, not sure) before the big meal. Occasionally one of the men that appeared to be in an inner circle would take a microphone and say a word or phrase that would be echoed by the crowd, and then the speaker would repeat it with the tone of, "I can't *hear* you...," and the crowd would up the volume. Then back to waiting. Some people were taking photos with their phones. Some were texting. There was a prayer at one point. There was a passing of a "handshake" from neighbor to neighbor – you slid your hands between your neighbor's and then touched your heart. A little speech was given by the vice-mayor of Baubau. The guide whispered to Jesse that her talk had nothing to do with the celebration, that it was strictly political and for the wrong party, and if she had a brain she wouldn't need to read from notes!

There must have been some cue that I missed. People were removing the tops from the woks and starting to eat. In mine I recall there being a huge bowl of rice in the middle, surrounded by two deviled eggs, a whole fish (five-alarm spicy), a noodle dish, a little bowl of chicken (the man next to me demonstrated adding a sauce from another bowl to the chicken), a bottle of water, a can of pineapple juice, a large bunch of tiny bananas, some watermelon, an orange, a plate of various confections, and half a dozen coconut rice sticks wrapped in banana leaves. How to eat any of this while sitting cross-legged in a dense crowd was a puzzle.

Also puzzling were the ladies sitting directly across the woks from us, facing us – they were not eating. We had plenty to share, but no one was offering. I tried once to offer, and the woman looked away. Jesse's buddy explained that the woman sitting directly in front of each of us was the woman who made the food and decorated the wok. Or at least it came from her family and she was the family representative. Yikes – now I felt bad that we were barely eating, after having already had dinner, and not being entirely up to the challenge of how to eat a whole fish with just a spoon.

The guy next to me was helpful. He took the fruit juice from his platter and put it in my backpack, and indicated I should do the same with mine. He pulled out the half-dozen rice sticks in the banana leaves, and indicated that I must put them in my pack. Then he put the cover back on my platter, and his, and nodded an abrupt goodbye and left.

Luc passed the word that it was time for us to go. Not that the event was over, but time for us to leave. As we followed Luc back through the throng-lined walkway to our bus, he explained why there was such a crowd. Each family received one assigned space in the pavilion, and the family chose a representative to go inside. The rest of the family attended outside.

It felt surreal. I should have been outside watching. But Luc had told us we would have opportunities to be treated like royalty, just because we were tall white folks who traveled from afar. Our presence added a strange form of status to a local event.

Jesse rented a motorbike, borrowed two of our guides and went exploring. He had a great time, free from the old yachtie crowd. They rode into the hills and hiked to a waterfall with a swimming hole. He deepened his bond with the guides. He was pumped about riding the motorbike in the chaotic traffic with unfamiliar rules. For example, you don't stop for a red light unless you are making a turn.

That night the BPOers went out for dinner. At the restaurant we bumped into the first non-yachtie white family I had seen in Baubau, and I found I had the urge to shout, "Hey, Mister!"

Tim and Jesse went on Luc's tour-of-the-day; I stayed aboard for some quiet time. It didn't turn out the way I planned. Our batteries were low, so I started an engine to charge up, and I heard a POP from the engine room. Broken alternator belt. No big deal. While I was in there I also tightened the belt for the water pump, and then discovered that we had a slow fuel leak by our transfer pump. Plus there was some odd banging noise that at first I thought was debris banging against the side of the boat. No, it was our connection from the steering hydraulic piston to the rudder armature, come very loose. None of these was big trouble, having been caught in time. Then I noticed that our solar array was not providing a charge to our batteries. We never had any problems with the solar charging, hence I knew little about it. That was disconcerting.

I enjoyed hanging out on the boat and tackling the small jobs. Even the solar array tracked down to our usual problem – a corroded wire connection. By noon I was ready to relax, when Jesse showed up with his friend/guide Sahur, to show him the boat. Nice! Tools still everywhere, I explained to Sahur that this was what we did on our boats – we fixed things. While I had Jesse's help, I went up the mast to inspect for chafe aloft. All good.

I got a wee bit of quiet time before the next event. We all had to don long pants and look our best for a meeting and dinner with the mayor. Once again we were center stage, this time with tables and chairs rather than mats on the floor. The food and entertainment were delightful, though I nearly passed out when I ate a whole hot pepper hidden in a mild fruit salad! I gushed sweat, and cried for a while, and slowly recovered, all while trying to act like nothing happened.

Selayar

I was more than ready to move on, but it was sad for Jesse to say goodbye
to his new friends. They had been wonderful guides, wonderful people.

Our overnight sail was perfect. Moving fast on smooth water, on a moonlit
night, headed west. West toward home. I planned to take a break and fly home
from Singapore. I was feeling saturated with foreign foods and language
barriers and "Hey, Misters," and I longed for familiarity and belonging. But
Singapore was still a month away. We had four more stops in Indonesia, plus a
jump to Bali. I needed to breathe deeply and "be here now."

"Here now" was Selayar (or Salayar or Seleier), another small city. Noisy,
smelly, and the water too polluted to swim in despite the equatorial heat. I
skipped some of Luc's tours, and read books instead.

There were some fun highlights ashore though. We were guests of honor,
again, at a performance of music and dance. It was an annual show at an arts
center, and many of the performers were youngsters. Parents jockeyed for
position with their cell phones to get video of their kids performing. In this
strange land, I enjoyed the universal aspect of parents, kids and cell phones.

We had a memorable meal at a restaurant where they immediately start
bringing food when you sit down. A wide variety of foods, on small plates. If
you take food from a plate, you have purchased that dish, and usually they bring
more of it. Anything that you don't want you simply leave untouched. I had
shrimp and veggies and crab and beef and a couple things that I couldn't
identify. Plus a bottle of tea. All for $5. Best "fast food" ever.

Komodo

Every now and then along came a day that was simply magical. We had sailed the 170 miles to the island of Komodo. Except for a pre-existing village, the entire island was declared a national park because of the presence of the unique Komodo Dragon. The landscape was beautiful. If you gazed above the water, the beach, and the coconut palms, it looked rather like the red mountains of Arizona.

We were up by 6am to head ashore for our park tour. We were told if we arrived by 6:45 we were almost guaranteed to see dragons. We did. We were warned to stick together, and there was always a guide at the front and the back of the group. We got to hear the story of a tourist ten years ago that left the group to take pictures, and after a week of searching only his camera and eyeglasses were found… These giant reptiles mostly eat deer. They are somewhat like crocodiles – they hide and wait, and when an animal comes within range, they have a sudden attack. Their bite causes infection; they stalk the bitten prey until it succumbs to the infection. Mothers will sometimes eat their own hatchlings, too…

After our hike we all bought drinks and relaxed. Jesse started to kid around with some of the locals. Next thing I knew he was arm wrestling, and some wagers are being placed! He did well, winning a little cash and impressing the locals with his strength.

I was touched by a comment made to me by a fellow American BPOer. Politically, he was no liberal. "I wish every American could come visit this area. The people have been so wonderful; it would change American ideas about what it means to be Muslim."

We took the dinghy to nearby Pink Beach for some snorkeling. The water was clear, there was an amazing variety of fish, and the colors and textures of the coral were mind-boggling. This unheralded spot turned out to be a magnificent underwater gem.

The magic continued. Tim had arranged with one of the park guides to meet at 5pm; he would take us to the village for dinner. There were no restaurants in the village, but Abdullah said he could provide dinner at his house. The village itself was fascinating. The houses were mostly on stilts, which could protect them from a storm surge, but also protected them from dragons. Abdullah's house was on the edge of town, bordering the park, and he said it was common to see dragons there.

Walking down the narrow "Main Street" path, Abdullah stopped and asked if we wanted chicken for dinner. Uncertain about why he was asking, we said that would be great. He said we needed to give him cash to buy the chicken. We did, he took it into a nearby house, and came out with a bird. Then on to a nicer-than-average house, that our guide said was not his, but it belonged to his family, and we could have coffee and tea there. Apparently one could also rent accommodation space there.

While Abdullah took the chicken to his wife for cooking, and we sipped and waited, up the path came the only white person we had seen. Tim got into a conversation with her, and she joined us. Nina was from Holland, she was a nurse, and she had lived on the nearby island of Flores for several years. She also worked for an NGO that helped charitable organizations find projects that addressed local needs. We had a constant stream of questions for her. We learned, for example, that there was a desalination facility almost next door, with a solar array and batteries. Except it stopped working after less than a year, and the charitable organization that built it was done with their project, no longer around to fix it. Nina had found a Belgian group with the expertise to fix it, and that was looking for a project... In the meantime the villagers carried water from six kilometers away.

We learned that another group built public toilets for the village, with a proper septic system. Except that the system required a pump that was no longer working. I'm not sure if this was a question of "appropriate technology" or effective project management and follow-up.

Tim asked a lot about the government. Nina said, "I don't believe in governments. They come and go, and the politicians get rich and nothing changes for the poor." We were in a remote part of Indonesia (a country with many remote parts), and very few resources were sent this way. What the village needed, she said, was a fast boat to carry sick or injured people to a hospital. Five mothers had died in recent months from complications in/after childbirth. Sometimes a person would be bitten by a dragon and need urgent care for the infection. Tim asked about the government providing such a boat, and she laughed. No chance.

As it started to get dark, a generator cranked up, and our host fiddled with some wires until lights came on. There was electricity from 7pm to 11pm, usually.

Abdullah returned and invited us to follow him to his house. We sat on a rug over a section of the bare wood floor. Adjacent was a mattress – probably filled with kapok, which grew locally. No glass in the windows, of course, but pretty fabric that could at least keep out the sun, perhaps some of the rain. Corrugated metal roof. The whole structure swayed on its stilts when we moved. Tim asked in the course of conversation whether the house included a toilet. Abdullah laughed; a toilet would be a huge expense; they had the beach.

Abdullah's wife cooked in the next room. Cooked with a wood fire! Gas was too expensive. She was not introduced, and she did not sit or eat with us. She brought food, she nodded when we thanked her, she was happy to pose for a photo with her husband and baby daughter. The food was superb! Well, no, the chicken was tough. But the flavors were delicious and there were several dishes and the quantity was over the top. We ate sitting on the rug on the floor. At some point they turned on their television for their two kids and a neighbor friend. They got one channel, and they had to pay for it. I was surprised they would allocate money to TV, but when I saw the kids passed out asleep in front of it, I could see that it might be valuable.

We learned that the relatively hefty fees we all paid to the national park went almost entirely to the government in Jakarta. The guide received about $3 for the entire tour – roughly 1% of the fees collected from our group. Nothing went to help the village, except of course for providing the job opportunities.

All three of us came away wishing we could fix the broken down projects, and help Abdullah and the village as a whole. We did what we readily could – we paid a generous amount for our meal. Abdullah would not say any amount that he expected; it was up to us. We gladly paid as much as we had paid in any restaurant, plus we had already bought the chicken.

Abdullah escorted us back to our dinghy. The long ride home was beautiful, the stars brighter than we had seen before in Indonesia, and the water was calm and phosphorescent. What to make of it all…? Was there more we could do for these people? Is the way to leave the world better than we found it to become a Nina – to live in an emerging area for years and help with sustainable development? Is there a way to be useful from our distant homes?

Pirates and Volcanoes

As we were preparing to leave for Lombok we got word that a 60′ German sailboat crossing from Lombok to Bali had been attacked by pirates! This part of the world had a long history of piracy. But according to Luc no yacht had ever been attacked; the piracy focus had been on stealing oil from tankers, etc. Obviously the news was disconcerting. We had no details about the circumstances, and whether the people were held for ransom, or…

One could argue that this must be have been a one-time event. One could argue that there would now be heightened awareness/patrols, and so things would be safer now than before the event. Argue whatever; I couldn't help thinking a lot about the subject. We discussed contingencies – who would do what if people tried to board the boat. We discussed the use of our meager makeshift weapons, concluding that they would merely enrage attackers without deterring them. We reviewed the priorities of making a lot of noise and light, calling our fellow BPOers on the radio, setting off emergency beacons and hiding them.

We set sail for Lombok in close convoy. It was beautiful sailing, and during the night we pulled ahead of the group. We were still within sight of the other boats, five miles away. The distance didn't seem like an issue, until two fishing boats approached us. Suddenly the body/mind went into high alert…fight or flight. At what point could you determine hostile intent, and at that point how much time would you have? The mind goes into overdrive. Of course the boats went on with their fishing and all was well. But we "closed ranks." The internal/mental stress was intense, even though "nothing happened."

After arriving at Lombok, we heard a different story about the "piracy." Luc said he knew the boat, which was actually American, and the owner, whom he described as eccentric. The marina staff said he took on an equally eccentric German woman as crew shortly before he left. They said the woman reported (by VHF radio?) a sexual assault. They said the boat sailed to Christmas Island (Australia), not to Bali. They said the "pirate attack" was actually the Australian Coast Guard arriving to investigate.

The locals had an interest in minimizing the event, so it wouldn't affect their business. But it seemed almost certain that there was no piracy. Interesting, though, how much we were affected by the mere suggestion. Perhaps this had been a good "drill" – to get us thinking and talking about how to be safe.

Concurrent with our pirate experience, the volcano on Lombok erupted. A minor eruption, but enough to close the airport in Bali, downwind. The airport reopened after two days and all seemed to be okay, except…the whole boat was covered with a layer of dust/ash, inside and out. This was beyond annoying; it felt like a violation of my personal space. I didn't want to open the hatch over

my berth, because my sheets would get covered with dust. But you had to open the hatch, it was so hot. I didn't want to breathe either, but again…no choice. Each day I hoped/wished it would be done "ashing." I wanted to get both pirates and active volcanoes behind us!!

Lombok and Bali

Lombok is the next island east of Bali, and the primary activity planned was to leave the boats and fly or ferry to the well-known Hindu island full of resorts. We only had one full day in Lombok before Jesse and I planned to go. Jesse convinced Tim and me to rent motorbikes with him for the day, and ride to a waterfall 2+ hours away.

Riding in Indonesia was a scary/fun challenge. We were used to driving on the left at this point. But in Indonesia that seemed to be about the only rule. Lots of creative driving, especially when it came to passing, which was pretty much all the time. If the road was wide enough for, say, one car plus two motorbikes, many drivers expected that combination to fit, without any regard to "sides" of the road. For example, a car might pull halfway into the right lane to pass a motorbike, despite the fact that a motorbike was approaching – it would still fit in the remaining half a lane. In fact, cars tended to pass like this even if there were *two* oncoming motorbikes, side by side. This arrangement wouldn't fit, but it was assumed that the two oncoming bikes would get into a single file when they saw the car approaching in their lane.

More frequently it was bikes passing cars or trucks. The bikers would pull up until almost touching the car, waiting for a chance to pass. Several might all pass at once, filling the passing lane, zipping back to the left (or maybe only to the middle) just before hitting oncoming traffic.

There were also more unexpected obstacles. Tim had a momma goat and her kid run out in front of him, and the kid began nursing in the busy road. There were motorbikes carrying loads the width of a car – often display cases used for selling something on the side of the road, packed up on the back behind the biker.

It became our quest to make it to the waterfall. Tim's bike overheated. Jesse found a bike shop where they added coolant. Before long it overheated again. Jesse found another shop. This time the guy pulled the cover off the engine, exposing an air filter thoroughly clogged with dust and volcanic ash. He cleaned it out with compressed air, and the problem was solved.

We got lost. And we must have looked lost, because a man offered to help. When we said we were looking for the trail to the waterfall, he told us people could not go to the waterfall without a guide. But no problem – he was a guide! The waterfall was good. Cold water! The day was an adventure of a different kind, and fun.

Jesse and I took the ferry to Bali, to spend three days at a resort near Ubud. The resort was quiet. Relatively cool up in the hills. Cooler still in the air-conditioned room! There was a shower with hot water. Another shower outdoors, by the private jacuzzi/pool. Great place for a romantic getaway. Or a recharge break from your yacht!

We got massages at the resort. We rested in the air conditioning. We took the shuttle into Ubud. Hundreds of little shops and restaurants, and sidewalks filled with mostly white people speaking many languages. We bought our share of crafts. We enjoyed strolling through the monkey forest. We attended two dance performances.

Three days at the resort was about right. We were starting to grow accustomed to the air conditioning and good food and over-the-top service. Maybe we would like to stay another month...?

No. Back to the boat and the grit on the deck and below, and the stifling heat. The crew rigged the emergency manual pump, never before used, and we took turns pumping seawater to wash the gritty decks. This was hard work, but after an hour of sweat I felt much better about being back aboard. We had a big supply of food delivered to us, and we were ready to leave the damn volcano behind.

Kumai – Orangutans vs Palm Oil

In a word, our 3 ½-day passage from Lombok to Kumai, on the south coast of Borneo, was HOT! The dark transom steps were at times too hot to stand on, and of course the metal fittings would get hot, but never before had I experienced such heat on my feet just pacing the off-white deck. We had a very welcome wind blowing off of Bali the first night. After that it was motorsailing, or simply motoring, most of the way.

Like so many other places we had been, Kumai turned out to be quite different from what I expected. Kumai was not the remote national park ranger station we had been led to believe. It was a busy port, with ships coming and going constantly. The waterfront had not only the usual docks and mosques and boats large and small, but also huge gray concrete structures, some seemingly with no windows and others with narrow slits for windows. They were a mystery. Later we learned they were full of nesting birds, with the nests harvested for bird's nest soup – popular in China, especially for pregnant women. I thought it was strange that enough birds would choose to nest there, and I wondered how the birds found enough nesting materials in such a densely populated area (dense with both humans and birds). We could hear their constant chatter, a mile or more away.

We came to Kumai for one reason: to visit the national forest where there were orangutans. We joined a river tour boat shortly after we arrived, we returned the following night after dinner, and we made our departure from Kumai the next morning. We never even put our dinghy in the water; never went ashore except on the tour. Our only business besides visiting the park was to replenish our supply of diesel, which was brought to us anchored in the river.

We shared a tour boat with our friends from *Tahawus*. We all lived on the open upper deck, while the crew and cook lived below, and our guide went back and forth. The food (five meals plus tea and snacks) was excellent. The sleeping quarters were the same upper deck where we ate and sat watching the jungle glide by. At night mattresses appeared from below, and mosquito nets, and it was pleasant to sleep with the sounds of the jungle all around. We simply pulled to the side of the river and tied to some vegetation for the night.

We made three stops near places in the park where food was provided for orangutans, and they commonly came to eat. Sometimes they wouldn't come, as the food provided was not their favorite. They preferred to eat durian fruit over the bananas and jackfruit provided in the park, so they often didn't show when the durians were ripe. We saw many orangutans.

The orangutan habitat was being threatened. The biggest threat stemmed from the commercial production of palm oil. This oil was in high demand for its low cholesterol and other desirable properties. As a result, forest was being cleared at a dramatic rate, and being replaced with palm oil farms. The diverse natural habitat was being replaced with a monoculture.

Our guides were members of a group called O Green. They called each other "brother," and they were on a mission to save the orangutan and lands that were their home (both the animal's home and the people's home). They did the tours to raise money and raise awareness. They fought the fires that were started to clear the land. They

organized the townspeople, school children especially, to plant seedlings in burned areas.

They raised money to purchase private land across the river from the park. A few hundred meters in from that river bank it was all palm oil farming now. They hoped to purchase the remaining strip of river bank to protect the habitat and beauty. They had purchased one kilometer. They dreamt of much more, though they knew it was a distant dream; there might not be time before the palm oil growers purchased the land.

I found it interesting to be near the "front lines" of such a battle. Putt-putting up the jungle river for hours, seeing the monkeys and the birds and the fireflies and the remote beauty, and seeing the magnificent orangutans…and seeing in the distance the palm oil trees. The "O Greens" indeed seemed to be a band of brothers, and I stood on their side of the battle.

"Orangutan" means "person of the forest," and let's just say it: they are totally cool.

I received a long list of questions from the students at Lewiston Middle School…

What do you like to do when you're bored on the boat?

I rarely get bored. Tim listens to audiobooks. Jesse reads or works on writing poetry and music. Sometimes I read, and occasionally I like to solve Sudoku puzzles. But there are always tasks to be done to maintain the boat, plus researching our next port and how to get there.

How long do you stay on the islands you go to?

Some of my Blue Planet Odyssey comrades have called our travels through Indonesia a "forced march," meaning that we are constantly on the move with no time to relax. Most places we go we are there for about three days only. One reason for this is that the BPO is covering a lot of distance in a relatively short time. (A friend who has been sailing the world for years asked how long the BPO was, and I said about two and a half years. She said, "Can't you make it five?" Most cruisers would go much more slowly and spend a month in places they like. Or maybe a year.) A second reason we are moving fast now is that it is late in the season. The wind will be turning against us any day now. We are hoping to complete our next passage – about 450 miles to a harbor near Singapore – before that happens. We can sail against the wind, of course, but it can be very unpleasant if the waves begin to build.

Did you or others ever fall off your boat?

No. We are extremely careful about this. Especially at night, when there is usually only one person awake. The boat is normally on "autopilot," so it will keep right on sailing if the person on watch goes overboard, and likely no one would notice until the next person comes on watch, up to four hours later. So if you go overboard you are in a heap of trouble. We have harnesses that we sometimes wear, which can clip into "jack lines" that run the length of the boat. You clip in if you need to do something outside the safety of the cockpit.

Was the German sailboat and the people on the boat saved?

Apparently the report of a pirate attack was wrong. It was posted on a widely read website for cruising sailors, but we don't know who posted it or why they had such poor information. Don't believe everything you read on the Internet!

How often do you fish?

Usually we troll a lure when we are at sea, and we catch a fish every few days. Recently we stopped, because we are eating so much fish ashore – we don't really want to have more fish on board. Fish and rice are the main foods here.

Have you liked being on a boat for so long?

Yes, but I'm sure looking forward to coming home in two weeks. I know when I get cold in Maine's winter I will have thoughts about how nice it will be on the boat again. But I want to see family and friends, and eat all my favorite foods, and watch a Patriots football game, and take a hot shower whenever I want… I will be home for almost three months, after which I think I'll be happy to get back aboard for the remaining year of the voyage.

Have you ever gotten homesick?

Occasionally. Then I remind myself that I am doing what I've dreamt of doing, and I won't be doing it forever, so I better appreciate being where I am, even while I'm missing home.

Did anything ever jump into the boat?

Sometimes at sea we find flying fish on the deck in the morning. A few times we found tiny squids, which I still don't fully understand. If you remember my posts from the Galápagos Islands, we had sea lions climbing aboard, which was quite a shock the first time. We had to block off the steps up the back of the boat to try to keep them off, since they would shed and poop on the deck.

What sorts of things did you see on the pink beach? Why is it called a pink beach?

Pink Beach has a slight pink color from bits of coral in it. We could swim right from the beach to spectacular snorkeling – clear shallow water, and a seemingly endless variety of coral shapes and colors, and fish shapes and colors. Did you see the animated movie Finding Nemo, with the crazy-looking fish? I think we saw those fish, and more.

How do you get internet?

Different ways at different times. Sometimes we only get it ashore, often at a restaurant. Here restaurants usually do not offer Internet, but they have very good cell phone service. (Everyone here seems to have a cell phone.) I have purchased a data plan using the cell system. When we are really lucky there is wifi close enough on shore that we can connect directly from the boat. Almost every place we've visited has Internet, one way or another, though it is usually much slower than what we get at home, and in some places it is restricted so that you cannot access some sites.

What's the best place you've visited and why?

Hard to choose, but I'll go with the Marquesa Islands. Beautiful, rugged, remote, good snorkeling, manta rays, good fruit, and of course friendly people.

Could you touch the Komodo Dragon?

Absolutely not! They are dangerous; sort of like a crocodile on land. And their bite gets very infected. They kill large prey by biting them and then following them while the infection weakens/kills them.

What's the most interesting kind of wildlife you've ever seen?

Each is different and interesting in its own way. The sea lions for their acrobatics. The crocodiles for their primordial scariness. Whales for their magnificence. The Komodo Dragon for its strangeness. The orangutans for their personalities. If I had to choose, I would go with the orangutan, though that might just be because we saw them so recently.

Is it expensive to sail around the world?

Yes, at least the way we are doing it. Boats cost a lot to buy and maintain. Food and fuel costs add up. Some countries charge a pretty penny to visit. We are paying for all of this from our life savings. But some people manage to do it for far, far less. They start with a smaller boat. They do more of the maintenance themselves. And they have some skill/trade that allows them to earn money along the way. They may stop somewhere for months when they find a job, and earn enough money to keep them going to the next opportunity.

How often do you eat the food that the people on the island usually eat? What do you eat on the boat?

Great question. When we are in port we frequently eat ashore, especially here in Indonesia where food costs very little. Often what we eat is the same as what the locals eat. Lots of fish and rice, plus fruit and eggs. When we eat on the boat we have more meat, and canned goods when we run out of fresh.

How often do people give you gifts? What's the best one you've received?

Generally the only gifts we receive are people's smiles and welcoming attitudes. In Indonesia they are trying to promote tourism, and we have been given T-shirts and sarongs by the Tourist Board, plus they have provided guides/translators and welcome/farewell dinners and dance performances. At the Pacific Islands we were sometimes given fruit and coconuts, and once fish. When we went to ceremonies we would be given flowers. Receiving fresh fruit, right from the trees, was my favorite.

How many volcanoes have you seen? Does it ever scare you?

We have seen many, many islands that were formed by volcanoes. But most have been inactive for centuries or more. Only the one on Lombok erupted, and that eruption was not life-threatening to anyone, as far as I know. So only Lombok was a little scary; mostly it was just a nuisance.

You said you felt violated when ash covered your boat. What do you mean by that?

The boat is my only "personal space" (and even this I have to share with two others). I like to be able to retreat to the boat to relax, and maybe to be alone in my cabin. But ash was everywhere – in my personal space. I felt like my privacy was intruded upon, and there was nowhere I could go to fully relax.

While you were on this wild adventure, on a scale from 1-10 how fun/exciting was it?

It seems to me that you only get a few wild adventures in a lifetime, and they are all special. On an extended adventure like this, the fun/excitement ebbs and flows. You can't be excited all the time!

> **Have you ever gotten a disease?**
>
> Not on this trip. Nor has anyone else on our boat. But some boats have dropped out of the BPO due to health problems.
>
> **Have monkeys ever chucked poop at you before?**
>
> No. But Jesse got peed on by an orangutan high overhead. Our guide said that will bring him good luck!

East Belitung

It was a two-day passage from Kumai to East Belitung. Mostly motoring. Hot. The highlight for me was crossing longitude 110 degrees east. This was 180 degrees from my home in Maine – literally half way around the world.

The Tourism Board once again went above-and-beyond to welcome us. They provided guides – delightful people willing to go out of their way to help us. The Board provided both a welcome and a farewell dinner, gifts, local entertainment and an air-conditioned bus. All greatly appreciated. But it was hard for me to envision East Belitung as a tourist destination. The number one tourist attraction seemed to be an abandoned open pit tin mine with a pool of strangely colored water at the bottom!

At the farewell dinner/celebration, there was music and dancing, plus a demonstration of rattan stick fighting. Two shirtless contestants would enter the "ring." On cue from a referee, they would stalk each other, thrust and parry, trying to hit each other on the back. The referee would keep the fight orderly, and stop it at some point. Then he inspected the contestants' backs for welts. The contestant with fewer welts was pronounced the winner.

After their demonstration, they asked if one of us would accept the challenge, and Jesse stepped forward. He battled fiercely and valiantly, and came away with a serious "caning" that he was still recovering from two days

 later. I guess the Tourist Board didn't impress upon the locals that they should not beat up on the visitors! But Jesse was a hero for his bravery and style, if not technique.

Trying to Make Sense of Our World

I enjoyed talking with Jesse about world events and what role we could play in them. Both of us (he more than I) had been reading books that triggered these topics.

We both read a book about how/why the aboriginal people of Australia were suffering (still, in spite of many well-meaning efforts by the government and others to atone for past wrongs). The book was called *Why Warriors Lie Down and Die*. It showed that most "help" provided by the dominant culture was provided within a context (language, laws, knowledge base, worldview) of the dominant culture, and often it had unintended consequences that made conditions worse.

We both read Howard Zinn's *People's History of the United States*. This book, while not necessarily new information, was upsetting – to understand how rich capitalists have controlled our own history, at the expense of most people. We had visited some places where, unlike the USA, money was not King; where people didn't own much, but they were happy and healthy. What to make of this contrast…?

What should we do about the Syrian refugees? Jesse read his "friends" posts on Facebook, and many suggested that we should not help the refugees, because they were Muslim (and therefore potentially terrorists…?), or because we had to look after our own (as though we didn't have a hand in making the mess to begin with…?), or other poorly-reasoned reasons. I was amazed at the lack of empathy in that youthful crowd.

While I was more sympathetic, I also tended to be frozen, not knowing what I might do that would make any difference. I had a hard time thinking beyond the issues I saw first-hand. Contemplating what we heard about in the news was overwhelming. Jesse and I talked about this, and also talked about trying to improve world conditions through engineering. Jesse said he had always thought of engineering projects in terms of technical contributions, but now he saw the importance of the social/political aspects that are part of any development project. Maybe he will become an engineer not only with "heart," but with an understanding of people and an ability to communicate well.

People ask how we spend our time on the boat. Trying to make sense of our world is one answer that I've probably never mentioned.

And Then There Were Four

After two days of no wind, we got wind directly in our faces en route to our final Indonesian stop at Nongsa Point Marina, across the strait from Singapore. The going was unpleasant, but everyone made it in time for our meetings with Jimmy Cornell to discuss what lay ahead for the Blue Planet Odyssey.

We were now north of the equator again, just barely. I'm glad that Jesse got to sail "across the line." I would have liked to jump into the ocean with him to celebrate, but it was at night in uncomfortable seas, and no one was of a mind for celebration. Instead it was a toast at the marina bar after arrival.

Our meetings with Jimmy went smoothly. *Chapter Two* announced, as expected, that they would not be continuing across the Indian Ocean. *Joyful* had made it to Australia, but they still had health concerns, and they withdrew. So now we were four: *Blue Wind*, *Tahawus*, *Maggie* and *No Regrets*.

Jimmy explained that the old plan to sail to Sri Lanka in the spring would not work with our current schedule, because we would likely encounter headwinds going from Sri Lanka to Chagos. Maybe it was good that we had headwinds getting to Nongsa Point; everyone was crystal clear that they would like to avoid that!

The alternative that we adopted was a different route, south along the west coast of Sumatra, which we would do in leisurely cruising fashion for the month of April. This coast was rarely visited by yachts. Even Jimmy had never been there. Then we would strike west to Chagos, assuming we could get permission from the Brits to stop there. After Chagos we would sail to Mauritius and then Réunion. There we would wait a couple months for the Southern spring, and sail on to South Africa.

Nongsa Point was effectively a suburb of Singapore. Expensive restaurants, lots of security, no town nearby. We didn't care. Jesse and I cleaned and packed and prepared for a few days in Singapore before flying home.

Chapter Two hosted a farewell potluck party. I would miss them. I would  miss all the BPOers for the next three months. And I realized I was going to miss *No Regrets*. I liked her. She had been a good home for the past year. When a nice breeze came up in the afternoon I wished we could set sail and go…onward. Oh well, I would remember that feeling for my return.

Tuti, our translator/guide, and Jesse

We told the boys to stay out of our
dinghies, but when we came back to
this face, it was hard to be angry.

Collecting for the mosque

Jimmy,
Zeke,
Luc

SOJOURN AT HOME

Absence made me more appreciative of the comforts of home. A well-stocked supermarket an easy mile away! Hallie had always called the supermarket my "happy place;" now more than ever. I lost 25 pounds while living aboard. I was trying to gain some of that back.

Television was so seductive! I enjoyed snuggling in on the sofa to watch a favorite show. The next show was interesting, too. And the next. Whole days could drift by without actually doing much of anything. I looked forward to taking another long break from TV on *No Regrets*.

Surprisingly, I coped okay with the cold; a mild winter helped. It was the lack of sunshine that bothered me. At noon I felt like the morning must be about to start. Just when it seemed like brightness might happen, the sun was on its way back down. It didn't seem right.

Other observations: houses in the US were crazy big and far apart. There were almost no people on the streets. (What did I expect? It was winter!) I seemed to spend a huge amount of time "dealing with things" on the phone or online – reconciling the COBRA payments for health insurance, researching new health insurance, dealing with fraudulent charges on a credit card, making and changing appointments, unfreezing/refreezing credit reports, stopping service on a lost cell phone, getting a replacement through the insurance we had been paying each month, weighing whether it was worth $48 to reserve a seat in advance for each return flight versus taking what would be available at check-in, discovering that you couldn't access info you needed online without first updating the app, and the update failed. And modern society's most irritating thing – the automated phone systems that give you a limited set of choices, none of which match the reason you have to call in the first place. I had been avoiding most of this mishegas while on the boat. Thank you, Hallie, once again, for keeping our household operational in the "real" world.

I thought a lot about the non-functional solar-powered desalination system in Komodo. Could I learn enough to fix it? Could I find someone to fix it? I contacted Nina, who was trying to get an NGO to take on the project. She reported that she was still waiting for their answer… I contacted my cousin whose career was teaching and practicing "appropriate technology." As expected, she replied that the situation was classic – bringing a high-tech solution to a community that didn't have the infrastructure to maintain it. Yes, no question about that. And yet, it seemed like such a good solution – to use the things the village has in abundance, seawater and sunlight, to produce the fresh water that they needed! Maybe this technology could be made more reliable and be replicated in village after village. Or maybe a low tech solar still would make more sense; but how large would a still have to be to serve a village…?

In the shorter term I found a way that I could "act locally," by joining a Community Solar Farm. This is similar to putting a solar photovoltaic array on your roof, except that nine households band together to build a shared array. That would be my contribution to the health of the planet for the time being.

BPO and Crew Updates

While I was home, Tim informed me that he was planning to leave again in Mauritius (two-thirds of the way across the Indian Ocean), and later return to the boat in Brazil. Joining us in Malaysia, and also going as far as Mauritius, would be Chris, an acquaintance of Tim's who had a little sailing experience. I'd be set for 4 to 5 months. Then I'd be returning home for six weeks, waiting for the Southern spring. Then I had no one signed on for four months and 5,000 miles, from Mauritius through Brazil. Bob was thinking about returning for that leg, but he wasn't sure.

I posted a blog entry asking if anyone was interested in crewing. Three days later I heard from Liam, a friend of a friend. He lived only two hours away, so we met for lunch, and we said "Yes" to each other. A little scary to sign on a nearly complete stranger, but I trusted my ability to judge character. After all, I met Tim and Bill via the Internet; why not do it again via my blog? One crew signed, one more needed. There would be more uncertainty after Brazil, but that was far over my horizon.

In BPO news, *Blue Wind* had withdrawn. They were going to ship their boat by freighter to the Mediterranean. Our Blue Planet Odyssey fleet was now but three: *Tahawus*, *Maggie*, and *No Regrets*.

MALAYSIA & THAILAND

The plan had been to leave the boat in the Singapore area, while we took our break. Then Tim decided he would instead like to sail during that time, and he enlisted Bob and wife Barb as crew. They would sail east to Borneo and then return to the Singapore area, and I would rejoin where I left off.

It didn't work out quite that way. They sailed most of the way to Borneo, but were pummeled by headwinds, and never made it. They returned to Singapore early, and they continued up the west coast of Malaysia. Tim informed me that *No Regrets* was near Penang, about 400 miles north of where I had left. I was irritated about this because it meant leaving a "gap" in my circumnavigation, equivalent to about 3 days' sail. Oh well, there was a price for having partners.

Two days of airplanes to get from Boston to Penang, traveling with a spinnaker and various boat gear – 100 pounds of baggage. The airline's maximum weight per bag was 23 kilos; the spinnaker was 22. The local hop from Singapore to Penang had a maximum total weight of 40 kilos; my total must have exceeded that slightly. But they accepted my payment for the 40-kilo maximum – $50 baggage fees for a flight that only cost $68 for myself. No problem.

Chris met me at the hotel/condo that I had booked at the marina in Penang. It was nice to start to get to know him; also nice to be in a condo with separate rooms and separate baths. The drawback was that the boat wasn't there. Tim and crew had sailed further on to Langkawi, a 3-hour ferry ride away. But we spent two days in Penang, as did Tim, getting our visas for our return to Indonesia. I got to cross paths with Bob and his wife as they were about to head back home to Canada. Bob would be coming back to sail aboard *Maggie* to Mauritius. Then he would either go home to help care for his newborn granddaughter or he would join me from Mauritius to Brazil. He/I would know soon.

When we finally arrived at the boat, she looked a little sad. Lots of dirt on the outside, and in some areas inside. Stains on the deck and top sides. She had a crack in one of the pilothouse windows. She was low on fuel (not a small task, carrying jerry cans and siphoning through a filter into our tanks). The port side cabin sole/floor had cracked, making for a spongy surface and the risk that it might give way completely, potentially causing injury We needed propane. Food stores were very low. One of the fuel transfer pumps wasn't working (again). The forward fuel gauge had broken irreparably.

But no worries. It was fun, despite withering heat, tackling some of the problems. Cruising: fixing your boat in exotic places... I focused on the cabin sole, epoxying in four supports to brace the damaged floor. It was satisfying to use the skills I had learned in the building of my own boat, even though that boat still wasn't finished after 23 years!

Philosophy and Politics

Having Chris aboard was inspiring long/deep philosophical conversations. One night over dinner and beer at a pleasant Indian restaurant, we talked at great length about how privileged we were, and what responsibilities came with that. Not privileged to be living on a boat in Malaysia, but privileged to be white males raised with means in North America, with opportunities open to only a very small percentage of human beings. We didn't have to struggle to feed ourselves or to keep our families safe. We had the luxury of time and comfort, from which we could choose the actions we took.

Chris asserted that everyone has choices about how they want to live; whether they want to live within the norms of our society or live in some other way and/or place. Tim vehemently disagreed, asserting that most people have no such choice, because they are so exploited by our capitalist culture that their reality doesn't extend past their next paycheck and car payment; forget dropping into some other place and culture. Tim seemed to believe we carry a responsibility to take direct action to right wrongs (he was quick to admit he wasn't presently doing so), while Chris seemed to believe his responsibility lay in learning more about spiritual/mystical realms beyond what our brains readily perceive, and then look again at the question.

I found another difference of opinion between the two very interesting. Chris asserted that most people act like robots, being reactive to incoming stimuli, rather than making choices from a more aware state. He saw his current "job" as expanding his awareness and growing personally beyond the robotic condition. Tim believed that if people act like robots it is because they have been treated like robots by our exploitative capitalist corporations, and he saw focusing on personal awareness as a narcissistic excuse for doing nothing to improve the lot of the oppressed. Beyond this being a very entertaining conversation, it made me wonder...do people have to grow in some spiritual sense to live a fulfilling life? Or do they only need an environment where they are valued and not worked to exhaustion?

From there we worked our way to the topic of denialism… How can people still watch professional football, Tim asked, when they know that a third of the players will suffer serious brain injury? Whatever the mechanism is that allows people to enjoy the football game, he asserted, it is the same mechanism that has us ignore the oppression of the working-class people of the world…

Another night we had cocktails aboard *Tahawus*, and I expected some fireworks with Tim and Norm being in the same space. Norm leans to the right, while Tim obviously leans left. To my great surprise there were no fireworks when the subject of Bernie Sanders came up. While Norm didn't have the passion for Bernie that Tim had, he did think Bernie was the best of the available candidates for president.

Since politics didn't generate much heat, the conversation moved on to Islam, and the subjugation of women in Muslim culture. Here Chris asserted in essence that we Westerners should keep our noses out of a culture that we don't understand. That Western interventions, thinking we know what other cultures should do, have led to terrible things (the destruction of most of the American Indian cultures, for example). We should at least tread lightly, and not assume we have the answers. This led to the never-before-seen bonding of Tim and Norm jointly standing against a common enemy…uh…that is…fellow BPO rally member, citing examples of women being stoned, and being treated as whores if they didn't wear the required uniform, and having to walk four steps behind their men, and not being allowed to drive, and not being given access to education. Should we take some action about all this? Do we display our Western culture as an example of what's possible, and help others move toward it if they think it is an improvement? How do we reconcile the extreme examples of subjugation of Muslim women with the many happy and well-educated women we met in Indonesia?

Oddly, perhaps, that conversation made me think of the South Pacific Islanders, whether Marquesans or Tongans or Tuvaluans, where most of the people seemed to be very happy, content with their lives. But now comes TV and the Internet, and young people longing to travel to Los Angeles so they can do serious shopping! Sowing seeds of discontent, it seems. Is there a similar impact of Western society seeping into the Muslim world? Leading women to want equality and education sounds like a good thing. But are we also increasing the level of unhappiness? Maybe sowing seeds of discontent is a good thing, when big change is what's needed…?

Whether it was societal responsibilities or politics or religion, one member of our crew saw the need for class revolution; the other looked to personal awareness. One said expand consciousness of the evils of the exploitation of the many by the few; the other said expand your personal consciousness to experience dimensions beyond our limited/limiting minds. It looked like I was in for an interesting four months!

≈≈≈

Our introduction to Thailand was touristy, but much more international than Malaysia. As soon as we cleared in at Ko Lipe we found an ATM and got a local SIM card and bought smoothies and had dinner at a beachfront restaurant.

Wind was rare in the northeast monsoon season. We motored a few miles to a place reputed to have excellent snorkeling. The snorkeling was only fair, but it was wonderful to spend some time in the water. The days were all about the heat, and largely the nights as well. At 9pm it was comfortable below only with a fan on. It was slightly more pleasant on deck, but there one was accosted by brilliant lights of squid fishing boats all around.

We took a mooring at a national park for a night. We wondered how well maintained it might be. The water was 80 feet deep and not very clear, so we had no way to inspect. No problem, for us. But we met the crew of another catamaran that used a similar mooring, and during the night found themselves on the reef. They were lucky that all they lost was one propeller.

Another engine problem arose. Our control unit began giving an alarm that it couldn't shift the port engine in/out of gear. While on our mooring, once things cooled off a bit in the evening, we removed the shifter control cable and found that indeed it was nearly impossible to move the shifter lever. We decided to go back to the mechanic Tim had used in Langkawi. We didn't bother to clear out of Thailand or into Malaysia. Unlikely that anyone would notice or care. The mechanic fixed us up, a minor corrosion problem. Chris was beginning to understand the cruiser's definition of cruising…

We took the dinghy up a river on Ko Tarutao, to see the Crocodile Cave. (They say there have been no crocs for many years.) You tie the dinghy to a dock in the jungle and follow a short trail to the cave mouth. There you climb aboard a plastic raft and pull yourself through the cave via a rope. 100+ meters into the darkness, you climb through knee-deep muck onto dry (but very dark) land, and continue on into a large cavern. Interesting limestone formations; bats on the ceilings. But in the cavern the air felt old and thick, and I began to feel dizzy. I was happy to turn back.

At the river mouth we stopped at the park facility to get a cold drink. We met a German man who had been traveling around SE Asia alone for five years. Living simply. A Buddhist. Staying in a tent on the beach. Said he had lost faith in America, since George Bush's reelection. He couldn't believe Trump was taken seriously, but on the other hand he thought no president could do much on his own (as the thwarting of Obama had shown), so it didn't make much difference. We didn't hang out for long, but I felt a connection with him. He seemed to emerge from another world of simple solo traveling, smile, sip his hot water, and quietly retreat back to his world.

We got underway for Ko Bulan Le, about ten miles north. The breeze was directly on our nose, so we motored. But there was a breeze! So nice. We needed to charge batteries and make fresh water anyway. We anchored and swam ashore to look around at a pretty beach. There was a little resort with a restaurant. Trip Advisor said that almost everybody loved the place, if you're looking for a very quiet, very remote island vacation.

There was one other sailboat anchored, and it was incredibly small – maybe 26'. Ashore there was a long-haired weathered graybeard, snoozing in the meager shade of an inflatable kayak. Had to be the sailor! I chatted with him. He left Belgium 21 years ago and was slowly working his way around the world! I told him we left the USA 14 months ago, to which he replied, "Zoom!" Another interesting spirit of simplicity, low impact, quiet. I asked if he would return to Belgium, and he said, "Belgium is good for beer, mostly. No, I'm not going back."

Tim made a delightful fish and mushroom curry dinner. It was pleasantly cool at sunset. The islands visible in the northern distance had a dramatic appearance, raising my desire to explore further. And to make the day complete, I was *so* happy I wasn't aboard the tiny boat next to us, 21 years into a voyage with no end in sight!

We picked up a very well-maintained mooring off of beautiful Ko Rok Nai. We had heard about good snorkeling on the reef, and sure enough – it made our top-five list of underwater theaters. The water was clear, and both the fish and the coral won awards. One fish was all bright purple on its sides, with a streak of yellow along its top and bottom, with a black and white face. From time to time I nearly laughed out loud, despite my mask and snorkel, because I recognized some crazy-looking fish from the animated movie Finding Nemo!

Thankfully we did our swimming early, because as we were wrapping up, tour boats were arriving from all directions, and the reefs got crowded. We moved east, to Ko Muk, anchored off the beach, dinghied ashore, had drinks at a resort, bought half a cake for Chris's birthday, and took Chris out to a delightful dinner on a deck high on the rocks overlooking the cove.

Nearby was the Emerald Cave. After our experience with the tour boats we were motivated for an early start. We picked up a mooring and swam to the barely-noticeable cave mouth, uncertain if we were in the right place. Despite the diminutive entrance, we continued to swim into the cave and the passage stretched on for 80 meters. The route went around corners so we needed a waterproof flashlight in the darkness. Then daylight appeared ahead, and we swam out of the darkness into a hidden paradise formed at the center of an old volcano. The water ended at a little soft sand beach inside. Rock walls towered straight up all around, with a patch of distant sky above. The only access was the way we had come. Trees and vines clung to the vertical walls. It was cool and quiet and magical. We lingered, letting the serenity of this world-apart wash over us. When a stream of kayakers began to arrive, we left quickly; we wanted to remember this amazing place empty, silent.

We sailed up the ten-mile-long west side of Ko Lanta. I had never done cruising like this before – anchoring most anywhere off of beautiful islands and eating dinner ashore night after night. But why not? The food was good, and cheap, and the weather was…shall I say…steady? That is, it was too hot and not enough wind. But because of these conditions we anchored off of any beach, even where there wasn't any protection. If the wind died and the boat turned sideways to the small seas, it might get a little bumpy at night. But nothing worrisome. There hadn't been a hint of rain, and barely even a cloud, since I arrived in Malaysia.

We did have one problem, but it was of our own doing. Returning to the beached dinghy after dinner and gelato, we found that the tide/waves had risen just enough to splash over the side. The dinghy was full of water; our gas tank and battery box and other gear were floating in it. Luckily nothing had floated out.

We tried to pull the boat clear of the waves but we couldn't budge it with its load of water ballast. Chris went back to a shop to borrow a bucket; I manned our pump. Waves continued to splash in, but between the two of us we bailed faster than they splashed, and we got ourselves launched and clear of the beach. To our delight the electric start still functioned and the motor came right to life. No harm done.

Bad Day

The day started with receiving an email from the British Foreign Office, denying us permission to visit Chagos (in the middle of the Indian Ocean). I think it was incredibly inhospitable for them to say we cannot stop over at their little atoll for a break on an ocean passage! I couldn't imagine why they would say no to us, but it certainly colored my image of the British administration.

Next we learned that one of us had nudged our drinking water valve, and during the night we had unknowingly emptied 20 gallons of fresh water down the drain. Hence we had to tolerate the banging of the watermaker for 4 hours to replenish the supply.

We motored to Phi Phi Dom, a popular tourist spot where we thought we might get lunch and top up our cell data plan. It turned out to be *too* popular – ferries and longtail boats coming and going constantly, buzzing right past us as we headed in. We thought it might be more peaceful at the head of the bay, but it only got worse. We turned around and left.

I was excited about continuing on to Ko Hong, a very dramatic set of islands 20 miles east of Phuket. Along the way I noticed that our batteries didn't seem to be charging. Ironically we had a good sailing breeze for almost the first time, but we ran the engine anyway, trying to test the battery controller and alternators to see what was wrong. My concern was heightened when I discovered that the starter battery isolator switch had been left in the wrong position, so our starter battery also had very little juice. There was a risk that all batteries would be drained so low that we couldn't start an engine…

We made it to Ko Hung and were surprised to find a restaurant there. It turned out to be relatively expensive and the food was mediocre. And there were mosquitos. Oh well – a good day to have behind us.

We changed plans, reluctantly foregoing the inviting islands ahead, and made for the Royal Phuket Marina, where we would be able to find a mechanic. The marina was crazy expensive. And our first night there was miserably hot, with mosquitos (potentially carrying dengue fever and malaria, of course).

I lay awake much of the night thinking about our electrical system. Could the belts be slipping on the alternators? I had dismissed this idea because the problem occurred on both sides. But identifying nothing else that we could fix ourselves, I replaced the port side belt in the morning, and behold! we got a steady charge on that side!

So we tried the starboard side, but the belt there was nearly new and replacing it made no difference. My next thought was that the starboard alternator was fried. We had a spare alternator that had been rebuilt in Panama but which had never been tested. We took out the old alternator and we asked a local guy to test both the old and the rebuilt one. He said the old one looked very bad; he thought we should put in the rebuilt one. He would get back to us with a price to fix the old one, which might take a few days.

So we installed the rebuilt alternator. The result? The engine wouldn't start! It wouldn't even turn over. Thinking our rebuilt alternator must somehow be mis-wired, we disconnected all its wires and tried to start the engine with effectively no alternator at all. *Still* wouldn't turn over! Now what?! We were almost at wit's end. We were paying big bucks to stay in a fancy/miserable marina full of mosquitos and no wind, and we didn't have a working engine and we didn't understand why and we didn't know whom to contact about it for help. For maybe the second time on the trip, I was ready to quit and go home.

I hoped I had "hit bottom" emotionally and would soon be on the rise. Ironically, we had hit bottom on the way in to the marina and were stuck in the mud until the tide rose.

Even though it seemed that our engine problems must relate to swapping the alternator, we tried replacing the starter motor with a spare. (Yes, Chris White, sometimes you DO have the spare parts you need, and it IS worth carrying the extra weight aboard.) The engine started right up! And the rebuilt alternator put a good charge to the batteries. Suddenly we were back on track, again in control of our destiny.

We got a crew working on our cracked pilothouse window. They ran off to buy new glass, but upon return they said it would take ten days to get our desired tempered or laminated glass. They knew we were in a hurry, so they brought heavy window glass. We considered that unsafe and sent them off again to find the thickest acrylic sheet they could find. They returned with a nicely cut piece, but it was not thick enough to generate the level of confidence we wanted to have at sea. Plus the tint was darker than our other windows. Our pilothouse now had a black eye.

For safety we kept the original sheet of glass, plus we procured a sheet of plywood big enough to cover any broken window in an emergency. This was something we would have to fix again, perhaps back in the USA, but for the time being we had done the best we could.

We didn't want to wait for the alternator repair. We arranged to meet the guy at Ao Chalong, where we would be clearing out of Thailand in a few days. We gave him the bad starter motor to rebuild, too.

We learned that we were entitled to free chilled coconuts, as a benefit of paying big bucks to stay in the marina. That was a delightful perk! I could almost learn to like it there, if money were no object and we had A/C on the boat…

And Then There Were Two

Tahawus decided to stay in SE Asia for another year, or longer. The BPO now consisted of *Maggie* and *No Regrets*. We had a goodbye dinner in Ao Chalong, along with Daphne and Ruy from *Blue Wind*. Sad to say goodbye to people we had built such a bond with.

And then there were two…crew…on *No Regrets*. Chris announced that he was feeling claustrophobic on the boat, and it wasn't his kind of travel. He wanted the low budget backpacker experience. He would leave us in Sumatra. If we didn't find a replacement in time, Tim and I would continue without a third.

We checked out with the Thai authorities. It was the most paper pushing that I'd seen anywhere on the trip! But all in air-conditioned offices, so we didn't care.

We didn't want to actually leave for Sumatra just yet, because we would arrive on Sunday. That meant special fees; Luc advised us not to. Yes, Luc was going to meet us once again in Sabang, our first stop in Sumatra. So we retrieved our rebuilt alternator and starter, and sailed around the south end of Phuket to a neat little anchorage off an almost hidden beach. Tourists came and went constantly in longtail boats until sundown. Everything we saw along the southern Thailand coast was touristy – tour boats by the dozens, resorts and restaurants and bars wherever you look, and local girls hanging out in the bars inviting the foreigners to join them…

I was excited to be moving on. The Thai coast was beautiful, and the people had been sweet. But I never connected much with either, so oppressive was the heat. (End of poetry.)

I had some trepidation about Sumatra based on accounts I had read – people being unfriendly, anchorages not providing shelter from sudden squalls. But, as they say, "your mileage may vary" – we would have our own experience.

≈≈≈

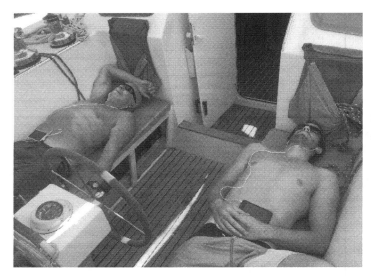

Trying to beat the heat

Thailand is definitely *not* a Muslim country!

SUMATRA

Sumatra is one of the 6,000 inhabited Indonesian islands. Population 50 million. The eastern side of Sumatra borders the Malacca Straits, famous for its volume of shipping and history of piracy. The western side of Sumatra borders on the Indian Ocean. It has legendary surfing, made famous by the Endless Summer and other surfer films. Although we were "returning" to Indonesia, our time in Sumatra would be nothing like the whirlwind tour of Indonesia-to-the-East that Luc led us through. That is, except for our first stop in Sabang, where Luc was once again meeting us.

We had a good crossing from Phuket to Sabang. We had some wind, and it was nice to only motor some of the way. We mostly sailed with just our working jib – slow but easy and comfortable, and about at *Maggie*'s speed. No encounters with pirates in the Malacca Strait…

Various authorities came aboard in Sabang. The quarantine people went looking for 'expired' medications and cans of food. They didn't find any out-of-date food, but they found lots of out-of-date medications, which they confiscated. Luc said their concern was that we might give old medications to Indonesian residents, and among their many regulations there was one prohibiting bringing these things into the country. No matter that Tim pulled up a medical journal with a study showing that 90% of medications are still effective 15 years after their expiry dates!

What did matter was that the government was trying to promote tourism, and welcome yachts, and Luc was connected with the officials in charge of that. When Luc told them what happened, they pressured the quarantine folks to return our medications just before we departed Sabang. We had to promise that we wouldn't let officials elsewhere in Sumatra see the items, since regulations were being violated in letting us keep them. There were four other yachts in the harbor, and one of them was not so lucky. The quarantine guy apologetically asked if there was anything in their old meds they couldn't do without. The skipper got his EpiPen back. Then the official poured gasoline on the rest and lit it! Obviously the effort to be more welcoming to yachts was still a work in progress.

Some of the authorities who came aboard asked for beer. I wasn't prepared for that. The area was very strictly Muslim, and alcohol was illegal except at resorts. I gave them each a can of beer. I should have said no, and offered soda instead. Luckily, there were no repercussions.

Most important for successful clearance, I had my new "boat stamp." While I was home, I ordered this rubber ink stamp via the Internet, and it turned out to be essential in dealing with the Sumatran authorities. It simply had the name and documentation number of the boat, but it conveyed "official." Lots and lots of multi-copy forms, and they wanted the boat stamp on each copy.

One other glitch checking in. Tim had removed our American flag and put up a United Nations flag instead. This didn't go over well with the officials. We were told later in the day to please fly our proper country flag. Again, no repercussions beyond some scowls.

After dealing with the officials, Luc had a little tour bus pick us up, plus the crews of *Maggie* and new friends aboard *Gaia*. Off we went to lunch. Then to a bank with ATMs to get our Rupiah. Then to a tiny museum (locked; hasty phone calls to get someone to open it). Then to the open market to get some fruit. Then back to the harbor so we could nap before going out to dinner. It was fun to hear the comments of Jim and Helen on *Gaia*, "We've been cruising for 21 years, and never had all our needs met on Day One like this before. Maybe there is something to be said for participating in a Rally!"

To understand Sumatra you had to think tsunami. Recent history was divided into BT and AT – before or after the tsunami of 2004. Sabang had many structures erased, but it was not deadly. On the nearby "mainland" of Banda Aceh many thousands were killed. The total number of people who died on Sumatra that day was close to 200,000!

We visited a junior high school. The kids we met with were only 3 years old when the tsunami hit, but they knew their family stories. One girl told of her father feeling the big earthquake and hurrying the family to high ground. But her brother was off playing, nowhere to be seen. A tourist risked his life to search for him but couldn't find him. Later they learned he had gone to higher ground with other villagers, and everyone was safe.

Our guide also shared his tsunami story. He was on Banda Aceh, and saw many people killed, even though he was a kilometer inland! People in his family were lost. He said he was very depressed for months, until his faith pulled him out of it. That got Tim's attention; Tim jumped right in there with the question: how did he reconcile such a disaster with his faith in Allah? The answer was that the Quran says "disasters are caused by our own hand." He believed that mankind was not living right, and God was providing a warning or correction.

Several people acknowledged positive things coming from the disaster – much of it in the form of outside help from NGOs and foreign aid and agencies like the American Red Cross. It was hard to imagine the impact of the tsunami. We ate at one beachside restaurant that had BT and AT pictures posted. The AT one showed a foundation – nothing more.

At the junior high school, we tried to discuss climate change with the kids. But they spoke almost no English, and our translators had an annoying practice of answering our questions themselves rather than relaying them to the kids. We learned a little...most of their fathers fished...they liked to swim and snorkel...and ride bicycles. But they were so shy, we couldn't get them to ask us any questions. Very frustrating! They were beautiful, and I hope they enjoyed having an unusual day at school. One group came up with an interesting idea after we learned that they still didn't have an adequate tsunami warning system. Why not use the mosques, which were everywhere and all had blaring speaker systems, to spread the warning?

This part of Indonesia was almost entirely Muslim, and strict about the rules. One female guide/translator declined to shake hands – no contact with men other than her husband. But for the most part the customs were similar to the areas we visited five months before. A group of young ladies working at a restaurant giggled when I came in and indicated that they liked my beard. That happened once before back in Tual. Okay by me!

Crew Update

Probably it was for the best that Chris left. He got seasick in relatively mild conditions. I doubted that was the major concern, though. He said he felt claustrophobic on the boat. I suspected this had more to do with Tim than with cabin space. Tim treated him like a son whose behavior he disapproved of. Loving, but Tim repeatedly brought up the question of what Chris was doing to right the wrongs of the world, and admonished him that his "inner journey" was self-indulgent and pointless.

Chris didn't seem to have the self-assurance to say something to the effect of, "Tim, this is what I am currently up to, and I'd like your support; or at least respect my choices and back off on the criticism." Instead they would re-engage in the discussion, in one form or another, until Chris was fatigued. I could take some blame, too, given that I stayed out of it and just watched and listened. I probably could have made the same statement above on Chris' behalf, with some effect.

Tim was angry at Chris for backing out. I was angry at Tim for driving Chris out. But it was a relief when Chris left. I silently forgave Tim for being the crazy-but-wonderful man that he is. We moved on.

We needed crew. How do you get someone to fly to Sumatra on short notice, and sail with strangers on a boat across the Indian Ocean? One answer is that you list with a service called Offshore Passage Opportunities. People who wish to crew pay to subscribe. We could list for free. Here's what they sent to their subscribers:

> *Padang Sumatra to Mauritius*– We have a crew request for Zeke Holland. He is presently on an around the world passage with Jimmy Cornell's Blue Planet Odyssey. He knows this is short notice for a passage that starts and ends so far away, so he says he is not looking for crew to pay boat expenses, but you do have to get to and from the boat. If you are interested please e-mail Zeke with a brief resume and questions (like where in the heck is Padang). Please note that it might take a little bit of time for him to respond since he cannot get to the internet every day. He e-mailed:

> "Chris White Atlantic 42 catamaran seeking 3rd crew from Padang, Sumatra, May 1, to Mauritius (perhaps via Cocos Keeling) around July 1. Candidates must have a little offshore experience and be comfortable in the galley (cooking is shared). The boat has the expected equipment for a circumnavigation: watermaker...AIS...radar...chart plotters in both the cockpit and the pilothouse...fridge/freezer...wind, solar and hydro generators...life raft. Accommodations are basic but comfortable."

We got one serious response. TC was Australian born, living in France, working in England; he was a contract lawyer who worked half the year and found sailing opportunities for the other half. Good sailing experience. References. He could meet us before we left Sumatra. I was ready to sign him on, but Tim wanted to know more, and sent this email:

> Zeke tells me you've been corresponding and that you are pretty eager to join the remains of the Blue Planet Odyssey (with only two boats remaining I've labeled it the Blue Planet Oddity). I'm encouraged and hope things work to make it happen. I'll leave it to Zeke to "vet" your sailing skills and history. For me, I'm just as interested in you as a day in day out companion in a smallish environment so I'd appreciate your telling us a little about your non-sailing interests: food, music, hygiene, literature, politics, philosophy/religion, people you admire/worship, thinking about climate change and its causes and possible solutions, the current US presidential race. Just throwing out a pretty pedestrian list of stuff so please feel free to add other items about yourself and your life that might give us a fuller sense of our potential boat mate. And feel free to ask questions of your own.

In fairness, let me say that I am a sort of deck-side Marxist, atheist, and reader of mostly non-fiction stuff such as Naomi Klein. You read her? I am not terribly hopeful about our species (reading The Sixth Extinction for the second time) with a current maybe overly intense fascination with the complicated although seemingly ubiquitous state of global denial about a variety of social/environmental/philosophical issues. Blah blah.

I'll save you my rants although, if you join, I hope you're up for discussions on all things globe threatening or changing.

I feared Tim might scare away our one good prospect. But when TC took Tim's questions in stride, I was confident things would work out. He and Tim had a chat via Skype, and we all said yes.

Meanwhile, there was the matter of crew for the following leg from Mauritius to Brazil. I received word from Bob that he would not be joining for that leg. But I had a new lead. Nora, Bill's daughter, who had sailed with us for a week on the US East Coast, said she would like to join for that leg. This was a surprise and a conundrum. For starters, she was not ready to commit. She had applied for a job. If accepted, that would take precedence over sailing.

I wasn't ready to commit either. Although Nora knew how to sail, and was somewhat familiar with the boat, she had no offshore experience. She had been very seasick when she was aboard, and she readily admitted that this was a recurring problem. Then there were interpersonal questions. Was I willing to spend months with a beautiful young woman aboard? Would Bill like or dislike the idea of her joining, especially for the potentially rough weather around South Africa? Tim was outspokenly against the idea. His stated reason was her inexperience, but when he said it I sensed that he didn't think it would go well to have a beautiful young woman aboard. He would indicate his disapproval at every opportunity, even though he would follow by saying it was my decision. I couldn't help but think: what if something terrible happened? Bill would blame me for failing to protect his daughter, and Tim would be pointing the I-told-you-so finger.

Nora said she could commit in two months. I had other things to focus on in the meantime.

Trying to Leave Sabang

We thought we were free to leave Sabang at any time, but Luc told us that the Harbormaster wanted to give us a port clearance paper. Tim dropped me ashore near the Harbormaster's office, and waited in the dinghy for what we thought would be a short and simple matter...

I thought they would be expecting me, but instead it was a challenge to get across why I was there. I was granted an audience with the Harbormaster. I explained that we wished to leave for Padang, with stops along the way. It turns out you cannot specify Padang as your next port, apparently because it has multiple locations/harbors, and you have to be more specific. I had heard of one of the choices, so I picked that.

I filled out the departure form and applied my boat stamp. He pulled out a *No Regrets* file and inspected it in detail. Why did my crew list show two people but we arrived with three? I pantomimed that Chris took off in an airplane to go (eventually) home. He called Immigration to check on this. Okay, no problem.

But wait, what about my name…? One form showed my middle name, another didn't. He looked at my passport, and again things seemed to be okay. Then he called in someone who spoke a little English, and the two of them had a long and serious-sounding discussion, in Indonesian. After several minutes I interrupted to ask my 'translator' to explain the issue to me. "Oh, we are talking about a Thai boat that came in recently and broke many rules. We're not talking about you." Then he said we were done. I asked if the Harbormaster wasn't going to give me a clearance paper, and he said no, all done. My translator got up to leave, and I started to follow, when the Harbormaster called me back, pointing to a pad of clearance forms and saying something that I imagined would translate to, "Where do you think you're going? You need a clearance paper, fool!"

Then he called Quarantine, and one of their guys appeared. I needed to go to his office. No, not when done with the Harbormaster. Now. Off we went, and he and two very pleasant associates started filling out forms. One was actually completed on a typewriter, for those who know what that is! Many signatures and stamps, and then the forms were assembled into a "health book" that I was to show authorities on our way south, should any authorities care to intercept us. Next he pulled out a ledger and started writing out the fee for each form. At this I objected, saying we were told we had no fees to pay. "No, not you, Captain. You do not pay. The officials in the blue building pay us." I was dismissed with smiles and my health book, and walked back to the Harbormaster office.

The Harbormaster handed me the clearance form and said it cost $5 US. I explained that I didn't have US money, and he agreed to accept 40,000 Rupiah (about $3). However, I only had a 100,000 note. I showed it to him but didn't hand it over, asking if he could make change. Another guy in the office, who had become my new translator, handed me 50,000 in exchange for the note. Close enough. All done? Yes, but the Harbormaster would like a gift of $1 US. I tried not to lose my cool (actually, had been trying for the past hour). Nodding toward the payment just made I said, "Didn't I just provide a gift?"

"No problem, Captain. It is not required. Goodbye, and I hope you have enjoyed Sabang."

All part of the adventure. Frustrating, especially with the language barrier, but I had become much more relaxed about it than at the start. Worst case it would delay us a day and cost a few dollars. At least, I guessed that was the worst case. I suppose they could have thrown us in jail for giving beer to locals. On that subject I did one thing right. On the Customs forms filled out on entry, there was a question: "Alcohol in cargo." They could see we had alcohol, but I told them we didn't have any "cargo," and wrote "None." They warned me that all alcohol must remain aboard. One of the other boats made the mistake of listing two cases of beer in the "cargo" section. Their beer was confiscated.

≈≈≈

By noon Tim and I were underway, with no plan yet for where we were going. There were some islands a dozen miles southwest, with no description in our very limited cruising guide. It seemed surprising that no one had mentioned this enticing area; we headed that way. We had a little wind, and finally tried out the spinnaker that I had carried to Panang from home. It seemed to be in good shape, and we had a fine sail.

The sun was low when we reached the islands and hunted for a protected anchorage. We were approached by a fishing boat carrying two young men; we tried to ask if it was okay to anchor there. I wasn't sure they understood, but they said no. I pointed to the next spot west, and they nodded yes. They waited while we anchored and then came alongside (banging into us). They asked for drinks. We said no. They asked for ice, which made us laugh. We have a freezer, but not one effective enough for making ice. They left.

It was a touch unnerving, as we were now in a *very* remote area. No boats except an occasional local fishing boat, and no signs of civilization ashore. We would be completely vulnerable if someone came with ill intent. I found in such situations that the only thing to do was to trust in the goodness of people. And we had encountered nothing but good, half the world around.

That night there were strange creatures making thin phosphorescent scribbles in the water. Random hairline trails of light. If I shined a flashlight at one, there would be no creature visible, and the trail would be erased. But as soon as the light was out a little scribble would slowly begin again, and forge a crooked path a couple feet long. There were dozens of these wispy trails alongside us. I never did figure out what made them.

To Mainland Sumatra

In the morning a few fishing boats came by to check us out; all just waved and moved on. We set sail and headed south to mainland Sumatra. The west coast of Sumatra is a surfer's paradise. We hailed an anchored catamaran for local advice and learned that the Australian owner had been cruising/surfing the area for twelve years. He warned us that we were at a beach that was popular with the locals, and it could get busy/noisy. That sounded okay, though we weren't prepared for the kids who piled into our dinghy when we launched it from the beach, or the teenagers on inflatable torpedoes zooming by, with those in the tow boat taking photos of them and us.

This entire area had been erased by the tsunami. It took a direct hit. About a third of the population was killed! It was very hard to imagine. It was beautiful there, and the beach was crowded with kids playing. Tim took a taxi into the city of Banda Aceh to see the Tsunami Museum. In the city there was a huge barge that was washed five kilometers inland (!), left there as a monument. I decided to forego the photos and maps and statistics and monuments, and just try to commune with the wonder and power of the natural forces of our planet. A little challenging when being constantly buzzed by teenagers wanting me to pose in their pictures…but…all part of the adventure…

Mind-Fullness

The mind is an amazing tool, but one that might be improved with an OFF switch.

Our boat batteries needed replacing. They were an unusual model, not readily procured outside the USA. Tim suggested we call a distributor in Australia to see if we could get them shipped to Cocos Keeling – remote islands belonging to Australia, where we planned to visit if the wind blew favorably. This seemed to be our best hope. But my mind went to the perhaps unfavorable wind. We could have $3,000 worth of batteries waiting for us at Cocos Keeling, and be beating into headwinds until we gave up and just headed west across the ocean, leaving them behind!

We left the overpopulated beach and motored south against a very light wind. Our boat speed added to the breeze, making it pleasantly comfortable, and the sky became mostly overcast, adding to the coolness. But the wind gradually increased until we were having difficulty motoring into it and its small waves. Here's where my mind went: The northeast monsoon/season changes to southwest that time of year. And the SW winds are stronger and bring rain and squalls. In northern Sumatra, where we were, there are very few anchorages sheltered from the SW. Those that exist, like the one we headed for, are open to the NW, which tends to be the wind direction in the squalls. Maybe this was the start of the SW monsoon, and we were going to have a miserable time trying to get south.

Then the engine unexpectedly slowed down, and simultaneously the alternator stopped charging. After a few seconds it returned to normal, but this repeated several times. I couldn't make sense of it. If the alternator belt had slipped, the engine would have sped up, not slowed down. If perhaps there was a clog in the fuel line, the engine would slow, but that wouldn't cause the alternator to stop charging. We switched to the other engine and had no further problems. Later we ran the first engine for a fifteen-minute test, with no problem! The mystery remained. My mind abhorred such mysteries, and it had me thinking that we had a serious electrical problem that was beyond our ability to troubleshoot, nor would any of the 50 million people in Sumatra know more than we did. Thus it was likely that we were going to have a disabled boat in a no-help place, and the voyage would be over.

As we approached our chosen anchorage the wind was trying to blow us onto rocks. My mind was calculating what we would do if the engine quit at that point. Did we have room to set the jib and jibe away, or would we be ending our adventure on those rocks? We got into the cove with no problem, of course, and we anchored with good protection from the SW. But there was thunder. If we got a NW squall, and the anchor started to drag, we would have very little room to the rocky beach. Well, my mind said that at least that would be the simplest way to end the trip – insurance paying for the boat broken on the rocks, and we just wading ashore and buying a ticket for home.

Not that these thoughts were wrong... It's just that they got in the way of enjoying a pretty day in a pretty anchorage in a very, very foreign place.

Hendra

Another 30 miles down the coast we anchored at Pulau Raya. Two young men in a fishing boat came alongside, and one did not wait to be invited to come aboard. To me this was a major breach of protocol, but he was so charming – and he spoke pretty good English – that I forgave him. His name was Hendra. He taught himself English by speaking with people who came to help after the tsunami, and with yachties. He asked for beer. We lied and said we had none aboard. But we said if he caught a big fish we would buy it from him in the morning.

Tim asked lots of questions, including if there were orangutans in the jungle nearby. "Oh," Hendra says, "I have one of those." I assumed he misunderstood the question. But no. He said he had a two-year-old orangutan that he raised like a member of his family. Tim asked if other people did that. "No, just me." Tim asked if the authorities might not approve of this. "In the city it would be a problem. Here, not a problem."

In the morning the two of them were back, but no large fish. We chatted. They smoked. Tim told them, "Save your money. Save your body." They understood but didn't appear likely to quit the habit. Hendra wanted to know how much a boat like ours cost. I blanked out with the number of zeros on Indonesian currency, while Tim told him 50 million Rupiah. That seemed like a big number to him, and to me. But later I realized it was only about $4,000.

Offshore Islands

Simeulue is the northernmost of a chain of islands 80 miles offshore from "mainland" Sumatra. We poked into an almost land-locked bay to try to anchor where the chart said it was 27 feet deep. There were a few houses/shacks there, and children calling to us from shore, and it looked inviting. But way too deep!

Sure, we could find 27 feet, but a wind change would have put us on shore. We went back outside and anchored along the coast. Fishermen in canoes stared at us.

We motored down the east side of the island to its major town, Sinabang. Despite having 20,000 residents and a commercial harbor, it was not even mentioned in our little cruising guide. The channel was buoyed, which was helpful since the layout didn't correspond very well with our chart. I had to keep reminding myself not to take the charts too seriously here.

We went ashore and had an Indonesian dinner, bought ice cream for dessert, got bread, and gasoline for the dinghy. Lots of young boys wanting money, or whatever was in our shopping bag, or to swim with our life jackets from the dinghy. One kid was very persistent, and he seemed to think if he said something enough times I would understand him. Exasperated, I started speaking to him in the same manner in English. It was absurd and funny, especially when a teenager thoughtfully explained to me, "He not understand what you say!"

The teenager and a buddy of his were sweet. He wanted to ask me questions but was very unsure about his English. His friend knew more English words but he was too shy to speak to me. So they would confer about how to form a question, and the outgoing one would ask it. One thing they asked, which surprised me, was my age. When I told him 62, he didn't believe me – he thought I must mean 42!

I was happy to leave Sinabang. Too much commotion when we went ashore. Especially when we walked by a school where the kids apparently were on recess! A cacophony of shrieks and "Hey, Mister!" and "What is your name?" Almost everyone was friendly, although we did have two young men flip us the finger as they went by on a motorbike. I also noticed an older woman give a disapproving stare at Tim's legs. His shorts were too short, plus his shirt nearly covered the shorts, so the net result was probably disrespectful.

We headed south to the islands of Belayar, into a passage between the two islands that gradually got narrower but remained deep. We anchored in a nook among mangroves, with no sign of humanity in sight. But we could hear the distant town sounds – an occasional vehicle, and the ubiquitous call to prayer.

I was awoken in the morning by Tim talking with two fishermen in a canoe.

They had a good-sized red snapper, and we bought it from them with the proviso that they fillet it for us. Well, I don't think fillet is in the Indonesian language or culture, but they did cut it into manageable pieces. They asked for food, and we invited them aboard for PB&J's. Tim loaded them up with crackers and snacks before they left. They wanted to know what our various electronics and winches did; it was fun trying to communicate that without a shared language.

We continued south to Lasia. Beautiful and empty. We swam ashore and walked on the soft white sand beach. Lasia was the first place we had been in Sumatra that had no cell/data connection at all. For one night I couldn't play "Words with Friends" with Hallie. "WWF" is an online Scrabble-like game, and Hallie and I had been playing it as a way of being together. I missed having that connection with her!

We sailed east to the Banjak island group. Had another visit from fishermen. We declined the big octopus they wanted to sell, but we had a chat, with assistance from an English-Indonesian dictionary. Other fishermen passing by asked for beer. We always said no. There was good cell/data connectivity once again. Made chicken and pasta, rather than fish and rice, for a change.

Next day we sailed right into a squall that lasted half the day. First really heavy rain since forever. Took advantage and washed my sheets. I expected sunshine an hour later for the dry cycle but didn't get it. Things did dry out in late afternoon, just in time to have sheets to sleep on.

Sailed to the Bay of Plenty surfing spot. About a dozen surfers there, some from a big power catamaran where I imagined they lived aboard for a week or two. There was a surfer's guest house ashore. Possibly we could get a meal there, but it didn't seem worth the effort to rig the dinghy and go exploring to find out. After a busy sailing day it was nice just to be at rest in a beautiful anchorage.

A canoe paddled toward us, and to my great surprise I saw it was paddled by a bule (white person). His name was John, from Florida. He worked at the surfer camp six months of the year, and had for several years. He said he had never seen an American boat come into the bay! It was fun and refreshing to speak English. I invited him aboard, but he had things to do.

Tim and I watched a movie, which was becoming a common evening activity. The bugs convinced us to stop before the end, put screens in and retreat to our cabins. I wanted to read, but I didn't want to use the light and attract the bugs to my berth. I wanted to continue my online game with Hallie, but we had no internet connection here. As my mother used to say, mockingly, "It's a tough life!"

Well, it was a strange life. In some ways it was a cruising paradise. No other yachts. Beautiful islands. Squally, but warm, and so far nothing overpowering. On the other hand, it was constant unknowns, running out of provisions with no immediate prospect for resupply, no restaurants, intense sun, and minimal ability to communicate with the local people. One moment it seemed wonderful, another moment I was awash in discomfort. I was trying to maintain my equanimity for another two weeks until TC would arrive. At that point I knew I would be in prepare-for-the-crossing mode, and I would be fully, contentedly engaged in that process.

Nias Island

We anchored in a beautiful little harbor at Lahewa on the island of Nias. Some boys jumped off the town dock and swam toward us. I was hesitant to let them climb aboard, but some of the kids were very young and they had to swim a long way. So I extended a welcome. More followed in their wake. Before long there were twenty kids aboard! It was a challenge to eventually get them all headed shoreward again.

We were tempted to leave the next morning. But we had spoken with the Harbormaster about maybe arranging a ride for us into Gunungsitoli (the big city of Nias, population 125,000), with an English-speaking driver. We had to go ashore to see the Harbormaster anyway, as he was holding our clearance papers.

There were several people in the Harbormaster's office, and we sat and chatted. After some coffee he asked if we wanted to go to the city; he would drive us himself for 600,000 Rupiah (about $50). We decided yes. But first Tim asked if we could complete our clearance, since we would leave the following morning. Yes, he said, but there was a minor problem… We had cleared out of Sabang for Padang, not for Lahewa, so we weren't really supposed to be there. But not to worry, he said. We would pay a small fine to make it right.

"How big is the fine?" I asked.

"Well," he sat back in his chair, "That's up to you."

Okay, I was a little slow, but now I understood the nature of our "fine." The key point was not really what it said on our papers, but that our papers were in his possession! I suggested 50,000 (about $4), a figure I had read in someone's notes about cruising in Indonesia. He asked if we had American money – $5 would be good. We didn't have American money with us.

But wait! There had been a soggy $5 bill in the seat of our dinghy since before we left the USA! I didn't remember how it got there, but we left it there as "mad money," and this was the perfect opportunity to use it. After a quick trip to the dinghy, everyone was satisfied. We got our clearance papers and piled into his air-conditioned car for the two-hour drive to Gunungsitoli.

The road was good – it was built after the tsunami. But there were many little bridges, and the roadbuilders didn't extend their good work to those bits. Tim suggested they didn't get enough money from Jakarta, and I think our host was a little offended by that. He said no, that workers in Indonesia sometimes just say, "Good enough; I'm going home."

The tsunami was not devastating here like it was in Aceh. Destructive, yes. But here the tsunami of 2004 was followed by a more deadly earthquake in 2005. What a place to call home!

We visited the Nias Museum. The Islanders had a fascinating culture somewhat like the Marquesans – lots of tribal warfare. Here they didn't eat their enemies, but they hunted heads. They made stone sculptures reminiscent of tikis. They had rugged houses and interesting tools. Nias was only 40% Muslim; it was predominantly Christian. Our driver said they all live together in peace; the kids go to the same schools. But sometimes the government overlooked their needs, he said, because they were "not as Muslim" as most of Indonesia. Houses on Nias all seemed to have electricity, and most sported a TV antenna. Not everyone had water, though. They collected rainwater off the roofs, but when it was dry they sometimes had to buy more.

Tim asked our guide what he thought about the United States. Sometimes good, he said, and sometimes not. He thought Obama was a good president because he did not tell everyone to be the same as Americans. But invading Iraq was the bad side of the US. He had always been interested in the US, since he would occasionally meet Americans on yachts, and once he worked on a tugboat that went to Diego Garcia to help dock a US aircraft carrier! But he said he would never have the money to actually go to the US. Several people had made similar statements, that we had the means to visit Indonesia but they did not have the ability to visit the US.

When Tim got around to the subject of alcohol, our guide told us that Nias had a traditional alcoholic drink distilled from coconut milk. Tim naturally asked how to get some. Well, he had a friend who would meet us if we had cash… Coconut moonshine!

It had been a long and tiring day, so we weren't too happy to look out from the pier and see kids climbing on the boat! They swam away as we approached, but others then swam out. We yelled at anyone who tried to climb aboard. It took several iterations before they gave up and left, so we could sample our moonshine in peace.

Heading down the west coast of Nias from Lahewa, our next stop was Afulu. The entrance was exciting – appearing to have breaking waves all across it. Our cruising guide, limited though it was, gave waypoints for a passage in. Nerve-wracking, but no problem. Once inside, there was a huge peaceful bay.

We stopped at Hinako. This very remote place was made rather eerie by surf breaking in what appeared to be open water, no land in the vicinity. The chart showed shallows at some of those places, but others it showed being deep, which was disconcerting.

We were bound for Lagundri at the south end of Nias. We tuned in to an informal cruiser's "net" on the radio, and learned that another boat, *Convivia*, was also bound for Lagundri, and they were out of fuel. We offered to meet them outside the anchorage and pass them a jerry jug of diesel. As it turned out, they filtered a gallon or so from the dregs in their own jugs and got in without assistance. But they nevertheless invited us over for margaritas!

Todi was a local who paddled out to us on his surfboard. He spoke reasonably good English, though he had the Indonesian habit of saying Yes whenever he didn't understand what we said. We had a long talk with him, including arranging a tour and ride into town, for us and for the four *Convivians*.

In the evening he took us to his family's losman (guesthouse) for dinner. We didn't realize we would be the only ones there. Nor that ordering chicken with our curry noodles meant that they would have to buy/kill/prepare a chicken, and it would take over an hour! No worries, we got to meet Todi's mother, father, and wife, plus they had cold Bintang beer – a treat that we hadn't seen for weeks.

We also didn't realize when we followed Todi's lead to shore that we would be tying the dinghy just off the jagged coral, stepping onto the coral, and walking over 50 yards of coral and mud to get to solid ground. Tim had a case of the shore-sways, perhaps augmented by the margarita, and he went halfway into the drink. I blew out my flip-flop, as the appropriate Jimmy Buffet song goes. After the fine meal and large-size Bintangs, we had to find our way back through the mud and over the coral in the dark. We found the dinghy okay, except that the line tying it to the shore had untied itself, and it was hanging by its stern anchor 50 feet out in deep water. Whatever, a little swim after a big meal…quite nice.

In the morning Todi had a truck and driver lined up. We picked up the *Convivians* and rode through small surf to the beach. Locals helped us pull the dinghy above the high tide line and we were off to town. First stop was a gas station to buy 70 gallons of diesel for *Convivia*, and 10 for us. This was a little dicey because it was not legal for us to buy diesel – the government subsidized the price, and thus it was only for Indonesians. Foreigners had to buy at designated places at higher prices. Of course there was no such place nearby, and besides, the locals wanted to sell us the low-price fuel with their own small markup.

We tried to get a firm price before filling the jugs, and our guide said we could have the pump price (since he was already getting money from us for the truck and driver). But then the gas station wanted extra. Tucker from *Convivia* held the line, giving them a very small bonus, but basically saying no to their requests. Meanwhile our driver was watching a police vehicle fueling, and he looked very worried. We completed the deal, no problems.

After lunch and errands, our guide suggested we go to "The Village." We had no idea what to expect there, but Todi said we could see "stone jumping."

This was a boy's traditional coming of age ritual. The boy had to jump over a two-meter-high stone wall, some say with sharp sticks on the top, some say with no knowledge of what was on the other side (maybe the latter was metaphorical). We also heard it said that a man couldn't marry until he successfully jumped; others laughed at that.

The Village turned out to be atop a mountain. Or at least a very long steep hill, very far from the water. From the crest of the road we walked up 50 or so stone steps, to a remarkable place. It was expansive and very flat, as though the top of the hill had been sheared off or ground down. There was a wide, straight, paved-with-stones "Main Street" stretching out ahead, with houses and shops all along it. Halfway down was the King's house on the left, and a perpendicular street running to the right. I was amazed by the stone paving, and how wide the streets were and how flat. This was clearly a special place, a place of power! And surprisingly far from the sea.

As we walked toward the King's house, we were attacked by men selling traditional (maybe) carvings and necklaces and other souvenirs. They were unrelenting, following us everywhere, asking us to look again at their wares – it was for their children to be able to go to school, some said. I bought a carving and a necklace. In retrospect I might have bought several necklaces, but I felt that once I'd made a purchase I had to say no, no, no, in order to fend off the hoard and be able to breathe.

Having heard so much about the jumping, it seemed obligatory to pay to see a costumed young man jump. It was better in the stories than it was in practice, but I imagine in the days of old it must have been a major event with everyone watching and feasts and parties. Todi's grandfather jumped, so the days of old were only two generations back.

The King's house also served as a community house, hosting feasts. It was built upon colossal tree trunks; it was huge; it was massive; it had a very solid, very flat wooden floor. The whole Village seemed like a museum, but the houses (except the King's) were lived in. Not much interpretation/history was provided. The Village was one of the most impressive sights I had seen on our entire voyage, and I hadn't even known it existed.

We were thinking of renting surfboards for a first-ever try at surfing. But first there was a leaky hatch to repair. And more research into a possible battery replacement configuration. And I wanted to replace the fuel filters on the starboard side, because that engine seemed to labor at times. That turned into a long hot messy process, as did trying to bleed the fuel system after, and get the engine to start.

Then Todi came by for a visit, paddling his surfboard with one hand because he had my sandals in the other. He had seen my "blowouts," and had offered to get them fixed for $2. He delivered them back repaired and asserted they were "very strong," which indeed they proved to be.

I wanted to clean some of the beard off our waterline, and say goodbye to our new friends on *Convivia*. And go aloft to check that lines weren't chafing at the masthead. So…we didn't get surfing. That was disappointing, since we were at a primo surfing destination. On the other hand, we weren't going to get our first lesson out on the big reef break, but on the tiny beach break, which was certainly not what the primo surfers came here for!

TC and a Little Regret

TC had agreed to meet us at Tua Pejat, capital of the Mentawai Islands, south of Nias. It would have been easier for him to meet us in the big city of Padang, but this way he could get a little local cruising in before we began our ocean passage. We could get to know each other, and he could get to know the boat.

Padang would be our point of departure from Indonesia. Luc would meet our fleet of two there and help us with the authorities. Upon departure we would anchor at one or more Indonesian islands on our way out/south, even though technically we weren't supposed to after clearing out. We needed to work our way south to get out of the Inter-Tropical Convergence Zone (ITCZ, aka the doldrums) to find wind. Padang is at the equator, which is why we had calms and squalls and shifting breezes in all directions. South lay the trade winds that would carry us across the Indian Ocean.

South also lay the Australian islands of Cocos Keeling. We hoped to stop there. It sounded like an interesting place, and it would break up the long passage. It was a toss-up whether the wind would allow us to get there without beating to windward, however. If the wind came in our face, we would skip Cocos and head west, destination Rodrigues, part of the country of Mauritius.

I was champing at the bit to head back out to sea.

When we arrived in Tua Pejat on a Saturday afternoon, we met a local who spoke good English, who acted as our guide/translator for an hour or two. We asked about buying diesel, and he took us to a store a quarter mile up the road, where the owner said he would provide 40 liters of diesel (two jerry jugs) for 8,000 Rupiah per liter. We agreed to return on Monday with containers.

On Sunday, everything was closed. And "sun" was what the day was about. Intensely hot, stuck in a harbor where we didn't want to swim, I tried to simply be semi-conscious, and let the minutes ease by. When the sun got low we went ashore in search of dinner. We found one restaurant open, but it had no breeze and it had no cold drinks. Instead we bought sate and some other indeterminate food from street vendors, plus two cold beers, and returned with our take-out back to the boat.

In the morning Tim went for the fuel. He returned saying he had found a much more convenient source. Though somewhat more expensive, it was right on the dock, so we didn't have to transport heavy jugs a quarter mile. We emptied the jugs into our tanks and decided to go back for another round.

The "fuel dock" was the one where the police boats were tied, and the guy helping us wore a police T-shirt. He repeatedly told us we needed to go somewhere to see the authorities, which we were hoping to avoid. We gave him a photocopy of our passports, which quieted him briefly, but then he again indicated that we needed to see someone else (probably the Harbormaster). We said okay, as we left with our fuel…

It was time to meet TC's ferry. We saw a policeman in the ferry terminal, and having accidentally made eye contact with him, I asked if a white guy had just arrived on the ferry. He laughed and said we were the only white guys here. He didn't seem to care about our checking in, but of course I didn't raise the question.

I saw someone who appeared to be from a surf camp. The ferry hadn't arrived yet, he said; he was waiting to meet guests. He warned that the Harbormaster might charge us as much as 500,000 Rupiah. "You just meeting your mate and then leaving? I'd just go. The police aren't going to waste their fuel coming after you. But you didn't hear that from me!"

The ferry arrived, and we found TC. We bought some breakfast at the ferry terminal, we made an escape plan. We bought a few fruits and veggies, then quickly to the boat and off we went! No problem. It didn't feel great, though, to be sneaking out. (For a little perspective, the only other yacht in the area was anchored two miles away, because they never checked in to Indonesia at all! They were avoiding all towns big enough to have a Harbormaster, but they had to get close enough to bring their dinghy in to buy fuel.)

We headed for one of the highly touted surfing spots, as a nice area to show TC, and with the idea that maybe we could buy a tasty dinner there. Anchoring turned out to be problematic; too deep in most places. After trying several unsatisfactory spots, the sun was getting low. We finally went right next to the resort and anchored between two reefs, off a little beach. We hoped that would give us a sandy bottom, but it was too dark now to tell.

As we came ashore with hopes of dinner, a local man told us we were not anchored in a good place. Why? The government wants to protect the coral, he said. We were having trouble understanding what the man's role was. He said he didn't work for the resort, but he also didn't seem to work for the government. Tim blew him off, saying we would just stay for an hour to visit the resort and then leave.

The resort was empty, except for the bartender. The guests had all left earlier in the day; new batch tomorrow. Yes, they could provide dinner, but at a "US price." It would have been by far our most expensive meal in Indonesia. No, thanks. We bought some cold beer to go, made dinner aboard.

During the night a squall came through, strong wind swinging the boat 180 degrees, and with tremendous lightning/thunder striking around us. Worrisome, but no problem. In the morning we could finally see the bottom. All coral…no sand. I'm sure we broke some coral in the squall.

I felt like the whole previous day, except declining dinner, was regrettable…out of integrity. Or as the sailing community says, not "leaving a clean wake."

"No regrets," you say…? Well, yes, I regret leaving a dirty wake that day. But I think regrets come in all sizes, and we ought to have different words for them. I regret that I didn't put more beer in the fridge last night. That's obviously not what the boat name was about. The boat name was about high-level regrets – things one might regret on one's deathbed. In my case, not giving a circumnavigation a go. Or even higher-level, like all of us regretting our collective lack of bold action in the area of climate change.

Near Miss

On the overnight sail to Padang, TC took first watch, I came on at 2300. Nice night; heat lightning in the distance over Sumatra; some fishing boats around with blazing fish-attraction lights; a large ship 7 miles ahead. The ship was coming our way, but the AIS indicated we would clear by 2 miles. TC went below to sleep. I watched the ship on AIS and radar.

Something didn't seem quite right with the radar, but it took me a while in my not-fully-awake state to put two and two together. The big blip ahead on the radar couldn't be that ship! AIS said the ship was 7 miles away; the radar was only displaying a 6-mile range. It showed the big blip as less than 2 miles away! Binoculars. Yes, ahead just slightly to port were two red strobe lights. Probably one of those huge fishing platforms, not lit up tonight. Or a fishing boat anchored or drifting, taking a break. I came to starboard a few degrees to be sure we would miss it.

I enjoyed the night for a few minutes, then looked again at the radar. The blip still seemed to be in the same relative bearing, and closer of course. I could see the dim red strobes now without binoculars, and we didn't seem to be clearing them. There must be current setting us to port, I thought. I came to starboard another 10 degrees.

Then things started to happen quickly. I could see the outline of the fishing boat, and it was big and completely black and closer than I expected. I turned another 10 degrees to starboard, just as it dawned on me that this boat was not anchored or drifting. It was underway and moving fast across (maybe) our bow! All my turning to starboard kept moving us into its path! I turned sharply to port and watched as a black 80-foot boat steamed silently past, not 50 yards away. Not a single light aboard other than the little red strobes – no running lights, no cabin lights, no work lights on the deck. Eerie. Never mind that I had the right of way, which counts for nothing in those waters. I had nearly steered us directly into a collision. Angering. Humbling. Trembling…

Padang

We had been told there were "supermarkets" in Padang, and we had high hopes since we needed to buy our food for the next three weeks or more. The supermarket turned out to be just another smallish shop, with an odd assortment of items on display. But wait! You could go out back and up the rickety stairs and find more. Still didn't find what you wanted? Ask! The Chinese (as usual) proprietors came up with most things on our shopping list, from mysterious invisible locations. For a few items, someone ran down the street and returned with the item!

A lot of logistics did not work out well here, in part because we arrived just before a four-day holiday that we didn't know about, and in part due to language issues, and probably in part simply because this was Indonesia. Before we arrived, Tim had contacted "Charlie," referred to us by one of the surf charter boat operators. Charlie spoke pretty good English, and we were told he could provide supplies and hardware and help us find whatever else we needed. But when Tim went to meet him on the dock, he wasn't there. The ensuing phone call added to the confusion, as each claimed to be on the dock waiting for the other! Tim found Erik, who spoke good English, and got him on the phone with Charlie. Turned out Charlie thought he was meeting us in Tua Pejat, 80 miles away! That was an unfortunate miscommunication. But Erik adopted us and was extremely helpful.

Luc tried to arrange a tour for *Maggie, Gaia,* and us. This also didn't work out. But Erik located a large car, and a group of us went exploring. We had heard that strawberries grew in the area. With visions of freezing piles of strawberries, and ideas that we would drive up in the hills with coolness and beautiful views, we had Erik tell our driver to take us to strawberry country. He took us initially into the city, but that was okay because we needed to change money (unload our remaining Malaysian and Thai and Singaporean cash for Rupiah that we could spend at the market). And next door to the money-changer was a fancy coffee shop where Tim and I satisfied our sweet tooths with "momos" – mochas with milk and Oreos, in a blender with a little ice…

Back in search of strawberries, we did not go into the hills, but followed a long plain, largely covered with rice paddies. Eventually we turned toward the hills and went up just a little. Everywhere now there were plants for sale – nurseries, one after another. And then we "arrived" – at what I wasn't sure, but it had a gate and it was closed for the holiday. Our driver persisted, asking various people and finding a back way in. It had the appearance of a university agricultural extension farm. Beautifully laid out small plots of dozens of crops; hydroponic lettuce; gourds grown on trellises overhead with the fruit hanging down below. After much searching and asking around, a strawberry plant was located. Yes, one plant; no berries.

Oh well, it was a little adventure, and in a comfortable car with air conditioning. Though we never got up into the hills, it was just as well because by that time it was pouring rain and you couldn't see anything anyway. The "momos" turned out to be the highlight of the day!

Last stop on the way home was to pick up our clean laundry. On the boat we sorted out the clothes between the three of us. TC said his only pair of trousers was missing! He and I got back in the dinghy and returned to the laundry. Closed! The light was on, so we banged on the door. The lady from the shop next door looked at us like we were crazy and said they had gone home. With charades language we explained that TC's trousers were missing. She got on her cell phone; told us the laundry person would come back. We waited as it got dark.

Eventually a lady on a motorbike pulled in, nodded at us, and opened the shop. We did the charades again, and she understood, but waved her hand at the shelves with bundles of clear-plastic-wrapped laundry ready to be picked up. I had hoped she would say, "Oh yes, I forgot the trousers that are drying out back." Instead she picked up a random bundle as if to say, "You want to search for a needle in a haystack?" But she turned the bundle over, and TC pointed to the bottom item in the plastic – his trousers!

Indonesian Authorities, Again

Luc would provide transport to Immigration, Customs, and the Harbormaster, which of course were not located close to one another. We were to start a 9am, but Luc's ride/guide/translator canceled at the last moment. At 10 Luc called from a taxi, telling us to meet him ashore in five minutes. We got to the only place around for landing a dinghy, and waited, but no Luc. Phone calls…neither Luc nor his taxi driver knew where we were…could we tell them? Actually, no. We were at the only dock we could find near the anchorage; that meant nothing to the driver. Tim started cornering passers-by on the street until one agreed to take his phone and tell the taxi driver where we were.

We went to Customs first, because it was closer than Immigration. I pulled out my sheaf of papers from the authorities in Sabang, and they asked for the Vessel Declaration Form. I handed them the pile of papers, but there was no such form. "I'm sorry, but you have a problem. You need the form from Sabang." Luc was masterful in this situation. With great authority he announced: "There is no problem because these people did everything properly in Sabang. I know, I was there, I saw them. The Customs office in Sabang must have made a mistake and not given them the paper. And now they need to leave in the morning, 6am."

That was a great try, but the response was, "This is not really my job. I help you only because I speak some English. We have to refer this to my superior, who is busy now."

Luc told them to call the office in Sabang. They didn't have the number... Luc made calls to get the number for them. He told them to call and get the form faxed or emailed, and meanwhile we would go to Immigration. Everyone said Yes, and off we went.

The Immigration office was daunting. It was big, crowded with people waiting. Master Luc brushed past the crowd and walked into a glass-walled office. He had been there before working on *Maggie*'s visa renewal (another long story), so he went directly to the official he had dealt with. The official said we needed to take a number and wait. Luc said no, we were not renewing visas today, we were leaving the country – very simple, stamp the passports, no wait. Several officials conferred; one took our passports and said he would process them.

It took half an hour, but the passports came back stamped. By now it was noon. There was no point in returning to Customs until lunch ended at two, so we stopped for our own lunch and our final provisioning.

We dropped Tim and TC off at the dinghy landing, since they weren't needed for Customs and Harbormaster. They would get our frozen foods into the freezer. Then back to Customs, where we waited for the guys to return late from lunch. Our English-speaking helper arrived. No, they didn't call Sabang... We would need to speak with his boss.

The boss showed up a little later and was briefed. He agreed to call about the missing form, for us and for the other two boats. We waited. When he eventually returned he had a copy of the missing form. Hallelujah!

Next he needed to round up an assistant and they had to come inspect the boat. We had hoped to avoid that. He said he had to take photos of the boat; I gently let him know that I had photos that I could email to him. Yes, he would like my photos, "But you understand that I must come inspect the boat." We called Tim to bring the dinghy back to the dock, and we all went to the boat. Our inspector took a few photos, and then we did the important one – the three crew plus the two inspectors posing aboard. This was the essence of the "inspection" – proof that they came aboard.

As we returned ashore it was approaching 4pm, and we were concerned about getting to the Harbormaster in time. Luc had a plan. On the way back to Customs, where they still needed to complete the forms, they could drop me at the Harbormaster so I could make my presence known and start the paperwork. They would require the Customs clearance, but Luc would bring that as soon as it was ready...

The Harbormaster folks were joking around amongst themselves. It seemed like they would be helpful, but it was hard to tell. The group included two women, which I thought was a good sign. Women tended to be more helpful, and kept the men from being jerks. I started answering their questions.

The guy joked that it was going to cost 15,000, but don't worry, he said, it is Rupiah, not dollars... And then he looked at my "health book" from Sabang.

"Where is your clearance from Quarantine?" he demanded.

"But we are *leaving*, not arriving," I protested, trying to channel Luc. "Quarantine should not be necessary." Apparently I was wrong about that.

Another guy stood up and said, "Follow me." I followed him out of the building to his motorbike. I hopped on behind him, and he drove me through rush hour traffic to Quarantine. Inside, he stared at an office that was locked. Not good. A lady in uniform was nearby waiting for someone, obviously anxious to go home. He asked her if she could help this poor "bule" who needed to clear out. She rolled her eyes. She said the office was closed. I tried to give her the pleading puppy dog look. My escort tried to charm her, said some persuasive things, and she called to someone out in the parking lot to bring the keys. My new friend winked at me.

I filled out forms and did the boat stamp thing to make everything look official. The woman was very nice, once resigned to getting home late. She asked about our trip. She stamped the necessary stamps and handed me the papers. "All done?" I asked.

"Yes, but you need to pay." The cashier window said it was closed, but we were on a roll at this point. Someone took my money (about $2), and it was back to the motorbike, back to the Harbormaster. My driver said goodbye, he was going home. I tried to pay him for being my taxi. He gave me a very genuine smile and said, "No, my friend." I wanted to hug him.

Two things had happened while I was gone. One was that Luc showed up with the Customs papers, completed. The other was that the shift changed, and nobody knew where I was. Luc called Tim – did Zeke return to the boat?? No. Luc had the good sense to stay put and wait. With a little more waiting, a little more struggling with the language, a little more money (but no "gifts" requested), it got done. **We were cleared out of Indonesia!**

INDIAN OCEAN

Our first stop after clearing out at Padang was the Macaronis Resort in the Mentawai Islands west of Sumatra. Technically we were not supposed to set foot in Indonesia after departing, but we had read that many sailors stopped in this remote area. We thought we might be able to top up our fuel there (wrong) and get a last restaurant meal (right). And get a last good night's sleep at anchor before embarking for Cocos Keeling.

Cocos (Keeling), as it is officially named, is a small group of islands 700 miles SSW of Padang. They are under the jurisdiction of Australia. They are by no means on the direct route to Mauritius or Rodrigues, but boats have to sail south anyway to pick up the trade winds, so they are perhaps 300 miles out of the way. Whether we got there would depend on the wind. Particularly once we reached the trade winds, which could blow from the east (good) or the south (bad). If the latter we would give up on Cocos, turn west, and go the remaining 2200 miles to the island of Rodrigues.

We motored almost the whole way to the Mentawais. Hated to burn our fuel so early, but we expected to get more wind as we went south. We rendezvoused with *Maggie* 50 miles further south, and at last we were again headed out to sea. Still motoring, but happy. The well-worn Indonesian courtesy flag came down. The air and the water were a little cooler. The Sumatran islands were fading on the horizon. Many wonderful memories of the Indonesian people remained.

Cocos is at 12 degrees South latitude. We were at 3 South. We could reasonably expect to find trade winds at 8 South, 300 miles ahead.

As we approached 5 South we found good wind. But it died after a few hours; back to motoring. It was an overcast gray day, which was a good thing, but a side effect was that I didn't know what time it was. I misread the numbers on my wristwatch and had dinner ready at 3pm! But it was yummy still at 5:30.

As we approached 6 degrees South there was a squall, and then good wind from the SE. Could it be the start of the trade winds already? The forecast showed light winds in the area from every direction. But we were on a close reach directly toward Cocos making 8 knots, sometimes nine. It lasted a few hours. Then squalls and calms and motoring.

We crossed 8 South, where we thought we could legitimately expect trade winds. We got some unfavorable SW wind, and uncomfortable seas from multiple directions. By afternoon we could see clouds overhead moving in the direction of the SE trade winds, but on the surface we still had SW.

At midnight we crossed 9 South. Just before Tim came on watch at 3am, a big line of rain clouds passed overhead, and the wind started to build from the SE. When I awoke 4 hours later, Tim said, "Come out and behold the majesty!"

The SE wind was approaching 20 knots; seas up to 4 meters; patches of blue sky between gray and white clouds; pelagic birds soaring by with their wing tips inches from the waves; and *No Regrets* surging along at 9 knots. Trade winds at last! A bumpy close reach, but a welcome one.

The squalls continued. Winds from 5 knots to 35 knots. But the following morning we arrived at Cocos. The anchorage was beautiful. And empty. The only signs of humanity were a shack on the beach, a dock, and two other sailboats. One was *Tom Tom*, with our singlehander friend Chris aboard. He left for Rodrigues shortly after we anchored, but not before we had a drink together. He told us we could buy very expensive diesel, and that Friday a freighter would arrive with fresh produce, so we should provision Saturday morning. In the meantime, things were going to be rather quiet. He clued us in to a wonderful feature: wifi right in the anchorage, from a hotspot on the beach!

Cocos (Keeling) was unlike any place we had been. For starters, what place has parentheses in its official name?! Cocos is two atolls, 15 miles apart. The northern one is small, no harbor, no people. The southern atoll is a ring of islands around a lagoon four miles wide. Three islands are of importance – Direction Island, Home Island and West Island. Culturally, each is distinctly different from the others.

Direction Island was where we anchored. In fact, it was the only place where yachts were allowed to anchor. The anchorage was beautiful and well protected, and the island had the nicest beach of the atoll. But nobody lived on Direction Island. Twice weekly a ferry came from Home Island, two miles away, and brought people who wanted to "go to the beach." There were several little shelters…walking trails…a big cistern of rainwater…a few hammocks and beach chairs…a barbecue hearth…and the wifi internet router. Except on ferry days, it was just us yachties. No fishing boats, nobody paddling out for handouts. Just sitting on the boat in the trade winds and gazing at the beach and palm trees was delightful.

Home Island was where the people of Malay descent live – about 500 people, very Muslim. There was a well-stocked grocery store, though prices were high – a banana cost about $2. There was a restaurant that opened on certain nights if there was enough interest…a post office…a bank that opened for a few hours a week…a primary school…the Shire Office, where we paid $50

(Australian) to anchor for a week…a marine services building with impressive tools and equipment…a crafts shop that they opened for us when we showed interest (but nothing compelling inside)…several other little shops…and a fuel depot open at 7:30am for one hour twice a week, and two hours on Fridays. No cars, but some golf carts and motorbikes and 4-wheelers. The pace was pleasantly slow.

Lastly, West Island, with ferry service from Home Island half a dozen times a day ($2.50 each way; half hour ride). About 150 people lived on West Island, most of them white, most of them government workers and their families, and ex-government-workers who liked it and didn't go back home to Australia. There was an airport with a few flights per week. There was an expensive grocery store…some tourist shops (but not many tourists; TC told us that most Australians had never heard of Cocos)…a "hotel"…not much else. It all seemed rather unreal…artificial…out of place. It was also rather high-end, over-infrastructured. There was a bus that made three stops, because the ferry landing was several kilometers from the "town." You could buy beer. One Home Island resident referred to it as Naughty Island!

The division between the Malays on one island and the Aussies on the other, plus the yachties at a third was…well…interesting. It seemed to work. It was an interesting history that got this atoll inhabited in the first place. The Malay people originally were brought there in the 1800's as a harem (and slaves) for a white sea captain who wanted to create his own little world apart – 600 miles from the southern tip of Sumatra, 1100 miles from Western Australia. The recent incorporation into Australia was agreed to by a close-to-unanimous vote.

On Friday, when the fuel depot was open an extra hour, we made two dinghy runs to buy diesel at $8 (US) per gallon. Plus we had to buy petrol/gasoline to fuel the long dinghy rides. Then we hailed the police boat to come by to clear us out. We were free to leave anytime during the weekend. I took my bedding ashore to wash in the rainwater stored there; it was a perfect drying day. Since the squalls had gone away, it was beautiful beautiful beautiful.

The next day we shopped for what limited fruit and vegetables we could find. We were ready to go, but…

I felt so *good* there! The air temperature was warm; the constant wind felt cool. The anchorage was protected, the holding solid – made for sound sleep. I had shaved and cut my hair, which made me feel lighter, happier. It was quiet – we were far from the generators and the mosque in town. The things that had been going wrong were getting fixed. We had splurged and bought a case of expensive beer. The good internet was allowing me to get my "fix" of Words-with-Friends with Hallie. Swimming was wonderful, the water clean and clear, and the sharks were small and didn't bother you. The air was clear and clean. I had clean sheets and pillowcases. I washed my hair. My body felt good; my soul felt good; no worries; no hurry.

Yachties leave 'signatures' on Direction Island.

Kids' mural in the Shire Office. Not sure how much an umbrella will help in adapting to climate change…

2,000 Miles to Rodriques

We dove to do a last scraping of barnacles and noticed that a chunk was missing from the bottom of one daggerboard! This must have happened when Tim and I were cruising off Sumatra. There was a time when we just drifted for a while because we had a decent cell signal. We were deep into emails when we suddenly noticed there was a coral reef right next to us. An engine was quickly engaged, and we thought we got away clean. Apparently not. Another item for future repair.

I felt a twinge of sadness about leaving beautiful Cocos, and a little reluctance to leave the smooth anchorage for the open Indian Ocean. Instead of Goodbye, the Cocos Islanders like to say, "See you next time around!" Yes, I hope so.

We set out with *Maggie* in beautiful trade winds, about 16 knots on our quarter. Relatively small seas, and relatively small swell coming north from the Southern Ocean. I appreciated having a peaceful first day for the adjustment to the motion-of-the-sea.

We had only been underway an hour when we had our first casualty; our computer died. The most important function of the computer, at least at sea, was to control the modem that allowed us to send email and receive weather charts via the radio. Tim had a spare laptop, and he had loaded it with the necessary software. We were quickly up and running again. Thank you, Tim!

Lots of birds; lots of flying fish. Near perfect sailing. We had a bird (shearwater?) land on our bow in the evening, and during the night she moved back toward the cockpit, just a few feet from where we sit. She preened for hours, then tucked her head under a wing and snoozed. In the morning she flew off for ten minutes, then landed on the bow again. Until we put up the spinnaker, intruding on her space – then she left.

We had some major spinnaker excitement. We were setting our asymmetrical, and the sock was difficult to raise. We had all our attention on the situation aloft and didn't notice the wind starting to fill the sail with a wrap in it. We couldn't get the wrap out; the sheets were twisted together so we couldn't ease them out; we couldn't get the sock down; we had a mess. We lowered the halyard and managed to pull the tangle aboard before it dragged in the sea. The hoop at the bottom of the sock was broken. I don't know if that was a cause or an effect of our struggles.

We stowed that spinnaker and broke out the old Parasailor – the spinnaker with a slot and wing, shown on the cover of this book. Except the sail was no longer a Parasailor since we repaired its latest tear by removing the wing and filling in the slot with solid fabric. This time the sock control lines got twisted/jammed/fouled. The spinnaker was flying okay, but the sock was not right, and one of the control lines was yanked from my hands and swung up out of reach. We managed to grab it with the boat hook, and we pulled the sail down, half socked. Then we raised it in its sock again and sorted everything out as it went up. The sail worked beautifully – it seemed at least as stable and effective as when it had the Parasailor wing!

After another beautiful sailing day, we were tempted to leave the spinnaker up through the night. But after the reminders of how things can go wrong with spinnakers, we decided to switch to the screecher. The change reduced our speed by a knot or more, but we were staying apace with *Maggie*; no need for speed.

We received an email around mid-day from Chris, the singlehander aboard *Tom Tom*. He reported that his forestay had broken, and although his mast was still standing he was in rough seas and was concerned about it. He had rigged several lines to provide support to the mast, but everything was tenuous in the rough conditions.

We scheduled a call on the SSB radio. His voice betrayed his exhaustion and fear. We let him know we were headed in his direction, but we were 575 miles behind him. He appreciated our being there even if "there" was four days away.

That evening I got on the SSB radio net – a loose association of boats crossing the Indian Ocean and checking in on the radio daily. Our friends aboard *On Verra* were only about 25 miles from the position I estimated for *Tom Tom*. But they didn't have email at sea, so with Chris not on the net (probably trying to sleep), it would be hard to make contact. They offered to alter course toward Chris, and try him on the VHF radio as they got closer. Chris was still sailing, with greatly reduced sail, and he was not asking for assistance. Hopefully he would be able to sail slowly into Rodrigues, but we would try to "have his back."

Day 5

A beautiful sailing day. It struck me that we were in a particularly empty ocean. For five days, not a boat or a light or an airplane. Just water and waves, sky and clouds, occasionally birds and fish.

On Verra was already west (downwind) of *Tom Tom,* and 35 miles away, so they did not connect by VHF radio. But *Tom Tom* was on the radio net that night. His wind has decreased to 20 knots, and he was continuing to sail slowly on. He sounded like his usual self – upbeat! It was nice to chat with him a little, and clear that he appreciated the contact.

Day 6

A frustrating day for us. Not quite enough wind. But worse, the wind constantly shifted to the east (begging for the spinnaker) and then the south (requiring that the spinnaker come down). At sunset the breeze freshened and came south, and stayed there. We were happily sailing with mainsail and screecher at nearly 8 knots, hoping the conditions would hold.

We got an update from *Tom Tom* on the radio net. All the other boats reported winds of 20 knots or less; Chris had 25 to 30 knots. That didn't seem fair, but he was okay.

Day 7

We completed the first week of the passage and crossed the halfway point. Baked bread to celebrate. During the day the weather deteriorated, with heavy rain at times, and wind gusting to 30 knots. Twice we went out to reef, and both times the wind and rain increased just as we got outside. Oh well. At dark I was glad to have two reefs in for the night, not so much that we needed it then, but probably we would at some point before morning.

We lost our wind instrument data, making night sailing in the gyrating seas difficult. But a reboot of the electronics brought it back.

Dolphins visited.

Lost a(nother) fishing lure.

Day 8

Very wet on board. Especially in the pilothouse, but gradually the wetness was working its way toward our sleeping quarters. Boats ahead reported rough conditions and overcast, but at least not pouring rain. Hopefully we would get a chance to dry out soon.

Day 9

The day started out dry, but it didn't last. A ship passed us only a mile away, according to the AIS, but we couldn't see it in the rain. After seeing no ships for 9 days, it was eerie to have one pass close by…invisibly.

The wind was up and down, backing and veering, so we always seemed to have the wrong sail combination set. Our track looked like we were drunk, wobbling north and south in the wind shifts. We flew our small spinnaker for a while. Then the wind decreased to 14 knots and stayed there, leaving us underpowered. We put up the big spinnaker, the old Parasailor. Within minutes the wind was back to blowing over 20 knots, and we were screaming down waves, sometimes hitting 15 knots (while I tried to prepare lunch!). We talked about getting the sail down…thought we would wait for a break in the rain…then the wind eased, so maybe we would keep it up…

…and then it was no longer a spinnaker, but a flapping mess of ragged sailcloth! Major tears all along the foot and up one leech. It was the third time we had torn this sail, and I knew it was done. Not worth repairing yet again.

Hell

When I came on watch, TC and I put in a second reef. When Tim came on watch four hours later, he and I put in a third. Very rough; difficult to sleep in the crashing and banging.

The wind came far around to the south, so we were broadside to the waves. That brought spray flying across the cockpit and kept us inside the pilothouse all day. On most of our passages I had spent long hours staring at the sea and the sky. But now we were hunkered down inside. I read five thriller/mystery novels – probably as many as I had read in the rest of my life! They became my transport to another world, to escape this hell, and pass the time and miles.

The wind stayed south, across our course, and it stayed strong. It was a wild and crazy ride. Almost impossible to sleep, until you were so worn out you just didn't care what was happening around you. Then you might pass out for an hour.

The conditions bordered on torture. For starters there was the whoosh of water rushing by your ear at 10+ knots, while your berth was moving like a carnival ride. That part was relatively pleasant. The water was very lumpy, and some of those lumps got between the catamaran's hulls and slammed into the bridge deck – the structure that connects the hulls, that comprises the floor of the pilothouse, and the underside of my berth. Some lumps hit with a dull thud.

Others hit like a wrecking ball, with a deafening crash and an impact that wracked the entire boat. It felt like the boat, and the crew, were being shaken apart.

Then there was the wail emanating from the wind generator. It had an internal brake that engaged at about 35 knots, so the blades wouldn't spin themselves into oblivion. The brake had the vibrato electronic hum of a Jedi warrior's lightsaber in combat, but with an intensity more like the air horn of a large truck closing fast and wanting to pass. Add those two sounds together, and you have the wail that told me, lying in my berth, that the wind was still howling outside over 35 knots.

Then there were the waves that broke against the side of the hull, since we were sailing crosswise to them. These were different from the blasts under the bridge deck. The crash lifted the boat sideways as though it might flip over; sheets of salt spray flying at the pilothouse windows. All the hatches were closed except for one on the sheltered/downwind side. One wave sent such solid water over the top of the pilothouse that it flew in that one open hatch.

This all occurred in darkness, of course. You couldn't see the waves coming. The hardest thing on one's stomach was the anticipation. When you heard one about to hit, or felt the boat begin to lift, you couldn't help but tense up, bracing for what may or may not come next. The ones under the bridge deck came with no warning – just a sudden impact from below. It wore on one's nerves. If you needed to move, it would have been foolhardy to try to stand without at least one hand firmly on a handhold.

One wave lifted our man-overboard horseshoe buoy out of its bracket on the lifelines. It caught on a line on deck, so it didn't wash overboard, and its automatic strobe light began to flash. A bonus feature of the carnival ride: visual chaos. It was almost humorous going out to retrieve it – trying to do it quickly before a wave drenched me, while being blinded by the flash of the strobe.

Adding to the pandemonium were the items flying about the cabin. Books flew off of shelves where they had been securely (we thought) wedged in place. My plastic glass of water flew off the table to the floor. Locker doors unlatched and banged open and shut. Our plastic granola container crashed to the floor and spewed its contents. Silverware rattled. Dishes (and a Thermos, a coffee maker, and miscellaneous other items) banged about in the sink, where they had been stashed to keep them from flying elsewhere. Plus the surprisingly loud sucking/gurgling sound made by the sink drain as waves rushed by its exit. The bilge pump alarm occasionally trumped all other noises for twenty seconds, while some of the seawater that found its way into an engine room was returned to the sea.

Underlying it all was the constant gnawing fear of whether the boat and rig could withstand the incessant pounding. Could the crew...?

At dawn the tension eased somewhat. The waves didn't look as awful as I had imagined in the dark. The wind eased back to 30 knots, instead of 35. It was a sunny day, and that lifted my spirits even on a day when the priorities were to get some food down and get some sleep. Ideally we would bear off and run with the waves; it would be much easier, probably even fun. But that was not an option, as we would miss Rodrigues. We had to hold our crosswise course. The wind was ever so slightly aft, for which I was very thankful. Just a little more forward and the crashing and banging would become even worse. It was tempting to bear off just a little. But what if the wind went even higher (in strength or direction)? We would have to make up that lost distance to windward, and it could be even more difficult than what we were experiencing. So our course was just a degree or two to windward of our destination, those degrees providing a very slim margin of error/safety. 250 miles to go. If we could keep our speed up (without breaking anything important) we would have just one more night of hell, and arrive the next day.

Later in the day the wind gusted to 40 knots. Tim and I discussed lowering the mainsail altogether (it was already triple reefed); he in favor, me thinking conditions might ease a bit. As we talked, a wave picked up the back of the boat and sent us surfing at 22 knots! That was a record for *No Regrets*, and it was a record that I had no desire to ever break! We dropped the mainsail.

The noon to noon run was 206 nautical miles. We were tickled to receive an email from Jimmy Cornell congratulating us on an impressive run!

Day 13

By noon we entered Port Mathurin harbor on Rodrigues. We just managed to clear in before the authorities shut down at 4pm. We had a beer and dinner with Chris from *Tom Tom*, who safely made it in the day before. I was very much looking forward to some real sleep!

Twelve days and a few hours to cover 2,000 miles. After a slow start, the passage ended fast. It was the most unpleasant passage I had ever made. Glad to have it behind me. We lost one spinnaker; broke the sock used to raise and lower another; lost the blades from our hydrogenerator; had our wind generator shake loose from its brackets (but it was already back together and functioning); the throttle control for one engine was not working. And we lost three fishing lures while catching zero fish!

Tim tried to rig the spinnaker sheet without disturbing our guest, but she flew off.

Photos of waves never convey their relentless movement, power, majesty, awesomeness. Still one has to try...

Rodrigues

I liked Rodrigues. It had a Caribbean flavor – people primarily of African descent, pretty laid back, a little crowded in the town but empty in the countryside. Some cafes, an open market, a supermarket, western (French) foods.

Monument and a little park in tribute to the slaves that were brought to Rodrigues early on, and the freeing of them, also pretty early on (at least compared to the US).

Graduation!

My Middle Schoolers were about to graduate. I passed along congratulations and my (unsolicited) commencement thoughts…

Middle school is a long "passage," and I'm sure there were rough times and smooth sailing…periods of adventure and others of boredom…doldrums and trade winds… Probably you did not write a blog about your time in middle school, but perhaps you should start…or at least keep a journal. Because you get to write your own story. Your life is your story. It doesn't have to be grand…it doesn't have to make for exciting TV…it is simply…yours.

I hope you have learned something about the world from me. Our world is not as big as we often think. With a little time you could sail a boat right around it! And everywhere you would find people. They speak different languages, but they all smile the same. Most of them understand that we all share one future — that what happens in the United States affects the people of Tuvalu, and what happens to Tuvaluans will eventually impact us all. With airplanes and TV and Internet, we are all connected. With climate change, we are all connected.

Although we name the different parts, we have One Ocean, One Planet, One Future. And you have a story to write, with a new chapter beginning in high school. Take pride in your story; have no regrets!

~~~

After a pleasant few days in Rodrigues, it was time to move on to Mauritius, about three days away. We were an hour from clearing out with the Rodrigues authorities when we had a crew problem.

I should have seen it coming… It started three days before on our island tour by minibus. We were all piling back into the bus after a stop. Tim was climbing into the back as TC got in the front and closed his door…on Tim's hand. Tim made a lot of noise about it, though he wasn't badly hurt. I'm not certain if TC even knew it happened. Probably he did, but decided it wasn't his problem. He said nothing. The incident seemed to pass, but it came up again a day later – Tim saying to someone else that there was no contrition on TC's part. At this point I should have seen the similarity to what happened a year ago with Bill and the winch handle incident.

As we prepared to leave, Chris dinghied over from *Tom Tom* to say goodbye, and he jokingly brought up a sensitive topic, asking who signs the papers with the authorities – who is *really* the captain of *No Regrets*…? While I was responding that it was purely a matter of convenience that I sign the papers, TC made a comment about my being the real captain, plus something disparaging that I didn't catch about Tim being old. Chris departed, I went below, and shortly after I heard Tim shouting at TC…repeatedly calling him an asshole…saying he now understood why women don't stick around with him! I held my breath wondering what would happen next. TC was hurrying silently to his cabin. After a minute I peeked through his door. He appeared to be packing his gear! Oh, no! It wasn't that we needed him to get to Mauritius, but we had assured the police and immigration officials that we were departing with the same crew we arrived with. We wouldn't be allowed to leave without him until he purchased a plane ticket out of the country. Plus, I would be stuck with the aftermath…Tim's one-sided story, starting with the hand in the door, and no contrition.

I waited a few minutes, hoping everyone was cooling off. Then to the pilothouse where Tim was; I asked what happened. He vented, and he seemed to relax a little as he spoke. Then I stuck my head into TC's cabin and suggested that he ask Tim what set him off. To my surprise and relief, he cheerfully said he would. A few minutes later I heard him going up and saying, "Can we clear the air?" We all got through it.

So many different aspects to sailing…

To Mauritius

The three-day passage was pleasantly uneventful. We had a steady 20 knots for the first half; the wind gradually tapered off until we had to motor the last 80 miles. Easy going. Beautiful night sky.

The last night had me taking stock. As soon as we arrived, TC would be booking a plane and be gone. Tim would stay for a week to help with boat tasks, then he'd be gone. I would have three weeks to close up the boat, then I'd be gone. It was my last night at sea for two and a half months. For Tim it would be over six months.

Mauritius was a major milestone in the plan. I considered it the two-thirds point of the circumnavigation – eight time zones away from home. I looked forward to spending a summer in Maine. Beyond that lay something special: Africa!

Approach to Port Louis, Mauritius

Clearing in at the Customs Dock

Le Caudan Marina

For me, Mauritius was primarily about getting the boat to a safe place to leave it, arranging to fly home, and getting things ready to head to sea again upon return.

We cleared in at Port Louis and found a parking space at Le Caudan Marina, part of an upscale downtown waterfront. The marina was not expensive, but then again it wasn't much of a marina. It was a small boat basin with concrete walls. Initially we were told there was no room for us (despite Jimmy assuring us that they were "expecting" the BPO boats). But it was so close to the Customs dock that we walked over, identified a space on the wall, and got the okay to tie there. Occasionally a swell got in there, primarily from passing ships, which made it scary to be tied to a concrete wall. After the first night we rafted to another boat, which was far better. But I didn't like the idea of leaving the boat unattended there in my absence.

Hoping for a better option, we took the bus to a private development 15 miles south, that had a marina with well-protected floating docks. The slips were all for the homeowners, but sometimes they sublet. Very secure. Not much in the way of amenities; no showers. It was far more expensive than Le Caudan. But I felt much better about leaving the boat there; Tim would help me sail there before he departed.

We arranged to have our damaged daggerboard fixed while I was away. We talked with a sailmaker about fixing our broken spinnaker sock. That didn't work out, so we replaced it with the sock from the torn Parasailor. We gave the shreds of that sail to the sailmaker; he said they would use the material to make bags and other items. I was happy to be rid of it and know that the material would be reused. We talked with a battery company and decided not to try to replace our batteries there. We took our nonworking computer to a shop; they said the motherboard was shot; they copied all our files off the hard drive. We would have to replace the board or the whole machine while home.

We changed the oil in both engines. We cleaned a stuck valve for the starboard head and serviced the port head. We repaired a broken support for our cockpit floorboards.

We didn't see much of the island of Mauritius. We were in a city, but it was a well-guarded, high-end waterfront section, not the *real* city, which was teaming with people and vehicles. Our "tours" consisted of our bus adventure to the marina and walking through the city on errands. I didn't much care about seeing the pretty parts of the island, but I felt like I didn't do the country justice. I was glad we had visited the delightful part of Mauritius that was called Rodrigues!

Immigration

There must have been a time when crews abandoned their boats in Mauritius, and/or when multiple boats were damaged while their crews were away. I say this because Mauritius had extreme regulations when it came to skippers leaving the country. When my passport was stamped into the country, it got the word "skipper" written over the stamp. That restricted my freedom to leave by air...

We had to hire a "guardian" to be responsible for the boat in my absence. We needed a letter from the guardian, indicating not only that he was responsible, but that his fee was prepaid through my return date. I needed to have a paid airline return ticket. I was required to take these documents to Immigration in advance, and get a letter authorizing my departure.

I dressed in my best – long pants and a button-down shirt – and walked the half mile through the city and the heat to the Immigration office. I was directed to a room that had two large desks in front, and dozens of chairs looking like church pews. But nobody was in the room. I waited a while, and then started asking people in the halls. There was a staff meeting going on; it should be over soon.

Eventually a person in uniform appeared at one of the desks, and I explained my situation. She understood what I needed, which was a good sign. She gathered all my paperwork and told me she would take it to the supervisor. I waited.

The supervisor appeared and asked a few clarifying questions. Then we got to, "Are you the owner of the boat?"

I tried the simple answer. "Yes."

For the first time on this trip, that answer wasn't good enough. He said, "But the document states that the owner is No Regrets LLC."

"Yes, that is correct. I am a member of the LLC."

"How do I know that?" he asked.

Therein lay a problem. No one had ever challenged the boat ownership. I had never been asked to make a connection between the LLC and myself. I doubted that I had a satisfactory document on the boat, but I could see that I was at an impasse. "I will go back to the boat, find a document, and come back."

As I walked back to the boat I called Hallie, even though it was the middle of the night at home. She didn't answer; I left a message that I had a time-sensitive administrative issue. Aboard, I looked through the boat's file folder, and I found something. It was a document from the State of Delaware stating that the LLC had been formed, and that the initial members were Tim, Bill and myself. That seemed rather flimsy. Membership could change. But then again, how could they ever know what the up-to-the-minute membership was?

I was reasonably optimistic as I walked back to the Immigration office when it reopened after lunch. The supervisor was late returning, so I waited once again. When he appeared he was ready to help me. He stared at my document for several seconds. "But Mr. Holland, I cannot accept this document."

Gulp, I said.

"It has no official seal. No ribbon. Not even an official letterhead. Anyone could have typed this."

It was true. Probably because this was some sort of online receipt, it had no letterhead. It said "State of Delaware" at the top, but just in regular type. I had to go out on a limb. "My friend, everything is done online in the United States now. Nothing has an official seal anymore. It is the only proof that I have."

This was a desperate lie. Back home I had the original documents with a letterhead and seal. But I wasn't going to get a copy in time, nor was it clear he would accept a copy.

He pondered. He wanted to help, but clearly he felt that he would be breaking some rule. So I tried this. "I have the *No Regrets* boat stamp…"

You could see his administrator brain battling with his compassionate brain. At length he murmured, "I will accept this document with your stamp."

Yes! Except the stamp was back on the boat, and it was Friday afternoon. "I'll get this stamped and bring it straight back."

"We're closing soon. We don't have time to process your letter. You'll have to bring it Monday."

"I can't bring it Monday. We're relocating to Black River this weekend. I can run to the boat and be back in 25 minutes." I had "I'm begging you" written on my face.

He winced. "Twenty-five minutes."

It was still hot. I couldn't run all the way. I was a few minutes late. Well, maybe 10 minutes late. Maybe showing up with my clothes drenched in sweat would show that I made a good effort.

In fact, when I returned, panting, my new friend had all the paperwork ready and waiting. We both signed, and I had the letter I needed to be able to fly home. Thank you!

There was an interesting addendum to all this. Shortly after I got home, I received the boat's renewed Coast Guard documentation certificate. In the box labeled "Owner," where it used to say "No Regrets LLC" it inexplicably now read "No Regrets LLC, Zeke Holland managing member."

Closing Up

For a week I did almost nothing but clean the inside of the boat. Plus a little time at the pool, checking out the nearby restaurants, and half a day of exploring the island by car with the *Maggie* crew. A week wasn't quite long enough. I had hoped to empty every locker and clean inside. Didn't get that far, but I cleaned the walls, the ceiling, the floor, the counters, the fridge, the freezer, the settee cushions, the heads. I threw out every bit of food that I thought might go bad or get bugs. I threw out some that I wasn't even sure what it was – mysterious looking stuff labeled in uncertain languages. I gave a few items away to the security guards.

I showed our "guardian," Xavier, how to start the engines; the starboard one was very reluctant to start. He arranged for a mechanic to come in the morning before I left. Of course with the mechanic there, it started right up. Xavier would be coming once a week to start the engines; he said he would call the mechanic again if there was a problem. Xavier also volunteered to spray our tiny ants while I was away. He seemed to know his stuff and be very helpful, which made it easier to leave the boat. *No Regrets* and I had been taking care of each other; I was reluctant to leave her alone.

Journey to the Airport

I planned to leave at 11am for the journey via three buses to the airport. But it was 1pm before I had everything put away and closed up. No matter – my flight would leave late at night, so I had all day to make my way there. The bus service was not simple or quick. When I mentioned to Xavier the day before that I would be taking the bus, he raised his eyebrows and quipped, "You better leave now!"

The first bus arrived right away. I was armed with Google Maps to see where we were, plus a list of all the stops on the route, up to my stop. I thought I was prepared, but… It was surprisingly difficult to match where we were with the name of a bus stop. Most of the stops had nice rain shelters, but no names on them. And you couldn't simply count stops, because the bus didn't stop if no one was waiting to get on or off. When I thought we were close, I asked the ticket-taker, who said he'd let me know. Stop after stop went by… Maybe they had added a dozen stops not on my list-from-the-internet. He didn't steer me wrong – when he told me it was my stop, we were in the expected town.

Next I had to walk to the town roundabout to get my second bus. But the town didn't seem to have a roundabout! I asked, and two people assured me I was going in the right direction, and the bus stop was just ahead. My bus was #163, but only some of the buses showed numbers! I asked another person waiting. "You can take any red bus, but not an express." Sounded reasonable, but when I started to board a red bus and asked the ticket-taker to confirm the destination, he looked at me like I was crazy, and said no, it didn't go there. Then someone directed me to the next bus approaching – an express…#163. That worked.

When I got off, I confirmed that I wanted bus #198 to get to the airport. Yes. At the stop there was one other person waiting, so I asked if I could get #198 to the airport at that stop. Yes. But after several minutes he said, "To the airport? You need to be on the other side of the road!" Normally I'm very good with my sense of direction, but that didn't help much with meandering bus routes.

On the other side I again checked with a person waiting. Yes, you want #198, but it will say Mahebourg – it may not have a number. Many buses went by. Finally a #198. But it didn't stop! I asked my friend, "Do I need to jump in front of it to get it to stop?" He replied, "It was full."

Many more buses went by, and along came one for Mahebourg. My friend indicated I should take it. But the ticket-taker said it didn't go to the airport; it would go to Magnien. Well, whatever. It was rush hour, and I figured I should take what I could get and figure it out when we got "there." At the next stop there was a huge crowd. The bus had a sign: Capacity 65 seated, 5 standing. We packed everyone in, more like 65 standing, to the point that it was nearly impossible for anyone to get out at the next several stops. Everyone (almost) was smiling about it.

I didn't know it until we got there, but Magnien was where the airport was. As I exited I saw a sign for the airport in 2 kilometers. I could just walk. But I didn't want to walk along the highway, and I saw several people walking down a paved path through the sugarcane, so I ventured there. After 100 meters or so I saw a man getting into a car; I asked if this path would lead me to the airport. No. But he was driving to the airport – please hop in! The airport was just a stone's throw over the sugarcane. But it started raining at that moment, so the ride was especially appreciated. Naturally he dropped me right at the international departures door. People everywhere want to be helpful!

My airport odyssey took only three hours, and cost about $4 instead of the $60 to take a taxi. Now I had 5 hours before boarding my plane. But at this point it was like being on an escalator – just letting it carry me along for the next 30 hours to home.

Crew

Nora and I had been updating each along the way. No word from her hoped-for employer. Good, for me. Bob had declined to crew for the leg. Good, for Nora. I decided to trust my instincts, ignore Tim's admonitions, and offer her the position. She said yes, but then delayed purchasing her plane ticket, which worried me. Then when she was about to put money down, my worry changed to uncertainty that she fully understood what she was signing up for. I sent the following to both Nora and Liam.

> Full Disclosure…
>
> I've always known that the crossing from Mauritius to Durban is challenging, but I've only recently read up on the details. Here's a summary.
>
> The distance is over 1400 miles – nearly half an ocean. We may start in trade winds, but they quickly disappear, and the winds become subject to weather fronts. Jimmy's book on ocean passages says one can expect anything from 0 to 50 knots. But what makes this area challenging is the current. It flows west, with us but against the SW winds that blow hard with frontal systems,

making for steep/rough seas. Then when closing with Africa the current joins with the southerly flow west of Madagascar to become the infamous Agulhas Current. This current is similar in strength to the Gulf Stream off of Cape Hatteras, and one doesn't want to be there when a SW frontal blow arrives.

To complicate matters, the fronts tend to come through every few days, so you can't time a departure from Réunion to miss them. We will almost certainly have to deal with one, and likely two. Of course, cruisers make this passage and many experience greater challenges elsewhere. But odds are that this passage will include the most uncomfortable conditions of our circumnavigation.

Liam, I hope I'm not reporting anything you didn't already know and are prepared for. Nora, I know I have not spelled this out to you, and I want to be CERTAIN you understand fully before you buy your plane tickets. If you would rather join us in Durban, and avoid this crossing, that's okay – I will try to find other crew just for Mauritius to Durban.

Nora replied:

My dad and I both read through the description that Jimmy provided on making the passage to Durban. I was aware before committing that we are highly likely to sail through rough weather and intense currents.

I was tentative to commit at first to this passage, but I did a bunch of research (including a number of video diaries from other cruisers) to get a better sense. It seems to me that this will be some rough sailing (big waves), but I'm up for the challenge if you are comfortable having me.

I was relieved that Nora didn't accept my offer to start in Durban, as I had no idea how I would get crew just for the potentially nasty passage from Mauritius. But "if you are comfortable having me" gnawed at me. It seemed to me that her commitment was conditional, rather than "all in." Like it would be my fault if things didn't work out. Was I being too picky about the words she used? I decided I couldn't just let it go, and wrote:

On a dark night when you are feeling sick and the waves are fearsome and it's driving rain and the boat is banging and crashing, and I say you need to get out of your semi-dry bed to help put in another reef...I just don't want to have any lingering thoughts that you hadn't really signed up for this kind of "fun." Sounds like you are "on board" come what may. There will be sunshine, joy and the satisfaction of accomplishment on the other side!

I note that your statement of being up for the challenge is conditional upon my level of comfort. I doubt you meant it that way, but since my comfort level is less than 100% (or we wouldn't be exchanging these emails), I'm hoping it is fair to reword your statement as "I'm up for the challenge, and hope you are willing to have me." Which I am. In this way we can both commit, whether comfortable or not. Is that fair? It might seem that I'm picking at words, but to me the distinction matters.

She agreed. She was in. Liam's cheerful reply to my "full disclosure" also made me smile.

I was aware that this leg would be one of the more challenging of the trip. Before I approached you I had read through other accounts of this passage (probably a bad idea) and studied my ancient copy of Jimmy's *World Cruising Routes*. Of all the sources, http://earth.nullschool.net/ was probably the most informative. I expect we can pick our days for the leg from Durban To Cape Town, but as you say, Réunion to Durban requires an all-in commitment and no bolt holes. Still, I think I prefer that to being shot at in the Gulf of Aden! I am still in, and eagerly looking forward to it.

I had a full crew for the challenging bit ahead!

The condo development where I felt it was safe to leave the boat for 10 weeks.

TO AFRICA

Tahawus was back! They sailed direct all the way from Thailand to Mauritius to catch up with our mini-fleet and rejoin the rally. Hooray!

There were only a few glitches to getting underway again. I updated all the apps on my iPad the day before leaving home, and all my electronic charts on the device disappeared! I had some desperate communications with the company. Things got corrected while I was at the airport waiting for my flight out of the US.

Nora and Liam were already at the boat when I arrived; no worries. The boat looked okay. The engines started right up. The daggerboard had been repaired, but when we tried to slide it into its case, it wouldn't go! The repaired area was too thick. A desperate call to our caretaker had him show up with a grinder. An hour later the repaired board fit, though much of its new antifouling paint and some of its new fiberglass were now gone. I could live with that.

We had planned to do major provisioning before leaving the marina. But we got word from other boats that due to an outbreak of hoof and mouth disease, many foods were being confiscated by the authorities in La Réunion, our next stop. Boats that had just stocked up in Mauritius lost hundreds of dollars of provisions. We still stocked up with non-perishables; no meat, milk, fruits, veggies, cheese…

We left on schedule to sail back up the coast to Port Louis, where I had checked in two and a half months before, and where we had to check out. It was only a three-hour sail, but I found it exciting and stressful. I was out of practice at sailing. So many details to forget; so many things that could go wrong. We didn't know if there would be any space available back at Le Caudan marina. But it was splendid to pull in and see *Tahawus* and *Maggie* there, and space to raft up alongside *Maggie*. Also delightful to have showers available. The complete BPO fleet (of three) assembled for drinks that evening.

I was surprised to discover how happy I was to sail into a place that was familiar. In the Rally we were always moving on to the next place, so it was a rare and pleasant experience to arrive and know where the shops were, where the showers were, what it would cost for dockage, etc.

In the morning we checked out. Off to "tropical France," Réunion Island, 130 miles away.

It was a challenging night for the new crew. Wind was mostly in the 20s, and at least once up to 30. Seas right on the beam, occasionally breaking against the side of the boat. Spray flying so we couldn't enjoy being outside. Both Nora and Liam were sick. But I wouldn't have known if they didn't tell me; they continued to be active and pull their weight.

La Réunion

We arrived at Réunion, a little bit of France in the Indian Ocean. The authorities searched the boat and confiscated the few things we knew they would take, plus a few more. No big deal. It was great to see Luc once again. The fleet had scheduled one "work day;" then Luc took us touring.

All the BPOers squeezed into little cars and headed to the mountainous interior of the island. Traffic was heavy and slow. I thought we might be making a mistake – wasting one of our few days there, sitting in stop and go traffic. But once we headed up, out of town, the scenery became pretty, and then splendid, and then magnificent. The highest peak on the island is over 10,000 feet. We drove crazy narrow switchback roads that rose from sea level to 7,500 feet.

The road we drove was new. Yet there were villages here and there in high remote areas. Previously they had been accessible only by lengthy trek. They were referred to as "islands." I was puzzled as to why/how such communities started. Answer: runaway slaves! Before the French arrived, there were no people here. Very different from the Pacific, where the incredible voyagers in sailing canoes had found and populated almost every island. Réunion (and Mauritius) were too inaccessible. When the French began a settlement, they brought slaves to grow sugarcane.

There was still plenty of sugarcane growing, still harvested by hand. The pressed stalks, once waste, were now used to generate power for the island – enough for six months of the year. (Imported fossil fuels powered the other half of their needs.)

We had another day of provisioning and chores, and then a farewell dinner with Luc. Really farewell, this time; he would not be in the remaining BPO plans, sadly. Aside from the sailors themselves, Luc had been the heart and soul of the BPO for more than a year.

The 1400-mile passage to Durban, South Africa, could be challenging. The BPO had arranged for a weather router to advise us about conditions/route/timing. He sent us a weather update the night before our departure: "There's no extreme weather at this point that would be cause for concern. Conditions are ideal at this moment for the passage."

To Africa! This was getting exciting.

Love the name, but too small for our crew.

At the intersection of engineering and art, driving here required your full attention!

In places the road narrowed to one lane, as it did at this tunnel. We met a row of oncoming cars and had a standoff. We (and several cars entering behind us) had to back out.

You could drive to the village on the plateau, center. But there was also a village in the valley below, with access only on foot!

≈≈≈

Sometimes it was hard for me to believe… We were 60 miles off the southern tip of Madagascar, about to reach a waypoint where we would turn west for Durban, South Africa. It felt like a dream, but we were doing it.

When Nora started her 7pm watch the wind was 20 to 25 knots, and we left our small heavy-weather spinnaker up. We were surfing down the waves, occasionally hitting 14 knots. I tried to get some sleep, without success. It was different for me without Bill or Tim aboard. I couldn't relax the way I could when an owner/partner was on watch – totally leaving the well-being of the boat in his hands. Now it was in my hands, even when I was off watch. My stomach was in a knot. I hadn't fully found my sea legs, even after four days. I lay in my bunk and reminded myself that the conditions were perfect for putting this catamaran through its paces. The small spinnaker was the perfect sail; no fuss. Surfing on waves like this was one way that our vessel excelled. And the night was beautiful, clear, moonlit. Gradually the knots eased and I relaxed. No sleep, but an easing of the tension…

…until the surge of the surfing became more extreme, and the boat yawed wildly, and the spinnaker collapsed and filled with an explosive bang. Time to get out of bed and see what was happening. The wind was in the high 20's; the waves were building; the autopilot was having difficulty holding a steady course. I watched for a while. The moonlight shining under the spinnaker, the night cool but not cold, the beauty deeply pervasive, our speed in top gear. Maybe we could continue in this magical groove…

But no. The wind hit 30 knots and it was clear the spinnaker had to come down. I woke Liam, if he was really asleep, so we would have "all hands" available. Turned out I needed him, as I was unable to pull the spinnaker snuffer down over the wildly flogging sail. The downhaul line threatened to lift me off the deck and throw me into the ocean. Once under control, continuing with just the half-rolled jib, we were still making 7 knots.

By then it was time for my watch. The boat was fine. Winds occasionally hit 35 knots, but no problem now. I needed sleep, and I needed to keep an eye on the many ships coming and going along the same route we were sailing. We checked for ships, and anything else of concern, every 10 minutes. I could relax on the settee with an alarm set and doze off for a few minutes between checks. After about a dozen such cycles I felt pretty good. The moon set, the darkness grew intense, but I was far more relaxed than earlier. When Liam came on watch at three, I got some sound sleep.

When we left Réunion the wind had been bending every which way, around those incredible mountains. It seemed to be anything but the predicted SE wind. At one point or another each boat was turned back toward where we started. We joked on the radio that Jimmy Cornell had hired the weather router to feed us happy information that had nothing to do with the actual conditions! But after a few hours of climbing away from the island we did indeed get the SE wind that scooted us toward our waypoint off Madagascar, 600 miles away.

On Day 3 we had light winds, and we motored for half the day. It was sunny and peaceful. I decided I'd had enough of the dry mouth side effect from the Scopolamine seasickness patch we were all using, and I removed my patch. That may have been a mistake. Usually I acclimated after two days, but this time I was still shaky after four. It seemed like I wasn't getting any credit for the first two days with the patch, and I had to start adjusting from scratch after removing it. Whatever, we were all getting by, limiting our time in the galley, lying down a lot, nibbling on crackers through the day and night.

What a difference a few hours can make! The wind fell to near zero; we were motoring in relatively calm seas with a bright sunny day. French toast for breakfast. We all took showers and had naps. Spirits were high, even though I was concerned about the lack of wind.

We had to stay alert in this location due to the huge volume of shipping. The ships followed the same route we did, from the southern tip of Madagascar to Durban. We saw as many as two dozen ships at once on the AIS display. Normally the range of AIS was about 25 miles, but there must have been some fancy repeater system in the area, because we were seeing data from ships 200 miles away.

We didn't see *Tahawus*, though; probably our puny transmission signals didn't reach the repeater. Last we knew we were about 35 miles ahead of them, and 150 miles ahead of *Maggie*. Chris on *Tom Tom* was following, three days back. We checked in with each other on the SSB radio morning and evening. But *Tahawus* wasn't present at that morning's check. After the variable weather of the past 24 hours, they could have passed us. We weren't racing, of course, but we liked to be ahead...

What a difference a few hours can make! After motoring most of the day, a pleasant sailing breeze came up in the evening. Pleasant for an hour...until it built to 25 knots, and Nora was waking me up to put in a second reef. On my watch I put in the third. Very "bumpy." Dawn brought only gray and more gray.

Since leaving Réunion we had been unable to access Sailmail via the SSB radio. No emails to/from home, no weather updates; very frustrating. We were doing our SSB radio net twice a day, and *Tahawus* would give us the weather synopsis. The outlook for our expected crossing of the infamous Agulhas Current, 10+ miles out from Durban, was not encouraging. A brief strong SW wind was forecast, which was exactly what we didn't want blowing against the current. I reapplied a scopolamine patch, in preparation for potential nastiness.

We thought about slowing down to wait for the wind to shift. But our weather router assured us that the current was not running hard; it was only about one knot. So, we did exactly what the experts advise against: we crossed the Agulhas Current with a strong southerly wind.

We made it...Durban...1400 miles in nine days. *Tahawus* arrived 3 hours before us; *Maggie* arrived a day later. It was a challenging passage, with a little of everything, but not much pleasant sailing. As Nora put it, this ocean was either on or off, not much in between. We had winds to 37 knots (top gust 55 knots according to *Tahawus*), and twice we had to motor. Some very lumpy waves. Awesome lightning displays. Whales welcomed us to Durban.

At the end of a rough passage I commonly listed what broke or went bad. For this one the only damage was our paper towel holder, which leapt off the counter and broke its back on the floor! It was still a mystery why we could not connect to Sailmail.

Liam and Nora both wrestled with seasickness (me, too, initially). They figured out ways to manage it, and they were always cheerfully on time to stand their watches. Good for them both! They were no longer offshore newbies. I had experienced crew!

Liam managing the queasies

Nora managing the queasies

SOUTH AFRICA

There was a very welcoming Point Yacht Club at the Durban Marina, with food and wifi and hot showers. However, after waiting two days to meet with various authorities, we were frustrated. Although we were thrilled to be in Africa, we had seen nothing but a yacht club.

When all three boats were finally cleared, we arranged a Great Leaders Tour to notable historic sites. We visited the gravesite of the Zulu chief/king Shaka, who in the early 1800's built the Zulus from a collection of small tribes to a powerful warrior nation. Although Shaka eventually went a bit off the deep end and was killed by his half-brothers, the Zulus remained a major force.

We visited the former home of Chief Albert Luthuli. Luthuli was president of the African National Congress and recipient of the Nobel Peace Prize in 1960. The (white, apartheid) government refused to issue him a passport to travel to receive the prize. An outpouring of foreign support led to Luthuli being allowed to go to Oslo the following year to receive his award and receive the accolades of most of the world. In 1966 (with the US in the midst of its own racial/social upheaval), Robert and Ethyl Kennedy flew by helicopter from Durban to Luthuli's home. The photos of Kennedy with Luthuli, in this simple remote place, without entourage, seemed very "real." Two men committed to common ideals, speaking with each other, not to reporters.

Each stop seemed to hit "closer to home" for me. Number 3 was the home of Gandhi. When the Brits determined that this area was ideal for growing sugar cane, they assumed a supply of cheap (black) labor. But they found that the Zulus would not work for them. The Brits needed slaves, but they had abolished slavery. Their solution was to bring indentured servants (not-quite-slaves) from India. *Lots* of them. Hence the very large Indian population in the Durban area. But they were not treated well, of course, and Gandhi came as a young lawyer to help with their legal issues. His plan was to come for 6 months, he remained in South Africa 21 years. Gandhi was a wealthy and well-educated man, but in South Africa he was "colored," second class. This experience changed him, forming his views about overcoming oppression through nonviolent action.

Gandhi's house was in the middle of a large "dormitory township." That is, where the non-whites were to sleep, even though they came to Durban each day to work for the whites. This remained an area that most tourists shied away from. We were the only ones on our rainy day. Being there hit a nerve, and the absence of tourists deepened the impact. We were standing in Gandhi's own house…where his beliefs took root. What an honor to stand there…to sign the guestbook…to compare his day to our day. What stand would he take against injustice today…?

We continued to the site where Nelson Mandela, at age 75, after a lifetime of struggle against oppression, cast his vote in South Africa's first democratic election. In his words: "I voted at Ohlange High School in Inanda, a green and hilly township just north of Durban, for it was there that John Dube, the first president of the ANC, was buried. This African patriot had helped found the organization in 1912, and casting my vote near his graveside brought history full circle, for the mission he began eighty-two years before was about to be achieved." After voting, Mandela is said to have walked to Dube's grave and said, "Mr. President, I have come to report to you that South Africa is now free."

South Africa remained a complex tangle of competing interests, of course; still in flux. As at home, the economic injustice remained, despite the end of apartheid. Land ownership by blacks was disproportionately small. Unemployment overall was at 24%; for young blacks it was 50%. Still, so much had changed in a few decades. I used to think that "history" was old news and had little to do with "now." Somehow my education failed to instill the idea that history is an ongoing process, happening today; that the events of the past have set a direction to the flow of events to come, and it is by collectively taking a stand that we have some ability to redirect the course of those events.

Wildlife

The Great Leaders Tour was just the opening act. We wanted to see more of the country and learn more history, and above all we wanted to see the African wildlife. Master tour guide Greg Garson planned out a remarkable six day exploration for us.

All the big animals were fantastic, but for me the most amazing was the giraffe – out of proportion, yet elegant and graceful, and curious about us. Incredible that she and I share the same home planet!

Midlands and Mountains

It was a long drive through the Midlands.

A memorable stop was the site where Nelson Mandela was captured (and then imprisoned for 27 years). Mandela himself wanted no memorial of significance at the spot, but recently an evocative sculpture was done and a museum built. The museum told the story of the man and of the fight against apartheid.

Many students were there on field trips. Many of them wanted their picture taken. A little like Indonesia but without the "Hey, Mister!"

There was a path from the museum to the sculpture. The artwork appeared to be a collection of odd-looking metal posts. It morphed as you approached…

We drove into the Drakensberg Mountains. It was misty/cloudy in the afternoon when we arrived, but wow…air so clean…silence so deep…the place had a wonderful and spiritual feeling. This area used to be home to the Bushmen, or San People. There are rock paintings done by them, some 5000 years old, some from 150 years ago.

Ardmore Ceramics

Imagine the
aromas at
the curry and
leather
goods shop!

Waiting...

Eight days after our tour, we were still in Durban. We were itching to move on, but the weather would not cooperate. It looked like we would have a "window" coming; then the window would close before it arrived. Twice. Although it was spring, it was cold like the depth of their winter, and the winds kept blowing from the unwelcome SW. The conditions would change rapidly, so there were brief periods that seemed inviting, but the forecast said no.

We made a list of boat tasks to do, and we crossed almost all of them off. One thing I was pleased about was we had a sailmaker repair the spinnaker snuffer that originated with our asymmetrical spinnaker. Its hoop/bucket had broken, so we had substituted the snuffer from our old Parasailor. But the latter was bulky and awkward and complex. Our repaired snuffer would be more manageable and simpler to use.

We had a mechanic look into why our starboard engine was reluctant to start. We had multiple "battery people" give us options for replacing our old batteries, but none of the options were very attractive. We decided to carry on with what we had.

We cleaned. We had diesel delivered. We searched for an outfit that could fill our propane tanks (our American fittings were not compatible with South African), and eventually succeeded in doing so. We repaired a lifeline, tightened alternator belts, inspected aloft, cleaned and lubed stuck zippers, lubed hatch dogs, inspected our repaired daggerboard, tested a temporary windlass repair, re-repaired our cockpit floorboards and reglued gaskets on hatches.

With most of our chores complete, we were reading a lot. Going out for a meal almost every day. Tagging along when others made a shopping run, even though we didn't really need to. Starting to think about the schedule ahead post-Brazil...how much time in the Eastern Caribbean...how much in the Bahamas...when back to the USA...and who would be aboard, as I would probably be looking for crew once again.

All the crews seemed to be getting a wee bit irritable, even though we put on happy faces. Would we ever get a good forecast to get out of Durban...? Jimmy wisely had told us to allow a month between Durban and Cape Town, despite it being only 800 miles. I didn't think we would click off so many of those days waiting to get started!

Just across the dock from us, we met Webb Chiles, a well-known singlehander and author. Liam poses by Webb's boat *Gannet* to show how tiny it is! Chiles has done a circumnavigation aboard that little boat. (He sailed direct to Durban from Darwin, Australia – 55 days at sea.) In the foreground is *Tom Tom*, sailed by another singlehander, again to drive home just how small *Gannet* is.

The Wild Coast

The area between Durban and Cape Town is known as the Wild Coast. Weather changes in a flash. Winds blow hard along the coast in one direction, then switch and blow hard in the other direction. There is the always-looming specter of the Agulhas Current, and the impact it has on the seas.

"Did you see the email from our weather router?" Norm was asking. "He says we have a short window first thing tomorrow to get as far as East London or Port Elizabeth." I had just been talking with Rob and Carol on *Maggie* about leaving the boats for another week, flying to Cape Town, and touring the area; hoping for changes in the weather pattern by the time we got back. But Norm was clearly beyond ready to depart, even if it entailed some marginal weather.

We all studied the email and consulted our various wind prediction websites. It took a while to adjust to this new plan. As we discussed it, a consensus emerged that we shouldn't wait until morning, but rather get going at dusk. This might put us into some nasty wind initially, but the hope was it would avoid even nastier wind at the other end of the hop, 2+ days later. Edd, our BPO rep, told us we needed to get moving ASAP with clearing out. Even though we weren't leaving the country, we had to do forms for Customs, Immigration and the Port Authority before we could leave for another port!

Nobody seemed to know definitively what the process was. Edd was told when we checked in with Immigration that we didn't need to see them to leave, but the Port Authority told us otherwise. At Immigration they couldn't find my inbound forms, even though they were done at the same time as *Tahawus*, whose forms they had. So I filled out the inbound forms as well as outbound. They briefly asserted that our crews needed to present themselves, but when we said we'd have to drive back to the marina to fetch them, the officers decided it wasn't necessary…

Two hours of forms and walking between the three offices, and we were "out." The plan was to go at 6pm, and hopefully sail as far as Port Elizabeth (about 370 miles), with an option to stop at East London (250 miles). There was no place to stop closer than 250 miles, so we had to be prepared to deal with whatever the weather would bring for two days. Nora and Liam had their Scopolamine patches on; I popped a Bonine.

Tahawus went first, on schedule. *Maggie* was about to go next when a nasty looking rain squall blew in. They decided to wait a few minutes. But daylight was waning. The wind was still blowing when *Maggie* backed out of their slip into the narrow channel, barely wide enough for them to turn in. As they tried to back and turn, the wind blew their bow down toward *No Regrets*. We were all on the dock, helping them with their lines, unable to get aboard in time to fend off. Some shouting ensued… *Maggie*'s anchor overhangs their bow, and it was one inch (literally) away from taking a chunk out of *No Regrets* when their boat magically stopped its approach. The magic must have been their bow thruster, which had been repaired the day before!

It was nearly dark as we motored toward the mouth of the harbor. Surprisingly large waves began rolling in. Ahead we could see the end of the protective breakwater, lit up periodically by the flash of an adjacent navigation light. Huge surf was crashing over it! What were we getting ourselves into!?

I might have turned back if *Tahawus* wasn't ahead, apparently doing fine. As we motored past the breakwater and turned directly into the seas, wave tops were breaking around us, and we were plunging down off of crests into steep troughs. I was glued to the helm, adrenaline pumping. Nora and Liam were both sick already!

[Later, on the radio, we heard ships calling Port Control for permission to enter the harbor. Permission was denied. "The port is closed due to the seven-meter waves breaking across the entrance." We didn't see 7 meters, but it was exciting, and funny to think that large ships were being denied entrance.]

My hope at this point was that the big, steep seas were caused by the shallow water along the shore, and we motored toward open ocean. Doing so would likely put us in the stronger current, with the wind opposed to it, so while the deep water might help, there was also a risk that the wind-over-current would make things even worse! I called *Tahawus* on the radio for a status report. Norm seemed cheerful enough; we plowed onward.

As we edged offshore we found ourselves surprisingly in a counter-current flowing north. This moderated the waves somewhat. But we could only motor into the mess at about 5.5 knots (with both engines), and that gave us only 3.5 knots made good against the current. This was going to be a long night.

Chris, the singlehander aboard *Tom Tom*, had recently quipped that I was "singlehanding with two passengers." That was a nasty comment, and not close to the truth about my crew. But for this night I was getting a taste of singlehanding. I stood watch all night, and let Nora and Liam try to sleep. Not sure they got any more sleep than I did, though!

We got out of the counter-current and into 3+ knots of Agulhas current going our way. The wind came up at a good sailing angle. Things were looking up. I was feeling "chuffed" (new British word I learned, meaning very pleased) about being at sea and mastering a challenging situation.

The second night the skipper made French toast for dinner – trying to make something the crew would eat. Everyone had some. Good. The crew was still feeling green, but their spirits remained positive.

The night sky was spectacular. But it was too cold to stay outdoors and enjoy it for long. We put up our small spinnaker for some relatively comfortable downwind sailing. Naturally it didn't stay that way. About 4:30am, I was awoken by the surge of the boat, and went up to find the wind was approaching 30 knots. We were sailing beautifully and very fast. With the extra boost of the current, we hit 20 knots over the ground. But the spinnaker was at its limit, so time to bring it down…always a challenge in the night…Liam and I did enough shouting to wake Nora who says she can sleep through anything…the three of us succeeded in getting it "snuffed"…and switched to just a reefed jib…still going fast. When the wind gusted over 40 knots I was very happy to have the spinnaker down!

The morning brought superb sailing. Blowing about 30 from behind, with a big push from the current, waves surprisingly manageable. On a midnight radio check-in with our fellow BPOers, *Tahawus* and we committed to carrying on for Port Elizabeth. *Maggie* would stop at East London.

By mid-afternoon we had 40 miles to go. The forecast gave us until 8pm before the wind would turn and blow hard against us. We would need all of that time. We could already see clouds ahead signaling the change. As we approached the coast we lost the boost from the current. With ten miles to go, the wind faded. We motored and made it in just as the last light faded and the new wind began to blow.

The Wild Coast? *Tahawus* was just a few miles behind us. Before they made it in, the weather window was long gone. They battled winds of 40 knots, gusting to 50, on the nose. Despite their hefty engine they could barely make way against it. We stayed up to take their lines when they got in around midnight. Wild, indeed.

≈≈≈

I was disappointed with what we found at Port Elizabeth. The yacht dock was not readily accessible to boats our size; they told us to tie to the fisheries pier instead. Giant tires kept us off the concrete wall but painted black smudges on our topsides. There was a surge as well as the crazy wind. Uncomfortable motion, grinding noises, and rubbing against those tires. It didn't seem right to be in port and still have difficulty sleeping. Nora still felt seasick. At one point the boat lurched as I was stepping from the deck to the cockpit, and I ended up in a pile on the floor with a bloody scalp.

We were amidst a hive of activity of fishing boats coming and going, nets hauled up on the jetty, deckhands gawking at our boat (lots of compliments). A short walk away was the yacht club, with a bar and restaurant, and hot showers. Things began to look better. But our primary task was to identify another weather window for moving on. I wished the weather window would include some warmth, too – winter did not seem to have yielded to spring yet in these parts.

Uncertainty

We were pinned in Port Elizabeth for a week. It looked like we had a window for Cape Town, but once again our window closed as it approached. We remained tied to the fisheries pier. We were lucky, the fishermen said, that the fishing fleet was out, or there would be no space for us. A big fishing boat came in at night, and the pier came alive with workers shouting and trucks and horns and a general cacophony.

The port area was fenced/gated. I felt imprisoned, even though we were free to go out and in with the help of a gate attendant swiping an ID card for each of us. I had just one experience in "PE" where I felt like I connected a bit with the local community.

We needed fuel. I loaded jerry cans into the dinghy (which hadn't been in the water since Rodrigues, maybe 5 months ago…?), and (after coaxing the outboard to life) motored over to the fuel dock, which was just another pier with big tires over the side and a row of fishing boats tied up. A guy there latched on to me immediately, offering to help (expecting a tip, of course). I couldn't understand 80% of what he said – a little worse than average when I spoke with the fishermen here. My friend grabbed three of my five jerry cans and headed down the pier, to what destination I knew not. I grabbed the other two and followed. Up ahead he had a conversation with someone, and made an about-face, headed back my way. He said a lot to me – what I think he was saying was that they wouldn't fill jerry cans; but he would find someone who could help.

He disappeared into one of the fishing boats, to fetch a member of the crew, I thought, but he was gone for a very long time. I waited and chatted with several fisherman, a few of whom I could understand. They go out at night for small sardine-like fish. They can harvest 25 tons. Their catch gets sold overseas as bait for tuna fishing! The world economy operates in strange ways. They were interested in where I was from, and they liked hearing the list of places we had been. What did I think of South Africa, they asked. I told them in addition to the natural beauty I liked the people and the social complexity. "Many cultures," one said. Eventually my friend reappeared. He said the guy was coming soon. I wasn't sure who was coming or what he was going to do for me…

Anon a well-worn micro pickup vehicle (you couldn't call it a truck) arrived, and I met Fabian, the driver. The jerry cans went into the back, as did my friend and another helper who had glommed on. I wasn't sure how hard to close the tin-weight door; but nothing broke. Off we went. I immediately liked Fabian, and not only because I could understand him. I couldn't be sure what held his vehicle together, but I think it might have been the speaker wires, because the one component that was top quality was the stereo! Did I mention that I liked Fabian? He asked if I like reggae, and he allowed as how he liked to listen to reggae all day long.

Trains carry iron ore to this port to load on freighters. We waited for one to pass. Then on to the gate of the fenced-in port. Oops – he didn't have his ID with him; can't get back in after leaving, with no ID. So back to the fishing boat, Fabian muttering about the foolishness of the authorities/system. Then back to the gate, and a mile on down the road to the petrol station. No problem getting both diesel and petrol there, and I could pay with a credit card. I even earned a 25 Rand credit to be used on anything in the store. I gave the credit to my friend.

Fabian drove to our boat, where we deposited the diesel jugs, as my crew and others wondered where I had been for the past hour, and why I was returning by car when I left in the dinghy! Fabian took me (and the petrol for the outboard) to the fuel dock. I asked about his family. He said he has four children and a fifth on the way. A boy…he already knows…modern technology, you know… He also has a grandchild. Having a child younger than your grandchild seemed interesting. He said this child will definitely be the last. I said, "I bet you said that after #4, too," and he burst out laughing. Did I mention that I liked Fabian?

I had already paid Fabian gas money at the store. I had the foresight there to get change for my big crispy bills issued by the ATM. A tip for my friend, a tip for the glommer-on, a tip for the guy who "watched" my dinghy while I was away. I think everyone was happy. Me, too. My friend jumped in the dinghy and started untying it, which had me puzzled, but one of the guys I could understand explained that he wanted a lift over to the other pier. No problem. The dozen or so fishermen hanging around all waved and said goodbye, and my delightful little Port Elizabeth adventure was complete.

The morning after we first arrived in PE, a salty looking motorsailer arrived, with an equally salty looking skipper. He introduced himself as Wavy ("Not my fault," he says). The boat was a training vessel. The crew of mostly 20-somethings was aboard for five months to get licensed. Great training weather here…go out and experience 50 knots anytime! Wavy was a delightful guy, and gradually we learned more and more about his adventures. He was a racing skipper; won the Fastnet race; was on an America's Cup crew; sailed on the record-setting catamaran Enza; rowed across the Atlantic singlehanded; currently was racing skipper on a Swan 60 raced all over the world, with him and his racing crew flown in for the regattas. They just ordered a new racing mainsail for $150,000… He also sailed across an ocean or two with just his four-year-old daughter as "crew." David Immelman was his real name…like Webb Chiles in Durban, a fascinating character to bump into on the dock.

Back to uncertainty… We learned it was not simple for US citizens to get visas for Brazil. They want you, or your authorized agent, to show up at the consulate closest to your residential address. I.e., mail my passport to an agent in Boston, even though I was required to have my passport with me in South Africa… There was a consulate in Cape Town, but it wasn't entirely clear if we could get visas there, or if it would issue them only for South Africans. They wouldn't answer our questions on the phone, so we would have to wait until Cape Town to learn our fate. If they wouldn't issue visas we would…umm…sail to French Guyana instead!?

Tim said he would prefer to rejoin in French Guyana anyway. But the plan remained for the BPO to sail to Brazil. Liam and Nora could to sail on to French Guyana if we were to arrive early enough, but there was no certainty about that.

So the crew onward from South America, Tim and his son Josh, had to wait and see, along with the rest of us.

First we had to get around the Cape of Storms, to Cape Town. After a week in PE, the weather forecast predicted a short window, long enough to sail to Mossel Bay. That's still on the Indian Ocean side, but it would chip away at the distance to go, increasing our chances of making Cape Town when the next opportunity came.

Mosselbaai

The sail to Mosselbaai (Mossel Bay) was pleasant. No racing to get in before dark, or before a front came through. We arrived at a pleasant marina, with floating docks and water/electricity available. Once again we were inside a fenced-in port, and had to pass through a gate to get out and in. But the town was very accessible and pleasant and, we were told, safe. It was a touristy area. It was considered "Western Cape," even though we were still on the Indian Ocean side of Cape Agulhas. The white people here spoke Afrikaans.

Just up the road was the Bartolomeu Diaz Museum. Diaz was the first European to sail around the Capes, attempting to reach India. He sailed to Mosselbaai in 1488. A replica of one of his vessels was built in Portugal and sailed here, where it was now on display in the museum. Great fun to go aboard and check out its interesting rig, and to imagine sailing aboard a small caravel with a crew of 33! I understand why early explorers found this area to be almost impassable, and in fact it is amazing they managed to round the Capes at all with no weather router or weather tracking ability, and no charts, and no knowledge of where shelter could be found ahead. Sailors today have it so easy!

I was feeling more and more "arrived." Hard to describe...I was just being present...not perseverating about the weather window...we would get to Cape Town soon enough... But it wasn't just getting around the Cape...I was more content on the boat...more comfortable with my own ability to voyage...to be the master of my vessel. The last day on the way from PE we were a dozen miles ahead of *Tahawus*...it was a rare pleasant sailing day...I decided to change course to go closer to the coast to see more of the scenery...let *Tahawus* sail on past us...no need to rush, no need to arrive first... I enjoyed both the side trip and the laid-back feeling, which had not been present much since, well, since Cocos Keeling, months before.

Word came from our weather router that we had a very favorable pattern coming, with plenty of time for us to get to Cape Town. It being so nice at Mosselbaai, we considered letting this window pass and waiting for the next one. But we needed to get our Brazilian visas handled at the Consulate in Cape Town.

Replica of
Dias' caravel,
sailed from
Portugal,
nested *inside*
the museum!

Into the Atlantic!

I knew I would be excited to pass Cape Agulhas and cross the imaginary line between the Indian Ocean and the South Atlantic, but when we actually did it, I was "pumped!" The sailing conditions were super. We were flying along at 9 knots with the big spinnaker up. As we crossed that line we also turned north, back toward the sun and the tropics, for the first time since Sumatra. Hooray! Whales were spouting in the distance.

We had a little ceremony to mark the milestone. Three Ships Scotch was tasted and offered to the sea. One could say that the major ocean milestones of this voyage were the Panama Canal, Thursday Island where we left the Pacific for the Indonesian seas, the Straits of Malacca where we transitioned to the Indian Ocean, and here – the transition to the South Atlantic and our furthest point south of the voyage. Making the turn north made my heart sing, a verse about the warm sailing that lay ahead, a verse about heading toward home.

Cape Town and Western Cape Region, in Pictures

Comfortably berthed at the Royal Cape Yacht Club. We were very, very lucky getting in. Our reluctant starboard engine quit, but we arrived amid a rare occurrence...a calm...so we could maneuver in on one engine.

Plenty of Cape Fur Seals as we neared Cape Town. They like to hold their flippers in the air to regulate their body temperature.

Table Mountain coming into view; approaching Cape Town

Table
Mountain
is such an
icon here,
one has to
ascend.
We chose
to forego
the cable
car (just
visible)
and climb;
3000 feet.

Robben Island
(where Nelson
Mandela was
imprisoned) in
the distance

Cape of Good Hope. Understandable why it gets more press than Cape Agulhas!

The lighthouse on the Cape of Good Hope appears as a tiny bump low near the point.

The old lighthouse —
decommissioned because
it was too high! Ships
sometimes could not see it
up in the fog/clouds.

To the interior…cool
mountain passes, following
the route of the Trekboers,
into the semi-arid Karoo,
into areas where some
speak only Afrikaans, into
vineyard country.

Klaudia has a twinge of uncertainty about this… Unfortunately (?) the men were over the weight limit for this activity.

Walking on eggshells…

Departure Time Approaches

I had mixed feelings about moving on. As always, I looked forward to continuing the voyage, reeling off some miles, getting into the life-at-sea rhythm. But it was very pleasant in Cape Town. The yacht club facilities (hot showers, Internet, restaurant, laundry, and water/electricity at the dock) were top notch. Everyone was friendly, and we had made some new friends. The exchange rate made things affordable for us. It seemed that you could get anything done/made for a boat, and done/made well. Why go anywhere else?

The boat I had owned 30 years before was built there. Many Atlantic 42 catamarans were built there. The popular Leopard catamarans commonly offered by Moorings and other charter companies were built there. This was a serious yachting centre. The boats at the yacht club didn't just sit and go nowhere. (Well, some did, of course.) There were races every Wednesday and Friday evening, and a constant stream of events at the club.

And...where to go...? We got our Brazilian visas, no problem (other than the high cost), and of course we would sail to St Helena and Brazil. But many people had told us of the wonders of Walvis Bay, Namibia, 700 miles up the west coast of Africa. It wouldn't exactly be on the way to St Helena, but it wasn't terribly far out of the way either. If we went there we would want to stay several days, because the cool stuff required a tour ashore. All told it might add a week to our itinerary. We could do that and still arrive in Brazil by the time I promised Liam and Nora.

We had been getting ready. Scrubbing the growth off the waterline (too cold here to get in the water and clean the whole bottom). Removing a faulty relay for the wind generator and installing a new switch in its place. Going to the rope factory where they sold remnants and loading up on new lines at fabulous prices. (Three of the "remnants" I bought were 80 feet long! I felt like a kid in a candy store, made two visits and wished we had time for a third.) Meeting with our diesel mechanic almost every morning to take the next troubleshooting step. (Still had troubles but hoped it would serve well enough.) Getting the standing rigging inspected and following up on replacing some damaged parts (which had to be fabricated). Installing a new motor for our windlass. Fixing the corroded wiring on an engine stop solenoid. Stocking up with diesel and propane. Replacing a broken hinge on our table. Always more to do.

We had to provision for about four weeks, which for us was a challenge both in planning and execution. We ordered frozen meats from a wholesaler. Then filled three shopping carts at the supermarket (and got a checkout line opened for us, and a lift in their van to get all the food back to the yacht club). We were almost ready. Just needed to settle bills, do laundry, fill water tanks, finish stowing everything, watch the weather, and...determine where we were going!

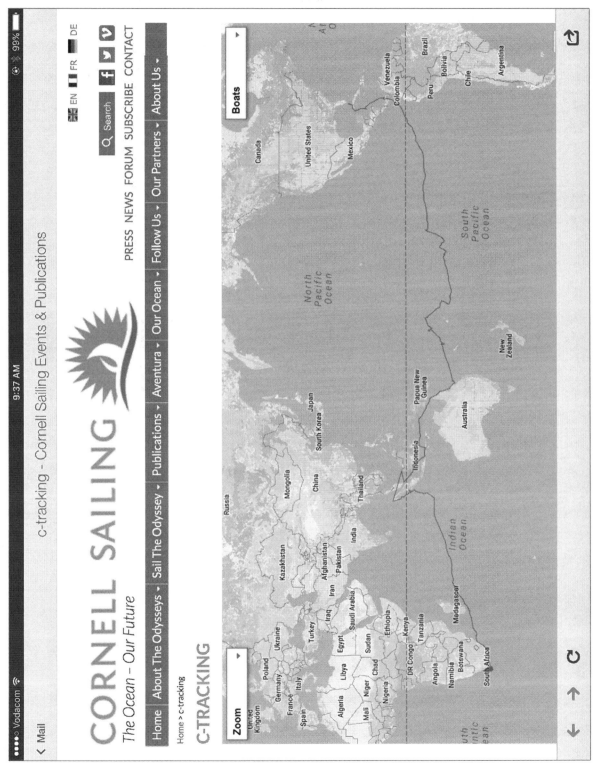

Our entire BPO track so far, as recorded on the BPO website.

SOUTH ATLANTIC

Namibia? Why not!

We decided to go; *Tahawus* and *Maggie* decided to head straight for St Helena. We would all check out together, along with our friends aboard *On Verra*. We had been told that checking out on a Sunday would be simple, a 20-minute process. But…

For starters it was a half hour walk to where the authorities were. We got cleared by the Port Authority, and Immigration was next door and held no surprises. But Customs was another matter. We had no paper clearing us into Cape Town. Normally one does not clear out of one port just to go to another in the same country. Not so in South Africa. But Royal Cape Yacht Club had handled everything when we arrived. They apparently did not clear us in through Customs. I pulled out our clearance into Durban, but that carried no weight. We couldn't be cleared out of Cape Town without a clearance in, the official insisted. I asked the gentleman what I was to do, given that the yacht club had told us we were properly cleared in, yet we didn't have the required paper. Well, we would have to clear in before we could clear out, and that would involve a fine for our delay in doing so. On Sundays no one was there to handle money, so we would have to return tomorrow. It seemed absurd, but there appeared to be no getting around it.

We walked the half hour back to the yacht club, where Diane was helping us. She said this had not been a problem in her thirteen years of clearing yachts in and out. She got on the phone and insisted that a supervisor must call her back within the hour, because we "had to" leave today. It was a good effort, but the rules apparently had changed and Customs was not budging. Our fine was to be 1,500 Rand (a little over $100) and must be paid in the morning.

So…what would happen if we simply left, I asked. Nothing. Our passports were already stamped. The next port would normally expect a clearance, which could be troublesome, but we could argue our case there. *On Verra*, bound directly for Grenada (6-7 weeks away!), had already given up and left.

"Diane, what would you do?"

"I'd just go," she said.

So we did.

≈≈≈

For the 700-mile passage, winds were fresh; occasionally down to 15 or up to 35, but mostly in the low/mid 20's, and directly behind us. The first evening brought whales all around, as the sun was setting. They were mostly in the distance, but just after Liam and I went below to sleep, Nora spied two crossing our bow. One dove just a few feet from the boat! Sorry, I missed it; no photo.

The Namibian coast is low and flat, and the air off the desert creates a mist over the cold Benguela Current coming from the Antarctic. Even though we came within five miles of shore, we could barely make it out. And even though our latitude was only 26 degrees south (Liam pointed out that this is the same distance south of the equator as Saudi Arabia is north of it), and summer was approaching here, it was *cold*. No lounging on deck! Night watch in the pilot house under a blanket.

No lights from shore; no airplanes; no chatter on the radio; no yachts; only an occasional ship; rarely even a cloud. We were getting into the groove of 24-hour sailing. I kind of wished we were settling in for a longer ocean passage, rather than stopping again and having to restart. Hopefully our Namibia adventure would prove worth it.

The US presidential election happened. Nora and I had sent in our ballots from Cape Town. (Liam is British and had to sit this one out.) I was shocked by Trump's win. I thought there would be a "silent majority," especially of women, that in the end would vote for Hillary. Like so many others assessing Trump's chances, I was wrong. There was a message in it for me, that I had a narrow view of my country; that my news sources had a similar narrow view of my country. Perhaps this election would provide a useful wake-up call about the social diversity of the country. Or do we just become more polarized and unable to work together?

We arrived at night. Exciting negotiating a busy unfamiliar harbor in the dark, the lights afloat mingling with the lights ashore. Creeping through the small boat end of the harbor, I was surprised to find a mooring, and we celebrated with a bottle of wine and a bar of chocolate.

In the morning we cleared Customs – they didn't even ask for a clearance from Cape Town! Then Immigration, found an ATM, found SIM cards and topped up data, got a map, and got wifi at the yacht club. Good start. Next we needed to find someone to actually rent us a mooring (we didn't know who owned the one we were on), and figure out how to rent a vehicle and where to go for some fun.

Sand, Beautiful Awesome Magnificent Sand

We struck out finding a mooring to rent. We asked at the yacht club, and no one knew. We found a number for the Commodore, who told us they had none available. The local boat tour operators said none were available. Yet there were plenty of empty moorings. The second morning we saw a charter crew cleaning a boat nearby, so I dinghied over and asked them. "Oh, the mooring you're on belongs to a boat that is up on the hard; just stay there, no problem." Jackpot!

We also struck out finding a 4×4 we could rent and drive out into the desert. Nothing available. But while we were asking one of the waterfront tour operators about moorings, she booked a tour for two German women, and…we thought…maybe we should switch gears and do a tour instead of wandering about on our own. What a good move that turned out to be! We declined the harbor tour in the morning (cold, damp, and we had a fur seal hauled out on the back of our boat – we didn't need to book a tour to see 'em). We signed up for the afternoon tour to see the desert sand dunes.

Herman was our guide, and in his very cool Land Rover it was just the 3 of us and the two Germans. Herman turned out to be a rather special character. One of 6 people with permission to go anywhere in the Namibian national parks. A vast knowledge and a wicked sense of humor. We drove out the point that makes Walvis a bay. It was just a sandbar, largely covered with salt pools drying in the sun. We "peppered" him with questions about the salt works. He had the answers, and I think he warmed up more and more to us in appreciation of our thoughtful inquisitiveness.

Then south along the desert/beach. Fast! Herman was a test driver for BMW, and it became ever more clear that he was an expert when it comes to driving in sand. We got stories about overturned self-drives, and vehicles stuck in quicksand.

There were fur seals on the beach, some alive, some dead. There were springbok, jackals, and ostrich. But mostly there were sand dunes like none I had ever seen or imagined.

Herman dropped us off atop a particularly beautiful dune and told us to meet him at the bottom – lunch would be ready. Very nice to take off the shoes and walk in the hot sand. And a very nice touch that lunch included chilled local oysters on the half shell! And chilled champagne!

Herman referred us to a friend who could take us to see Dune 7 the next day. I didn't know exactly what Dune 7 was, but everyone said you had to go there. And we found you can't just go there – you have to climb it, and it is the tallest dune in Namibia.

The daily Walvis Bay fog recedes, revealing a nice sunny day from about noon to 4pm. The rest of the time was cold, though technically we were in the tropics.

This cape fur seal brought back memories of the sea lions in the Galápagos!

The oil rig in the background
was parked – taken off station
because it was not profitable
to operate with low oil prices.

Heading inland, Herman says we now leave the moguls behind and head for the serious dunes.

Dune 7

At our driver's suggestion, we opted for the ridge up the side rather than the direct frontal approach (while he snoozed in the car). The sand was fine and soft, making for difficult hiking.

Namibia to St Helena

We were off to St Helena, 1200 miles (about 8 days) away, halfway across the South Atlantic.

We took the "scenic route" out, hugging Pelican Point so we could see the huge fur seal colony there. Fun to watch their antics. Some performed alongside the boat, probably expecting us to reward them, as the tour boats probably did.

The wind was light and against us, so we motored for the first few hours, trying to get clear of the coast with its fog and local winds. We ran the watermaker for the first time in ages. After fifteen minutes or so there was a POP, and the machine sped up as though it no longer had any resistance. I feared that its reverse osmosis membrane had failed. As I experimented with it, we noticed water in the lockers under our settee. The plumbing had sprung a leak. Two hoses bound by a hose clamp had simply slipped apart. Fixing the plumbing was easy. Emptying the lockers to mop up the mess and dry it out was a pain.

The wind gradually came up and came more south, as expected, and we sailed through the night with the screecher. A full moon lit up the cold Benguela Current mist.

Two months ago we were approaching Durban, and I had the feeling that *wow*, this was Africa! It had been a wondrous time. Now leaving Namibia I had a similar feeling of awe that we were leaving Africa and heading for another continent across an ocean!

By the end of day 2 the air temperature was up over 70. A blanket could finally come off the bed. Sea temperature was up from a chilling 55 when we left, to 65. The nighttime fog/mist was decreasing. We were reaching in 20 knots of wind, doing 10 knots boat speed with a single reef in the main. I made a good dinner and celebrated with a beer. Everything that we needed was working as it should. We were out beyond the shipping routes, expecting a quiet night. Two hundred miles behind us, a thousand ahead. Perfect!

By day 4 the air temp was over 80; the sea temp up to 67. Wind was behind us at 15–17 knots...just what was advertised for this part of the ocean. The big spinnaker was up, and I imagined it might stay up for days.

During the night we once again lost the blades off our hydrogenerator prop. Third time. Annoying, particularly given the high replacement cost, but whatcha gonna do? We also started fishing for the first time. We hooked a beautiful tuna that could feed us for 3 days, but just as we gaffed it the hook came free. The gaff was not set well enough to hold it...so despite having it briefly on the transom steps, we lost it. We vowed next time to get it right!

I took a short, bracing shower on deck, and stretched out listening to good old rock music with the headphones. Ah, the way life should be! We hadn't been this warm and had such pleasant/relaxing sailing conditions since somewhere early on the Indian Ocean. Soaked it up!

Day 6. Nora and I had gotten into a routine in the morning, where we brought the small spinnaker down and put up the big one. As we were getting the big one ready to go, Nora noticed that the small block for the "snuffer line" was damaged – the sheave was gone, so the line was dragging over the pin/axle. We found a small snatch block that we could use to replace it.

As we worked on it we also noticed that the halyard had chafed entirely through its protective outer braid, exposing the inner strands. We needed to cut off the worn end, but later; I decided to go ahead and raise the sail. It went up half way and stopped. Something fouled aloft. We brought it back down, and at that point noticed that the halyard was also chafed through the braid further along, where it would pass through the masthead block when the small spinnaker was set. The frayed braid was apparently jamming in the block aloft.

Okay, so we would need to rig a new halyard at our first opportunity. But the damaged one could work for now. We covered the two worn spots with white rigging tape. The tape would prevent the frayed bits from jamming, and the white would be visible from below so we could adjust the halyard to avoid wear at those critical points. Up went the big spinnaker again; it set fine.

I looked through the binoculars to check where the white tape was, relative to the block. Something was still wrong. The line appeared to be off the sheave, jammed into the side of the block. Not good; we decided to bring the sail down again. Except…now it was really jammed…it wouldn't budge up or down!

We could still use the snuffer to get the sail mostly under control, and luckily the wind was relatively light. But to get the sail down was going to require a trip up the mast – not a pleasant experience at sea! The motion of the waves gets amplified by the height of the mast. Aloft in the bosun's chair, it was almost all I could do just to hold on. I could not budge the halyard. There might have been creative things to try, using the power of a winch below to free it, but I knew I had very little time before I would be exhausted from the effort to hold on. The only practical thing to do was to release the snap shackle on the halyard, and let the snuffed spinnaker fall to the deck or over the side. I had meant to bring a line aloft to help with such contingencies, but I had forgotten it. I yelled to my crew below to be ready to pull the sail out of the water if necessary. With a great deal of effort, I pulled the pin and watched the whole thing drop. Right on top of Nora!

Nora was bruised, but not seriously injured. Allowing this to happen was a terrible lapse of judgment on my part. I was struggling with my end of things, and I simply didn't focus on what was going to happen below. I think Nora recovered from the event before I did. I was upset for a day about my failure to put safety first.

The halyard was still jammed aloft, and that wasn't going to get fixed until we were in a quiet anchorage. We had ideas about rigging the blocks aloft differently, but that also had to wait. We had a line long enough to replace the damaged halyard, but that, too, had to wait. For the time being we were not flying a spinnaker, as the wind was allowing us to use the screecher with fair results. If we needed a spinnaker, we would have to lower the screecher to the deck to borrow its halyard. That would be tricky because the screecher would end up sprawled all over the deck. But it would be the only practical way to set a spinnaker until we sorted out the problems.

The wind went light. We motored for a couple hours, including when we had the highlight of the day – crossing the Prime Meridian. To celebrate our return to the Western Hemisphere, I let the boat drift for a few minutes and jumped in the ocean. No other takers for that ritual, though. Maybe next time. We changed our clocks two hours to St Helena time, which (naturally, given our zero degrees longitude) is the same as UTC / Greenwich Mean Time. Still 340 miles to go. I wasn't in any rush, except that it would be nice to arrive before the other boats departed.

A pod (gam?) of whales swam by about 75 yards away. Not much other life though. No dolphins; very few birds.

We lowered the screecher to the deck and raised the spinnaker. Wind had been about 10 knots all day; we glided along at a quiet 5 knots. Peaceful. Sixty miles to go.

Locating a small island in mid-ocean used to be an exciting time, especially if the sky was overcast so you couldn't get sextant sights. Even with good sextant readings there might be a nagging doubt about whether you added when you were supposed to subtract, and thus you might be off by 30 miles – enough to never see the island. But now we take GPS for granted. We know exactly where we are all the time, and there was no drama about seeing St Helena at dawn.

Arrived before noon; picked up a mooring next to *Maggie* and *Tahawus*. No problems with the authorities. Everyone was friendly; people said hello; drivers waved. We explored some. We booked a tour for Thursday – our Thanksgiving activity. Nora and I walked the 699 steps up "Jacobs Ladder" to see the view. We all took showers ashore. In the evening we had a very pleasant welcome/farewell gathering of the "three ships" aboard *Maggie*. The others would set out in the morning, since they had already been there a week. We would stay three days, then follow in pursuit.

St Helena

St Helena is about nine miles by six miles. It is inhabited by 4,000 "Saints," as the locals are called. And 5,000 "machines," according to our guide, referring to cars. Our guide was Robert Peters, the go-to guide among the yachties. He was 80 years old, a former school bus driver, and a man full of stories about island life when he was a boy.

It was at times challenging to understand Robert...the Saints have an interesting variant on the British accent. We got into some serious confusion when we couldn't distinguish between "story" and "distillery!" But yes, we did visit the distillery – a Brit who retired and decided he would like to make spirits, despite having no experience in the field. He had a still custom made in Germany and shipped to his very nice home on the island. With the help of some books, he started making Tungi (from local cactus). And then rum and gin and whatever else struck his fancy. We did a brief tasting and bought a sampler set from him (the only place on the island that will take a credit card!). But the real treat was just listening to him engage with Liam about the details of the still and the process. I had to drag Liam away, back to our tour.

One of the best parts of the tour was just driving on roads that were carved into the mountainsides. In many places there wasn't room for two cars to pass. Uphill had the right of way. Going down you had to look ahead and gauge if you could make it to the next wide-enough spot before meeting a car coming up. This made for slow going down at 4pm, when many of the workers in "downtown" headed for their homes on high.

We visited Napoleon's tomb. Napoleon was exiled to St Helena in 1821, and lived there until he died six years later. On his tomb the French wanted an inscription with the title "Emperor" but the Brits wanted "General." Unable to agree, there was no inscription at all. Nice spot in any case. His remains didn't stay put, though. France took them back.

On to Longwood House, where the Emperor/General was "imprisoned" for most of his stay. Beautiful house on a beautiful hilltop, which made it "guardable" by sentries at a discrete distance. The prisoner could look...in vain...at the distant horizon for a ship coming to rescue him. Apparently he didn't like St Helena, though many people would be thrilled to be exiled to Longwood House!

Another attraction on our tour was the brand-new airport. For many, many years there had been just one way to travel to St Helena, if you weren't sailing your own yacht. That was the "RMS" – the Royal Mail Ship. The RMS sailed monthly from Cape Town to St Helena, unloaded for a couple of days (5,000 machines, remember), then sailed on to Ascension Island before returning to Helena and Cape Town.

When I heard that an airport was opening on St Helena, I imagined a delightful old place being overrun by tourists. Well...not yet, at least. The British government spent many billion pounds flattening out a piece of the volcano for a runway, but it had such severe wind shear that it was not considered safe for commercial aircraft! More billions will probably go into modifying the surrounding landscape before the tourist hordes can descend. But now that I had gotten to know the island a little, I no longer imagined it would be drastically altered by an occasional jetload of visitors. When the RMS came in there was a flurry of activity, and then much of the island seemed to go back to sleep. I expect when there is regular airline service there will be some minor reduction in sleepiness.

We stopped outside the Governor's House, not so much due to interest in the Governor herself, but to see the tortoises that were imported many years ago. Several remained, including "Jonathan," born before Napoleon arrived!

The island was discovered in 1502 by a Portuguese sailor. Unlike many "discoveries" of that era, there were no inhabitants to displace, infect or enslave. I'm not sure how/when it became British; the tour wasn't big on pre-Napoleon history. But lemons were grown there, and sailors with scurvy were left to recover (eat lemons) and then join a crew again. And naturally it was a watering-place. The island was also used as a place of exile for the Zulu king Demizulu, and it held 3,000 Boer prisoners in the Anglo-Boer War. Based on my reading of Michener's *The Covenant*, Boers brought to St Helena were the lucky ones, in that few died there, while huge numbers died in camps in South Africa.

Back to current events. The Saints were incredibly friendly. People said hello and waved. They went out of their way to be helpful. What a nice "outpost" in mid-Atlantic. Almost made me want to stop at Ascension Island, too. But no, Brazil beckoned.

Approaching St Helena

What used to be a tramway is now 699 steps with a view.

View from atop the 699 steps. In the center are *Tahawus*, *Maggie*, and *No Regrets*. The bigger sailboat is Kat, of the Brazilian book/movie Pequeno Segredo (Little Secret).

Creative gardening; note
the egg in the nest.

St Helena to Fernando de Noronha, Brazil

It is 1700+ nautical miles from St Helena to the islands of Fernando de Noronha off the coast of Brazil. Here are snippets written along the way.

~~~

Flying the spinnaker most of the time. Having to remember protection from sunburn. Lots of lazy time. Since *Tahawus* got a 290-mile head start leaving two days before us, we don't feel like we're racing, so we are more laid back than if we were watching them on AIS. Fabulous blue ocean. Empty except for flying fish (one flopped off the pilothouse and onto Nora) and occasional birds. All quite pleasant. Just wish we had been able to buy fresh produce in St Helena, as we are already down to nearly nothing.

~~~

A whole world to ourselves, it seems. Endless ocean. No sign of other humans. On we march, hour after hour, day after day, and each mile looks the same. Another thousand to go, the chart tells us.

~~~

At last it is warm at night (and hot in the daytime). Like our joyous nights in the Pacific, one can lounge in the cockpit and feast upon the stars. Tonight we had the tiniest sliver of moon following the sun down – a welcome harbinger of more moon to come each night. Venus is so bright it casts a dancing reflection on the water.

~~~

Our attempts at fishing have been sad. The first day out we hooked a beautiful little tuna, and had it gaffed, yet it still wiggled clear of both the hook and the gaff, and we lost it. I'm sure by then it was dying, so it was a lose-lose situation. Fishing was very quiet for the next several days, which I took as our punishment for wasting a good fish. As the water got warmer (from 55 degrees off Namibia to 79 degrees with 750 miles still to go) we saw more action. Which is to say we had one get off the hook before we ever saw it, and we lost two lures. Lose-lose, again.

We might have stopped fishing at this point, but we are low on food. We need to get it right. Today we hooked a big one. We snuffed the spinnaker to slow the boat down. We eased the drag on the reel to prevent breaking the line. The fish had taken almost all the line before we got things under control…spent a long and arduous time grinding it in. A mahi-mahi, at long last! Big, beautiful, and still fighting as we got it up to the boat and gaffed it. And *crap*, we lost it (and our lure) again!

We were one unhappy crew at that point. But Liam rigged another lure, and though it was late in the day, we tried again. As the sun was going down we got another strike. A small tuna, with beautiful cobalt blue streaks. In comparison to the mahi-mahi it looked puny, but we got it aboard and we got it filleted, and it's going to provide us with two meals.

~~~

All day I have not so much as touched a line. Spinnaker flying, we are rolling along under the hot sun. We made an easy 177 miles noon-to-noon. I've eaten and napped and read, occasionally glancing at the chart plotter to confirm there is still no sign of another craft within AIS range.

I did do one little thing this morning – I deployed our new hydrogenerator propeller. About four days ago our last prop lost a blade. As a result we have had to run an engine nearly 3 hours per day to charge the batteries. But I had kept one of the old broken propellers in our "trophy collection" of bits and pieces that have failed along the way. I spent a day wondering if it would be possible to graft a blade from that old prop onto the newly broken prop…

It took a day to find the old prop, and only then did I realize that its blades were smaller. But it would at least be in the ballpark. Worth a try. Liam pointed out that we could trim down the other blades to match. Out came the epoxy, and we cut the blade off the old prop and epoxy-tacked it on to the newer one. Then (next day) a proper layer of epoxy. Then fiberglass tabs front and back to add to its strength. A little shaping, including trimming the other blades, and ready to go. We tried it, and it seemed to work, but it had more vibration than I had hoped. Decided to take it back off and add fiberglass tabs to the other two blades to try to keep them from breaking, since that's how these props keep failing. A final coat of epoxy last night, and today we deployed. It was quite a work of art, I think, for something improvised at sea!

It worked for half a day…then the grafted blade disappeared. Apparently the epoxy doesn't bond well with the plastic of the prop, and the blade managed to work its way out of the fiberglass sandwich. Crap! Back to running the engine again. With our fridge and freezer, plus all the electronics, we use a lot of electricity. Maybe in another day or so we will empty the freezer and thus remove one of the big draws. Too bad that our work of art isn't functional; into the trophy collection it goes.

~~~

I finished reading *The Covenant* – quite an accomplishment for this infrequent reader. I knew that the mixture of peoples in South Africa was complex, but the book made it apparent that they are even more complex than I knew. Some of the description of Apartheid was appalling. Again, I knew that Apartheid was ugly, but it was even uglier than I knew. Interesting that the book was written before Nelson Mandela was freed. Michener ends with a description of several possible scenarios for the future course of South Africa, most of them much more bleak than what has actually come to pass. I am struck by what a great man Mandela was, to bring about such a huge transition in a mostly peaceful and orderly way.

~~~

The sailing is peaceful and pleasant, which leads to thoughts about the next boat and/or the next time around. Would it be a catamaran? I'd like to spend some time sailing a monohull now, to do my comparative analysis. But probably I would go for a multihull. I like the sailing qualities of trimarans, but I would probably again choose a catamaran for practical cruising. Possibly even this same boat, or its 48-foot big brother. I'm intrigued, though, with the James Wharram catamaran designs… simple… Polynesianesque… and I find some of them beautiful. And being out of the mainstream, maybe more affordable.

There is boat-as-vehicle and there is boat-as-home, and a spectrum in between. Currently I am more in the former camp. My home is ashore in Maine; my boat is how I'm getting from here to there (or is it here to here, for a circumnavigation!?). If there is a next time I could see leaning more toward boat-as-home. Of course, Hallie might not like these ideas, but reality need not intrude on this reverie. I could see living aboard in a place that we like, until our visas run out and we have to move on. Maybe from French Polynesia we would head north to Hawaii instead of continuing westward, and then to the Pacific Northwest. I'd like to visit Denmark and Norway…maybe Iceland…go back to Réunion…see more of Africa…revisit Tuvalu…explore New Zealand. That doesn't make sense as an itinerary, but the point is to live in these places long enough to get to know them, rather than just spend a few days and move on.

So many things to do in this short life…

~~~

We are 8 or 9 days into our passage. I can't remember exactly, without counting up the X's on the chart plotter that mark our position each noon. Here's what today was like, in greater detail than usual…

I wake shortly after 7. Nora had taken over from Liam at 7, but Liam is still hanging out chatting. I make my rounds, checking for anything wrong on the boat. We have our big spinnaker up. It's a bit unusual to fly it all night, but the winds have been light and steady. Liam reports that the wind briefly went up to 20 knots on his watch. He was about to wake me up to bring the sail down, but the wind eased again, and it has remained light. I find two flying fish dead on the deck. They have so many tiny bones that we don't bother trying to eat them. I threw 3 overboard during my watch last night, two of them alive and kicking, but I didn't notice the third in time.

I set out our trolling line, and tell the universe I don't want another tuna, I want mahi-mahi.

Liam goes below for some rest. Nora offers toast, made from an excellent loaf baked by Liam, and I gladly accept. It is Nora's day to cook, but preparing anything for breakfast is optional. She cuts our last apple into thirds, for a special savor-it-because-there-ain't-no-more treat.

I dig out our spare outboard propeller, with the idea that maybe we could connect it to the hydrogenerator to make some electricity. But in the meantime our batteries are very low, so we start an engine. We run it in neutral just to charge batteries. Putting it in gear would likely collapse our spinnaker, plus we are trying to stretch our limited supply of fuel.

At 8am it is time for the radio net. That's another reason to be running the engine, since transmitting on the radio draws a lot of current. We connect with *Maggie* and *On Verra*, reporting our positions and sharing that nothing of particular note has happened overnight. We do not hear *Tahawus*, which is a little disappointing since we like to compare our position to theirs. We've been gaining on them roughly 9 miles per day. They're still about 230 miles ahead of us. Our update will have to wait for the evening net.

While the engine is running we should make some fresh water. Our tank is low after Nora and Liam took showers yesterday. Making water draws even more current than the radio; we do it only when the engine is running. It is also a noisy operation, sometimes driving us out of the pilot house, to the cockpit. It takes an hour of noise to make six gallons.

Though cloudy initially, blue skies win out, and it isn't long before the heat is intense in the sun. Time to put up our awnings, to provide some shade in the cockpit. It's delightful to sit in the shade and stare at the bright blue ocean. Easy sailing. Beautiful emptiness. I scan the horizon, half expecting to see a sail. Not likely!

Suddenly the watermaker starts banging rapidly. Nora and I both recognize the sound – we heard it before when we sprang a leak in the seawater supply line. I jump below to shut off the supply valve. We open up various lockers to see how much water is in the bottom. Sure enough, the joint that came open before has opened again. I get a bucket and a small towel to start wiping up the water. I look at Nora's face and laugh – how much she does *not* want to do this is written all over it! She says, "I didn't know I was that transparent," and joins in with another towel. At least we caught the problem quickly this time; much less clean-up than the first time.

We rummage through our plumbing supplies and find a combination of fittings that will be more secure. We trim off the worn end of one of the hoses; we find a hose clamp that has a wider grip. It all goes together easily, and we give the watermaker a test run. All good. But the lockers are going to stay open all day, drying out.

After a while Liam is up; he and I brainstorm how we can get some use out of the hydrogenerator. I'm leaning toward attaching the spare outboard propeller to the hub of the old prop (with all its blades broken off). Liam is leaning toward cutting new blades from some steel bookends and fitting them into a hub. We have two old broken hubs available, so we decide to each try our own ideas. Maybe one of them will actually work…

Our mechanical engineering projects keep us busy until a pasta salad appears for lunch. Delicious. Also with a savor-it-while-you-can flavor, as it contains our last bits of celery and carrot. Midday brings an assessment of the past 24-hour run, from a waypoint we set the previous noon. 165 nautical miles – a respectable run in the light wind.

In the afternoon I get my prop-on-prop graft assembled, and we try deploying it. Amazingly it starts working with minimal shakes or vibration. It doesn't generate much power though – maybe 4 amps. Still, that could mean running the engine twice a day rather than three times. Liam continues with his project, which will require several small batches of epoxy, and thus at least another day.

Dinner is ready. Cabbage salad, sautéed butternut squash, and a surprisingly good frozen pizza. We are working toward emptying the freezer, so we can shut off that current draw. There's still one more frozen pizza in it. Probably everything else could survive in the fridge.

As the sun is setting we bring in our fishing line (no action today), bring down the cockpit awnings, and tune in for the evening radio net. Connections are marginal, hard to make out what anyone says, but we do get the positions for *Maggie* and *Tahawus*. We've knocked another 10 miles off of *Tahawus*' lead.

Liam heads to bed. Nora and I sit in the cockpit for a while staring at the sky. The crescent moon is close to Venus, very pretty in the twilight. We pick out several satellites. She sees a fleeting shooting star. I could sit in the cool and stare at the sky for the 3+ hours until my watch, but I should get some sleep before I am on duty, so I turn in.

With the quiet conditions I sleep through until my alarm goes off at 10:53. Time to unhurriedly report for duty by 11. Nora briefs me on what the wind has been doing (not much), no ships, no nothing. She turns in, and I have the world to myself. When the sailing is peaceful, I love to be alone on my 11pm to 3am watch. When conditions are hairy, the watch can be terrifying, but that is half a world away tonight.

The batteries are low, so time to start an engine before I use the radio to check for Sailmail. Although the Africa station is now 3,000+ miles away, at this time of night it connects on the first try. I transmit a long email asking Hallie to post an entry to my blog, and several short emails about when/where we will make connections with upcoming crew. We're working out the details now for the Caribbean and Bahamas. It is wonderful to be able to send emails at sea, even though we sometimes spend hours in frustration, trying to get an adequate connection via the radio. We've learned what frequency and what time works well for the Africa station, but we will be gradually losing that. Next up will be a station in Trinidad, and we will probably go through a learning curve working with it.

The wind goes even lighter and shifts direction 30 degrees. Normally we would consider motoring at this point, but we have limited fuel given our battery charging situation, so we will just sail slowly. I adjust the sheets, with a silent apology to Nora for grinding the winch directly over her head. It will wake her up, but she will go right back to sleep.

Batteries charged, emails sent, engine off, I settle into writing what this day was like. Before I can even finish it, Liam appears and my watch is over. Time now to sleep 4 hours, and do it again. I could repeat days like today, happily, for weeks on end.

~~~

This is our last night at sea; we should arrive around dusk tomorrow. It has been a wonderful day. Clear, with a steady breeze. We were entertained by a bird that hovered in front of us, watching until we would scare up a "flock" of flying fish, and then he'd swoop in and try to catch one. We saw him succeed several times. A bird landed on the back of the boat, but he was off again after a few seconds. We also had a bird go after our fishing lure, but luckily he gave up before he got hooked.

Tonight we had two ships pass close by, on their way toward Europe/Gibraltar. One was on a collision course with us, and with our spinnaker up I was limited in what I could do to get out of the way. I gave him a call on the radio, and he changed course 30 degrees to pass behind us, thankfully. I also saw two airplanes. We must be approaching civilization!

~~~

Yesterday Liam deployed the hydrogenerator propeller that he had improvised from bookends. It worked well – very quiet and smooth, generating about the same power as my outboard prop concoction. But this morning it didn't seem to be generating much, so I pulled it up for inspection. The blades had all bent backward! We are back to using my solution. But this is no longer a big concern, as we approach our destination and we still have some fuel in reserve.

~~~

Nora won the bet on how far off we would be when we spotted Fernando de Noronha. Liam and I each owe her a drink. We were surprised by how high the land was, and especially by one prominent phallic peak that turns out to be a focal point from nearly everywhere on the island.

We arrived as the sun was getting low. We anchored and all jumped in for a quick refreshing swim; then watched the sunset. We opened a bottle of wine and were about to have a simple pasta dinner when we heard James and Ruy, our *Blue Wind* friends, approaching in their dinghy. They had recently arrived after sailing across the Atlantic from the Mediterranean. We welcomed them aboard (they had never been aboard *No Regrets*!), and shortly after we heard the *Tahawus* crew approaching. We opened another bottle of wine. We've never had so many guests in our little cabin! A nice welcome, and always fun to reconnect with James and Ruy. Ruy says he needs to go with us to see the authorities in the morning, because they speak no English (and we speak no Portuguese).

Eleven and a half days at sea on this most pleasant of passages. Hard to believe we are in Brazil. Hard to believe that Nora and Liam have sailed 6,000 miles with me. We are a seasoned crew now, and it's a little sad that our thoughts are turning to flights home (for Liam) or to other parts of South America (for Nora). But first we will enjoy being here for three days, and then two nights from here to Cabedelo on the mainland. Hallie will be coming to visit there.

Brazil! West side of the Atlantic! Only three time zones east of home!

~~~

Our collection of
hydrogenerator propeller
improvisations/failures

Approaching Fernando de Noronha

Fernando de Noronha

In the morning we were surrounded by dolphins! Dozens of them chirping in Dolphinese, mostly slowly swimming by as they caught their breakfast, but with some doing crazy aerial stunts. My guess was that they jumped out of the water to make a big splash, to scare the fish toward the pack. Nora suggested it was adolescent males showing off. Whatever their reason, they put on a delightful show for an hour.

We dinghied over to *Blue Wind* to pick up Ruy and headed ashore. The Harbormaster/Capitania loved Ruy (everyone did!) and was happy to help his friends. He drove us to Immigration to get our passports stamped, and then to the airport so we could get cash at the ATM there. He also said he wouldn't charge us for the previous day – Fernando was tremendously expensive and they charged a fee for each person for each day, as well as a fee for the boat. Looking at the form I had just completed indicating that the length of the boat was 13 meters, he said he would charge us the 10-meter price. Ruy translated, "Your boat is under 10 meters, right?" I replied, "Yes, we are 13 meters." Everyone smiled. They still collected over $300 from us for 3 days at anchor!

High on Nora's list of priorities was snorkeling. After lunch we took the dinghy to an area where we were told there was a wreck. We weren't sure exactly where it was, but we saw a light/shallow patch of water and dropped our anchor there. Turned out that our anchor rested on the deck of the wreck. It was fun checking it out, and a few fish, but the water was murky due to a high surf, and the fish were not plentiful. Nora will get more snorkeling chances in two months, in the Caribbean.

After a nap it was time to head ashore again as the three crews were meeting for dinner at a Brazilian style (of course) steakhouse. We had two rented dune buggies – the standard mode of transportation on the island. Not surprisingly, we were the first customers at the restaurant, since we were not on the schedule of Brazilian nightlife. Ruy took charge of arranging for our food – great meats kept appearing, sliced off the skewers at the table. When we were sated, the skewers appeared with roasted pineapples with a sweet glaze, an excellent dessert.

Back to the boats…unless you wanted to follow Ruy to the bar for some dancing. Our crew all went with Ruy. Again, we were way early. But the band was fun and we danced as best we could…not up to Brazilian standards, I'm afraid. When we got back to the boat, well after midnight, Nora said, "Is it really the same day that we checked in?" I had to think hard about that (through a fog of alcohol) – it had been a very long and remarkable day.

In the morning there were dolphins.

Ashore we did food shopping. Siestas on the boat. Then ashore and into the buggies to go to a beach. Wow, it was beautiful! Acres of superfine sand, pleasant surf, and nobody there. We played in the waves and walked on the sand, until reluctantly we had to leave to return the rented buggies, and the other two boats were preparing to leave. Ruy came out with us for one last drink, and he tried at length to get our cell service working. He shouldn't have, not because the phone effort failed, but because it was nearly dark by the time we ferried him out to *Blue Wind*. Captain James was clearly not happy that his crew was so late. Ah well, *Tahawus* and *Blue Wind* got off okay, and I hope James has forgiven both us and Ruy.

In the morning there were dolphins.

We all worked on cleaning the bottom of the boat, since this was our last chance to be swimming. Liam and Nora did a last visit ashore, while I soaked up a little alone time, and started dinner. When they returned we had just enough time to get the dinghy stowed and things put away and dinner consumed, and then get the anchor up as it was growing dark.

We had only 250 miles to go. We almost certainly could have left in the early morning and arrived before dark the next day, but by leaving in the evening and planning to sail through two nights we removed any risk of having to navigate up the river too late in the day. We were happy to go slow (double reefed in 12 knots of wind, to try to keep our speed down) and enjoy the peaceful ride.

Ruy sends a message to Daphne. Ruy was crew aboard *Blue Wind*. Daphne embarked aboard *Ransom*, then was invited aboard *Tahawus*, then fell in love with Ruy and moved to *Blue Wind*. But she was home at this point, and Ruy was indicating how much he missed her. I tried to share a pun with him, that he had a "heart on" for her, but it was completely lost in translation to his native Portuguese…

Here they seem to be born with rhythm.

Crew Update

Tim and his son Josh would sail with me to Barbados, where the BPO rally would end. Nora was making a plan to travel (ashore) in South America. But she was interested in doing more sailing in the Caribbean. It had been part of Bill's original plan to sail in the Caribbean with his two daughters. He had given up on that idea, as he realized that his daughters had busy lives, and couldn't very well leave their jobs to go sailing. Yet, here was Nora doing just that. Why not take a month off from his own job and sail with her? He and Nora both agreed to rejoin in Barbados, and Bill would bring his friend Harry as well.

We would have a full house for a month, from Barbados to Antigua. Then what? I wanted to sail with Hallie in the Caribbean. She could join when Bill and

Harry departed. And I had invited Jesse and his girlfriend Chelsea to come for a few days. That was still going to leave me well over 1,000 miles from the USA.

I knew once the circumnavigation was complete that we would be putting the boat up for sale. The three of us were not about to go cruising together or share ownership beyond this voyage. Where would we park the boat to show it? There would be much work to do, getting it emptied and cleaned and repaired and staged for sale. It shouldn't be too far from Maine/Vermont/Pennsylvania… We had Rhode Island in mind. We would list the boat with Chris White, the designer; he lived in that area.

One could sail direct from the Caribbean to New England, perhaps with a stop in Bermuda. But I had done that years ago, and I wanted to cover new waters. I wanted to explore the Bahamas on my way to the USA. Nora was willing to stay on to Abaco, in the northern Bahamas. I needed to fill in one crew from Antigua to Abaco, and two from Abaco to the USA. I wasn't picky about where in the USA. I figured once there I could round up friends for short hops, if needed, up the coast. Hallie might even be willing to sail that area.

After all that we'd been through to get this far, I was confident that crew would work out. I was less confident about how our partnership would fare with trying to sell the boat. But I wasn't going to worry about that yet.

What About Sex?

When we checked into our first foreign port, in Havana, and Tim was joking with the officials, they got on the subject of "chicas." Maybe it was the Customs guy who started it, commenting that we were "tres hombres" sailing with "no chicas." Tim being Tim, he asked if anyone knew some chicas for us. Me being me, I cringed and tried to change the subject. But that night, as we relaxed after dinner, three giggling young ladies came down the dock and asked if we wanted chicas. I had no idea how Tim would respond. "No, gracias. Buenas noches."

Some people when they met us wondered if we were gay. You could see the thought cross their faces. Three guys on a boat for months…no women…maybe they're gay…a threesome?…not likely… Usually the next question was, "Are you married?"

Almost every boat cruising around the world has a "couple" aboard, usually husband/wife, sometimes not married, sometimes same-sex, sometimes with children, sometimes with other (often temporary) crew. Jimmy once reported some statistics on this. I remember that we fell into the "all others" category – we were a rarity.

I know some people who will be disappointed to read this, but aside from when Hallie came to visit, the only sex that happened on *No Regrets* would have been solo-sex. Wait, they say, you and Nora sailed together for months…

That Nora was female and attractive was a concern. I checked in with my men's team about whether or not I should invite her – checking if I had a "blind spot." I listed the pros and the cons. Already having met me and sailed on the boat was a pro. Being prone to seasickness was a con. Being an attractive female was both – I'd love to have a beautiful woman around, yet I didn't want the potential distraction/frustration. Responses from the team: "How would Hallie feel?" "You would get more stress than pleasure from the arrangement." "The risks outweigh the benefits." I have a huge respect for this group of men. That doesn't mean I always take their advice.

Nora and I were in a supermarket checkout line in South Africa, and the woman behind me said something about my wife. Oh, I realized, she means Nora! My ego soared. For a moment I understood why some men have "trophy wives." I thoroughly enjoyed it whenever people assumed that the pretty young lady was this old man's wife or girlfriend.

Chatting with a shopkeeper, Nora and I told her about our voyage, the boat, crossing the ocean. Then I said I might buy something for my wife. I was oblivious to the woman-to-woman communication that happened in that instant. Nora explained to me afterward that the shopkeeper shot her a glance that said, "Did you know he was *married?*" Another stroke for my ego.

But no sex. In fact, Nora and I seemed to have an unspoken rule: no touching. Working together in the confined galley, we would awkwardly avoid bumping into each other. It kept the boundary clear. Sorry, guys.

Was it difficult being celibate? Sometimes. Probably would have been harder when I was younger. Sex is no longer the unstoppable force that it once was. Thankfully.

At one point when trying to work out the crew plan, there was a proposal that Nora and I might sail alone from Brazil to French Guiana, after Liam left and before Tim arrived. A week or two of quiet sailing in the tropical sun, alone together on the endless blue ocean. I squashed that proposal. Edging that close to the romantic sail-off-into-the-sunset dream would likely have my men's team saying told-you-so.

Brazil

We docked at Marina Jacaré, several miles up the Paraiba River, about halfway between Cabedelo and João Pessoa, in the easternmost part of Brazil. It was hot. And there tended to be loud lousy music at 2 or 3am. But the little marina was pleasant. Protected, but with an all-important breeze; nice showers (no hot water, but none needed); wifi; a bar/restaurant; and Nicolas (one of the owners) spoke English and was extremely helpful. Unfortunately, business was so quiet (many boat owners flew home for the holidays, including the crews of *Maggie* and *Blue Wind*) that Nicolas suddenly decided to take 10 days off, and with him went not only our translation service but also the food/drink service!

Liam returned home. Hallie arrived. Nora remained aboard while working out her travel plans.

There wasn't much in the area to hold our interest. A walk of a mile or two took us to a supermarket, a bakery, and a beach. The beach was pretty but not great for swimming. We took a small train into João Pessoa, which is one of the oldest cities in Brazil, and the state capital. Lots of churches; interesting old architecture; interesting murals/graffiti on walls. It was fun for a day, but there was no desire to go back…

We had a wonderful dinner for the three crews, before Liam and Rob/Carol left, prepared by Nicolas (before he left), funded by the BPO. We broke out our tattered BPO banner for the occasion. We also had a fun celebration of Nora's 30th birthday, with ceviche made by Klaudia, and key lime pie and chocolate cake and creative alcoholic drinks. And Christmas Eve dinner aboard *Tahawus*, again with lots to drink and lots of laughs. We had some good times, but we wondered how we would fill the hot days until our planned departure date of January 10.

For some variety, Hallie, Nora and I did a three-day trip to a bed and breakfast in Olinda, an old and beautiful town on the outskirts of Recife. This was a hit! The B&B had only two rooms, so we had the full attention of our hosts Sebastian and Yolanda, and we almost felt like we were part of their family for our stay. Delightful breakfasts on the veranda!

Our B&B was near the top of a steep hill. Nice breeze, nice view, and sometimes a challenge walking back home in the heat of the day or the swirl of too many beers with dinner. The road appeared to be paved with stones from forever ago.

We took a taxi to Recife, to the restored old waterfront…a water taxi across to the breakwater…fascinating sculpture and views of the city…the first synagogue (now a museum) established in Latin America…the open market that goes on for blocks, very crowded, very noisy, many aromas. It was an experience just to walk in the crowd through the mayhem.

At the market I bought cashew fruit. I loved eating cashew nuts, but I had no idea how they grew or the process of harvesting them. The nut hangs down from a fruit the size of a small apple. The fruit is edible, but you never see it because it won't keep. It is sweet but makes your whole mouth pucker. The nut is in a nearly impenetrable shell. The nuts are dried, then roasted until they catch fire. One has to be careful, they can explode. After the lengthy roast one still has to crack each burnt shell with a knife or other tool to extract the nut. No wonder the nuts we buy are expensive!

Back in Olinda we heard there would be local frevo music at the music school. When we found the place, it was all closed up. But there were people in the street, and beer being sold, so we waited. A man approached us and said something in Portuguese. When we didn't understand, he spoke to us in English. He asked if we were there for the frevo music, and explained that the maestro was late, but it would start soon. Have a beer, stick around, he insisted.

Everybody seemed to know this guy. He led us inside the school and introduced us to the just-arrived maestro. And then the music was cooking (the word frevo is similar to the Portuguese word for "boil" – the music is hot/intense).

The music was inside, but all the windows were opened and the crowd was outside. Some people danced in the street. One man in the street was playing a Brazilian version of the tambourine – like no tambourine we'd heard before…quite amazing and fun. We followed this with a late dinner. The one other group at the restaurant was a birthday party, and the guest of honor shared her birthday cake with us. Chocolate cake with lemon frosting – hit the spot!

Olinda and our B&B home were so enjoyable, I was reluctant to return to dull Cabedelo.

Although we were still 1900 miles from Barbados, and that much again from New England, I had the feeling that my circumnavigation was winding down. What would I do next? How could anything compare with the past two years? Could I adapt to living ashore? Would I end up on the couch in front of the TV, depressed?

I browsed online and found a 46' Polynesian style catamaran for sale at a very affordable price. I found this style of boat romantic; it was simple. Maybe we should sell our condo and live aboard. Maybe we would spend winters aboard in the Caribbean. Maybe I should sail around again…

Hallie pointed out that I was "coming from fear" – that I was trying to fill an anticipated void, rather than "being here now." And of course she was right. A long voyage quiets the nagging question of life's purpose. One's purpose at sea is clear…to get safely from A to B, and hopefully have a good time along the way. When the voyage winds down, the questions of purpose reemerge. How can I do something useful with my blink of time on this planet?

Marina Jacaré

Coconuts

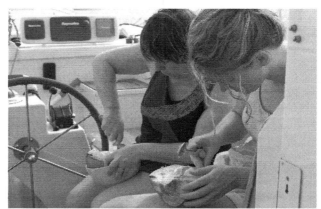

Entrance to our room in Olinda

The "canvas" is the trunk of a tree!

Sculptures on the seawall at Recife

Preparing to Go

Hallie and I enjoyed New Year's Eve on the beach at João Pessoa, thick with people, but everyone having fun and being cheerful. No ugly drunks…no snide remarks to the foreigners…no complaints about walking in front of other people as we wended slowly through the crowd. We bought kabobs and chocolate covered strawberries from vendors on the street. There were fully stocked bars put up temporarily on the street, too.

Nora left to travel in Argentina; Hallie left for home. Tim returned (last seen in Mauritius), plus our new crew: his son Josh. They had a day to acclimate before we cleared out. We drank/ate coconuts and then went to a local restaurant for their "prato feito" – the meal of the day, which was more than I could eat for $6. We provisioned. We had Nicolas prepare a farewell moqueca dinner for all four boats. (*Blue Wind* would also be departing, but heading in the other direction, toward her home near São Paulo.)

No Regrets had been sitting idle for three weeks. Things go bad when boats are idle. We tested the engines. Both started easily, but the tach stopped working on the starboard side and the stop solenoid failed on the port side. Oh well, not show-stoppers.

One downer was that *Tahawus* had lines stolen from their boat – staysail sheets cut right from the sail during the night! Ruy talked to some locals about it, and the consensus was that it must have been "the crazy guy" who lived nearby. Who knows? It colored our perception of the place, to have a boat boarded during the night while the crew was sleeping and have gear stolen. But it appeared to have been a weird one-time occurrence.

It would be a little under 2,000 miles to Barbados. Wind was expected to be favorable, though maybe light, plus there would be current with us. Maybe 13 days. Goodbye, Brazil!

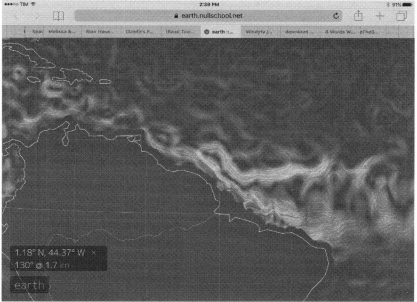

Current flows NW near the coast, doubles back offshore.

To Barbados

Day 3. It was very hot in the daytime; we were only 70 miles from the equator. But oh, the nights! Cool and spectacularly beautiful in the brilliant full moon. For the most part there was little to do but cook and eat and read books. The sailing was easy and comfortable, and with the help of the favorable current it was pretty fast. Our noon-to-noon runs were 170, 170 and 185 nautical miles. The last day was a big one because the wind came nearly abeam, allowing us to sail fast.

We were over 50 miles ahead of *Tahawus*, but they had given us a head start. Just as we were making sail after motoring down the river from Jacaré, they found that the tails of the halyards had also been cut/stolen! They had to go aloft to reeve new ones, and for that they needed to anchor in the sheltered river. And then on Day 2 they blew out their genniker, a go-to sail in the light downwind conditions. *Maggie* had an engine problem that delayed their departure. They had to wait a full day for the tide/current to again be right for them to go. No worries, there was no hurry to arrive in Barbados.

My day began with slowly waking from a deep sleep, wondering why there is so much noise of water rushing by. The current in the river at Jacaré was strong and audible, but not like *this*. It took me a minute to emerge from sleep enough to realize we were sailing. I checked my iPad to see the time. 6:30…I decided to snooze longer. When I awoke again it was 7:30 and starting to get hot.

After a brief "Good morning!" Tim said we should set the spinnaker. The wind had come aft again; the jib was at times backwinded by the mainsail. It took us 45 minutes to furl the jib, rig the spinnaker sheets, drop the mainsail, set the spinnaker and get all the lines squared away.

I was about to get a bowl of granola when Josh offered to make breakfast; leftovers from last night's excellent dinner, with poached eggs on top. It was more breakfast than I usually want, but I wasn't about to say no to such a good offer! While Josh prepared the food, Tim and I put up the awnings for some shade in the cockpit. We had considered leaving them up at night, but in a nighttime squall they could be a compounding nuisance, or worse. So we took them down each night.

0900 was radio check-in time. I watched the clock for twenty minutes prior, because twice already we had gotten distracted with boat tasks and missed the call. Today we had good reception and could hear both boats, although they couldn't hear each other. We relayed their positions. Not much else to chat about except how beautiful the night was, and confirm that we were all experiencing similar weather conditions.

Then time to do nothing until noon. Read. Snooze in the cockpit. Occasionally check for ships. Periodically silence our "AIS Connection Lost" alarm that triggered at inexplicable intervals. At noon we set a waypoint on the chart plotter, at our current position. Then we checked our distance from the previous noon waypoint. With the wind light and aft, it was our shortest day's run so far, but still about "average" with the help of the current.

I made wraps for lunch, using up a stew Josh had made from a fish head. The head was about all we had by the time we reeled that fish in. Something, probably a shark, took two-thirds of the fish along the way! The third we had left was still enough for a baked fish dinner, plus the stew that was dinner, breakfast, and lunch. We had been eating very well so far. And we still had some fresh fruit and veggies.

I tried to access Sailmail on the radio, to get a wind forecast. No luck getting a connection. We would keep trying every few hours.

There was a small ship ahead, coming our way. It appeared on AIS; it was a 177-foot military vessel. It changed course to pass very close to us. I listened on the radio, expecting them to call and "interrogate" us. They did get on the radio, but they were talking with another nearby ship. Still, they were circling up behind us, so I decided to call them and ask what their intentions were. They explained in broken English that they were on a military exercise, looking for a white boat with two {something I couldn't make out}. Had we seen such a vessel? I replied that I wasn't clear what size vessel they were looking for. Apparently they heard this as a "No." They thanked us and steamed away, to my relief. But two minutes later they hailed us again, asking where we were registered, where bound, where from. I braced myself for more, but that was all they wanted, and we were done with our encounter.

Time to think about preparing dinner. I defrosted some chicken…a stir fry over elbow macaroni…with some veggies and a little dried mango and some olives…

At twilight ugly clouds appeared to windward. We discussed whether or not to douse the spinnaker. Tim said yes; I hesitated because no squalls so far had "packed a punch." But these clouds were darker, more ominous, than any we had seen. In the interest of sleeping well, I agreed with Tim. Just as we were bringing the sail down, the wind increased. We got the billows stowed as gusts rose over 30 knots. I was very happy that we got it down! But, of course, 15 minutes later the wind was back under 20, okay for the spinnaker, and before long it was down to 14. No matter, where there was one squall there were probably more, so the spinnaker stayed down and we double reefed the mainsail for the night.

It was dark well before 7, when we had our evening radio check-in. This could be a noisy staticky intrusive hard-to-make-anything-out pain, or it could be a pleasant chat in addition to the exchange of positions and sharing of weather conditions. Tonight we could barely hear *Maggie*, and we couldn't make out their position. We traded info with *Tahawus*; they had closed the gap between us a little.

Silence again. Technically Josh was already on watch, but we tended to hang out for a while in the cockpit, letting the night wash over us, watching the moon rise, checking the clouds to windward to see if they were potential squall material. Then I set my alarm to 10:53pm and tried to settle in for some sleep. But I was not ready for sleep yet, and I lay awake with my thoughts. When the conditions were peaceful, as now, not sleeping didn't much matter. I could take cat naps during my watch later if I needed to. In challenging conditions I would be concerned about not sleeping when I had the chance.

At 2300 I was on deck. The moon was brilliant; the sky clear. The night air caressed me with coolness. The emptiness of our surroundings was enormous. We didn't have nearly enough sail up to move the boat well, and Josh reported that the wind had been light for his entire watch. I didn't want to shake the reefs out of the mainsail, because the activity would likely wake Tim. Tim chronically had trouble sleeping, and even more trouble getting back to sleep, so we tried to minimize nighttime sail changes. But Josh and I quietly furled the jib and slowly unrolled the big screecher in its place. This got us moving well enough. When Tim appeared at 0300, we shook out the reefs, too. And I got some real sleep until 0700 or so.

Tim and Josh would talk at length about politics, and I found their talks interesting. Tim blamed the ills of our society primarily upon a failed political system. Josh argued that no better system had been identified, and the problems stemmed from people, not the system. When would the rich and powerful recognize that they didn't need more wealth and power? Besides, the problems weren't so much political as economic. They both agreed that capitalism as we know it in the USA does not work for "the people."

I agree with Josh that change has to come not through big system changes, which the powerful would never let happen, but through individuals "waking up," and making many small changes that collectively might become a movement. It is very hard for me to be content with this approach though. The actions we can take, at least the easy ones, seem so tiny…it just leaves me feeling powerless, and I'd rather focus on something non-political…like sailing… I imagine this conversation will be recurring for me over the coming months, and probably far beyond.

Closely related to politics, especially in the Trump era, is "news." For over two years I was not plugged into the flood of media. I would get the news of important things through occasional updates from Tim or Hallie, a TV in a restaurant, a newspaper left at a marina. It was plenty. Most of the updated-by-the-minute "news" isn't news anyway – it is people's opinions about news, or worse, people's opinions about people's opinions. I think we would all be healthier and happier if we all tuned in to the BBC news (it's important to get an outside-the-USA perspective) once a week. That's all; just once a week. Unplug…

Day 10

We crossed the equator during the night, so no special celebration at the time. But in the morning the wind went light; we furled the screecher, reducing our speed to 2 or 3 knots, put a line trailing astern, and took turns jumping in. Refreshing! And always a fun experience to jump into water that you know is three miles deep. Of course it makes no difference if the depth is 10 feet or 10,000, but somehow the mind conjures up a fear of the deep.

Not much had happened on this passage. Each morning and evening we checked in with *Tahawus* and *Maggie*, and traded positions. Then we asked if anything exciting had happened, and for the most part there was silence. Boring, we would say, and let's keep it that way!

Without having our attention on problems, we focused mostly on our speed and our miles run from noon to noon each day. We had a brief period of doldrums, crossing from the predominantly SE trade winds of the South to the predominantly NE trade winds north of the equator. We were lucky to have flukey conditions for only one day. When the NE trades kicked in, that brought the wind on our beam (roughly 90 degrees from our course), which made for fast sailing. Plus there was the favorable current. The 20-knot winds kicked up some uncomfortable cross seas and made for unwelcome spray in the cockpit, but we enjoyed the possibility of recording a 200+ mile day. We did 217. The next day we got caught in some counter-current, as we strayed too far offshore. Yet we still logged 206. And the next day we worked our way back inshore, found the good current again, and set our all-time noon to noon record with 228. Three in a row!

All our fresh food was gone, so the cooks now had to get creative. I chopped and roasted almonds to add crunch to a can of green beans. I put dried mango and raisins and some chutney in leftover curry rice, for some interest and flavor. Our food had been excellent – better than I would normally have at home; but challenging now. We even ran out of onions, which I considered a major provisioning error. Never run out of onions! We celebrated Tim's birthday; Josh cooked whatever Tim requested, and we baked chocolate brownies.

Initially we saw many ships, rounding the NE corner of Brazil. But now we hadn't seen any for days. No airplanes. No trash in the ocean, either. No whales. Some pelagic birds, and frequently we had one or two roosting on the boat for the night. Once we had dolphins visit in the night under a brilliant full moon. That was magical. The night was so bright that you could see the dolphins underwater near our bows.

A line got snagged under the hatch above my berth, and it ripped the hatch open, breaking the "dogs" that hold it closed. I desperately tried to find replacements, to no avail. Then a wave broke over the deck, and I got to watch the seawater slosh onto my mattress and bedding. To say the least, I was not happy. I came up with a solution before another wave came in – lashing an aluminum bar across the inside hatch frame, and using "Spanish windlasses"

(twisting the lash lines) to tighten the hatch down to it. This was keeping the water out until Barbados.

Lots of reading: Ken Follett and Paul Theroux and one about the Quran that Jesse had been assigned in college. Lots of fiddling with the radio trying to send/receive email. Josh did lots of writing.

In the clear night sky we could see uncountable stars that most people in the modern electrified polluted world never see. I had a little sense of "home" – seeing the North Star once again.

Fish Attack

We caught a fish. A big fish. A "game fish" – jumping out of the water and "tail walking." I believe it was a marlin. He pulled most of the line out from our reel, so I had to tighten the drag to keep from running out. I fully expected him to break the line or free himself, but neither happened. Reeling him in was a challenge. But the real trick was what to do next. We thought it best to try to free him. With Tim tottering on the transom steps and me pulling the fish alongside the boat, we managed to get a line around his bill. Tim leaned over the side with pliers to try to pull the hook out. The fish did not cooperate. The pliers ended up in the deep, and Tim ended up with a puncture wound in the knee courtesy of the marlin's bill!

The hook was not coming out while the fish was alive, which was not going to be much longer. We changed the plan: land the fish and have marlin fillets for a month. Josh and I got a noose around his tail and hauled him up the transom steps. From bill to tail he was longer than I am tall. I filleted him right there; filled the freezer. That evening Josh made the best fish tacos ever!

As I returned to the pilothouse, covered with fish, Josh said, "You need to speak with your crew."

"Huh?" I didn't understand.

He gave me a serious look, and slowly, deliberately repeated, "You need to speak with your crew."

I looked at Tim. He was seated comfortably on the settee, knee bandaged, glass of rum in hand, bottle nearby. A wry smile hinted that he had something to say. I washed the fish off my hands and sat down. "So, how are you holding up…?"

Tim explained that the inner tissue protecting the knee had been punctured, and he was concerned about infection as well as damage to the knee structure. He thought I should get on the radio and seek medical assistance. I didn't see what assistance was needed or possible.

"Tim, I'm not the doctor here," I began. (Tim was.) "But suppose you spoke to a doctor; what do you think he would tell you?" I thought this was an inspired approach to a confounding situation.

"Clean the wound, bandage it, and take an antibiotic."

I gave him the "*And…?*" look.

"I did that. But I think we need to contact someone with local knowledge. Someone who knows what kind of infection could develop in a deep puncture wound from a fish."

I was concerned about where an emergency call might lead, but I could see he wasn't to be deterred. "Okay. Tim, you're the talker here, not me. Why don't *you* get on the radio and make the call?"

I had never even tuned to the emergency frequency on the SSB radio. Tim now did. "Pan-pan, pan-pan, pan-pan" – the code for an emergency a notch less critical than a mayday. "We are a sailing vessel 120 miles SE of Barbados, in need of medical assistance…"

The response? Nothing but static. Tim repeated the call; same result. I breathed a secret sigh of relief. What was another doctor going to do, in the remaining day before we reached Bridgetown…?

Tim came up with Plan B. He sent an email to Jimmy Cornell asking if he could arrange for us to be met by a doctor upon our arrival.

Bridgetown

We arrived the next morning. Nearly 2,000 miles in just under 11 days!

Jimmy had worked some magic. We were directed to a berth at a floating dock, where it would be easy for Tim to get off/on the boat. While there was no

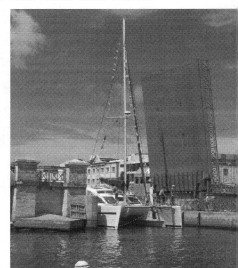

doctor waiting at the dock, someone was ready to drive Tim to a medical center as soon as we cleared in with the authorities. His consultation with the doctor was short and sweet: keep taking the antibiotics; if it gets worse then get on a flight home and get medical care in the USA!

We couldn't stay at the Immigration dock, but our local assistant arranged for us to move to The Careenage, which entailed arranging for a crew to open the narrow drawbridge, despite it being Saturday and a holiday. The Careenage was right downtown with easy access to everything. And he said we could temporarily tie alongside the wall, rather than the usual stern-to, to make it easy for Tim to get off/on. People were going out of their way to help.

Downtown Bridgetown was convenient, but noisy. Buses roaring by. Music blaring at night. People walking in the park a few feet from the boat. Plus everything cost too much. Welcome to the Caribbean! I was not happy there at first. But I knew by now that I felt that way at most new places. I needed a day or two to adjust.

Blue Planet Odyssey Completed!

Months earlier, when *Tahawus* arrived in Durban several hours before *No Regrets*, my competitive feathers were ruffled by the Cornell Sailing post leading with "*Tahawus* first boat in Durban." So I made a point of quickly sending a photo to Jimmy, before *Tahawus* arrived. I knew it would appear on the Cornell Sailing website…

NEWS
First Blue Planet Odyssey boat arrives in Barbados
By Cornell Sailing on 22.01.2017
Event(s): Blue Planet Odyssey
Destination(s): Atlantic Ocean, Barbados

No Regrets in the Careenage at Bridgetown

Jimmy and his wife Gwenda arrived and sponsored a little celebration. *Tahawus, Maggie,* and *No Regrets* comprised the entire fleet of finishers. Tim wasn't there – he had caught the first plane home after consulting with the doctor. Josh went with him. But Bill had arrived, along with his friend Harry. And Nora was back from her travels in Argentina.

The four of us attended the little BPO ceremony. It was fun to see Jimmy and Gwenda, and to congratulate ourselves, but it felt odd to be ending the rally without yet having completed my circumnavigation. No ocean crossings remainded, but we still had nearly 2,000 miles to go, and I was still patching together crew.

I was chatting with Carol, from *Maggie,* over a rum punch, when she said, "If I don't see you again…"

Yikes! This possibility hadn't yet sunk in. It was hard to imagine not rendezvousing again with *Maggie* and *Tahawus,* after sailing so far and so long together. We would stay in touch, but it was a sad thought that after all we had been through we were sailing our separate ways. I felt sad about the other friends we made along the way, too – the many crews who turned back or wanted to stay in the South Pacific or had health issues or shipped their boat home or…whatever. We had a bond, and I wished they (and Luc!) could have been there to acknowledge the completion and swap tales.

BPOers Bill, Zeke, Jimmy, Klaudia, Norm, Martin, Rob, Carol, Mirko, Nora

CARIBBEAN

The bridge opened at noon the next day, to let us out of the Careenage. We had done a tour of Barbados and seen some beautiful areas, but overall I was unimpressed. One of the few things I thoroughly enjoyed on the island was attending a cricket match versus Guyana. The cost was $5. I struggled to understand the game, which went on too long for me, but I enjoyed both the sport and the feeling of being a part of a local crowd, rather than a tourist.

Barbados sights, including the "screw dock" – a Victorian-era technology for lifting ships out of the water for maintenance.

Sprinting Through the Eastern Caribbean

We sprinted through the Caribbean. From Barbados to Grenada, Carriacou, Union, Tobago Cays, Bequia, Martinique, Antigua, Barbuda, Nevis, St Kitts, Statia, Ile Fourchue, St Maarten, Tortola, Virgin Gorda, Norman Island, St John and St Thomas. Eighteen islands (a dozen countries) in six weeks. Doing this was crazy – clearing in and out constantly, not settling in to enjoy the local flavors. But we accepted that we had a tight schedule, and we had a good time. Grenada was my favorite. The island was especially pretty, the sights interesting, the prices low by Caribbean standards, and I felt that the people were the most "real."

On a blustery beat from Carriacou to Union Island, a sailboat hailed us on the VHF radio saying they needed assistance. They had engine problems, they said, and they were having trouble sailing into the strong wind, and they asked if we would give them a tow. A tow!? Seriously…?? I was angered that they would even put us in the position of having to judge the severity of their problem. I stayed off the radio, while Bill diplomatically said, "We will gladly provide whatever assistance we can in an emergency. But this is not an emergency. You are sailing okay even though you are making limited headway; you can turn downwind and head for an alternate anchorage on Union; you can turn back to Carriacou. Trying to take you in tow is risky, and likely to turn a challenging situation into a dangerous one." They eventually turned back toward Carriacou.

At Tobago Cays a local named Sydney came by in a boat, selling T-shirts. That didn't interest me, but he got my attention when he said he also had banana bread. We bought a loaf. I asked in jest if he couldn't bring us a lobster dinner, too. No, but his buddy Free Willy would indeed provide this service. The price tag was high, but it was too good an opportunity to pass up. Willy came by later to confirm our reservation. But when our scheduled 6pm came around, no Willy. As 7pm approached, I gave up and started water for pasta. Willy appeared before the water was hot. It was worth the wait and the cost. Big lobsters, somehow still hot, plus baked potatoes and plantains and veggies and rice. A feast!

We stopped in the huge and beautiful anchorage at Admiralty Bay, Bequia. Ashore we went for smoothies. The woman at the shop gave me a long stare. When I asked what was up, she said I looked so much like her father that she thought I was he. I had a tan, but not close to her skin color. But who knows what color her father was? I asked about the white hair and beard. Yup, the same as her father.

The next day in Martinique we went into a bakery (of course), and a man gave me an overly friendly, "Hello!" I gave him a blank stare back…and asked if he was on a yacht. No, he lived in Martinique…and he continued to insist that he knew me. Instead of walking off mystified, I wish I had thought to ask if he also knew my daughter who makes smoothies in Bequia!

In Antigua we gawked at the superyachts and the superduperyachts, as we got Harry removed from the crew list, and prepared to meet Hallie. I Skyped with her and learned there had been some stresses back home, plus a snowstorm threatening her flight out. She was looking for some understanding and support from me. But I had no space for her concerns, and I went into a rant about the crazy stresses I'd been through for the past week. I hadn't realized how much the constant moving and dealing with the formalities and trying to keep to the schedule had got me wound tight, until I lost it on that call. And Hallie of course had no idea that I hadn't spent the week enjoying rum punches in the sunshine by the beach. My rant was cathartic, and luckily Hallie was understanding. Our call ended well.

That evening we took the long walk up to Shirley Heights, where Harry treated us all to a farewell dinner. I chatted with the bartender about sailing to Antigua 30 years earlier, before navigation was revolutionized by GPS. We had approached the island in the dark. We were sailing in tandem with another boat that had radar, and they thought with radar they would be able to find the entrance to English Harbour. But the entrance was not discernible on their radar, so we had a problem! We made a call on the VHF radio, asking for help identifying the entrance. To my surprise the call was answered by the bar/restaurant atop Shirley Heights – the same one we were visiting 30 years on. They said they would flash the lights of the restaurant to help us locate the entrance. They did, and we found our way in. Our bartender remembered doing this for other boats. No longer, though, as the bar no longer monitored VHF radio. Of course, with GPS and a chart plotter there was no longer the need, as boats know exactly where they are (if the electronics are working).

With Hallie aboard, we spent two days exploring the north coast of Antigua, then made the 25-mile crossing to Spanish Point on Barbuda. This was one of my favorite anchorages – still remote…and beautiful…and the best snorkeling we had seen in the Caribbean. Next we motored to the west side of Barbuda and anchored off of an endless, empty beach. There was a pretty resort there, but when we dinghied ashore we found that it was closed, and for sale. This presented a problem. We needed to check out of Antigua/Barbuda, which required that we get a water taxi across the lagoon to the town of Codrington, and it wasn't clear how we were going to find a boat to take us. We wandered around the closed resort until we surprised a caretaker. He called a water taxi for us.

Checking out was still a challenge, as it was Friday afternoon, and when we walked to the Immigration office, we found it locked. There was a phone number on a sign, but we didn't have a local phone. We tried walking to the Customs office, hoping for better luck. It was locked up, too, again with a phone number. We went into a shop across the street, bought eggs, and convinced the proprietor to let us use her phone to call Customs. No problem, Customs was open a few minutes later, and the Customs man called Immigration to tell them we were coming. We got back there 5 minutes before closing and completed our formalities.

We stopped at Statia (more formally, Sint Eustatius). We planned to stay just one night, but still we had to clear in, then pay our $35 harbor fees, and then clear right back out. Then we discovered there is an additional $10 national marine park fee. We asked about getting a map of hiking trails on the island. No problem…$2. But if you actually walked on the trails you needed a "trail tag"…$10 per person. But would be good for a full year…

I liked Statia. Off the beaten path…only a handful of boats…no cruise ships…no hawkers…no pushy taxi drivers…people very friendly. But the "nickel and diming" was unpleasant. Too bad we weren't staying longer – we would have bought trail tags…

At Tortola we said goodbye to Bill. Hallie, Nora and I continued on through the British Virgin Islands. At Soper's Hole we met Jesse (my son) and Chelsea (his girlfriend), joining for a short vacation. It wasn't much of a vacation, though, as the wind howled the entire time they were aboard. Too bad; next time… We dropped them at Charlotte Amalie on St Thomas. Hallie, too, said farewell at St Thomas, and my good friend Steve came aboard. Steve had sailed across the Atlantic with me 30 years earlier. At the time he had no sailing experience, but he was a man you wanted to have at your side going into battle. Now he had sailing experience, too!

Our "charter operations" in the Caribbean was finally over, and Nora, Steve and I could focus on sailing once again. We made a big provisioning run, and diesel and water, and we were ready. But we learned that *Tahawus* was about to arrive at St John. We back-tracked one island so we could rendezvous with our BPO-mates. We celebrated the reunion (and re-farewell) with an abundance of wine, conch ceviche (conch caught by the boys), and key lime pie. Then it was time to continue our journey.

We sailed to Isla Culebra, at the east end of Puerto Rico – an area often called the Spanish Virgin Islands. I liked the harbor at Culebra – it was big, with cruising boats from all over the world. And there was a nice bar/restaurant called the Dinghy Dock – what could be more welcoming than that! Steve was familiar with Culebra; he rented a car for us and played tour guide, taking us to see the beautiful beaches.

Then to "mainland" Puerto Rico, and a marina with all the amenities: showers, trash disposal, water, electricity, and a nearby restaurant. At Nora's suggestion we rented a Jeep for a day and drove up to El Yunque national rainforest. The visitor center alone was impressive – a huge structure nestled peacefully into the forest. If this was our tax dollars at work, I thought it was money well spent. We hiked to a waterfall for a high-pressure shower. We ventured on to San Juan, visited El Morro fort, and walked through some of the old city. Great day!

For the next several days we cruised along the south coast of Puerto Rico, and then to Boqueron. We took a taxi to Mayaguez to the Customs office to clear out. Puerto Rico didn't require that we clear out, but the Bahamas would want to see a clearance when we arrived. So we requested a "courtesy clearance." The officer asked when we were leaving, wrote the date/time on an empty form, stamped it, and said, "Fill it out before you get there!"

≈≈≈

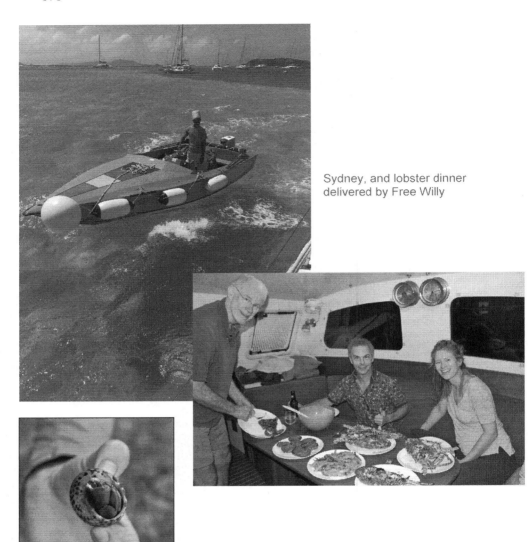

Sydney, and lobster dinner
delivered by Free Willy

Steve takes 360-degree photos to post on Google Earth

BAHAMAS

I liked Puerto Rico. If we had some slack in our schedule I would have stayed in Boqueron and let some messy weather pass. But already we had crossed the Dominican Republic off our itinerary to allow more time for the Bahamas. So off we went, motoring. Not unpleasant, initially. But as we got offshore the swells increased, squalls came and went, and at times the wind blew…dead against us, even though we were "supposed" to be in favorable trade winds. There was a major depression just north of us – close enough to see the lighting over the horizon at night. Not conditions for a happy crew!

All the motoring was raising a question as to whether we had sufficient fuel. I "answered" that question by forgetting to turn off a fuel transfer pump, resulting in our pumping several gallons overboard through the tank vent! Crap! Mia culpa; bad enough that we burn fossil fuel at all, and here I was pumping it into the ocean.

Between needing a break and needing fuel, we headed for the Dominican Republic after all. We had heard that Ocean World Marina was a good destination – a modern marina (showers), easy Customs clearance with no bribes, and fuel would be readily available. Those three pluses turned out to be accurate. But this place had minuses, too. It was a resort and theme park. Music played constantly, occasionally nice, mostly bad. We got to hear the overly enthusiastic announcer for their dolphin show thrice daily. It was a playground for the wealthy, with a casino and a cigar lounge and a Las Vegas-style nightclub show. No connection to the larger community, except for providing jobs. And maybe if the place were busy and thriving I would have gotten into the spirit, but it was nearly empty. Huge docks designed for superyachts were bare. The terrace lounge had seating for a hundred or more, four seats in use.

At least we got to take a run into the nearby town of Puerto Plata. The supermarket offered pickup/delivery for yachties to shop there. Of course they were thinking we would be doing major provisioning, but our lockers were full. Still, we bought a little more food. The highlight was our driver taking us the scenic route through the historic district, past the oldest cathedral in the DR, and allowing us to stop at the local produce market (after we had already bought all we wanted at the supermarket).

Oh well…the people were friendly, and it was fun to speak a little Spanish again. With full tanks, full freezer, and counters overflowing with produce and other items we couldn't squeeze into lockers, we set out once again for the Bahamas. The wind was still against us, but it was moderating and veering. Soon it would be sunny and pleasant except for the lingering swell from the gale.

Besides a hot shower, there was a special highlight before we left the DR. I got an email from a student at Yale who was preparing for mock treaty negotiations in a climate law class. (Yes, there is such a thing.) She was representing Tuvalu against the industrialized powers, and her web search took her to my posts from Tuvalu, especially the last one where I waxed philosophical about the conundrum of climate change and climate refugees. I went back and read my own post at **zekethesailor.net/2015/07** and it made me cry. That time seemed long ago and far away…but my feelings for the people and their beautiful culture remained close to my heart.

We stopped to anchor at Turks and Caicos. We didn't check in, we just "Q-flagged through." That is, we kept up our yellow Q flag to indicate that we had not cleared, and we simply anchored without leaving the boat. "Provo Radio" contacted us as we approached. They told us to call once we were anchored to give them identifying information about the boat and crew. When we called, they said to stand by on channel 16; they never got back to us.

We waited until 8am to leave, so we could see the coral heads on our way out. Turks and Caicos is essentially the same geography as the Bahamas, with miles of very shallow water surrounded by extremely deep water. Navigating the shallow banks can be rather stressful, and requires good visibility to see the coral. We called Provo Radio again as we were getting underway, told them we never connected to give them our vessel information. They said to stand by on channel 16 and…you guessed it…they never got back to us.

Our tentative plan had been to clear into the Bahamas at Mayaguana. But we would have arrived there around dusk, would have had to anchor and wait for daylight to dodge the coral close to town, then clear in, and most of the day would have been gone. We decided to keep going through the night and get closer to the Exuma island chain.

The day was nearly picture perfect, running under spinnaker with almost no waves. But also with not much wind. For a large portion of the day our speed was under five knots, and sometimes under four. I was getting frustrated that we were going so slowly and we were again facing a time crunch for a crew change. I was thinking about just wanting to get home and relax and not be dealing with boat problems (the last good burner on our stove was no longer working reliably!).

Then we caught a mahi-mahi, and that changed everything! Incredibly, it was the first mahi-mahi we had landed on the entire voyage. Sometime before we had hooked one, but we failed to bring it aboard. That really upset me, and the thought that we might not catch a single mahi-mahi on an entire circumnavigation did not sit well with me. This one was a beauty, and suddenly we had lots of my favorite fish in the freezer as well as in our bellies.

Somehow after catching the fish my outlook was entirely different. Instead of feeling like we had time pressure to get somewhere, I felt like we were already "there." Gliding slowly along on a perfect day, not exactly sure where we were going or when we would arrive, we were in the perfect place, content, with everything we needed…including a delicious dinner shared with good company, an empty horizon, a flat sea, a pleasant spinnaker breeze, a crescent of moon, and stars already brilliant that would become even more so on my watch, after the moon set.

We sailed south of Acklins Island and then headed north to go outside of Long Island. Running under spinnaker all day long, mostly out of sight of the low islands, we saw only one other boat. But that boat was slowly converging with us. They had only a tiny foresail up, so they must have been motoring, although they weren't moving very fast. On a collision course, and getting close. We had the right-of-way, and I assumed they would change course slightly to pass behind us, but no change was happening. I got a closer look with binoculars; no one visible on deck. Time for a call on the radio. He answered, "Yes, I see you."

I thought that was sufficient communication. But apparently not, as we continued on a collision course. So I called again and asked his intention – to pass ahead or astern of us. "Ahead, I guess," was the reply. Apparently he had no intention of altering course. I changed course and let him pass ahead. No big deal. But what the hell was he thinking? Did he have any clue what he was doing? Sailors like that are dangerous!

In the evening we put into Clarence Town, on Long Island. There is a nice anchorage there. But we went to the marina since we had to clear in, and I thought it would be nice to have some freedom to walk around town and chat with people. We told the clerk at the marina we needed to clear in, and she called the Customs official. Turns out that although Clarence Town is a port of entry, it isn't staffed. There was a $100 charge for the official to drive from the other end of the island. I spoke to him, suggesting that we might leave the marina, anchor out, leave our Q flag up, and clear in elsewhere the next day. No such luck. Now that he knew we were there, we had to clear in and pay the fee…

I walked into "town," but there wasn't much town anymore, after Hurricane Joaquin a few years back. Two big beautiful churches. Many houses with missing roofs. The grocery store boarded up and covered with vines, its sign still barely legible. A sad corner of paradise…

We motored all day in a calm to Conception Island, which is a marine park. No people. Beautiful anchorage. Maybe ten boats, but room for fifty. Steve and I swam ashore and walked the length of the beach. Sand so fine it felt like flour. Columbus is thought to have made his second landfall there.

Still without wind, we motored to Rat Cay – reaching the exotic Exumas at last! They are a long chain of sandy cays, with a deep Sound on one side and a shallow Bank on the other, and many cuts between. Over the next few days we visited Little Farmers Cay, Great Guana Cay, Staniel Cay.

At Staniel Cay I wanted to see Thunderball Cave – seen in the old James Bond movie. I decided to try the "shallow route" into the harbor rather than add a couple miles to follow deep water. This turned out to be dicey, as it appeared to be even more shallow than the 1 meter indicated on the chart! We read the water as best we could, and our depth sounder at one point indicated 2.6 feet…which should have had us digging a little furrow in the sand. But we never did touch, and if we had gone aground we would have simply waited on the sand for the tide to rise in an hour or so. Next time, though, I think I'll go the long route…

We anchored near the cave and dinghied over to snorkel. It was smaller than I expected, but it was cool. Shafts of sunlight here and there from the high ceiling inside, lots of fish, and a familiar impressive shape to the mouth opening on the far side. Beautiful coral outside that mouth.

Steve and I went ashore at the marina, disposed of our trash (for $6.45), and walked into town to a very well stocked "convenience store." We bought fresh fruit, freshly baked coconut bread and zucchini bread, chocolate, cookies, lemons and limes, asparagus, and lettuce. Hooray! You can't always get what you want in these Cays, so load up when you can!

A cold front was approaching; the last days we had available were predicted to feature northerly winds and squalls – just what we didn't want for our crossing from the Exumas to the Abacos. So we kept moving, to make the crossing before the weather arrived. Up the Banks side to Hawksbill Cay, then across for a brief stop at Nassau, then overnight to the protected Sea of Abaco. Nice sailing on the unruffled waters on the inside route to Hope Town. I didn't know what to expect there; I thought many boats might take to the harbor to be protected as the front went over. Would we find a mooring?

When we made our way through the narrow entrance, the scene was not reassuring. The harbor was packed with boats, practically on top of each other! We spied two empty mooring balls and randomly chose one. The moorings were so tightly spaced that we couldn't tie on with our usual bridle – we would be hitting the boat behind us. But the mooring system included two pennants; hanging on them directly squeezed us into the parking space.

I headed ashore quickly. I wanted to make sure our mooring was a rental, and not someone's private spot. No problem. Meanwhile another boat entered and picked up the last mooring nearby. Later what I had feared happened to them. Another boat came in, shouting that the first boat was on their mooring and had to move! Move where?? I guess they found another spot somewhere… In listening to the exchange (voices were raised, but the boats were so close we would have heard them anyway), we learned that the mooring was reserved by virtue of having a milk jug tied to it! How would a newcomer know? Nothing was written on the milk jug.

Hope Town was seductively pleasant. Well protected. Restaurants here and there. Friendly people. Fresh bread. Hot showers at the marina, with no timer – endless hot water!! Laundry facility right there, adjacent to the bar. Nice walking through the little town. And a fascinating lighthouse to visit.

The lighthouse was a marvel. The light still burned kerosene. Its turning mechanism was mechanical. Two keepers cranked a 700-pound weight to the top every two hours (they slept? in the tower). The 8,000-pound rotating lens sat in a bath of mercury. You could turn the whole 4 tons from a standstill with a hefty one-handed push. Very impressive mechanical machinery.

Seductively pleasant. Tempting to just stay indefinitely. Why go anywhere else? Hmm, well, there was crew flying out and crew flying in at Marsh Harbour, a few miles away. And better provisioning there. I managed to overcome the inertia, though not before Steve took the ferry to catch his plane; Nora and I motorsailed to Marsh Harbour. Although yachties speak ill of the commercial hub, it turned out to be a pretty nice place, too.

Farewell to Nora

It was time for Nora to leave. I found it hard to believe it had been 7+ months and 8,000 miles since she joined in Mauritius. What a wonderful crew and wonderful friend she turned out to be! Having to cobble together a crew is not without an upside. Nora wrote about her experience, providing an entertaining alternate perspective on sailing aboard *No Regrets:*

> We had just left Mauritius and we were doing an "easy" overnight sail to Réunion. Easy is one of those relative words. If you've been sailing around the world and living aboard a boat for a year, sure it's no problem. However, if you're used to living in an apartment (which, I'm sure I don't need to mention, is stationary), constant three-foot swells take some getting used to. Liam and I had just joined No Regrets, and this was our first passage.

I took the first night watch, in which I threw up four times, once every hour. When I wasn't throwing up, I was deep breathing, trying to stave off the next bout of nausea, making sure we didn't run into any tankers, and calculating whether it was easier to throw up in the galley sink or overboard. I chose overboard, on the windward side. I was too seasick to grab a safety harness, so every time my stomach demanded, I would carefully scoot my butt along the wet deck (directly over Zeke's bunk) to the lifelines, and hoped whatever remained of my lunch wouldn't be stuck to the side of the boat in the morning.

When Zeke came to start his shift he asked, "What were all the moving-around-on-deck noises from?" We were only sailing with the jib; with any more sail we would have arrived in Réunion too soon and in the dark. In other words, there were no good reasons to be scooting around on the deck on my butt, especially without a harness. All I could muster as a response was "Uh, I've been a little bit seasick" – a huge understatement. It was all I could do to get into bed and slam my eyes shut. I can be seasick or asleep, but luckily never both at once. I went to bed still wearing my rain-jacket and now soggy pants.

Did I know I was going to be seasick? Yes, I knew. I have always been susceptible to motion sickness, and it was the thing I was most concerned about before starting the trip.

It has been a long-time dream of mine to travel, and I couldn't imagine a more exciting and unique way to visit places I wouldn't have had an opportunity to see otherwise. Prior to joining No Regrets, I had been stuck in a job that wasn't a good fit, which helped me decide it was time to follow my dream. Before I could leave, I had to quit my job, move out of my apartment, and sell my car. After tackling my fear of quitting my job and living off savings, I was not going to let a little throwing up get in my way!

Once we arrived in Réunion, I got to experience the perks of traveling with the Blue Planet Odyssey. Luc showed up with rented cars which we drove through the incredible mountains and the Piton de Fournaise volcano. Also, while in Réunion I got to know the lovely people aboard *Maggie* and *Tahawus*. Traveling with Rob and Carol, and Norm, Klaudia, and the boys was an unexpected gift of the trip. They became my traveling family and celebrated my birthday, Christmas, and New Years with me, and countless happy hours, during my months away from home, family, and friends. I will miss having them around!

Réunion was a great break from my intense at-sea nausea. But when we began preparing to depart for South Africa, it occurred to me that I might be seasick for the entire 9 to 10-day journey. The longest ocean trip I had done without touching land was two days. I knew I would be seasick, but I didn't know if I would adjust after three days like most people. My anxiety began to build the night before we left, and I fervently hoped I wasn't going to throw up every hour.

When we left, my stomach was in knots, in anticipation of the nausea. Once we were out of the island wind shadow we were in the waves of the Indian Ocean. I experienced the same symptoms as before; sluggishness, nausea, but I had discovered my technique for coping with nausea! I would curl in to the end of the settee, close my eyes, and let my body relax. This and some breathing could keep me from getting sick. I would crack my eyes open when I wanted to see what was going on, then quickly close them again. This allowed me to function when we needed to reef the main, or switch sails. After being on deck I would peel off my foul weather gear and curl back up on the settee until I was needed again.

I found the Indian Ocean weather to be predictably unpredictable. If I didn't like the current weather, I had only to remind myself, "Don't worry," because it would change in about 8–12 hours to something completely different. This kind of weather made staying hydrated a challenge. Not because I didn't have enough to drink, but because I discovered I hated peeing when we were underway. I had to climb down the stairs, through the galley, and past my bed to get to the head. A nausea-inducing trip, when the waves were large. On windy days, I then had to get my pants down without falling, as the boat bumped and slammed its way through the waves. This usually resulted in one hand on a grab bar and one hand for the pants; it's harder than it sounds. It always took longer than desired, battling nausea and my bladder. Once sitting, I had to learn to time things precisely because on 30-knot wind days, I could "catch air" between myself and the seat when a big wave hit. No one tells you these details before you go on a long sailing trip!

During this passage, we had a light wind day, which provided us with the opportunity to take showers. So, five days into the passage, I took my first shower on the boat (and by shower, I mean cold water spritz, from a sink-like sprayer), on the back of the transom steps. It is quite an incredible experience showering with a view of nothing but ocean and blue sky around you. From the transom steps, I would watch the water bubble and swish past. It always reminded me how fast we were traveling through the water, when there was no land to watch.

The day before we arrived in Durban, we had 35-knot winds, and huge waves again. We had previously had some calm sailing so the immediate switch from calm to heavy winds caused me to feel especially seasick. I was ready to see some land. The next morning the wind died, and we motored into Durban. I got to see my first whales of the trip as we entered the city harbor. We pulled up next to *Tahawus* in our assigned slip and were immediately greeted by Edd, our Point

Yacht Club contact, who met us with South African beer. Hallelujah! I have never been happier to see a pail of frosty beers. All the difficulties from the passage faded away immediately because I WAS IN AFRICA!

I finally found my sailing groove on our way into Cape Town, our last stop in South Africa. We had unusually calm seas as we rounded the Cape, and I remember savoring the hour between 7am and 8am before Zeke and Liam were up. That particular day, I spent the clear, blue-skied morning watching a seal play in the surf of our wake, as Table Mountain came into view.

I have learned that there are two types of cruisers in this world: those who sail to go places, and those who enjoy sailing so much, they would be happy to skip most places and just keep sailing. I am the former. I enjoy sailing, but I think sailing is more interesting when you get to visit a new exciting place.

As we prepared to leave for Cape Town, I became even more aware of which kind of sailor I am. As we approached our date, Zeke couldn't believe we were leaving Cape Town in only two days. He said, "There is still so much to do!"

"I know!" I exclaimed. "I still really want to see the Botanical garden, hike Lion's Head, and check out more restaurants." While I was listing all the activities still on my to-do list, I was watching Zeke's blank look. It turns out Zeke had a different list in mind, that looked more like this:

- Schedule rigging inspection
- Finish scrubbing port hull
- Provision for the next 30 days
- Lubricate door latch
- Find hinge for cabin table

Trust me, the list was longer. Zeke and Liam's attention had shifted back onto the boat, while I was still trying to cram in more activities. They had the right idea, surviving the Atlantic crossing was certainly the priority. I just wasn't quite ready to shift from tourist back to sailor.

In contrast to the Indian Ocean, the sailing across the Atlantic was idyllic. Not only were we able to visit the beautiful sand dunes of Namibia and the remote island of St. Helena, we had beautiful downwind sailing. Downwind is the best sailing angle on a catamaran. Although I needed some time to adjust to the motion again, it was much better than sailing upwind. I truly loved our relaxed, 15-knot winds, and sunny days, as we made our way towards the warmer waters of Brazil.

I departed *No Regrets* in the Bahamas. I'm amazed to say that I sailed over 8,000 nautical miles, to 18 different countries and 32 islands. I feel immensely lucky to have seen the places we saw, thankful for the

> month I got to sail with my Dad, and all the wonderful people I met
> aboard *No Regrets*. I am particularly grateful to Zeke for taking a chance
> on someone who told him she gets sick in cars. I truly admired his
> thoughtful leadership and generous spirit and I can't imagine having a
> better captain. Would I do it again? I would happily sail across the
> Atlantic Ocean again. As for the Indian Ocean… I guess it would
> depend on how much I dislike my next job!

In the evening, my new crew arrived: Bob, who sailed with us from Bora
Bora to Australia, and Joe, a newbie who was a work associate of Steve. We
would have a week of cruising Abaco, and then would turn our attention to the
Gulf Stream and returning to the USA.

I thought it would be fun for the new crew to visit Hope Town. It was
unexpectedly fun for me, too – to return to a place I was familiar with. When
was the last time I had sailed into a familiar harbor!? I think we did it only once,
in Mauritius. It was also fun that we received a steady stream of compliments
from other sailors: they liked our boat; they knew and respected Chris White's
designs; we had the best-looking catamaran they had seen…

We visited Man O'War Cay and Great Guana Cay (another one). We waited
a day for the wind to calm down before tackling Whale Cut, where the water is
too shallow to proceed up the sheltered side, and one must venture into the
ocean for a couple miles. While that doesn't sound like much after crossing
oceans, the Cut can be extremely dangerous with breaking waves when the
conditions aren't right. It was a bit of a letdown, though – just choppy; no
breaking waves. In an hour we were back in protected waters. We sailed 30 miles
to Allans-Pensacola Cay. It was a beautiful day and a beautiful sail to a beautiful
uninhabited island with a secure anchorage. Idyllic!

But it was our last night in the Bahamas. Again we left a little earlier than
planned. Although the weather was good, it would soon be deteriorating. So
said Chris Parker, the weather guru for the area. We went ashore, hiked the
beach and the island, swam, and chatted with crews of two other boats (there
were 5 in the anchorage; it is a world apart from the boatropolis of Hope Town).
Joe cooked the last of our mahi-mahi. Thank you, fish, for providing another
great meal!

A last spectacular starry night at anchor… *No Regrets* felt like home. What
would it be like to shift to a home ashore…? It would be nice to reconnect with
Hallie, at least.

Clarence Town had many
structures with unrepaired
hurricane damage. But there were
exceptions...

Hawksbill Cay, Exumas

Hope Town's iconic lighthouse

The William H Albury, built at Man O'War Cay, and being restored there 50+ years later.

One sailor's trash is another sailor's art

Joe and Bob

HOME

With the weather fair, I wanted to ride the Gulf Stream some distance north. I had no desire to put in at Florida. I wanted to get to North Carolina quickly. There we would meet with the builder of the boat, John Lombardi, and talk with him about doing some repairs before we put the boat on the market. Our three-way partnership was intended just to complete the circumnavigation, no partner was about to buy the others out – we had to sell. We had contacted Chris White about listing the boat for sale. But we weren't listing it before we got back to the USA and addressed some of its accumulated problems.

Winds were light when we left. But the day was beautiful and the shallow Banks were delicious, so we set the spinnaker and ambled slowly along. So what if it took an extra day to get to the USA? After sailing all day, the water was still only 15 feet deep, and there were no waves; really enjoyable. At one point the wind went extra light, and Bob and I went for a "swim." That is, we hung on to a line trailing behind the boat. Two and a half knots can feel like a standstill on a big catamaran, but it is plenty fast when you are dragging in the water behind it!

During the night we made it west to the Gulf Stream (we had coordinates for its path provided by Chris Parker, the weather guru). We turned right to ride the Stream northward. The wind was lighter than we would have liked, but as a result the Stream was very tame – none of the steep breaking waves that it is infamous for. The sailing was slow but our progress with the current was impressive. We hit ten knots over the ground, with just nine knots of wind. We easily did a 200+ mile day.

As we moved north, east of Florida…Georgia…South Carolina, the wind fell to almost nothing, and it forced us more west than we wanted, pushing us to the edge of the Stream. *Then* it got lumpy. I didn't understand why the ride was so smooth up to that point, and with the same wind/current it got choppy toward the western edge, but that's what happened. We motorsailed to move out of the area, and soon it had calmed down. But the current was gone – we were across.

I had thought we might continue on to Southport, NC, but being out of the current and with no wind, we motored into Charleston instead. I really enjoyed Charleston on the way south, two and a half years earlier, so it seemed a fitting place to "cross our wake" and complete the circumnavigation. Mission accomplished.

I had sailed around the world!

≈≈≈

Bob, Joe and I worked our way up the Intracoastal Waterway to Wanchese, North Carolina. Along the way we did one last overnight sail, and I wrote to Hallie about it probably being my last for some time. She replied, "You seem so happy when you are sailing through the night, as if you are connecting to your soul, your spirit, and the heart and soul of the earth. Your peace. The ocean is your muse, your mistress."

Indeed there is poetry in sailing through the endless darkness beneath the shooting stars.

We made a plan to meet with John Lombardi, who built *No Regrets* eighteen years before. He would be the perfect person to do the work needed. Plus it might be fun for him, to see one of his creations return many years later.

Along the way I was contacted by John's brother Chris, a yacht broker, saying he had a client interested in an Atlantic 42, as is. I didn't take Chris very seriously; every broker has an "interested client" when they want to get your listing. But he said his client wanted to fly in to see the boat right away. That sounded serious. As we worked our way north from Charleston, the three of us polished the stainless steel and tried to clean what we could. In Wanchese, Bob and Joe departed, and Hallie arrived. We had the boat hauled and the bottom washed, but there was no time to get the boatyard going on anything more. The stove was corroded and barely functional; the countertop was badly worn; the floors in the hulls were cracked and sagging. Oh well.

Hallie and I had four days to remove as much "stuff" from the boat as possible. I had no idea some of the junk we had carried all the way around the planet! We rented a storage locker, bought plastic bins, and filled as many bins as we could. We bought heavy duty garbage bags and made generous use of the nearby dumpster. While I wouldn't have called the boat ready-to-show, I had never seen it look so clean.

And then she was sold.

Yikes! I was not ready to leave her. I was not ready to say goodbye to standing watch alone in the middle of the starry night. I was not ready to let go of my wonderful home, that had carried me safely across the oceans. *No Regrets* did not mean no sadness; I felt deliriously happy and achingly sad at the same time. Her new owners are wonderful people who are making a major investment to bring her back to near-new condition. And who better than the original builder, unabashedly proud of his creation, to lead the refit? It was time for me to let go.

And…there was a sweet little trimaran parked right next to *No Regrets* at the boatyard. I wondered if she might be for sale…

AND...?

I will choose a multihull next time, too. At least for cruising in the tropics, which is the kind of sailing I want more of. The Atlantic 42 was an excellent design, and well built. Thank you, Chris White and John Lombardi. If cost were not a factor, I would prefer a slightly larger boat, that would have better capacity to carry all the equipment and supplies we "need," and still perform well. But I also believe that any seaworthy boat will do. If you have one, go!

Shared ownership was wonderful for me. Thank you, Bill and Tim, for your partnership. It allowed me to sail on a boat that I probably couldn't afford on my own. It also brought a richness to the experience, beyond just sailing. It is an interesting challenge, having partners. Also having ever-changing crew. I feel privileged to have shared a powerful experience with each of the crew, without exception. We learned from each other, we cooked for each other, we endured discomfort together and made light of it, and we had each other's backs. The logistics of shuffling crew were difficult, but when I wasn't feeling desperate about filling the next position, I loved sailing with new people.

I acknowledge Tim, in particular, for sharing his unique, passionate and edifying view of the world. You wouldn't know it from my narrative (because I didn't recognize it along the way), but Tim was a hero in my saga. It was Tim who introduced me to the Blue Planet Odyssey. Tim who taught me to go to the village, rather than stopping for fear of being unwelcome. Tim who infected me with compassion for the birds and the fish and the working people of the world and the injuries we inflict on our ecosystem. Tim who jumped ship, impelling me to step up to Unequivocal Captain.

People ask about the value of sailing in a rally. Many consider it an unnecessary expense, and it limits your freedom to choose where/when to go. For me, it worked brilliantly. It had me seeing people and places that I would have blindly sailed by on my own. I didn't have to do as much research; it helped with clearing in and out. The Blue Planet Odyssey, with its focus on climate change and ocean health, led me to connect with the middle school kids, adding another dimension to the journey. It led us to Tuvalu, where the concept of climate justice became real for me. Thank you, Jimmy Cornell.

The rally was also a great fit for our unique situation of sailing with three captains. Without the rally there would have been conflicts over where to go and how long to stay. In retrospect, I'm not sure our partnership would have held together if we didn't have the next rendezvous laid out for us.

The best part of a rally, though, is the camaraderie. We were all going into battle together. There is a joyous spirit in that. I still feel that connection with my BPO-mates, including those who stopped along the way.

Two and a half years of sailing without turning back seems like a fading dream. I miss the onboard sense of purpose. There was a single, overriding focus: getting safely to the next destination, and hopefully having a good time along the way. The "doing" wasn't simple, but the "being" was. The priorities were clear; no internal conversation that I *should* be doing something else; no feeling pulled in multiple directions.

I miss living in a rhythm with the natural world. Being outdoors. Diving into tropical waters. Seeing the dolphins and the stars. Feeling the movement of the planet: the wind and the waves. Experiencing a harmony resonating with my soul. I am blessed to have such amazing experiences to long for.

People wonder about my marriage; about being apart for most of the two and a half years. We missed each other. Hallie said up front that four months was the longest we should go without seeing each other, and that's the way it worked out. But many people assume that Hallie was suffering at home during those months. Indeed, she sometimes resented that I left her with all the responsibilities of home ownership, bills, taxes, etc. But she also was proud of mastering the areas that had been my domain before. She enjoyed her freedom to do what she wanted, when she wanted, how she wanted. She was not suffering!

Hallie supported me every nautical mile, whether in spirit, or handling my financial affairs back home, or flying to join me in Tahiti and Australia and Brazil and the Caribbean and Wanchese. Always there with the love and support. A partner on so many planes! (Get it?) Regarding family, it was a special experience to sail with Jesse through Indonesia. And parent/child sailing was a recurring theme, Tim with Josh, Bill with Nora. How cool is that!

Sailing around the world was deeply satisfying – a huge project successfully completed; a dream realized; a source of a little swagger. But in retrospect I see that the Journey was more than a sailing trip. It was a Journey of the heart. I wonder about Stephanie, who paddled her dugout canoe out to *No Regrets*, offering fruit, and asking for a blanket. I gave her my sweater. Was that helpful? Or was it an inappropriate solution to a problem, like the solar-powered desalination system for Komodo? Does the village there have fresh water now, without having to carry it six kilometers?

Is Tuvalu any closer to controlling its future? What can I do, what can my town and my country do, to prevent the cyclones from drowning their culture?

Will they still dance for their children and for mine? Do we need to give up some conveniences? Pay a little more for cleaner technologies? Save Tuvalu, save the world…

I think of Kathy and Chief Joseph in Tisvel. They seemed so content with their lives and their beautiful little village. Are they still? Will they be, when the Internet arrives? These people have no power to steer the course of events on Earth. But they are not irrelevant. They are our extended family. They could teach the wealthy and powerful so much, about living well on a small planet.

Meeting these people and seeing their homes has changed me. More important than any sailing swagger, the experiences along the way have opened my heart. I like people more. I leave more generous tips. I get teary watching dramas on TV. I look forward to talking with people, rather than dreading it. I am more relaxed. More appreciative of the food, water, comforts, security, and opportunities I have. I'm more committed to using energy from renewable sources and voting for candidates who take climate change seriously. I'm much more willing to say yes to invitations.

People around me seem unable to separate from their screens; from the endless flood of "information" streaming at them. They bond with a "community" of like-minded people they may have never met. They feel animosity toward differently-minded people they almost certainly have not met. It is an addiction. Step away; unplug! We all have to focus on the next destination; toward peace and sustainability. Find a connection with our Earth: more outdoors; more nature trails; more sailing; more growing of gardens; more appreciation of who someone is rather than what opinions they hold. This is the Journey of our One Planet into our One Future.

Our planet is beautiful beyond words. The colors of the sea and the sky. The glassy calm and the squall. Sunrise and sunset. The dolphins gliding effortlessly at the bows. The moon peeking through the clouds. The phosphorescence shimmering in the wake. My photos are mere hints, suggestions that you go see as much as you can. Don't let your mind diminish the beauty with comparisons to what you've seen on a screen. Let the unfiltered beauty flow into your heart until it is full, and then open your heart to more.

It's not all that big, Earth. We humans are already straining the capacity of our Home, and not being very thoughtful about the course we are steering. Those of us who are lucky enough to have our basic needs met, who have food and water and security, who are also the big consumers of resources – we need to pay more attention to the well-being of our vessel. How do we create a future that we won't regret?

Some people cruise the world with young children. Some people cruise the world in boats much smaller and more affordable than mine. Some people set out without the means to complete their trip, and they find a way to support themselves as they go. Some people set out with no ocean sailing experience, but they read and practice and prepare and they go. I admire them all, for going. Of course you need to have a seaworthy boat, and of course you need to learn how to cope with the things that can go wrong. But if you do your homework, you can sail around the world. Literally, or metaphorically.

When I sailed across the Atlantic as a young man, I thought it might be enough to satisfy my sailing urge once and for all. But eventually I was itching for more. Sailing around the world, I again thought it might be enough – maybe future adventures would be ashore. But no, I have not had enough of the sea. However, I think now it will be easier to turn and sail for home. I've been around, and it was great. Home is good, too!

It's all Journey…

This book has a companion website: **www.satisfyingsail.com**. All the photos in this book, and a few more, are available there – in color. You can also order a full color edition of the book there, you can leave comments and questions, and you can connect with me. If you go to Tisvel, Vanuatu, please post a comment about what you find. If you are thinking of sailing from Panama to French Polynesia and you need crew, drop me a line!

Some photos were generously provided by others. Thanks to Dena Singh (cover photo, taken from *S/V Libby*), Timothy Liveright, William Hickson, Nora Hickson, Liam Kearney, Bob Shanks, Chris Dale, Klaudia Zayonc, and Bill Worthington (photo of me, below).

Thanks to Jimmy Cornell for creating the Blue Planet Odyssey, and allowing me to include screenshots from the Cornell Sailing website. Thanks to Molly McGrath at Pink Eraser for her enthusiastic support.

Hallie and I live in Brunswick, Maine, where I am very, very slowly building a little trimaran for coastal sailing. And dreaming of the moonlight dancing on waves across an empty tropical sea.

Fair winds,

Zeke

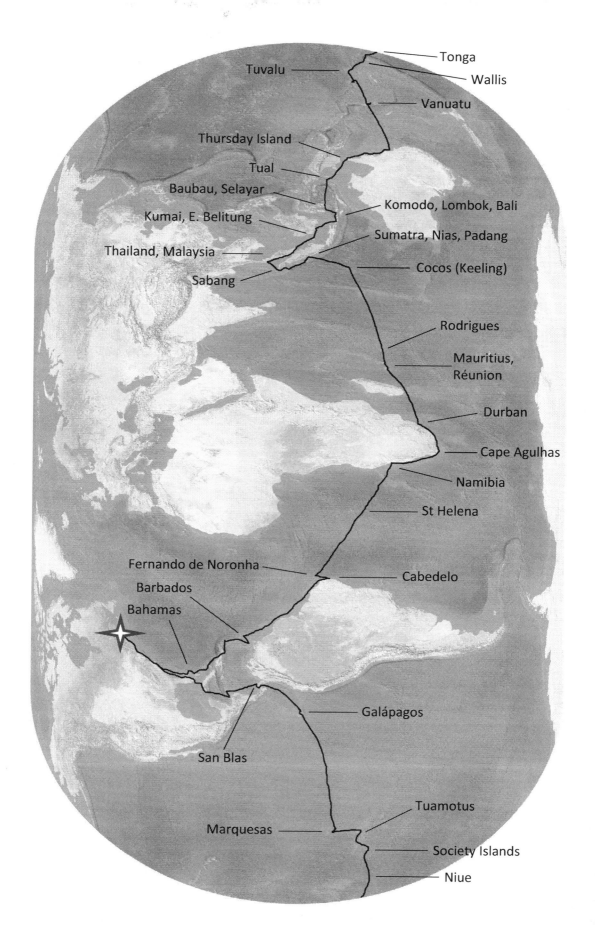

63049296R00230

Made in the USA
Middletown, DE
25 August 2019